New Focus on Success

Allgemeine Ausgabe

Cornelsen

New Focus on Success Allgemeine Ausgabe wurde geplant und entwickelt von der Verlagsredaktion der Cornelsen Press GmbH & Co. KG, Berlin.

Verfasser:	Michael Macfarlane, Oxford; David Clarke, Witten

Berater/innen:	Reinhard Ehrke, Flörsheim
	Philipp Fehrenbach, Leinfelden-Echterdingen
	Thomas Pache, Euskirchen
	Dr Gabriele Schneider, Chemnitz
	Elke Uthoff, Osnabrück

Verlagsredaktion:	Jim Austin
Redaktionelle Mitarbeit:	Christine House, Eleanor Toal, Andreas Goebel, Fritz Preuss
Gesamtgestaltung und	
technische Umsetzung:	Sylvia Lang
Bildredaktion:	Uta Hübner

Erhältlich sind auch:	Audio CDs
	Workbook
	Schlüssel zum Workbook
	Handbuch für den Unterricht

www.cornelsen.de

1. Auflage, 5. Druck 2006

Alle Drucke dieser Auflage sind inhaltlich unverändert und können im Unterricht nebeneinander verwendet werden.

© 2002 Cornelsen Press GmbH & Co. KG, Berlin

Die Internet-Adressen und -Dateien, die in diesem Lehrwerk angegeben sind, wurden vor Drucklegung geprüft (Stand: August 2002). Der Verlag übernimmt keine Gewähr für die Aktualität und den Inhalt dieser Adressen und Dateien oder solcher, die mit ihnen verlinkt sind.

ISBN-13: 978-3-464-04985-3
ISBN-10:   3-464-04985-X

Druck: CS-Druck CornelsenStürtz, Berlin

 Inhalt gedruckt auf säurefreiem Papier, umweltschonend hergestellt aus chlorfrei gebleichten Faserstoffen.

Vorwort

New Focus on Success ist eine völlig neu bearbeitete Fassung des alten *Focus on Success*. Es baut auf dem mittleren Bildungsabschluss auf. Das einbändige Lehrwerk erfüllt die Anforderungen im Fach Englisch für die Fachhochschulreife.
New Focus on Success ist in zwei Bereiche unterteilt, *Refresher Course* (Units A–E) und *Main Course* (Units 1–12).

Das Konzept

Zu jeder Ausgabe von *Focus* gibt es ein Workbook und Audio-CDs. Die Themenschwerpunkte sind hoch aktuell und reflektieren vielfältige Aspekte des heutigen Lebens. Besonderer Wert wurde auf den handlungsorientierten Charakter vieler Übungen gelegt. Bei der Themenauswahl wurde den Problemen und Möglichkeiten einer globalisierten Welt Rechnung getragen. Die Lernhilfen im Anhang vermitteln wichtige Techniken und Strategien, z.B. wie man mit neuen Vokabeln umgeht, Fragen zum Text beantwortet, Zusammenfassungen schreibt oder sich Informationen aus dem Internet besorgt.

Refresher Course

Die Rahmenhandlung des kompakten *Refresher Course* spielt in einer Reiseagentur, die alle fünf Units thematisch miteinander verbindet. Hier werden wichtige Grundstrukturen wiederholt und das Fundament für einen erfolgreichen Unterricht gelegt. Die Übungen, die auf die Texte folgen, festigen das Verständnis (*Looking at the text*), trainieren Wortschatz und Grammatik (*Working with words* und *Looking at grammar*) oder beinhalten andere praktische Aspekte der Sprache.
Die Bearbeitung der einzelnen Units des *Refresher Course* ist fakultativ und kann den Bedürfnissen des jeweiligen Kurses angepasst werden.

Main Course

Der *Main Course* ist das Herzstück des Lehrwerks. Seine 12 Units behandeln das jeweilige Schwerpunktthema aus unterschiedlichen Perspektiven.
Die erste Seite, *Focus*, bildet den Einstieg in jede Unit. Hier werden die Lernenden in das Thema der Unit eingeführt.
Den beiden anschließenden Haupttexten folgen jeweils Verständnisfragen (*Looking at the text*), Wortschatzübungen (*Working with words*) und Übungen zu den wichtigsten sprachlichen Fertigkeiten (*Writing, Speaking, Listening*). Eine Reihe von handlungsorientierten oder interkulturellen Übungen (*Culture check*) ergänzen das Spektrum. Nach dem zweiten Text wird auch noch die Grammatik durch Kurzübersichten (*Looking at grammar*) und dazugehörige Übungen (*Practising grammar*) gefestigt. Den Abschluss jeder Unit bildet ein fakultativer Zusatztext, *Further Reading*, der das Schwerpunktthema vertieft.

Anhang

Hier finden sich ein übersichtlicher, zum Nachschlagen wie zum Durcharbeiten geeigneter Abschnitt mit Lernhilfen, der Grundwortschatz, alphabetische und chronologische Wörterverzeichnisse sowie eine Übersicht über unregelmäßige Verben.

 CD X/X Dieses Symbol weist darauf hin, dass sich der Text bzw. Dialog auf der CD befindet.

Inhaltsverzeichnis

Refresher Course

Main Course

Anhang

A Blue Sky

Track 2

Blue Sky Adventure Travel is a travel agency in Fulham in London. The company specializes in exotic adventure holidays such as backpacking in Australia, canoeing in Canada and snowboarding in the Alps.

Blue Sky has five full-time staff, and they include Michael and Kate King, who own
5 and manage the company. The three employees are Jasmin Chopra, Joshua Atkins and Andrea Cooper. Jasmin runs
10 Blue Sky's website, while Joshua and Andrea help Kate look after customers who call at the travel agency in Fulham Road.

But at the moment things are not going too well at Blue Sky. Business is growing so
15 fast that the company is beginning to have problems finding staff.

For example, the website is taking up a lot of time. At present, Blue Sky is only advertising holidays on its site, but now Michael wants to sell holidays there as well. This means a huge amount of work for Jasmin. She seldom leaves the office before 8.00 pm and she also works most weekends as well.

20 Meanwhile, Michael and Kate, who live above the shop, never take a break and they are beginning to have more and more arguments because of misunderstandings. Although they often quarrel, Blue Sky's problems are not unusual. Many other successful businesses in the EU have similar difficulties. There are simply more jobs than there are people to fill them, particularly in IT.

25 Jasmin has already installed a Jobs@ button on Blue Sky's website, but Michael doesn't expect many replies. Everybody has these buttons nowadays, and good unemployed IT specialists in booming London are difficult to find.

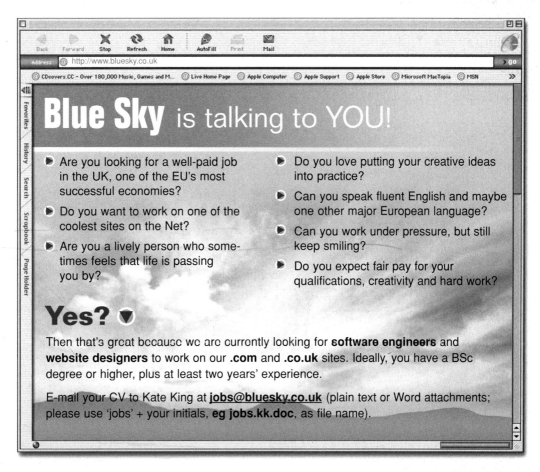

Blue Sky is talking to YOU!

- Are you looking for a well-paid job in the UK, one of the EU's most successful economies?
- Do you want to work on one of the coolest sites on the Net?
- Are you a lively person who sometimes feels that life is passing you by?
- Do you love putting your creative ideas into practice?
- Can you speak fluent English and maybe one other major European language?
- Can you work under pressure, but still keep smiling?
- Do you expect fair pay for your qualifications, creativity and hard work?

Yes? ▼

Then that's great because we are currently looking for **software engineers** and **website designers** to work on our **.com** and **.co.uk** sites. Ideally, you have a BSc degree or higher, plus at least two years' experience.

E-mail your CV to Kate King at **jobs@bluesky.co.uk** (plain text or Word attachments; please use 'jobs' + your initials, **eg jobs.kk.doc**, as file name).

1 Looking at the texts

Say if these statements are right, wrong or you don't know because the information is not in the texts. If the statement is wrong, correct it.

Yes, that's true/right/correct.

No, that's false/wrong/incorrect. It says in line ... that ...

I don't know. It doesn't say anything about ... in the texts.

1 Blue Sky specializes in <u>budget</u> holidays for young people. *wrong - exotic*
2 The company has <u>five</u> employees. *wrong - three*
3 Jasmin Chopra is an IT specialist who has come to Britain from India. *?*
4 Joshua helps look after customers who visit the shop. *right*
5 Jasmin often has to work late. *right*
6 Michael and Kate live in a flat <u>near</u> the shop. *wrong - above the shop*
7 <u>Kate</u> doesn't think the Jobs@ button will help much. *wrong - Michael*
8 Blue Sky will only accept job applicants from EU countries. *?*
9 All applicants must have experience of working with Java. *?*
10 The Kings think two years' practical job experience is the same as a BSc. *wrong*

The applicant must have a BSc degree or higher, plus at least two years experience.

2 Working with words

A Find the noun form(s) of these verbs in the texts. They are in the same order.

Example (to) travel *travel*

1 (to) employ *employee*
2 (to) specialize *specialist*
3 (to) live
4 (to) practise

5 (to) qualify *qualification*
6 (to) create
7 (to) design *design*

B Complete the e-mail below with words from the box.

> ad ▪ Computer Science ▪ course ▪ disability ▪ German ▪ hard ▪
> home worker ▪ hope ▪ interest ▪ IT jobs ▪ university ▪ websites

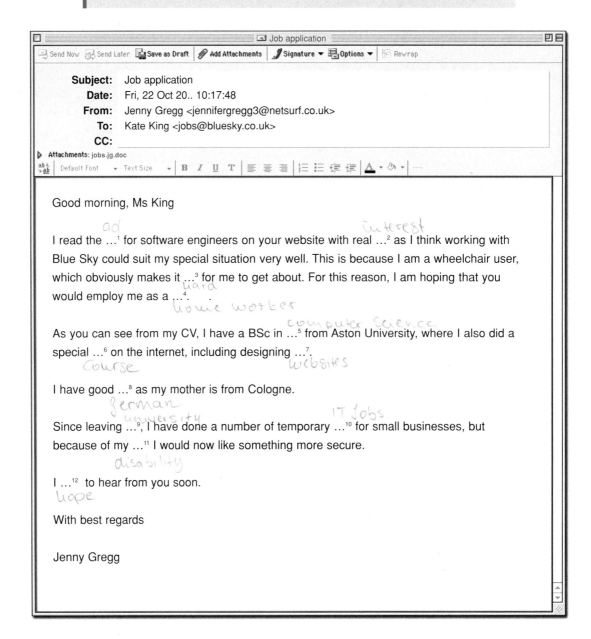

Job application

Subject: Job application
Date: Fri, 22 Oct 20.. 10:17:48
From: Jenny Gregg <jennifergregg3@netsurf.co.uk>
To: Kate King <jobs@bluesky.co.uk>
CC:

Attachments: jobs.jg.doc

Good morning, Ms King

I read the …[1] *ad* for software engineers on your website with real …[2] *interest* as I think working with Blue Sky could suit my special situation very well. This is because I am a wheelchair user, which obviously makes it …[3] *hard* for me to get about. For this reason, I am hoping that you would employ me as a …[4] *home worker*.

As you can see from my CV, I have a BSc in …[5] *Computer Science* from Aston University, where I also did a special …[6] *course* on the internet, including designing …[7] *websites*.

I have good …[8] *German* as my mother is from Cologne.

Since leaving …[9] *university*, I have done a number of temporary …[10] *IT jobs* for small businesses, but because of my …[11] *disability* I would now like something more secure.

I …[12] *hope* to hear from you soon.

With best regards

Jenny Gregg

3 Looking at grammar: simple present

Grammar

Remember

1 The company **specializes** in exotic adventure holidays.
2 Jasmin seldom **leaves** the office before 8 pm.
3 Michael **does not/doesn't expect** many replies.
4 **Do** you **love** putting your creative ideas into practice?

■ Wir benutzen das **simple present**, um **bestehende Situationen** (1) und sich **ständig wiederholende Ereignisse** (2) auszudrücken.

■ Daher kommen die folgenden **Signalwörter** mit dem **simple present** häufig vor: *always – never – often – seldom – rarely – ever – hardly ever – sometimes – occasionally – now and then – generally – normally – regularly – usually – every day/week/month/... – on Mondays/... – ...*

■ Ist kein Hilfsverb bzw. eine Form von *be* im Satz vorhanden, dann bilden wir die **Verneinung** und **Fragen** mit *do/does*. (3) (4)

A Read the checklist. Then use the simple present to make correct statements about what Blue Sky does (✓) and does not do (✗) for its customers. Start the sentence with either *Blue Sky* (third person singular) or *We* as the subject.

Examples Supply all tickets to your final destination. ✓
Blue Sky supplies all tickets to your final destination.
or *We supply all tickets to your final destination.*

Provide other meals. ✗
Blue Sky does not provide other meals.
or *We do not provide other meals.*

Blue Sky Adventure Travel

Checklist

Read this leaflet carefully! It tells you what we do ✓ and do not do ✗ for you.

1 Provide accommodation with breakfast. ✓
2 Arrange baggage insurance. ✓
3 Take out health insurance. ✗
4 Supply visas. ✗
5 Pay airport taxes. ✓
6 Guarantee a seat on trains and/or buses. ✗
7 Order foreign currency. ✓
8 Hire local guides and/or instructors. ✓
9 Supply sports or other equipment. ✗

B Ask questions with *do/does* about the <u>underlined</u> words. Use the question words in brackets. Look at the example first.

Example   Jasmin gets home <u>at about 8.30 pm</u>. (when?)
When does Jasmin get home?

1   The Kings live <u>in a flat above the travel agency</u>. (where?)
2   Halina Piatkowski starts work <u>next Monday</u>. (when?)
3   Joshua goes to work <u>by bus</u>. (how?)
4   Kate and Michael often quarrel <u>because of business worries</u>. (why?)
5   The new software engineers come from <u>Poland</u>. (where?)
6   The cheapest holidays in Alaska cost <u>over £2000</u>. (how much?)
7   Blue Sky hopes to find staff <u>by putting a Jobs@ button on its website</u>. (how?)

C Read the information in the box and then ask questions with *who?* and *what?*

Grammar

Remember

1   **Who likes** going on adventure holidays?   (Subjekt)
2   **Who do** you **like** best, Kate or Michael?   (Objekt)
3   **What happens** if we miss our bus?   (Subjekt)
4   **What does** Andrea **enjoy** doing after work?   (Objekt)

■ Ist *who* (1) bzw. *what* (3) das **Subjekt** des Satzes, bilden wir Fragen **ohne** *do/does*.

---

1   Blue Sky specializes in <u>adventure travel</u>. (what?)
2   Joshua often meets <u>his girlfriend</u> after work. (who?)
3   <u>Andrea</u> works with Joshua in the travel shop. (who?)
4   Andrea Cooper works for <u>Blue Sky Adventure Travel</u>. (who?)
5   If you click on the £ button, <u>you get a list of cheap flights</u>. (what? + happen)
6   <u>The new website</u> attracts a lot of customers every day. (what?)

4   Looking at grammar: present continuous

Grammar

Remember

1   Business **is growing** so fast at the moment that Blue Sky needs more staff.
2   We **are** currently **looking for** software engineers.
3   But at the moment things **are not going** too well at Blue Sky.
4   **Are** you **looking for** a well-paid job in the UK?

■ Wir benutzen das **present continuous**, um auszudrücken, was gleichzeitig während des Sprechens oder Schreibens geschieht. (1) (2)
■ Daher kommt das **present continuous** mit den folgenden **Signalwörtern** häufig vor:
   at present – at the moment – currently – now – just
■ Die **Verneinung** wird mit *not/n't* gebildet (3), **Fragen** durch Umstellung (4).

! Im normalen Gebrauch haben u.a. die folgenden Verben **keine continuous form**:
   want – wish – like – prefer – love – dislike – hate – mind – need – notice – understand – hear – seem – look like – know – think (Sinn: glauben, meinen) *– believe – remember – mean – own – belong to – cost*

A Put the verbs into the correct form of the present continuous. Be careful about negative statements and questions.

1 Michael ... (interview) a software engineer at the moment.
2 Just a moment, please, Kate. I think my phone ... (ring).
3 Why ... (you/just sit) there, Joshua? Do something useful while the files ... (download).
4 – Jasmin says that Ranjit is always so tired.
   – Are you surprised? At the moment he ... (run) his own business and he ... (look after) the children almost on his own.
5 Look, Michael, just calm down. All I ... (say) is that we should discuss our problems in private.
6 – How ... (you/get on) with the new catalogue, Andrea?
   – Well, I ... (not work) on it at all at present. I ... (deal) with customers instead.
7 We ... (advertise) on our website and in several papers but we haven't had any luck so far. Now Michael ... (even + think about) advertising in Eastern Europe.
8 The customers ... (not complain) about our holidays but they don't like waiting so long.

B Put the verbs into the correct form of the simple present or the present continuous.

Most of Blue Sky's customers ...[1] (be) young and successful people who ...[2] (work) 60-hour weeks and ...[3] (earn) very good money. These people ...[4] (normally + not have) much leisure time, and ...[5] (spend) their working week in offices. They ...[6] (like) to make up for this during their vacations, when they ...[7] (go) on exotic adventure holidays to far-off places. There they ...[8] (only + not enjoy) a complete change of scene, but they also ...[9] (get) some physical exercise.

At the moment, business ...[10] (slow down) because of a shortage of qualified staff. Some economists ...[11] (think) that this ...[12] (become) the most serious problem in Britain. The government ...[13] (now + try) to attract foreign workers to Britain. They ...[14] (even + offer) free English courses and cheap accommodation to people who ...[15] (accept) this offer. Currently, nearly 60,000 French people ...[16] (work) in London, for example, and the number of EU citizens who ...[17] (move) there ...[18] (rise) fast. Normally, British people ...[19] (welcome) these newcomers. They ...[20] (help) the British economy, while they ...[21] (also + add) to London's flair.

C Express these ideas in English. Use the simple present or the present continuous.

1 Können Sie bitte einen Moment warten? Herr King telefoniert gerade.
2 Joshua wohnt bei seinen Eltern in Fulham, aber zurzeit besucht er seinen Bruder in Brighton.
3 Normalerweise geht Andrea zu Fuß zur Arbeit, aber momentan fährt sie mit dem Bus.
4 Michael will nicht so viele Stunden arbeiten, aber zurzeit verkauft er so viele Reisen, dass er zwei neue Mitarbeiter braucht!
5 Kate kann nicht kommen. Sie spricht gerade mit einem Kunden.
6 Schließt Blue Sky auch Krankenversicherungen für ihre Kunden ab?

Where's my money?

When John Barton arrived in Winnipeg, Canada, for a canoeing holiday in the wilderness, he had some big disappointments. When he got back to the UK, he wrote a letter of complaint to his travel agency, Blue Sky.

John Barton

43 Victoria Road
Abingdon OX14 6KM
Oxon

Blue Sky Adventure Travel Ltd
77 Fulham Road
London SW3 2HB

23 September 20..

Dear Sir or Madam

I booked one of your 16-day 'exotic adventure holidays' in Canada last March, and at first I was more than satisfied. I found your staff in Fulham very friendly and helpful, and everything went fine until I landed at Winnipeg International Airport on 5 September.

Then my troubles began. To start with, from what it says in your catalogue, I was expecting to stay the night in 'a pleasant hotel on the edge of town'. In fact I spent it at a motel on a busy freeway near the airport. I did not sleep at all because trucks were racing past my room and planes were taking off all night.

At 9 am on Day 2, I was waiting outside the 'pleasant hotel' for your 'comfortable van'. I nearly missed it because I wasn't looking for the rusty old minibus that came to collect us.

As I was loading my canoe 'at a little village at the end of civilization', two big groups of tourists arrived. Where did all these people come from? Were they going to the same place as I was? If so, my destination in 'the solitude of the earth's last true wilderness' would be a bit crowded. And it was, of course.

I could easily go on like this for pages. The fact is that hardly anything was as good as your catalogue said. Our Canadian guides were friendly and helpful, but said they did not take any responsibility for 'mistakes' in the catalogue. They just advised me to contact you about a refund when I arrived home, and that is exactly what I am now doing.

Please see the enclosed list of complaints and let me know the size of my refund as soon as possible.

Yours faithfully

John Barton

Encl: list of complaints

1 Looking at the text

Answer the questions.

1 In what way was John Barton satisfied with Blue Sky?
2 Why was John's overnight stay in Winnipeg a nasty surprise?
3 Why did John nearly miss the bus on Day 2?
4 What made John think that his destination 'would be a bit crowded'?
5 How does the reader know that John has a lot more complaints?
6 How did the Canadian guides react to the complaints?

2 Working with words

Find synonyms or words of similar meaning in the text for these words and expressions. They are in the same order.

1 reserved	5 speeding	9 real
2 started	6 expecting	10 claimed
3 nice	7 came	11 errors , mistake
4 crowded	8 loneliness , solitude	12 get in touch with

3 Looking at grammar: simple past

Grammar

Remember
1 I **booked** one of your holidays last March.
2 I **found** your staff in Fulham very friendly and helpful.
3 I **did not/didn't sleep** at all.
4 Where **did** all these people **come** from?

■ Bei der Bildung des **simple past** unterscheiden wir zwischen **regelmäßigen** und **unregelmäßigen** Verben. Bei den **regelmäßigen** Verben hängt man -ed an den Infinitiv. (1)

■ **Unregelmäßige** Verben haben eine **eigene Form**, die man sich einfach merken muss. (2)

■ Wir benutzen das **simple past**, um **völlig abgeschlossene** Handlungen zu schildern. Daher benutzen wir häufig folgende **Zeitangaben**, um zu verdeutlichen, wann die Handlung passiert ist:

yesterday – the day before yesterday – three/four/... days/weeks/... ago – last week/March/... – in 1998/... – when I was at school/... – in those days – ...

■ Bei Vollverben **ohne Hilfsverben** bilden wir die **Verneinung** mit *did not/didn't* (3), **Fragen** mit *did* (4).

A Fill in the correct forms of the simple past. Be careful about negative and irregular forms (see p 206).

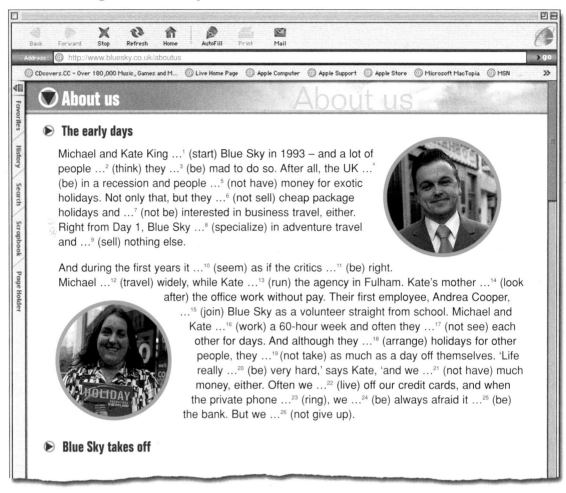

http://www.bluesky.co.uk/aboutus

About us

The early days

Michael and Kate King ...[1] (start) Blue Sky in 1993 – and a lot of people ...[2] (think) they ...[3] (be) mad to do so. After all, the UK ...[4] (be) in a recession and people ...[5] (not have) money for exotic holidays. Not only that, but they ...[6] (not sell) cheap package holidays and ...[7] (not be) interested in business travel, either. Right from Day 1, Blue Sky ...[8] (specialize) in adventure travel and ...[9] (sell) nothing else.

And during the first years it ...[10] (seem) as if the critics ...[11] (be) right. Michael ...[12] (travel) widely, while Kate ...[13] (run) the agency in Fulham. Kate's mother ...[14] (look after) the office work without pay. Their first employee, Andrea Cooper, ...[15] (join) Blue Sky as a volunteer straight from school. Michael and Kate ...[16] (work) a 60-hour week and often they ...[17] (not see) each other for days. And although they ...[18] (arrange) holidays for other people, they ...[19] (not take) as much as a day off themselves. 'Life really ...[20] (be) very hard,' says Kate, 'and we ...[21] (not have) much money, either. Often we ...[22] (live) off our credit cards, and when the private phone ...[23] (ring), we ...[24] (be) always afraid it ...[25] (be) the bank. But we ...[26] (not give up).

Blue Sky takes off

B Use these sentence elements to form simple past questions. You must add some missing words. Look at the examples first.

Examples   Blue Sky + tell/John/truth? – Yes, it did.
Did Blue Sky tell John the truth?

where/you + buy/tickets? – At Blue Sky.
Where did you buy the tickets?

1 John + complain/Blue Sky/his holiday? – Yes, he certainly did!
2 when / you + book/holiday? – In March.
3 where/we + land/Canada? – At Winnipeg.
4 what/John + like/Blue Sky? – Everybody was friendly and helpful.
5 the minibus + collect/tourists/motel/all right? – Yes, it did.
6 why/some tourists + complain/their first night/Canada? – Because they spent it in a noisy motel.
7 what/John + do/village? – He loaded his canoe.
8 John + expect to see/other tourists? – No, he didn't.
9 who/unhappy tourists + speak to/their complaints? – The Canadian guides.
10 what/guides + advise/them to do? – Contact their travel agents in the UK.

Grammar

Remember

1 At 9 am on Day 2, I **was waiting** for your 'comfortable van'.
2 Planes **were taking off** all night.
3 While I **was loading** my canoe, two big groups of tourists arrived.
4 I **was not/wasn't looking for** the rusty old minibus.
5 **Were** they **going** to the same place as I was?

▪ Wir bilden das **past continuous** mit *was/were* + *-ing*-Form des Vollverbs.

▪ Wenn wir ausdrücken möchten, dass eine Handlung zu einem **bestimmten Zeitpunkt** (1) bzw. während eines **bestimmten Zeitraumes** (2) in der Vergangenheit im Gange war, benutzen wir das **past continuous**.

▪ Wir verwenden das **past continuous** auch, um zu verdeutlichen, dass eine Handlung im Gange war, als ein neues Ereignis (plötzlich) eintrat. (3)

▪ Da bei dem **past continuous** immer ein Hilfsverb (*was/were*) vorhanden ist, werden **Verneinungen** mit *not/n't* (4) und **Fragen** durch **Umstellung** (5) gebildet.

A Put the verbs into the correct form of the past continuous. Be careful about negative statements and questions.

When Kate arrived at the agency, there were no customers, so she was pleased to see that everybody ...[1] (work) hard. Andrea ...[2] (tidy) the catalogue displays and Joshua ...[3] (help) Jasmin. In fact, the only person who ...[4] (not do) anything useful was Michael. And what ...[5] (he/do)? He ...[6] (play) solitaire.

A woman complained to Michael that she did not mind waiting as long as the assistants ...[7] (look after) other customers or ...[8] (use) the phone. But she did not like waiting if they ...[9] (make) coffee or ...[10] (chat) to each other. When Joshua heard this, he said: 'Did she say "chatting"? How did she know? ...[11] (she/listen) to our conversation? If so, she would know that we ...[12] (talk) about work.'

B Put the verbs into the simple past or past continuous.

Michael King of Blue Sky is phoning John Barton about his complaint.

JOHN   Hello. Abingdon 169784.
MICHAEL Good morning. Mr Barton?
JOHN   Yes. John Barton speaking.
MICHAEL Oh, hello, Mr Barton. It's Michael King of Blue Sky here. Sorry I haven't phoned before but when your letter ...[1] (arrive), I ...[2] (visit) one of our resorts in Austria.
JOHN   That's OK.
MICHAEL Well, of course we ...[3] (be) very sorry to hear that you ...[4] (not enjoy) the holiday you ...[5] (book) with us.
JOHN   Well, as I ...[6] (point out) in my letter, a lot of things just ...[7] (not agree) with the catalogue – or with what your assistant ...[8] (tell) me, either.

MICHAEL That may be so, Mr Barton, but there are always two sides to these things, aren't there? For example, you say in your letter what you ...[9] (hope) to find –

JOHN Now hold on, Mr King. I ...[10] (not write) what I ...[11] (hope) to find at all. I ...[12] (write) what I ...[13] (expect) from what you and your catalogue ...[14] (lead) me to believe. That's my point.

MICHAEL OK, then, perhaps so, but that doesn't apply to other things, does it? For example, that you couldn't sleep because trucks ...[15] (make) a lot of noise and planes ...[16] (take off) all night. That's just your subjective opinion, isn't it, Mr Barton?

JOHN Oh, come on, Mr King, you know very well what I mean. And as for that awful minibus – really!

MICHAEL Ah, yes, the minibus. Well, we ...[17] (e-mail) Winnipeg about that yesterday and they ...[18] (answer) immediately. That minibus ...[19] (come) to collect you because the van ...[20] (give) trouble, that's all. You really can't argue with that, can you?

JOHN Well, perhaps not, but –

C Express these ideas in English. Use the simple past or the past continuous.

1 Unser Reiseführer Jeff fragte uns: „Was habt ihr gerade gemacht, als der Bär aus dem Wald kam?"

2 Carol sagte: „Wir waren alle gerade dabei, unsere Zelte in die Kanus zu laden."

3 Dann sagte Jeff: „Ich verstehe. Ihr habt euch alle gerade gebückt (*bend down*). Ich nehme an, dass die meisten von euch mit dem Rücken zum Wald standen, richtig?"

4 „Ja, das stimmt," sagte John. „Daher haben wir den Bär zunächst gar nicht bemerkt."

5 „Bären sind sehr neugierig (*nosey*)," sagte Jeff. „Dieser wollte nur wissen, was ihr gerade gemacht habt."

6 „Einige von uns haben tatsächlich panisch reagiert (*panic*)," sagte John. „Manche haben sogar geschrien, als sie den Bär entdeckten."

7 „Schließlich sind alle nur noch wild herumgelaufen, als der Bär da stand und uns anstarrte (*stare at sb*)."

A gap year

Susan Wood, a school-leaver, is planning to have a gap year before training to become a nurse. She wants to work during the first months of her gap year and then spend a few months travelling. Here, Susan is talking to Andrea Cooper of Blue Sky Adventure Travel about her plans.

Track 3

ANDREA	Good morning. Can I help you?
SUSAN	Hi. Well, I'm leaving school in July and then I'm taking a gap year. I'd like to spend three or four months of it travelling. I feel I'll never have another chance if I don't do it now.
ANDREA	Sure. That's what a lot of adventure travel customers say. Now, are you thinking of any particular destination?
SUSAN	Well, what about India – or Africa, perhaps? Of course, my parents would like me to go to Australia or Canada. They think it will be safer there, but that's not the point, is it? I'd like to go somewhere really different.
ANDREA	Yes, well, you've come to the right place. Look, let's talk about the basics first. For example, how are you going to pay for your holiday? Will you pay your way by picking fruit or something? If so, your parents are right. You can forget India and Africa.
SUSAN	Oh, no. That's no problem. I'm going to work here for a few months first, and I hope my parents will help me financially a bit, too. I don't want to work during my holiday, you see. When my money runs out, I'll just come home.
ANDREA	Yes, well, that will give you more choice, of course, but it's not quite that easy. Take India, for example. You really can find fantastic architecture and some of the best beaches in the world there, but on the other hand …
SUSAN	Yes?

5

10

15

20

ANDREA Well, you won't find European standards of comfort, for example. And
you aren't the only person who wants to see the Taj Mahal, of course.
Please accept that accommodation will sometimes be, well, very basic
and transport can be a big problem as well. I'm afraid some people just   25
don't understand that. That's why we've introduced our new "Honesty is
Best" policy.

SUSAN I know. I read about that on your website. In fact, that's why I'm here.
But what am I going to do, then? Fly to Florida?

ANDREA No, of course not, but if you want a more exotic destination like India,   30
then please choose a group holiday. You'll travel and live with young
people just like yourself, but you'll have an experienced English-speaking
Indian guide to look after you. Otherwise, I can already see that you are
going to have some nasty surprises.
Look, I'll just fetch a catalogue and show you what I mean. I won't be a   35
moment.

1 Looking at the text

Say what role the following play in the text. Read the example first.

Example   Andrea Cooper
She serves/helps/advises Susan (Wood) at Blue Sky / the travel agency.

1 July   3 Africa   5 the UK
2 three or four months   4 Canada   6 a group holiday

2 Working with words

Complete the text with words from the box.

architects ▪ beautiful ▪ building ▪ built ▪ coloured ▪ example ▪ garden ▪
love ▪ problems ▪ started ▪ succeeded ▪ technically ▪ white ▪ wife ▪ workers

The Taj Mahal Mausoleum in Agra, India, was
…[1] by the Muslim emperor SHAH JAHAN for his
favourite …[2], Mumtaz Mahal. Over 20,000
workers took over ten years to build the Taj Mahal.
Work …[3] in 1631, but the …[4] was not finished until
1653 because of a shortage of skilled …[5] and
technical …[6] with the dome*. The Taj Mahal is
built of pure …[7] marble decorated with …[8] stones
and glass. It stands in a water …[9] that is a good
…[10] of a 'shalimar', ie 'garden of …[11]'. Today,
many experts think that the Taj Mahal is not only
the world's most …[12] building, but also its most
…[13] advanced. Many …[14] have tried to copy the
dome, but so far nobody has …[15] in doing so.

* *Kuppel*

Grammar

Remember

1 You **will find** some wonderful beaches in India.
2 My parents think it **will be** safer in Canada.
3 I hope my parents **will help** me, too.
4 Look, I'll just **fetch** a catalogue.
5 I **am going to work** in the UK for a few months.
6 How **are** you **going to pay** for your holiday?
7 I can see that you **are going to have** some nasty surprises.
8 **I'm leaving** school in July and then **I'm having** a gap year.
9 Susan's plane **leaves** for New Delhi **next Monday**.

- Das **will future** bilden wir mit *will (not)* + **Infinitiv** des Vollverbs. Es hat dieselbe Form für alle Personen. Beachten Sie die Kurzform: *will not = won't*.

- Das **will future** benutzen wir für **zukünftige Situationen** oder **Ereignisse**, die mit **Sicherheit eintreten** werden (1), für **Vermutungen** (2) bzw. **Hoffnungen** (3) und für **spontane**, vorher nicht überlegte **Entscheidungen** (4).

- Das **going to future** bilden wir mit *am/is/are* + *going to* + **Infinitiv** des Vollverbs. Bei **Fragen** tauschen wir *am/is/are* und das Subjekt einfach aus.

- In erster Linie benutzen wir das **going to future** für Pläne und Absichten. (5) (6)

- Das **going to future** verwenden wir auch für **Situationen** und **Ereignisse**, die **bald eintreten** werden. Dies ist besonders so, wenn im Augenblick des Sprechens oder Schreibens bestimmte **Anzeichen** dafür bereits gegeben sind. (7)

- Für schon **entschiedene Vorkehrungen** und **feste Verabredungen** benutzen wir auch das **present continuous** mit einer **Zeitangabe der zukünftigen Zeit**. (8)

- Für **fest terminierte Vorgänge** (Fahrpläne, Stundenpläne, Programme usw.) verwenden wir das **simple present**. (9)

Im Zweifelsfall benutzen Sie *will,* das neutraler ist.

! **Beachten Sie:** Ich will nicht = *I don't want to* (und nicht ~~I will not/won't~~)

A Put the verbs into the correct form of the *will* or *going to* future.

1 Andrea thinks that Susan Wood ... (choose) a group holiday rather than an individual one.
2 Blue Sky ... (sell) holidays on its website as well as advertise them there.
3 Michael hopes that he ... (not need) so many new staff if he sells more holidays on the internet.
4 – Michael ... (be) furious, but I don't think Jasmin ... (finish) setting up that secure site by the weekend.
  – Really? I ... (go) and help her then.
  – Don't be silly, Joshua. Who ... (look after) the customers? Me, I suppose.
5 – It's already clear that we ... (be) in real trouble unless we find more staff.
  – You're right. To begin with, we ... (not be able to) offer our usual standard of personal service.
6 – Andrea says she ... (deliver) the catalogue to the printers on her way home.
  – Is that a good idea? I suppose she ... (have to) leave the office early then.

B Use these elements to form sentences with the *going to* future or the present continuous. Use the present continuous when there is an adverb of future time.

Michael/buy/new car.
Michael is going to buy a new car.

Jasmin + leave/Blue Sky/end/month?
Is Jasmin leaving Blue Sky at the end of the month?

1 Kate/talk/printers/about/new catalogue/tomorrow.
2 Blue Sky + pay/Christmas bonus/this year?
3 Jasmin/ask/Michael/more powerful computer.
4 – you + interview/German programmer/this afternoon/Kate?
   – No. She e-mailed to say she/not arrive/London/until/Tuesday.
5 Joshua/learn/computer programming. He/start/evening classes/September.
6 Blue Sky + move/new offices/Chelsea?

C Put the verbs into the correct future form: *will* future, *going to* future, present continuous or simple present.

1 We ...[1] (definitely + look for) new offices, but I don't think it ...[2] (be) easy because we want to stay in Fulham.
2 – I'm sorry, Michael. I can't stay until 3.30. I ...[1] (miss) my bus to Harlow. It ...[2] (leave) at 3.45.
   – I ...[3] (give) you a lift home if you work later.
3 – What time ...[1] (the film/start) tomorrow, Jane?
   – Well, it ...[2] (begin) at 8.00 but we ...[3] (meet) for a drink at 7. Why don't you join us? Jim and Sarah ...[4] (be) there.
4 – What ...[1] (you/do) during your summer holidays, Jim? ...[2] (you/go) anywhere interesting?
   – Well, what's interesting? I ...[3] (visit) my sister in Scotland for the first ten days and then I ...[4] (see) how I feel.
5 Look, it's true that about 30 people ...[1] (lose) their jobs when the firm moves to France, but things ...[2] (not be) nearly as bad as the press says. About half of them are retiring so they ...[3] (not need) a new job at all and the new owners ...[4] (pay) the rest six months' salary. This means that they ...[5] (have) enough money to live on until they find something else.
6 – We ...[1] (hold) a press reception next week to launch our new "Honesty is Best" policy. Let's hope plenty of people ...[2] (come).
   – Of course they ...[3] (come). Nobody ...[4] (want) to miss the chance of free drinks.

D Express these ideas in English. Use the correct future form.

1 Diesen Sommer bleiben wir zu Hause. Wir möchten mehr Zeit in unserem schönen Garten verbringen und unser alter Hund wird es auch genießen.
2 – Vergiss nicht, dass freitags der Zug eine Stunde früher fährt.
   – Wirklich? Ich werde fragen, ob ich um vier Uhr gehen kann.
3 – Sehen wir uns bei den Kings morgen Abend?
   – Ich glaube nicht. Morgen komme ich erst spät aus Düsseldorf zurück.
4 Morgen bekommen wir die neuen Computer.

If you just want to 'fly and fry', please don't come to Blue Sky!

Blue Sky is one of the UK's biggest specialist adventure travel agencies. From small beginnings in Fulham, London, we now have 15 branches nationwide and an award-winning website. Last year, we sold over 97,000 carefully selected adventure holidays in the world's most exotic places.

And our famous HONESTY IS BEST policy makes us the travel agent that you can really trust.

Will your dream holiday be a passport to paradise or a trip to hell? Come to Blue Sky to get the honest picture behind the hype.

Track 4

London A spokesperson for Thames Radio's *People's Voice* programme said they had had 'a huge flood' of e-mails and phone calls after its highly critical report about a disappointed adventure
5 holidaymaker. The report described the troubles of John Barton, 26, of Abingdon near Oxford, who said that he was 'deeply disappointed' and felt 'seriously misled' by Blue Sky Adventure Travel, the travel agency that sold him his holiday in Canada.
10 Mr Barton certainly had a long list of complaints. The catalogue called a motel on a busy motorway next to an all-night airport a 'pleasant hotel on the edge of town'. It also described his badly-overcrowded holiday destination as 'a little village in
15 the solitude of the earth's last true wilderness'. However, although many listeners also complained bitterly about misleading hype, some disagreed.

Susan Wood rang the programme in support of the agency. She said, 'Blue Sky now has an "Honesty is Best" policy. I read about it on their website and it 20 works really well. They were completely open with me and I feel very safe in their hands. I know I won't have any nasty surprises. I think it's a great pity that *People's Voice* didn't tell listeners this. In a way, they were misleading, too.' 25
Greg Snow, the producer of *People's Voice*, said, 'We certainly don't want to treat anybody unfairly, but the programme was about Mr Barton's problems.'
Meanwhile, Michael King, co-owner of Blue Sky, 30 doesn't seem worried. 'We have learned a lot from all the bad publicity, and we have reacted to it very quickly,' he said. He added, 'Our "Honesty is Best" policy means that this will never happen again.'

1 Looking at the text

Say who is talking and how you know.

> *a People's Voice listener* ▪ *a People's Voice spokesperson* ▪ *Greg Snow* ▪
> *John Barton* ▪ *Michael King* ▪ *Susan Wood*

Example

> I'm not saying everything was bad, but I certainly did not get objective information about my holiday.

I think this is John Barton because he says that he felt 'seriously misled' by Blue Sky.

> 1 We were surprised by the number of calls we had, even during the programme.

> 2 I agree with Mr Barton. We had a similar experience on a walking holiday in Norway last year.

> 3 We don't advertise, and certainly not on a programme about a dissatisfied customer.

> 4 There's no such thing as bad publicity as long as you're honest about your mistakes and correct them quickly.

> 5 I think People's Voice gave listeners completely the wrong idea about Blue Sky.

2 Working with words

A Find words and expressions in the Blue Sky advert on p 21 to fit these definitions. They are in the same order.

1 another adjective for 'largest'
2 one-word adjective for 'all over the country'
3 another verb for 'chosen'
4 one-word adjective for 'strange and exciting'
5 one-word adjective for 'very well-known for a good reason'
6 expression meaning 'fantastic holiday that meets all one's expectations'
7 a document usually needed to cross a border into another country
8 another noun for 'journey'
9 adjective + noun meaning 'complete and correct description'
10 noun meaning 'misleading and often foolish exaggeration'

B Complete the leaflet with the words from the box.

> around ▪ at ▪ by ▪ for ▪ from (2x) ▪ in (5x) ▪ of ▪ on ▪
> out ▪ to (3x) ▪ under

Beware ...¹ thieves

➡ They are mainly interested ...² cash, so don't carry more
...³ with you than you really need.

➡ When you get cash ...⁴ a machine, make sure that it is
separated ...⁵ the street ...⁶ an automatic security door.

➡ Thieves are attracted ...⁷ tourist sites. They know there
will be tourists there with cash ...⁸ them. Be particularly
careful ...⁹ such places.

➡ Remember that thieves often work ...¹⁰ pairs. One of
them asks you ...¹¹ help – the way ...¹² the station, for
example – and the other one cleans ...¹³ your pockets.

➡ Never leave valuables such as cameras ...¹⁴ your car.
Even if you hide them ...¹⁵ a seat, for example, thieves
know where to look.

➡ Never leave jewellery ...¹⁶ hotel rooms. Give it ...¹⁷ the
receptionist who will put it in a safe or, better, leave it
...¹⁸ home.

3 Looking at grammar: adjectives and adverbs

Grammar

Remember

1 Mr Barton had a **long list** of complaints. The catalogue called a motel on a **busy motorway** next to an **all-night airport** a 'pleasant hotel on the edge of town'.
2 Susan Wood thought the radio programme **was misleading**, too.
3 Michael King doesn't **seem worried** by the report.
4 Susan **feels safe** in Blue Sky's hands.
5 Many listeners **complained bitterly** about misleading hype.
6 John Barton said he was '**deeply disappointed**' with Blue Sky.
7 Blue Sky's "Honesty is Best" policy works **really well**.

Grammar

- Möchten wir **Personen**, **Tiere** oder **Sachen** näher beschreiben, benutzen wir **Adjektive**.

- Adjektive stehen unmittelbar vor **Nomen** (1) und nach einer Form von *be* (2) bzw. einem Verb wie *become, seem, remain* usw., das *be* ersetzen kann (3).

- Adjektive werden auch mit Verben der sinnlichen Wahrnehmung verwendet, vor allem mit *feel, look* (aussehen), *sound* (klingen), *smell* (riechen) und *taste* (schmecken). (4)

- Wir benutzen **Adverbien** zur näheren Beschreibung von **Verben** (5), **Adjektiven** (6) und **anderen Adverbien** (7).

- Weitaus die meisten Adverbien werden durch das Anhängen von *-ly* an das entsprechende Adjektiv gebildet.

! **Beachten Sie** aber folgende wichtige **Unregelmäßigkeiten**:

- Die Adverbien *early, fast* und *long* haben dieselbe Form wie das entsprechende Adjektiv.

- Einige Adverbien haben zwei Formen – eine wie das Adjektiv und eine auf *-ly* – mit unterschiedlichen Bedeutungen. Am wichtigsten sind:

close	nah	*closely*	sorgfältig, genau
hard	hart	*hardly*	kaum
high	hoch	*highly*	sehr viel
late	spät	*lately*	neulich
most	meist	*mostly*	meistens
near	nah	*nearly*	fast

! **Beachten Sie:** Die Adverbform von *good* ist *well*. (7)

A First, make a 4-column table like the one below. Then look at the examples that have already been filled in. Finally, read the texts on p 21 again and add at least ten further examples to the table.

Adjectives	Position	Adverbs	Position
best	after 'be'	carefully	before adjective
biggest	before noun	really	before verb
		highly	before adjective

B Put the adjectives into the adverb form only where necessary.

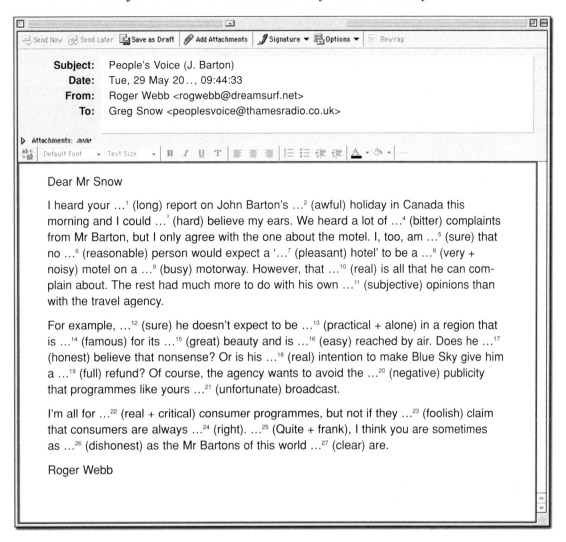

Subject:	People's Voice (J. Barton)
Date:	Tue, 29 May 20.., 09:44:33
From:	Roger Webb <rogwebb@dreamsurf.net>
To:	Greg Snow <peoplesvoice@thamesradio.co.uk>

Dear Mr Snow

I heard your ...[1] (long) report on John Barton's ...[2] (awful) holiday in Canada this morning and I could ...[3] (hard) believe my ears. We heard a lot of ...[4] (bitter) complaints from Mr Barton, but I only agree with the one about the motel. I, too, am ...[5] (sure) that no ...[6] (reasonable) person would expect a '...[7] (pleasant) hotel' to be a ...[8] (very + noisy) motel on a ...[9] (busy) motorway. However, that ...[10] (real) is all that he can complain about. The rest had much more to do with his own ...[11] (subjective) opinions than with the travel agency.

For example, ...[12] (sure) he doesn't expect to be ...[13] (practical + alone) in a region that is ...[14] (famous) for its ...[15] (great) beauty and is ...[16] (easy) reached by air. Does he ...[17] (honest) believe that nonsense? Or is his ...[18] (real) intention to make Blue Sky give him a ...[19] (full) refund? Of course, the agency wants to avoid the ...[20] (negative) publicity that programmes like yours ...[21] (unfortunate) broadcast.

I'm all for ...[22] (real + critical) consumer programmes, but not if they ...[23] (foolish) claim that consumers are always ...[24] (right). ...[25] (Quite + frank), I think you are sometimes as ...[26] (dishonest) as the Mr Bartons of this world ...[27] (clear) are.

Roger Webb

C Express these ideas in English.

1 Wir sind mit unseren Auszubildenden (*trainees*) sehr zufrieden. Sie sind alle interessiert und arbeiten sehr gut.

2 Wenn Sie einen wirklich schwierigen Kunden haben, holen Sie sofort Kate.

3 Diskutieren Sie Beschwerden bitte nicht am Telefon. Das kann leicht zu Missverständnissen führen.

4 Ich bin ziemlich enttäuscht. Der neue Katalog kommt jetzt eine Woche zu spät heraus.

5 Leider haben Andrea und Joshua kaum Zeit, um Jasmin zu helfen.

*Blue Sky has moved into new offices not far
from its old address, and now the company
is planning a reception to celebrate.
In this dialogue, Kate is talking to Ben Nelson,
who runs a party service specializing in
business events.*

Track 5

Ben	How many people are you expecting, Mrs King?
Kate	Please call me Kate.
Ben	Fine. I'm Ben.
Kate	Yes, well, let's see. We've invited about 80 special guests – you know, travel journalists, business friends and so on – but we've told them that they can bring some guests as well. I'm afraid I don't have much information at all.	5
Ben	That's OK, Kate. Lots of companies do that. My advice is to expect all the invited guests, and that about half of them will bring somebody with them.
Kate	What, about 120?
Ben	Yes, but don't forget the gate-crashers, will you? You'll certainly get a few 'unofficial guests' at an event like this.	10
Kate	Good heavens. I didn't think of that. But we can't do anything about it, can we?
Ben	Well, yes and no. A lot of unofficial guests could be journalists, and you don't want any trouble there, do you? But don't worry. Our security people are very good. They won't let just anybody in. And they videotape everybody who comes into the building, don't forget.	15
Kate	I'm glad to hear it. So what are we talking about, Ben? 150 guests in all?
Ben	Yes, that should be about right, I suppose.
Kate	OK, then, 150 it is.	20

* * *

Kate	Now, what about the food and drink?
Ben	Well, Kate, unless you want something exotic, I'd advise you to choose one of our set buffets. We have plenty of experience here. We really know what people like. You'll find the set buffets cheaper, too.
Kate	Well, that can't be bad after what we've just spent on this place. Tell me more.	25
Ben	Yes, well, there are four basic buffets – meat, fish, vegetarian or a mix of any or all of them. Potatoes, vegetables, cheese, fruit and a variety of bread are provided with all our buffets and we're also happy to make any changes you want. For example, you might like some sandwiches and prefer more poultry and pork, and no beef.	30
Kate	Yes, well, the main thing is that there's something for everybody. A mixed buffet sounds fine to me, Ben. Now, what about drinks?
Ben	Well, we have a standard programme there too. A wide selection of wine, beer, cocktails, soft drinks and spirits. No worries there, I promise you.
Kate	Good. That sounds great. Thanks very much.	35

1 Looking at the text

Answer the questions.

1. Why is Blue Sky planning to hold a reception?
2. Why are there likely to be more people at the reception than the 80 special guests?
3. According to Ben, why should Kate accept some 'uninvited guests'?
4. Why does Ben advise Kate to choose a set buffet?
5. Why does Ben say that Kate need not worry about drinks?

2 Working with words

Replace the underlined words with a synonym or word of similar meaning from the box.

> at present ▪ attend ▪ business ▪ difficulty ▪ firms ▪
> less expensive ▪ many different kinds ▪ one in two of ▪
> people ▪ receptions ▪ uninvited guests

1. Many <u>companies</u> give <u>parties</u> as big publicity events.
2. Some say <u>commercial</u> customers are better than private ones.
3. Kate's <u>problem</u> is that she doesn't know how many <u>guests</u> to expect.
4. <u>At the moment</u>, we think about 150 guests will <u>come to</u> the party.
5. About <u>half</u> the guests will bring somebody with them.
6. There may be some <u>gate-crashers</u>.
7. Yes, a set buffet will be <u>cheaper</u>, too.
8. Please provide <u>a good variety</u> of bread, okay?

3 Looking at grammar: countable and uncountable nouns

Grammar

Remember

- Nomen wie *guests, companies* und *journalists* sind **zählbar**. Sie haben eine Pluralform und können daher mit Zahlen und dem unbestimmten Artikel *a/an* benutzt werden.

- Nomen wie *bread, cheese* und *fruit* dagegen sind **nicht zählbar**. Sie haben keine Pluralform.

- Wollen wir ein nichtzählbares Nomen wie *bread* oder *wine* zählbar machen, dann müssen wir eine geeignete zählbare Mengenangabe wie *a/one loaf of ...*, *a/one bottle of ...*, *two packets of ...*, *three bars of ...*, *four slices of ...*, *five litres of ...*, *six glasses of ...*, *seven tins/cans of ...*, *eight boxes of ...* usw. hinzufügen.

- Die Sammelbegriffe *luggage, furniture, hardware* und *software* sowie die Nomen *advice, evidence* und *information* sind ebenfalls unzählbar und werden grundsätzlich im Singular verwendet.
  Um diese Nomen zählbar zu machen, benutzen wir *a piece of ...* (formell) bzw. *a bit of ...* (weniger formell).

Grammar

! Beachten Sie:

Das Nomen *news* ist unzählbar und deshalb im Singular, obwohl es auf *-s* endet. Um *news* zählbar zu machen, fügen wir ebenfalls *a bit/piece of* ... hinzu.

Die Nomen *people* und *police* sind Pluralformen, obwohl sie keine *-s*-Endung haben. Wollen wir diese Wörter im Singular verwenden, benutzen wir *person* für *people* und *police officer* für *police*.

Examples *There **were lots of people** in the shop, but only **one person** bought something.*
*A **police officer** said that **the police were** on their way.*

A Make a table like the one below and put the nouns in the box into the right column.

Give the plural form of the countable nouns. Be careful about the irregular nouns. Add a suitable countable noun to the uncountable ones to make it possible to use them in the plural.

> *advice · baby · boss · bread · child · chocolate · evidence · family · industry · information · interview · life · loaf · man · news · paint · petrol · police · roof · software · wife · wine*

kein

Countable		Uncountable	
Singular	**Plural**	**'Singular form'**	**'Plural form'**
baby	babies	chocolate	bars/pieces of chocolate

B Use the nouns in brackets to complete these sentences. Be careful about irregular countables and the plural form of uncountables.

Example The *men* (man) have already drunk four *bottles of wine* (wine).

1 Several ... (information) in this report are wrong.
2 There are three ... (evidence) that show the ... (thief) were at home at the time of both ... (robbery).
3 Please don't forget to buy a few ... (beer) on your way home.
4 Over 3000 ... (luggage) were lost at Düsseldorf airport last year.
5 I have just put 50 ... (petrol) in my car – it's so expensive these days, isn't it?
6 Two ... (police) were stopping all foreign ... (lorry) on the motorway today.
7 Four ... (car) were damaged in the accident and one ... (people) was injured.
8 John, when you have your two ... (interview) next week, let me give you two ... (advice): put on your best suit and don't be late.

4 Looking at grammar: *some*, *any* and their compounds

Grammar

Remember *eingeladen*

1 The invited guests can bring **some guests** as well.
2 You don't want **any trouble**.
3 Are **any journalists** coming to the reception? *Kommen einige Journalisten an die Rezeption*
4 May I have **some sugar**, please? *Kann ich bitte etwas / Zucker haben*
5 Would you like **some wine**? *Möchten Sie etwas / Wein*
6 About half the guests will bring **somebody** with them.
7 Kate didn't think **anything** about gate-crashers.
8 Have you seen Michael **anywhere**, Jasmin?

■ Wir benutzen *some* in **bejahten Aussagen** (1) und *any* in **verneinten Aussagen** (2) und **Fragen** (3).

! Drückt die Frage eine **Bitte** (4) oder ein **Angebot** (5) aus und man erwartet *yes* als Antwort, dann benutzen wir *some*.

■ Die **Zusammensetzungen** von *some/any* verwenden wir in genau derselben Art und Weise. (6)–(8)

A Complete the sentences with *some* or *any*.

1 – Kate, have we had ...[1] replies to our ad yet? *any*
    Antworten
    – No, but Jasmin said there are ...[2] on our website. *some*
2 – Excuse me. Could I have ...[1] salt, please? *some*
    – Of course, madam. I'll get you ...[2] at once. *some* *Sofort* *some*
3 I'm afraid we don't have ...[1] private parking, but you'll usually find ...[2] free *any* *some*
    spaces round the corner in Nelson Road.
4 Michael doesn't have ...[1] appointments this morning, but he's interviewing ...[2] *any* *some*
    job applicants this afternoon.
5 – Jasmin, can you lend me ... computer disks, please? *lehen some*
    – Of course. Take as many as you want.
6 Has Joshua had ...[1] luck finding a new flat? If not, there are ...[2] cheaper ones *any* *some*
    in the paper today.
7 – Can you eat ...[1] more salad, Kate? You can have mine. *some*
    – Thanks. I'd like ...[2] very much if you don't want ...[3]. *some, any*
8 Michael has been going to the fitness centre for three months now but he
    hasn't lost ... weight. *any*

B Complete the sentences with *some/any*, *somebody/anybody*, *something/anything* or *somewhere/anywhere*.
    (Substantiv davor) etwas jemand etwas

1 – I've found a cool apartment in Fulham but now I need ...[1] to share it with me. *Somebody jdn*
    – Well, what about me? I'm looking for a flat ...[2] in Fulham. *somewhere*
    irgendwo
2 – I can't find my umbrella ...[1] now and I know I left it ...[2] in the computer room. *somewhere* *anywhere something anything some*
    – Ask Joshua. He said ...[3] about an umbrella when he went to get the post.
3 – Did you buy ...[1] to eat, Kate, or are we going out to a restaurant again?
    – Well, I bought ...[2] fruit, but I suppose you want ...[3] cooked, do you? *something*
4 – Blue Sky needs ...[1] experienced in website management and they have asked *Somebody somebody*
    us to find ...[2] for them. I don't suppose you know ...[3] who might be suitable, do
    you? *anybody*

– You must be joking. We're looking for ...[4] ~somebody~ ourselves. I don't think you're going to have ...[5] ~an~ luck there.

5 – Michael wants ...[1] figures on travel insurance ~versicher~ prices, Joshua. If you aren't doing ...[2], you could help him. ~something anything~

– Yes, but I am doing ...[3], Kate. Michael told me to check ...[4] competitors' prices for him.

6 – Have you heard ...[1] more about that tanker accident off Brest, Joshua? ...[2] customers wanted to know. ~Something~

– Sorry, but I'm sure there will be ...[3] on the 12 o'clock news about it or can you find ...[4] about it on the internet?

5 Looking at grammar: *much, many, a lot of, plenty of*

Grammar

Remember

1 I don't think **many uninvited guests** will come.
2 **How many guests** are you expecting?
3 I don't have **much information** at all, Ben. ~Ich habe überhaupt k... viele Infor~
4 Do we really need **so much beer**?
5 **A lot of journalists** will come without an invitation.
6 We'll need **a lot of beef** because not many guests are vegetarian.
7 We have **plenty of experience** with business receptions, Kate. ~brauchst Erfahrung~

- Wir benutzen *many* mit zählbaren (1) (2) und *much* mit nichtzählbaren (3) (4) Nomen in **verneinten Aussagen** und in **Fragen**.
- In **bejahten Aussagen** verwenden wir *a lot of* sowohl mit zählbaren als auch mit nichtzählbaren Nomen. (5) (6)

! **Beachten Sie**, dass *a lot of* nicht nach *as, so, too, how* oder *very* benutzt werden kann.
  Examples *People didn't drink **as much beer** as usual.*
  *Don't worry. There won't be **very many gate-crashers**.*

- Wollen wir „mehr als genug" ausdrücken, benutzen wir *plenty of* statt *a lot of*. (7)

Complete the sentences with *much, many, a lot of* or *plenty of*.

1 – Hurry up! We don't have ...[1] time. ~much~
   – Nonsense. We've ...[2] time. Our train doesn't leave until 5. ~a plenty of~
   – Really? I thought it left ...[3] earlier than that. ~much~
2 – How ...[1] people work for Blue Sky now? ~many~
   – About 50 or 60, I think. ~so viele~
   – Good heavens, as ...[2] as that? ~much~
   – Yes. They've opened ...[3] branches recently, don't forget. ~many~ ~a lot~
3 You needn't go to the petrol station. There's ...[1] petrol in the tank and you won't ~much~ need ...[2] to get to Dover. Fill up in Calais. Petrol is ...[3] cheaper in France. ~much~
4 – This company employs ...[1] women, but not ...[2] of them have management jobs.
   ~a lot of~ ~many~

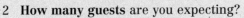

many (a lot of)

– Sure, but as far as I can see ...[3] women don't want top jobs. They prefer their
freedom, and you can't say ...[4] against that, can you? *much*

5 – How ...[1] cash have we got? *much*
much – Not ...[2], and we'll need quite ...[3] money this weekend. *much / a lot of*
– Oh, yes. We've got to buy ...[4] presents, haven't we? *many / a lot of*

6 – How ...[1] cigarettes does Harry smoke a day? *many*
many – Far too ...[2]. And he eats and drinks too ...[3] as well. He's going to have ...[4] health
problems when he's older. *much* *a lot of / many*

6 Looking at grammar: *(a) little, (a) few*

Grammar

Remember

1 Joshua should add **a little water** to his whisky.   (ein wenig Wasser)
2 Would you like **a few potatoes**?   (ein paar Kartoffeln)
3 People showed **little interest** in Michael's talk.   (wenig Interesse)
4 **Few people** work as hard as Jasmin.   (wenige Leute)

■ Wir benutzen *(a) little* mit nichtzählbaren (1) (3) und *(a) few* mit zählbaren (2) (4)
Nomen. Dies gilt für alle Satzarten.

A Complete the sentences with *(a) little* or *(a) few*.

1 – Would you like ...[1] more chips, madam?
– No, thank you. Just give me ...[2] sauce, please.
2 Poor Harry is only allowed to drink ... dry white wine with his meals now.
3 I'm not surprised that Kate and Michael have ...[1] personal problems. They
have very ...[2] time for each other and that's awful for a relationship.
4 – May I give you ...[1] advice, Joshua? Why not try thinking for ...[2] minutes
before you speak?
5 – How far is the hotel from the beach?
– Well, it says here it's only ... hundred metres away.
6 I'm afraid I've very ...[1] time to look into your complaint this week. Could you
give me a ring in ...[2] days, please? Then I'm sure I'll know ...[3] more.
7 There are ... food shops in town centres nowadays, just awful shopping malls
on the edge of town.
8 Some of our trainees show ...[1] interest in their work and ...[2] of them even take
the day off instead of going to college. I've very ...[3] understanding for people
like that.

B Express these ideas in English.

1 Die Nachrichten sind schlecht. Die Polizei kann die fehlenden (*missing*)
Touristen nicht finden.
2 Geben Sie bitte keine Kataloge mehr an Schüler aus. Wir haben nur wenige
übrig.
3 Heute brauchen wir kein Brot für die Party. Wir haben viele Brötchen.
4 Für unsere Party wollen wir viel vegetarisches Essen und wenig Fleisch und
Fisch.
5 Kann ich bitte etwas Salz haben?
6 Ich habe viel zu tun. Wollen Sie mir ein wenig helfen?

Focus

A Advertising is everywhere. Where have you seen advertisements during the last 24 hours, for example on TV, in magazines or on advertising columns in the streets?

B What sorts of advertisement were they? Think about brochures, posters, newspaper and magazine adverts (including classified ads), neon signs, TV and radio commercials, internet ads and sponsorship advertising.

C What do you think of these adverts? Use this language.

> *boring* ▪ *clever* ▪ *controversial* ▪ *daring* ▪ *erotic* ▪ *funny* ▪
> *hard-hitting* ▪ *sentimental* ▪ *shocking* ▪ *silly* ▪ *sweet*

D What do these adverts aim to do? Use this language.

> *Number ... persuades you to ...* ▪ *Number ... warns you not to ...* ▪
> *Number ... promotes ...* ▪ *Number ... draws attention to ...*

A People and society

Track 6 *Tara Newton joined the fast-growing advertising agency Pearson McCall a year ago. Here, she describes her new life in the world of advertising.*

Breaking into

Advertising

" I really got interested in advertising when I was in my college badminton team.

5 We were in the national league, and we suddenly found we didn't have enough money for training, equipment and travel. Fortunately, I'd had a summer job with a local video production company, and I knew the publicity manager. We had some meetings

10 and we put together a sponsorship deal. They got their name and logo on our T-shirts, and we got the money we needed. We were very lucky!

Anyway, I decided that a career in advertising was what I wanted most, and I applied for

15 various jobs. At my interview here, they seemed more interested in the sponsorship deal than anything else. Anyway, the interview

20 went very well – much better than I had expected, and next thing, I had a job!

I'm now a trainee

25 account manager, and it's very interesting.

An account manager is the bridge between a client and everyone here who is doing work for the client. They've just given me a client of my own for the first time, a company called Magic Moment Food and 30 Drink. We're working on the launch of a new drink called Starburst. It's exciting – and terrifying, too!

This is the story so far. First my boss, Julie Pearson, and I met the client to find out what they wanted and to give them general advice. 35 Then I wrote a report for the whole team here. That's especially important for the 'creatives' who are developing the ideas, images and words for the campaign. The first result is this ad. The clients love our latest design – and our new slogan: 40 "Starburst Beats Thirst".

I work closely with the media planners, too. Early on, they decide what media to use when, and how much. (In this case we're 45 going to start with a burst of TV commercials, and follow with ads in teenage magazines.) Then the media planners book the actual TV time and magazine space. In fact, 50 that's the topic of my next meeting with them, five minutes from now. "

(341 words)

1 Looking at the text

A Using your own words as far as possible, answer the questions on the text.

1 Why did Tara's college badminton team need money?
2 What was Tara able to do about it?
3 Why was this event at college important again later when Tara was looking for a job?
4 What job did she get?
5 How has her job changed recently?
6 Apart from her boss, which other people does she work closely with?
7 What do the people in the first of these groups do?
8 What do the people in the other group do?

B Put the paragraph headings in the correct order.

3 a Early progress in the new job
5 b How the advertising campaign is planned and arranged
1 c Tara's first practical experience of advertising
2 d Taking charge of a project for the first time
4 e The successful search for a job in advertising

C Give your opinion.

Which of the jobs that Tara talks about do you think might be especially interesting? Why?

I think I'd find the job of (media planning)	(very) enjoyable.
At a guess, I'd say (the creatives') work might be	(lots of) fun.
That's (probably) because	I like …
That's due to the fact that	I'm (quite) good at …

2 Working with words

A Match these words from the text with the list of synonyms.

fast-growing
- come new wadceno

Word from the text	Synonyms
1 *fast-growing* ▪ 2 *summer job* ▪ 3 *company* ▪ 4 *put together* ▪ 5 *deal* ▪ 6 ▪ *lucky* 7 *jobs* 8 *especially*	5 *agreement* ▪ 3 *business* ▪ 6 *fortunate* ▪ 1 *rapidly-expanding* ▪ 2 *holiday job* ▪ 4 *organize* ▪ 8 *particularly* ▪ 7 *posts*

B Rewrite the following sentence, using synonyms from **2A**.

Tara was especially lucky to get the job of trainee account manager with Pearson McCall, a fast-growing London advertising company.

3 Culture check: forms of address

Read the pieces of conversation from two situations. Decide the following.

1 When and where were these things said?
2 What rules do the speakers follow? Think about the changing situation.
   Who can and cannot suggest using first names?
3 In the same situations in Germany, what forms of address would people use?

Situation 1

A Please come in and take a seat, Miss Newton. Tara Newton, isn't it?
B Yes, Ms Pearson.
A Well, I'm glad you managed to find us all right. So, let's begin.

Situation 2 (an hour later)

A Congratulations! You've got the job.
B Fantastic! Thank you, Ms Pearson.
A Oh, please call me Julie. We're very informal here, Tara.

INFO

1 *Mr*, *Mrs* and *Ms* are the usual formal titles used when dealing with clients or customers.
   (*Ms* [mɪz] is for women when you do not know if they are married.)
2 In many companies, staff use first names with each other – even between junior and
   senior staff. This may seem very informal, but it is not really. It is nothing like the closeness of the German 'du' form.
3 As in Germany, changing from formal style to first names must come from the senior
   person, eg from Julie to Tara.

4 Listening

Track 7

A AIDA is a well-known formula used to create adverts like the one below.
Listen to Marcus McCall, co-founder and co-director of Pearson McCall, talking on
the TV programme *Money Matters*. Note the words that AIDA stands for.

A   means A…
I   means I…
D   means …
A   means …

B Listen again and note (in two or three words) each of the four AIDA features of
this CD brochure.

B People and issues

Julie Pearson, who interviewed Tara, is on a panel of experts discussing advertising at an international youth conference.

expertenrunde diskussion
Werbung   internationale Jugend-Konferenz
eine Frau wie sie

Carla Ms Pearson, as a woman yourself, can I ask how you justify the use of women in advertising? Advertisers use women to sell everything from cars to cans of cola!

Verkauf

5 **Julie** Well, I don't justify it. Quite simply, I don't allow that sort of thing at Pearson McCall. Our advertising just doesn't work like that.

Carla But a lot does. Why is that?

Julie Why? To attract attention –

10 the first task of any ad.

Carla But it trivializes women, doesn't it? It makes us look dumb. It turns us into sex objects!

Julie Well, I don't think it's as

15 bad as it was. Women are far more powerful than they were, and advertisers don't want to upset half the population! In fact, advertisers often succeed by showing

20 exactly that. Take this car ad, for example. The successful-looking woman here is clearly very powerful and elegantly dressed. She seems to have her own private jet, itself very

25 fast, powerful and elegant. And she doesn't just have an ordinary dog: she has two leopards! Speed, power and elegance again. And so the car takes on these qualities as well. It also seems powerful, elegant and successful – like the

30 woman. This woman probably runs a business empire with thousands of men and women working for her. She's in charge. And the car for her is this one.

This ad shows another thing, too. In the old

35 days, there were always words, words, words – the old 'hard-sell'. Here the picture itself does the speaking. And that's the way it is now. Everybody is far more sophisticated these days, and so advertisers have to be smarter and

40 subtler, too.

Stefan Err, changing the subject, Ms Pearson, isn't it a fact that all advertising adds to the cost of products? So why not ban it and save money?

Julie True, it adds about 3% to the cost of

45 things. But it also introduces us to new products and that increases competition, which forces prices down. What's more, without advertising, magazines and newspapers would be much

more expensive, and there'd be no money to

50 make your favourite TV programmes.

Pierre But you're missing the most important point of all. It's this. Advertising makes us buy more than we need. And manufacturers also package goods more and more expensively –

55 covered with loads more advertising, of course. That means we're using global resources more wastefully than ever before.

Julie That's an excellent point. But advertising is just part of the global market system –

60 and a vital part, too. Without it, sales go down, companies collapse, jobs disappear, taxes fall, hospitals close, and then the economy falls faster again. So … get rid of advertising, and we go back to the Middle Ages. Is that what we

65 want? Are we strong enough to do that?

(444 words)

5 Looking at the text

A Say whether the statements are true, false or unclear from the text. Correct the false ones, and say why the unclear statements are unclear.

1 Julie is one of the directors of Pearson McCall. *t.*
2 The youth conference seems to be an international event. *t.*
3 Pearson McCall does not use women in its advertising. *f.*
4 Pearson McCall made the advert shown on p 36. *f.*
5 Greater competition because of advertising reduces the cost of products by about 3%. *unclear*
6 Magazines and newspapers would be thinner without advertising. *thinner* *unclear*
7 Pierre agrees with Stefan – that all advertising should stop. *t.*
8 Julie does not disagree that advertising increases waste, but she sees no realistic alternative. *t.*

B Give your opinion.

1 Julie mentions a car advert during the discussion. What adverts and commercials are popular at the moment? Why?

People	really like	the advert for … .	I think it's because it …
	seem to love	the commercial for … .	It's due to the way it …

2 Do you agree with everything that Julie says?

I	totally	agree	with her when she	says	that …
	partly	disagree		suggests	

Personally, I think that	she's exaggerating.
It seems to me that	she's giving a one-sided view.
In my opinion,	she's got it about right.

6 Looking at grammar: comparison of adjectives and adverbs

Grammar

Remember

1 The woman is **stronger than** the man. In fact, she's the **strongest** person in the whole commercial.
2 Women are **more powerful than** they were. In fact, some of the **most powerful** people in the world today are women.
3 We're using resources **more wastefully than** ever before. The Japanese are actually the ones who use packaging **most wastefully** of all.
4 The 'creatives' are working **faster than usual** on this job. But they worked **fastest** of all six months ago when we did a very big anti-drugs campaign.
5 I don't think it is **as bad as** it was.
6 The old 'hard-sell' approach does **not** work **as well as** it did.

- Einsilbige Adjektive werden mit *-er* und *-est* gesteigert. (1) Dies gilt häufig auch für zweisilbige Adjektive, die auf *-y* enden. Dabei wird das *-y* zu *-i*, z.B. *happier, happiest*.
! **Beachten Sie:** *good / better / best* *bad / worse / worst*

Grammar

- Andere, längere Adjektive werden mit *more* und *most* gesteigert. (2)
- Adverbien, die auf *-ly* enden, werden mit *more* und *most* gesteigert. (3)
- Einige kurze Adverbien werden wie kurze Adjektive mit *-(i)er* and *-(i)est* gesteigert. (4) Die häufigsten sind: *early, fast, hard, late, long, straight.*
- ! **Beachten Sie:** *well / better / best*   *badly / worse / worst*

- Vergleiche stellt man mit *than* her. Man kann es mit Adjektiven (1) (2) oder Adverbien verwenden (3).
- Auch mit *(not) as … as* kann man etwas vergleichen. Man kann es ebenfalls mit Adjektiven (5) oder Adverbien verwenden (6).

7 Practising grammar

A   Match graph lines A–E and ways of describing changes 1–9.

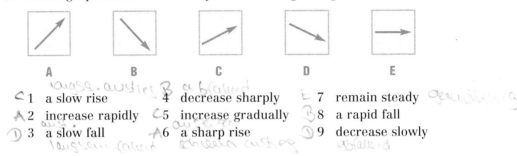

| A | B | C | D | E |

1   a slow rise   4   decrease sharply   7   remain steady
2   increase rapidly   5   increase gradually   8   a rapid fall
3   a slow fall   6   a sharp rise   9   decrease slowly

B   Look at the charts and read the statements. Say which statements use adjectives and which use adverbs. Then match the statements and charts.

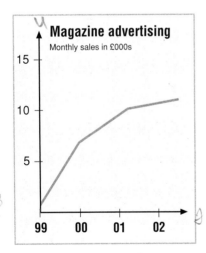
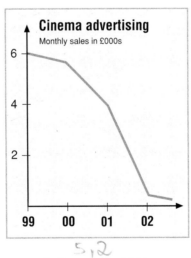
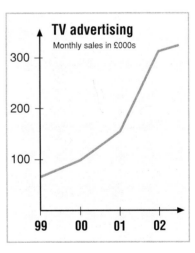

1   The sharpest rise of all came in 2001.
2   This decreased most rapidly in 2001.
3   The increase was greater in 1999 than in 2000.
4   This rose more slowly in 1999 than in 2000.
5   The fall in 1999 was not as sharp as in 2000.
6   This did not rise as rapidly in 2001 as in the previous two years.

C   Work with a partner. Each write four new statements about the charts. Exchange and read them, and match them to the correct charts.

8 Writing

⟳ Lernhilfen 4, S.146

Read the notes on the history of Blue Sky Adventure Travel and look at the chart. Then continue the story of Blue Sky. Use comparisons and this language.

> *remained (quite / fairly) steady* ■ *much more / less* ■
> *a little more / less* ■ *even more / less*

1993 Michael and Kate King start their adventure travel business from home.

1994 They move to a small office near their home.

1996 They hire their first assistant.

1997 They buy a shop with a flat above it in Fulham.
They also take on another member of staff.

1998 They hire a third member of staff.

2000 They set up their first website.

2001 They improve their website and launch a TV advertising campaign with Pearson McCall.

The Story of Blue Sky Adventure Travel

Michael and Kate King started their new business from home in 1993, but at first it only grew slowly. Then, in 1994, they moved to a small office near their home, and the business grew more rapidly that year than the year before. Although it remained fairly steady in the following year, sales rose quite sharply in 1996 when they hired ...

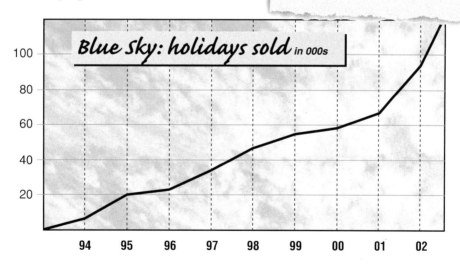

Blue Sky: holidays sold in 000s

9 Giving a presentation

⟳ Lernhilfen 5, S.150

Work with a partner to give a short presentation. First find a good advert that uses the AIDA formula. (The advert can be in German or English.) Your presentation should explain the following:

- what the advert is for;
- where it comes from;
- who it is aimed at – the 'target audience';
- how it works, (using the AIDA formula – see p 35);
- how well it works, particularly with its target audience, and why you both like it.

Further reading

The Ross family have bought a powerful, new home computer. After all the usual fun with computer games, everyone is now thinking about learning new skills.

A Read the adverts for different courses, and match them to family members' needs.

B Answer these further questions.
  a Can any of them travel together to courses and save travel costs?
  b How many hours is each family member likely to study?
  c How much is the family likely to pay for all the courses put together?

Dave Ross, 20, is preparing to leave his present job and set up his own motorbike courier service, and he wants to learn the necessary IT skills. He will need to run his accounts on computer, of course, and he also wants his own website and internet access to useful business information.

Susie Ross, 17, thinks she might train as a graphics designer and go into advertising. Her school art department has no computer facilities, so she wants to get some experience of computer graphics in some other way.

Mrs Ross has always avoided computers, but she has recently started a consumers' action group for safer food, and she aims to produce a newsletter, send letters to the media, etc. She needs basic word processing skills.

Sunningwall College of Further Education
is delighted to offer the following down-to-earth evening courses for people who find that they need new computing skills in their everyday lives. We realize that time is the enemy, and we concentrate only on practical skills which you can put to immediate use. Courses start the week of Mon 12th September.

Course IT101: Word processing
10 wks, Wed 6–8 pm, £60. Basic keyboarding and wordprocessing skills for letter-writing, etc.

Course IT102: IT for accounting
10 wks, Wed & Fri 6–8 pm, £130. Basic skills to keep a close eye on your home or small business accounts – income and expenditure, preparation of quarterly and annual accounts.

Course IT103: Going online
8 wks, Mon 6–8 pm, £50. Help with access to the internet. Also learn how to set up your own website.

Sunningwall Arts Centre Holiday Courses for Fun
Would you like to open up the potential of yourself and your computer to create beautiful art and design together? If so, join us for an intensive fun week (Mon–Fri, 10 am–5 pm) during the holiday period. Cost: £150 (20% reductions for senior citizens, students and unemployed).

Call Sally Lambert for further details on 01235 710359.

Focus

A Match jobs 1–8 and pictures a–h.

waiter · Kellner

1 waitress *Kellnerin* 4 carer *Altenpf* 7 shop assistant *Verkäufer*
2 farm worker *Landwi* 5 IT technician 8 personal fitness trainer
3 call centre operator 6 bank clerk

B Think about these jobs and the changing world of work. Do you think the number of people in each job is increasing or decreasing in Germany?

Anstieg   Abfallend

C Do you think the 'new' jobs are better or worse than the 'old' ones? In what ways? Which of the jobs above would you (not) like to try?

> *badly-paid / well-paid* ■ *boring / interesting* ■ *clean / dirty* ■
> *creative / uncreative* ■ *difficult / easy* ■ *outdoor / indoor* ■ *secure /*
> *insecure* ■ *stressful / stress-free*
>
> *be friendly and helpful at all times* ■ *be independent* ■ *do what*
> *you're told to do* ■ *gain useful experience* ■ *get a good salary* ■ *Gehalt*
> *learn new skills* ■ *meet customers / people / colleagues* ■ *work long*
> */ flexible / (ir)regular / reasonable / unsocial hours*

Old	jobs	like …		are	better	than	modern	ones	such as …
New		such as …			worse		traditional		like …

That's because the	new	jobs are	more …	than the	old	ones.
	old		less …		new	

I'd (quite) like to try …   because it's …
I'd be interested in trying …

I'm not interested in any of these jobs, but I'd like to try being a …

health management   learn – verdienen

A People and society

American career counselor Rob Harmer recently wrote this for young people seeking part-time work.

Thinking of getting a job?

You go to find a new CD in the record shop. The girl behind the counter is in your history class. And just recently, your mum came home from work with
5 this news: the part-time technician who fixed her office computer has just started his junior year in high school.

Over a third of all American high school students work during the school year, according
10 to the statistics. And in the last seven years, the number of teens with jobs has increased by 50%.

So, if you haven't already started work, should you get a part-time job now? Here are three
15 reasons to go for it:
- A job will show you the working world and help you decide your future career.
- The right job can give you a feeling of real job satisfaction.
20 • And of course the money is great!

But before you go any further, consider these 'test' questions very carefully:
- Are you sure you're on top of your school-work and you're getting good grades?
25 • Might a job affect family life badly? Could it mean 'forgetting' your domestic chores or arriving home tired and bad-tempered?
- Would you have to reduce extra-curricular activities, like sport? Or your social life?

30 If you answered 'Yes', 'No' and 'No', then follow these tips for success. But be careful about hours. Aim for 6–10 hours a week. Whatever you do, don't work more than 15 hours a week.

1 Think about what interests you   35
If you like what you do, you'll get a real kick out of it. If not, you'll be unhappy.

2 Look for job openings
Here's how to find out who's hiring:
- Choose places that interest you. If you love   40 movies, for example, try a video store.
- Look out for signs on storefronts.
- Check the classified ads.
- Ask friends and the school career counselor.
- Read the job boards at the supermarket or   45 job center or on the internet or at school.

3 Apply
Here are some useful ideas:
- Visit the business when it's not busy and ask to speak to the manager. Don't be scared!   50
- Expect to fill out an application form. For this you'll need your social security number, address, home phone number and at least two references.
- Don't worry about a resumé if this is your   55 first job.

4 Go for your interview
Here's how to make a good impression:
- Plan to arrive a little early.
- Follow the right dress code. If it's not an office   60 job, you probably don't need a dress or suit. Even so, look neat, cover up tattoos and take out that nose ring!
- Stand out from other applicants. Look your interviewer(s) in the eye. Smile. Show   65 enthusiasm.
- Be prepared. Think of questions they might ask. And what about your questions? Find out if there will be a math or aptitude test.

Finally, … good luck!   70

(469 words)

1   Looking at the text

A   Answer the questions on the text.
1   What do the girl 'behind the counter' and the boy who fixed the office computer have in common?
2   In addition to money and interest, what else can a part-time job offer?
3   What areas of life can a part-time job affect badly?
4   If somebody answered the three 'test' questions 'Yes', 'Yes' and 'No', what should that person not do, and why not?
5   Is it enough just to find a job which pays well? Why not?
6   In what ways can the American school environment help students find jobs?
7   How can you make yourself known to an employer? (two things.)
8   What can you do before an interview to help make it go well?

B   Give your opinion.
What sorts of part-time work would you most and least like to do? Why?
(Use language from **Focus C**.)

2   Working with words   ⊃ Lernhilfen 2.3, S.144

Making a word spider is a very good way of collecting and learning a word field – the vocabulary of a particular topic, eg jobs.

A   Copy and expand this word network with the following words from the unit.

> *aptitude test* ▪ *career counsellor* ▪ *classified ads* ▪ *experience* ▪
> *hours* ▪ *interview* ▪ *job boards* ▪ *resumé*

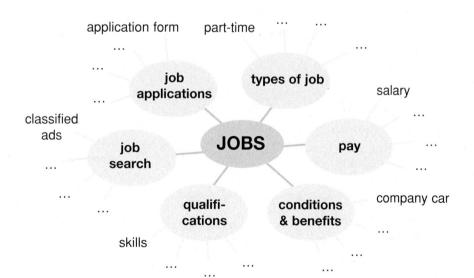

B   Add these words – and others that you know.

> *academic qualifications* ▪ *full-time* ▪ *hourly rate* ▪ *overtime* ▪ *overtime pay*
> ▪ *paid holidays* ▪ *paper qualifications* ▪ *permanent* ▪ *temporary* ▪ *wages*

C Use words from **2A** and **2B** to complete the following.

IAN   I'm going for a job ...[1] at the MediTech factory tomorrow.

SUE   Oh? How did you find out about it?

IAN   I saw it in the ...[2] in the newspaper. I just phoned and asked for an ...[3]. I completed that and sent it in, and they called me almost immediately.

SUE   That's good – you need the money, don't you? What's the ...[4] like?

IAN   Not bad. It's six-fifty an hour, and if I do extra time on Sundays, there's ...[5] at nine-fifty an hour.

SUE   Great! But what ...[6] do they want? Do you have to show them your exam certificates?

IAN   No, they'll give me the necessary training, but before that I have to pass an ...[7] to show that I've got the basic ...[8] that you need to do the job.

3 Listening

Tracks 10 and 11

A First, read the job advert quickly. Then listen to the two job interviews. Make quick notes on the following:

Name: ...

Age: ...

Day(s) available: ...

Language(s): ...

People skills: ...

General attitude towards work: ...

B Finally, decide who should get the job, and why.

CAFÉ CHARISMA

The Number 1 airport coffee shop

We are looking for part-time waiters and waitresses for well-paid weekend employment – Saturday and/or Sunday, 10 am–6 pm. Successful applicants will be hard-working, responsible and smart in appearance. They will also have good 'people skills', will be friendly, positive and good communicators. They will speak German and one or more other European language, including English. Experience an advantage, but not essential. Training given and uniform provided.

Apply (in English) to Frau S Kaufmann, Café Charisma GmbH, Postfach 70 40 56, 60313 Frankfurt am Main.

4 Culture check: meeting and greeting

Tony Ross has just got a part-time factory job. His new section head, Sue Wate, introduces him to the boss. Should Tony reply with a), b) or c)?

SUE W   Mr Riley, this is our new part-time production assistant, Tony Ross.

MR R   How do you do?

TONY R   a) Fine, thank you. How do you do?

            b) I'm fine, thanks. How are you?

            c) How do you do?

Tony sees an employee, Marie Carr, who was a friend at school.

What is the best greeting for him to use a), b), c) or d)? How could she reply?

TONY R   a) Good morning, Marie! How are you?   c) Hello, Marie! How do you do?

            b) Hi, Marie! How are you?   d) How are you?

Should Tony shake hands in either, neither or both of these situations?

B People and issues

Track 12

Today, women are doing jobs their grandmothers did not dream of doing 50 years ago. They have reached the top of large organizations, and they make up nearly half the workforce in most western countries. But there are problems, as this report shows.

Superwoman: *mission impossible?*

■ **By Lisa Price**

■ *Social Affairs Correspondent*

Shona Wilson has had enough. For the last few years, she has juggled the pieces of her life as wife, mother and busy advertising account manager.
5 But now another baby is on the way, and Shona has just made an important decision. For the next few years, she will leave the workplace and be a full-time mum instead.

10 ■ What has brought her to this point? 'For four years, I've been trying to do two full-time jobs – look after a family and do a busy job – and I'm exhausted. I've never been so tired.'
15 More importantly, she has felt increasingly guilty – for example on her morning walk to playschool with four-year-old Gina when she asks constantly, 'When are you coming home,
20 Mummy?'

■ Of course, she has had help. Husband Mark does what he can in the evening – when he is not away on business trips. Since Gina's and Luke's birth, she has also relied
25 heavily on her excellent nanny, Britta, who helps with the housework, too. In the end, though, she feels she must take full responsibility herself. 'I love my work and my financial freedom,' she says, 'but my real
30 dream is to bring up my children properly. So I'm ready to give up my career now to make sure my kids will be good human beings.'
■ Many other successful career women are making this decision, too. So is this the end of the 'Superwoman' dream, the idea that 35 women can have it all – a family and a career? Are women handing back the workplace to men and retreating to their 'proper place' in the home?

■ Certainly not. Today, women can choose 40 any role they want, and they can also change roles as they go through life. Shona says, 'I wanted to be Superwoman and have it all. Now I know I can do that, but I can't do it all at the same time.' 45

■ And, who knows, in another ten years she may be ready to start a whole new career. ■

(326 words)

5 Looking at the text

⟳ Lernhilfen 4.2, S.146

A Put the sentences in order to form a summary. Then compare the summary with the original text. What has changed? (Think about the details, use of direct speech, examples, style.)

a She has had help from her husband and from an excellent nanny.

b Many working mothers are doing the same.

c For four years Shona Wilson has continued her career while raising a family.

d She has reached this decision partly because of exhaustion.

e However, she now wants to be fully responsible for the way her children grow up.

f But they are not just going back to their old role in the home.

g Now, though, she has decided to concentrate on her family in the coming years.

h Instead, women are changing roles from career builder to homemaker and back again as they go through life.

i She also feels she is failing as a mother.

B Give your opinion.

1 Do you think Shona is right to give up work now? Was she right or wrong to continue work four years ago?

| I | definitely | think | she's | right | to | give up | now | because … |
| | tend to | | she was | wrong | | continue | then | |

2 You or your partner may be in the same situation in the future. What will you want (your partner) to do?

If	I'm	in the same	situation,	I	think	I'll	want		to …
	she's		position,		know			her	
	he's							him	

6 Working with words

Complete the comment below with the following useful words from the text.

> bring up ▪ career ▪ career woman ▪ change roles ▪ exhausted ▪
> guilty ▪ financial freedom ▪ full-time jobs ▪ give up ▪ have it all ▪
> make ▪ decision ▪ rely on ▪ take responsibility for ▪ workplace

In my opinion, Shona is right to … …[1] her successful …[2] and spend the coming years with her children.

Of course, it has been very difficult for her to …[3] this important …[4]: she clearly enjoys her work very much and the … …[5] it has given her.

However, she has tried to do two … …[6] for a long time, and she now feels …[7] in herself and …[8] towards her children. She believes that she can no longer … …[9] others to … …[10] her children for her, and that she herself must now … …[11] and … … …[12] the way they grow up. At this stage, she feels – rightly – that this is the most important thing in both her own and her children's lives.

To conclude, it was certainly not wrong of Shona to try to … … …[13] – to be a wife, a mother and a … …[14] – at the same time. It is now time to accept, though, that home will be her new …[15] for a number of years to come.

7 Looking at grammar: simple past and present perfect

Grammar

Remember

1 Women are doing jobs their grandmothers **did not dream** of doing **50 years ago**.
2 **For the last few years**, she **has juggled** her life.
3 **Since Gina's and Luke's birth**, she **has relied** on Britta.
4 Shona **has just made** an important decision.
5 Q **Has** Shona **ever tried** hiring a nanny? *einstellen*

   A Yes, she **has had** a nanny **for a long time**. She **hired** Britta **four years ago**.
6 For four years, I've **been trying** to do two full-time jobs.

Seit 4 jahren versuche ich 2 Vollzeitjobs zu machen

- Wir benutzen das **simple past** für abgeschlossene Ereignisse und Zustände in der Vergangenheit. (1) Häufig weisen Ausdrücke wie *ago, last (week), the day before* *Vorgestern*
  yesterday usw. auf den Gebrauch des **simple past** hin.
- Das **present perfect** wird benutzt, wenn etwas in der Vergangenheit begonnen hat und immer noch andauert. (2) (3) Hier soll man auf Ausdrücke wie *ever, never, all (his) life, since* (+ Zeitpunkt), *for* (+ Zeitdauer), *still (not), (not) yet* achten.
- Das **present perfect** steht auch, wenn etwas aus der Vergangenheit Auswirkungen auf die Gegenwart hat. Oft steht in diesem Zusammenhang das Wort *just*. (4)
- Wenn ein Aspekt der Vergangenheit plötzlich geklärt wird, wechselt man häufig vom **present perfect** zum **simple past**. (5)
- Die Vorstellung eines andauernden Prozesses unterstreicht man mit dem **present perfect continuous**. (6)

8 Practising grammar

A Complete Tina's story, putting the verbs in brackets in the correct tenses – simple past or present perfect.

Tina Rhodes ...[1] (always enjoy) buying fashion clothes and accessories. By the time she ...[2] (be) fifteen, she ...[3] (find) the allowance from her parents far too small so she ...[4] (decide) to get regular part-time work.

During the last two years she ...[5] (do) four or five different weekend jobs. The job she ...[6] (have) at an expensive hotel for the last three months pays quite well and the tips are good too, so she ...[7] (even manage) to save some of her pay.

But then the manager ...[8] (ask) her to work two or three evening shifts during the week too – or lose her weekend work.

Sadly, this ...[9] (already affect) family life and her school work badly.

B Complete the conversation between Tina and the manager. Put the verbs in brackets in the simple past or present perfect continuous.

TINA   Dave, you know I ...[1] (start) working evening shifts last month.

DAVE   Yes, and you ...[2] (do) a great job, Tina. I'm very pleased.

TINA   Well, there's a problem: I ...[3] (not do) a great job with school work because of this. And my parents ...[4] (put) a lot of pressure on me to stop.

DAVE   Well, I'm sorry, but they need to understand the situation here.

TINA   But I ...[5] (think) about it a lot. I'm afraid I really have to go back to weekends only or stop work completely.

DAVE   Mmm, let me think about it. We certainly don't want to lose you, Tina.

9 Writing: a letter of application

→ Lernhilfen 4, S.146

Follow the instructions below to write a letter of application to Frau Kaufmann of Café Charisma (p 44).

Paragraph 1
Say what you are writing about, referring to Café Charisma's advert in (name of newspaper) on (date).

Paragraph 2
Say briefly why you think you would be good at the job.
Refer to your language skills.
Refer to any useful experience you have.

Paragraph 3
Say what day(s) you could work, and also how soon you could start.

Paragraph 4
Add names and addresses of people, eg a teacher or a former employer (but never a family member), who can act as references.

Paragraph 5
Say that you very much hope to have the chance of an interview.
Say that you look forward to hearing from Frau Kaufmann in the near future.

10 Listening

Tracks 10 and 11

Listen to the job interviews again. Which of the following useful expressions do you hear?

Interviewer
1 Let's begin by talking about (you) a little bit.
2 I'd like to move on to (explain the way we work here).
3 Perhaps we could go back to (something you wrote in your letter of application).
4 Could you say a little more about (your reasons for applying for this job)?
5 Have you got any questions you would like to ask?
6 Thank you for coming in today. You'll hear from us shortly.

Interviewee
1 I'm sorry. I didn't quite understand the question.
2 To cut a long story short, (I need a job to help pay for college).
3 There are one or two things I would like to ask about.
4 I'd like to know a bit more about (the pay).
5 Am I right in thinking that (you pay overtime for evening work)?
6 Thank you for the chance of an interview. I'll look forward to hearing from you.

11 Speaking: job interviews

Work in pairs. Take turns to interview each other for a job at Café Charisma.
Try to use useful expressions from **exercise 10** above.

www.job-interview.net

C Further reading

You have won

a competition, and the prize is a return air ticket to Australia next summer holiday. You want to see the country, but you have to do it cheaply. A working holiday is the answer. But which one? You want:

- to work but not too much: you need time to enjoy yourself;
- to experience life in two or three places in just seven weeks;
- food and accommodation while you are working, and perhaps a little pay, (though you can pay for travel around the country yourself).

Read and choose, giving reasons for and against different types of holiday.

THE VISITOZ SCHEME

Springbok Farm, Goomeri, Queensland 4601
visitozscheme@onaustralia.com.au

Gives basic agricultural training followed by work (including work with horses, cattle, sheep and crocodiles) on farms throughout Australia.

No experience necessary, but enthusiasm and good English essential. 40–80 hour week, after training. 1–3 months, throughout the year. Basic salary according to skills and job. Food and accommodation, often with family. £10 application fee plus £340 course fee.

INTERNATIONAL VOLUNTEERS FOR PEACE

499 Elizabeth Street, Surrey Hills, NSW 2010
ivpsci@tig.com.au

Volunteers needed on workcamps. Recent projects include childcare for an urban Aboriginal community and working with children at a local primary school.

Applicants should be enthusiastic and ready to work hard as part of a team. Good English essential. 30–40 hour week. 2 weeks. November, January, July and September. Food and shared accommodation provided.

WILLING WORKERS ON ORGANIC FARMS (WWOOF)

690, Mount Murrindal Co-op, Buchan, Victoria 3685
wwoof@net-tech.com.au

A non-profitmaking company aiming to help organic farmers. Work available on approx 1,100 farms. Includes some places where the cultural exchange is more important than the farmwork, offering work choices such as typing, home maintenance, childcare, etc. From one week to 6 months.

Food and accommodation provided. Volunteers should take a sleeping bag. No fares or wages paid. Membership £17.

If you want information on jobs, you can visit:
www.summerjobs.com
www.monster.com or www.monster.co.uk

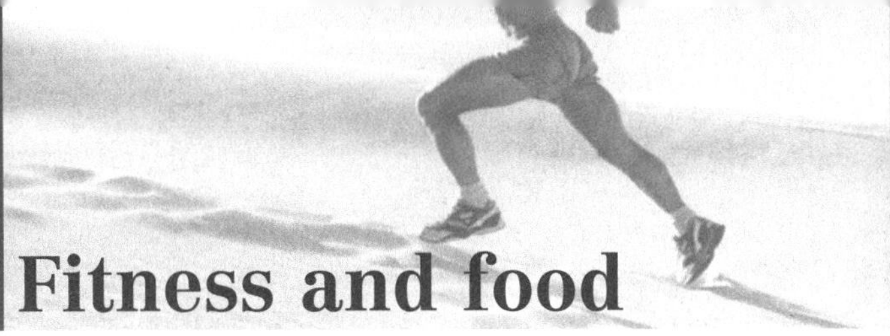

A Which of the types of food below do you really love? Do you absolutely hate any of them? What about other things that are not shown here?

B We all need a balanced mixture of protein (eg from meat and fish), carbohydrates (eg from bread and cereals), fat (eg from milk and other dairy products) and vitamins (eg from fruit and vegetables). With a partner, work out an enjoyable, healthy menu for one day. (You can add other things that are not shown here.)
www.lifebytes.gov.uk   www.foodfit.com

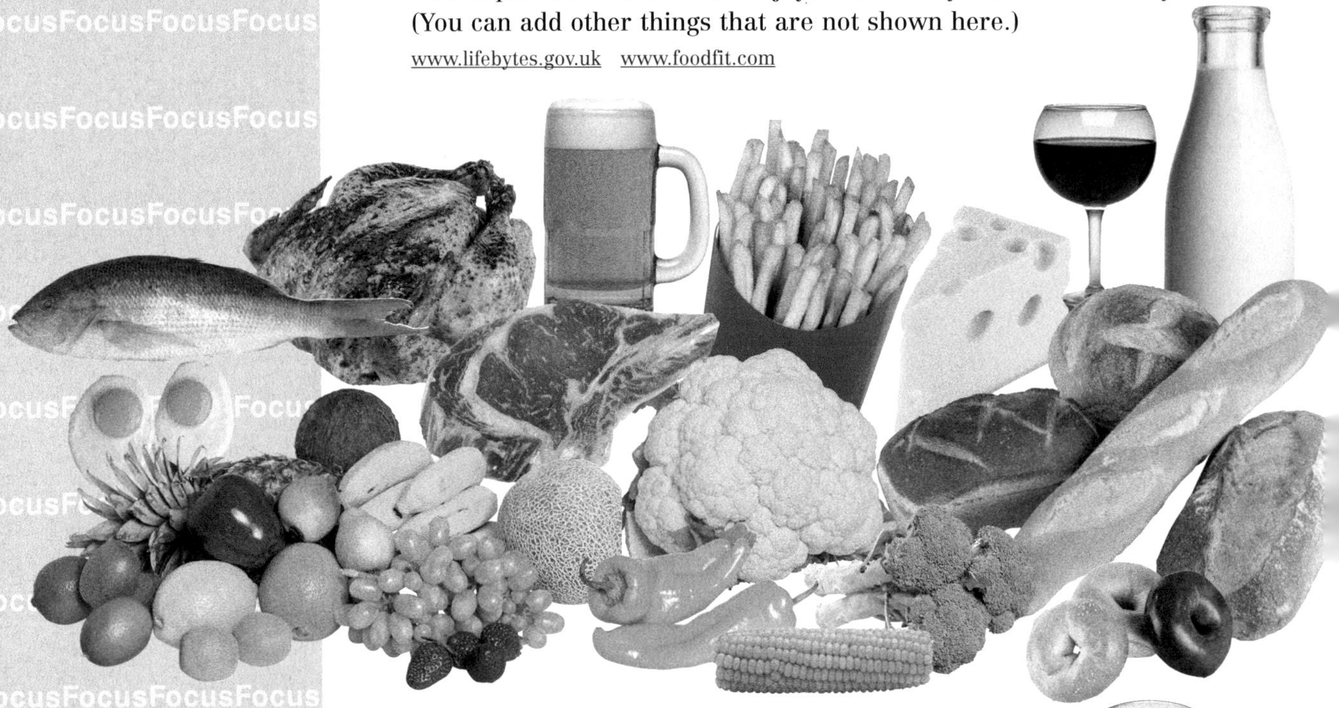

Use this language.

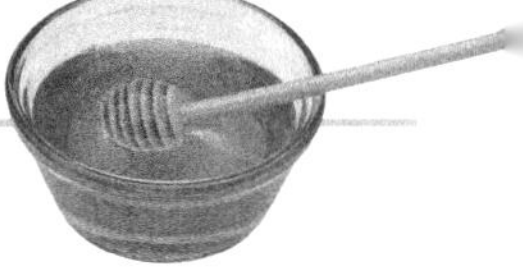

| I'd | really | like to | have | some (chicken). |
| | quite | | include | a few (chips). |

| I'd | rather (not) have | (any) ... | if that's all right. |
| | prefer (not) to have | | if you don't mind. |

| I'd | rather have ... than ... |
| | prefer ... to ... |

| But if we have ... and ... too, | that'll be | too much (fat). |
| | we'll have | too many (calories). |

But if we don't have any ... or ... either, we won't have enough (protein).

| Let's choose ... | instead. |
| Let's go for ... | instead of ... |

A People and society

Track 13

Personal fitness trainer Dave Stockman sees a lot of unfit people at the sports and leisure centre where he works. Many of them are older, but some are only in their teens. He also writes an advice column in the local newspaper, and here he has some advice for younger readers.

Body Matters by Dave Stockman

You're walking upstairs on your way to class. Someone starts talking about last night's episode of *Friends*, and you join in. But by the

time you're up the second flight of stairs,
5 you're out of breath, and you actually have to stop talking!

What's going on? You aren't really over-weight – well, not much – and you thought you were fit and healthy. But clearly you're not.
10 Why? According to recent studies, it's probably because you're not doing enough regular, vigorous, 'aerobic' exercise – especially if you're a girl. (By the way, the average 50-year-old British male is fitter than the average
15 15-year-old British female!)

What is an aerobic activity? It's anything that increases your heart rate and the amount of oxygen that your muscles burn. The experts say that just thirty minutes of aerobic activity a
20 day is enough to promote good health, keep weight under control, relieve stress and even make you sleep better. Now please don't think

that you have to start an extreme activity like long-distance running or that you need to go
25 and buy expensive exercise equipment. You don't even need to come to the sports and leisure centre, although of course you'll be very welcome if you do! Instead, here are three simple activities that anybody can try.
30 First, why not ride a bike to school every day? If that's difficult, make a habit of getting around by bike in your spare time. Secondly, if you go to school by bus, what about getting off a couple of stops early and walking the rest of
35 the way? Thirdly, you can get a natural workout through an informal fun game of basketball or football during the school lunch hour. (That way, your friends will be doing themselves a
40 good turn as well.)

The lazy alternative – minimum activity –
45 isn't a good one. Experts say that teens who enter adult life
50 out of shape are storing up long-term trouble. Over time, lack of physical activity is likely to contribute to health problems and may lead to heart disease,
55 osteoporosis and diabetes.

So ... when are you going to get active? Today? Good!

(356 words)

1 Looking at the text

⊃ Lernhilfen 4.2, S.146

A Answer the questions to form a summary.
1 Who does Dave Stockman address in this newspaper article?
2 How much aerobic activity is necessary?
3 How does it help?
4 What sort of activity is not necessary, however?
5 What are the dangers of very little activity?
6 What is Stockman's final piece of advice?

B Give your opinion.
After reading Dave Stockman's article, do you think schools should make students do more PE and/or sports?

Personally, I I really	think don't think	it would be a	good bad	idea move	to …

It seems to me To my mind,	we should	keep to … . change to … .	And here's why: … I'll tell you why: …

2 Working with words

⊃ Lernhilfen 1.2, S.142

A Find words and expressions in the text to fit these definitions. They are in the same order.
1 without enough air in you, so that you need to take in more air fast (lines 1–6)
2 fat (lines 7–15)
3 in good physical condition (lines 7–15)
4 energetic (lines 7–15)
5 elastic parts of body that push or pull to produce body movements (lines 16–22)
6 use and turn into energy (lines 16–22)
7 help, lead to (lines 16–22)
8 take away, reduce something bad (lines 16–22)
9 very hard physical exercise (lines 22–29)
10 training exercise for the body (lines 35–40)
11 not in good physical condition (lines 46–52)
12 help make something happen (lines 52–57)

B Complete the sentences with words and expressions from the text that you matched to the definitions in 2A.

TIM Tony's getting quite …[1]. He's only a small guy, but he must weigh 80 kilos or more.

SUE The main trouble is that he doesn't get any exercise. He was really …[2] when we had to run 50 metres to the bus stop the other day.

TIM I'm going to suggest that he comes to the gym with me for a …[3] once or twice a week.

SUE Yes, if he does that, he'll soon get a bit more …[4], and he'll …[5] off some fat too. Then perhaps I'll agree to go out with him!

3 Culture check: being indirect and polite

Dave Stockman is talking to Ann Riley, who wants to join the sports and leisure centre. Should he use forms a), b) or c)?

DAVE S   It's good to have you as a new member, Ms Riley. And I'll be your personal fitness trainer.

ANN R   I really hope to get into better shape – with your help.

DAVE S   a)   You were right to come for help.
        b)   I'm sure there's lots we can do to help.
        c)   You need a lot of help, and we're the experts.

ANN R   So what do I have to do to join?

DAVE S   OK, now first,
        a)   fill in this form for me, please.
        b)   you must fill in this form for me, please.
        c)   could you fill in this form for me, please?
        Then
        a)   perhaps you'd like a look round the centre with me.
        b)   you will look round the centre with me.
        c)   you can look round the centre with me if you want.

4 Listening

Track 14

First copy the plan of the sports and leisure centre below. Then listen to Dave Stockman and Ann Riley. Draw a line, showing their route around the centre. Match the numbers to the following parts of the centre.

bar restaurant ▪ *changing rooms* ▪ *fitness training room* ▪ *main gym* ▪ *pool room* ▪ *sauna* ▪ *solarium* ▪ *squash courts* ▪ *swimming pool* ▪ *tennis courts*

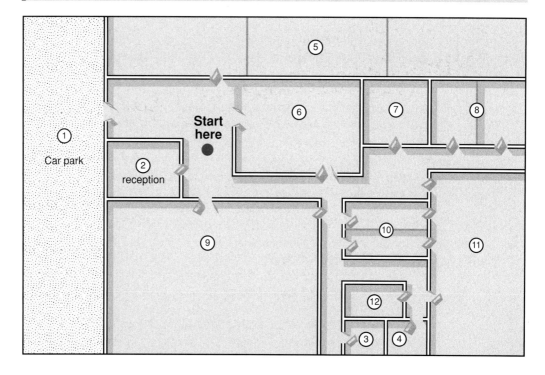

On Question Hour, *anchorman David Dampney and guests are discussing questions from the studio audience.*

DAVID D   Our next question comes from Susan Hill, housewife, mother and catering manager at a primary school.

SUSAN H   Thank you. My question is this: after so many food and health

scandals, including BSE and Creuzfeldt-Jakob Disease, should we change the way we produce food? Or should we change what we eat?

DAVID D   Lisa Brandt, you've written books and campaigned for years for natural, organic farming, and against factory farming. What do you say?

LISA B   The short answer is that we ought to change both. First, let's look at how we produce food. For 50 years farmers have gone for intensive, cost-cutting factory farming. That means masses of chemicals on the land and natural habitats destroyed for extra farmland. It also means keeping animals cruelly in tiny pens. And, until recently, it meant giving animals unnatural feed made with bits of dead livestock. And this of course was the source of BSE and CJD. So ... we're now beginning to pay the true price of so-called cheap food. A terrible price it is, too!

DAVID D   Alan Moore, as MP for West Oxfordshire, an area with many farms, do you think it's fair to blame farmers?

ALAN M   I certainly don't. Clearly, farmers have to produce cheaply because the supermarkets demand rock-bottom prices. That's because they're trying to undercut their competitors and attract more customers with lower prices – and keep on making very nice profits for themselves! Meanwhile, farmers are suffering terribly. Most are losing money, and many are going out of business. Things simply *must* change.

DAVID D   So it's the supermarkets that are to blame.

LISA B   And customers who insist on cheap food. And that brings me to the second part of the question. Should we change what we eat? I believe we ought to switch to organic produce.

ALAN M   That's easy for a rich author to say, but most people can't afford the luxury of organic food.

LISA B   I know it's more expensive, so why not eat more vegetables? Organic vegetables, I mean. And of course, we needn't eat so much meat. Why not eat meat – good-quality, organic meat – just two or three times a week? Then we'd all be much healthier.

(382 words)

5 Looking at the text

⟳ Lernhilfen 4.2, S.146

A Answer the questions on the text.
   1 What sorts of farming is Lisa Brandt for and against?
   2 How has factory farming affected the environment?
   3 Why has it also been bad for farm animals?
   4 Why do you think Alan Moore is particularly worried about farmers,
      and particularly angry with the supermarkets?
   5 What is Lisa Brandt's answer to the problem with expensive meat?

B Give your opinion.
   Do you think it is right that animals are killed for people to eat?

I really	(don't)	think feel	it's	right wrong	to … .	That's because …
I	(completely) (absolutely)	agree disagree	that … with …	since …		
I (partly) In some ways I		agree with go along with	what (name)	says, believes,	but …	

6 Looking at grammar: modal verbs

Grammar

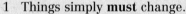
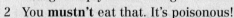

Remember
1 Things simply **must** change.
2 You **mustn't** eat that. It's poisonous!
3 We **needn't (don't have to)** eat so much meat. We can eat other things instead.
4 **Should** we change what we eat? Yes, we **ought to** change.
5 Some people **may** eat less meat. A few people **might** give it up completely.
6 Farmers **had to** start more intensive farming 50 years ago.
7 By doing this, they **could / were able to** produce more cheaply than before.

- **must / have to / need to** *(müssen)*
  Im Allgemeinen benutzt man *have to*. Wollen Sie die Notwendigkeit bzw.
  Verpflichtung besonders betonen, verwenden Sie *must*. (1)
  In der Vergangenheit wird *must* zu *had to*. (6)
- **must not, need not / do not have to / do not need to**
  (nicht dürfen, nicht müssen / nicht brauchen)
  Must not steht für Verbote. (2)
  Will man ausdrücken, dass keine Verpflichtung besteht, verwendet man
  need not / do not have to usw. (3)
- **can** */ be able to (können)*
  Wie im Deutschen, drückt *can* eine Fähigkeit aus.
  Die Vergangenheit von *can* ist *could* oder *was/were able to*. (7)
- **should (not), ought (not) to** *((nicht) sollen)*
  Diese Wörter stehen, wenn man jemandem etwas nachdrücklich empfehlen will. (4)
- **may / might, could** *(könnte)*
  Verwenden Sie *may* für eher wahrscheinliche Dinge und *might* sowie *could*
  für eher unwahrscheinliche Dinge. (5)

7 Practising grammar

A Choose the right modal verb to complete the sentences.

1 Charlie Reece wanted to start his own health club, but his friends thought he was crazy and said, 'Charlie, you ... do it!' (needn't / shouldn't)
2 But Charlie decided that he really ... try. (ought to / might not)
3 He started last year, and first he ... borrow a lot of money. (had to / must)
4 Luckily, his bank ... help him. (had to / was able to)
5 Now he is doing so well that he ... be able to pay all the money back this year! In fact, Charlie is nearly sure he will be able to. (may / might)
6 He says, 'I ... pay the bank back so fast, but I want to.' (don't have to / mustn't)

B Complete the farmer's story, using suitable forms of these modal verbs.

> *can* ▪ *have to* ▪ *may* ▪ *might* ▪ *must* ▪ *need to* ▪ *should* ▪ *ought to*

Until recently, Roger Giles was a farmer, but he ...[1] continue because the farm was losing money heavily. In the end, he ...[2] sell it. He then moved into town and opened a pet store so that he ...[3] continue working with animals. 'But,' he says, 'I really ...[4] succeed with this new business because I still ...[5] pay the bank back a lot of money.'

Of course, he ...[6] work very hard at his new business, but he ...[7] get up as early as he did on the farm. 'In the old days, I ...[8] stay in bed after 5 am because the animals needed attention. Now my problem is that I still ...[9] stop myself from waking up at 5 am when I really ...[10] to get up until 7 am. I know I ...[11] just turn over and go to sleep again, but I ...[12]!' As for living in town, he says, 'I suppose I ...[13] get used to it one day. I ...[14] even start to like it, but at the moment I really don't think so!'

8 Listening

Track 14

Listen again to Dave Stockman's tour of the centre with Ann Riley. Which of the following useful expressions do you hear?

Dave Stockman

1 Perhaps you'd like (a look round the centre with me).
2 If you'd like to ask any questions, please go ahead.
3 If you could come this way, let's start with (a look at the bar restaurant).
4 If you could follow me, let's go on with (a quick look at the swimming pool).
5 We need to turn left / right and go straight along here to (the next thing).
6 As you can see, (it has got all the latest exercise machines).

Ann Riley

1 I'd love to (have a quick look round).
2 Tell me, (what time do you finish in the evening)?
3 Can I ask (how much it costs for members here)?
4 If you don't mind me asking, (how big is the pool)?
5 Have I got it right that (members can bring guests)?
6 Thanks very much for (showing me round).

9 Speaking: role-play

Develop a role-play in pairs. Take turns to show each other round (part of)
a well-known local building, eg a college, a museum or a department store.
Try to use useful expressions from **exercise 8**.

10 Writing

⟲ Lernhilfen 4.4, S.148

An American exchange student is going to stay with you for a month and has
written you this letter.

> By the way, I really need to keep in
> training while I'm with you in Germany.
> That's because I'm going to take part
> in the pentathlon event in the Texas
> State high school athletics championships
> soon after I get back home. That
> means I have to do some general fitness
> training. It would also be great if there's
> somewhere I can train for the different
> pentathlon events - running, riding,
> swimming, shooting and fencing.
> Any suggestions?

Write a paragraph back with your ideas. You can use this language.

> *You can certainly do some general fitness training at ...*
> *I think you should / ought to ...*
> *You could try ...*
> *I'm not sure about ...*
> *I'm afraid there isn't anywhere local you can ...*

Start your paragraph like this.

I've had a good think about places for you to train, and here are a few ideas.
First of all, ...

How well do you rate on food safety? For each of the following, choose whether the statement applies to you often (**O**), sometimes (**S**), or rarely (**R**). (If you don't cook at home, answer the questions as you think you would act.)
Score yourself below and see how you rate.
Then read the commentary on the answers.

QUIZ:
Burger food safety

1	I don't worry about food safety matters.	(O)	(S)	(R)
2	I use the same cutting board for raw meat and vegetables.	(O)	(S)	(R)
3	I'm a one-plate cook. I put the cooked meat on the same dish that I used for the raw hamburger patties.	(O)	(S)	(R)
4	I make sure raw meat doesn't come into contact with any other food.	(O)	(S)	(R)
5	I wash, with hot, soapy water, everything that comes into contact with raw meat – my hands, the bowl and plate, knives, cutting board, and worktop.	(O)	(S)	(R)
6	I use the colour test – 'If it's brown inside and the juices run clear, it must be done.' – to make sure dangerous bacteria are killed.	(O)	(S)	(R)
7	I like my burgers pink inside.	(O)	(S)	(R)
8	I leave leftovers out at room temperature for hours, since they're already cooked.	(O)	(S)	(R)

Scoring

	Often	Sometimes	rarely
1	Often (5)	Sometimes (10)	rarely (20)
2	Often (5)	Sometimes (10)	rarely (20)
3	Often (5)	Sometimes (10)	rarely (20)
4	Often (20)	Sometimes (10)	rarely (5)
5	Often (20)	Sometimes (10)	rarely (5)
6	Often (20)	Sometimes (10)	rarely (5)
7	Often (5)	Sometimes (10)	rarely (20)
8	Often (5)	Sometimes (10)	rarely (20)

How you rate

40–80 points: It's time to do something about food safety. Or else look forward to a serious stomach ache.

85–120 points: It's been hit and miss with you and food safety. Now it's time to get serious.

125–160 points: With your terrific food-safety habits, you're a bacteria buster.

Commentary

1 Always think about food safety. Food-borne illnesses make 33 million Americans sick each year.

2 Cutting raw meat and vegetables on the same surface will contaminate the veggies. Don't do it.

3 Bad idea. Bacteria from the raw patties will get into the cooked food.

4 You should always keep raw meat apart from other food.

5 Washing your hands and the utensils that you cook with prevents the spread of bacteria.

6/7 You should cook ground beef to an internal temperature of 160° Fahrenheit (70 °C). Check with a thermometer. You cannot be sure just from the colour of the meat.

8 Store all leftovers in the fridge.

(Adapted from *Choices* magazine, Scholastic, March 2000)

Focus

A Describe what is happening in the cartoons.

B Explain the ideas that the cartoonists want to express. Use this language.

| In the (TV) cartoon, | the | idea | is that (the TV image is more real …) |
| In the one about (TV) | | joke | |

C What do the cartoons seem to be saying about people, machines and communications? Do you agree? Use this language.

| They all | seem | to be | saying | that … |
| All of them | appear | | suggesting | |

Personally, I	(fully) agree.	I think …
Speaking for myself, I	(completely) disagree.	I believe …
	(partly) agree / disagree.	I'm sure …

1

"Listen, John, we really need to talk. I'll send you an email."

2
"For goodness sake, Jimmy, get a life! The TV's on downstairs."

3

"No, damn it, I don't want to play Tomb Raider – I just want you to warm up my food."

4

"He's watching the Olympics so I'll get him to phone you back in two weeks, OK?"

5

We are taking over your house – you are obsolete!!

A People and society

Track 16 *Michio Kaku is a professor of physics at the City University of New York – and a futurologist. Here he describes how new technologies will affect life in 2020.*

- How old will you be at the time of the author's vision?
- How do you think day-to-day life will change by 2020? Read 'Molly' to find out whether the author agrees with you.

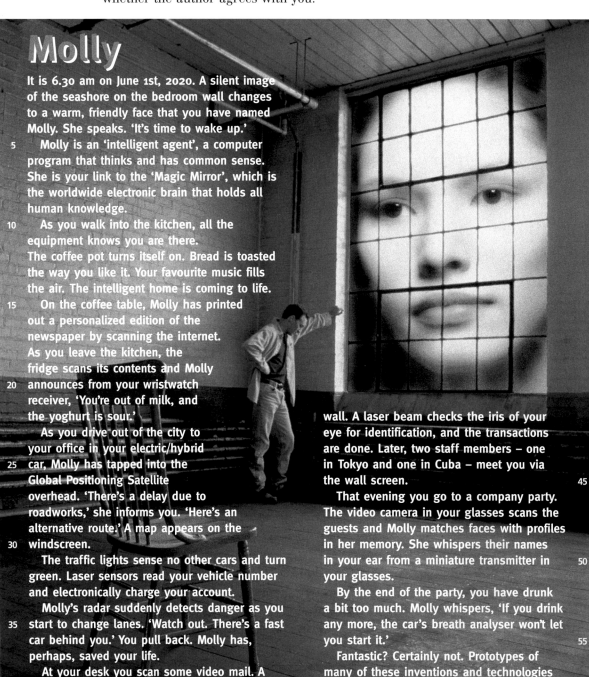

Molly

It is 6.30 am on June 1st, 2020. A silent image of the seashore on the bedroom wall changes to a warm, friendly face that you have named Molly. She speaks. 'It's time to wake up.'

5 Molly is an 'intelligent agent', a computer program that thinks and has common sense. She is your link to the 'Magic Mirror', which is the worldwide electronic brain that holds all human knowledge.

10 As you walk into the kitchen, all the equipment knows you are there. The coffee pot turns itself on. Bread is toasted the way you like it. Your favourite music fills the air. The intelligent home is coming to life.

15 On the coffee table, Molly has printed out a personalized edition of the newspaper by scanning the internet. As you leave the kitchen, the fridge scans its contents and Molly

20 announces from your wristwatch receiver, 'You're out of milk, and the yoghurt is sour.'

As you drive out of the city to your office in your electric/hybrid

25 car, Molly has tapped into the Global Positioning Satellite overhead. 'There's a delay due to roadworks,' she informs you. 'Here's an alternative route.' A map appears on the

30 windscreen.

The traffic lights sense no other cars and turn green. Laser sensors read your vehicle number and electronically charge your account.

Molly's radar suddenly detects danger as you

35 start to change lanes. 'Watch out. There's a fast car behind you.' You pull back. Molly has, perhaps, saved your life.

At your desk you scan some video mail. A few payments to some project consultants. You

40 insert your smart card into the computer in the wall. A laser beam checks the iris of your eye for identification, and the transactions are done. Later, two staff members – one in Tokyo and one in Cuba – meet you via the wall screen.

45 That evening you go to a company party. The video camera in your glasses scans the guests and Molly matches faces with profiles in her memory. She whispers their names in your ear from a miniature transmitter in

50 your glasses.

By the end of the party, you have drunk a bit too much. Molly whispers, 'If you drink any more, the car's breath analyser won't let you start it.'

55 Fantastic? Certainly not. Prototypes of many of these inventions and technologies are now coming out of the laboratory. The future is already here.

(Adapted from *Visions* by Michio Kaku, OUP, 1998)

(395 words)

1 Looking at the text

A Answer the questions on the text.
1 Who or what is Molly?
2 What four stages of your future day does the author describe?
3 Imagine Molly broke down at 6.25 yesterday morning. Say how it changed
  a) life at home yesterday morning;
  b) your journey to work;
  c) your party after work.
4 As you read the text, which future developments did you find
  a) most believable, and
  b) least believable? Why?

B Give your opinion.
1 What do you like or dislike about Molly?
2 If you have the chance to buy a Molly in 2020, do you think you will?

Something	I	quite like	about Molly is	her way of (checking) …
The thing		most dislike		the way she (checks) …
I'm pretty sure	I'll	buy	one	because …
No, I really don't think		get		as …

2 Working with words

A Copy and complete the table of word families with words from the text and adverbs that you know or can form yourself.

verb	noun	adjective	adverb
live	*life*	lively	(in a lively way)
personalize	person	*personal*	*personally*
sense	*sense*	sensitive	*sensitively*
inform	information	informative	*informatively*
appear	appearance	apparent	*apparently*
endanger	*danger*	dangerous	*dangerously*
fantasize	fantasy	*fantastic*	fantastically
invent	*invention*	inventive	*inventively*

(handwritten margin notes: rscheinen / efahrden / antasieren)

B Complete the following with the correct forms of words from **2A**.

…[1] in the 2020s is not quite as wonderful and …[2] as the futurologists used to think. We now …[3] in a world full of 'smart' technology. The trouble is that nobody has …[4] machines that never go wrong. And when something *does* go wrong, there is a real …[5] that things will get completely out of control. Take this morning: my fridge …[6] system …[7] went mad after I had gone to work, and told my 'intelligent agent' Pam that I was out of everything, and of course Pam then …[8] the supermarket. So, by the time I got home this evening, a small mountain of milk, yoghurt, fruit juice, cheese, etc had …[9] in my kitchen, thanks to the supermarket's automatic delivery service – and there was nowhere to put it all. …[10], I think it's time to go back to the old days and start deciding things for ourselves again!

*(handwritten margin notes:
1. Life
2. fantastic
3. life
4. invented
5. danger
6. information
7. apparently
8. informed
9. appeared
10. Personally)*

3 Listening

Track 17

A Helga White works in telephone sales for Handysystem GmbH, a mobile phone warehouse company that advertises in its own catalogue. Listen to Part 1. Say who is talking and what is going to be discussed.

Model	Talktime	Dialling	Memory	Internet access	Cost
Nexus 321 Code: 4563 €59.99	250"	Voice-activated	290 names & numbers	Yes	1 yr contract €45 per month; 10 hrs free calls per month
Star TR2 Code: 4564 €169.99	240"	Voice-activated	500 names & numbers	Yes	pay as you go €0.75 per min for first 5" per day; then €0.15 per min
Laser 101 Code: 4565 €139.99	260"	Voice-activated	99 names & numbers	No	pay as you go €0.30 per min peak, €0.10 per min off-peak

Track 18

B Now study the catalogue details. Then listen to Part 2 and say which mobile phone Helga should suggest and why. How much is the customer going to spend?

Track 19

C Copy this order sheet. Listen to Part 3 and complete it, including today's date.

Family name	First names
Address	
Tel	Date Order Ref

Source of information: Catalogue ☐   Website ☐   TV ☐   Magazine ☐

4 Culture check: being indirect and polite

A German speakers can sometimes sound too direct, and even rude, to English speakers. On the other hand, English speakers' politeness and indirectness can sound absurd to Germans. However, polite expressions are very important to English speakers – so use them!

> *please ▪ thank you ▪ certainly ▪ of course ▪ I'm afraid (that) … ▪ I'm sorry, but … ▪ Excuse me, but …*

Expressions for asking and requesting are also very important.

> *May / Can I ask … ▪ If you don't mind me asking … ▪ Perhaps you could tell me … ▪ Could you / I (possibly) … ▪ Would you mind if … ▪ I wonder if you / I could … ▪ Do you think you could …*

Tracks 17–19

B Listen again to the whole conversation. Which of the expressions above do you hear?

B People and issues

Letters to the editor

(Comments on the internet)

Last month, my husband and I bought a home computer for the children for educational purposes. Imagine my horror when I found them accessing a website which contained pornographic pictures. This was not our idea of 'educational' purposes!

5 I have banned the computer from our house, and I hope others will do the same. The internet has turned into a terrible monster. We must kill it before it corrupts the world.

S Turner (Mrs)

I was horrified to read of Mrs Turner's action. For the first time in history, the whole world has free speech and freedom of information, thanks to the internet. And Mrs T has banned it!

Of course, we – (me, too!) – dislike much that exists in Cyberspace. But
5 there is something she can easily do about it. She should check her ISP (Internet Service Provider) instructions. These will certainly show how to prevent access to 'adult' websites.

Luis Fernandez

As a political refugee from Myanmar (Burma), I have read the recent internet correspondence with fascination. I want to say that the internet is
5 absolutely essential for people who, like me, are struggling against our cruel, military rulers.

Through the internet, we stay in contact, at home and in exile. Here
10 in London, we have also regularly published our *Freedom Newsletter* on our website for the last three years. This has brought new hope to all who are fighting for freedom.

15 And they cannot stop us. The internet is unlike the traditional media. The censors cannot tear out pages. Nor can they jam us electronically.

Down with the dictators! Long live
20 the internet!

Sein Maung

Yes, Sein Maung is right that the internet is different from the traditional media. And not just because no one can censor it.

Think. Traditional media publishers have to try
5 to be truthful. If they fail, victims can take them to court and win large amounts of money. With the internet, though, anyone who has a PC, a phone line and the skills to create a website can start a newsletter. Good or bad, there is no control.

10 The message Sein Maung puts out is probably a good one, but there are bad ones too. Some websites push horrible racist politics. Others push conspiracy theories which attack people who cannot answer back.

15 Worse, what happens when a website gives us 'facts' that are actually lies? It now seems that there were many false propaganda reports in the Balkans conflict – reports of killings that never happened.

Diana Stein

(415 words)

5 Looking at the texts

 Lernhilfen 4.2, S.146

A Answer the questions on the texts.
1 Which letter writer depends heavily on the internet, and why?
2 Which of the other writers loves the whole idea of the internet, and why?
3 Which writer hates the internet, and why?
4 Summarize the other writer's feelings about the internet.
5 What can a) national censors and b) private individuals do to prevent access to unwelcome internet sites?

B Give your opinion.
Which of the letter writers do you agree with most and least? Why?

Personally, I I myself	agree most / least with feel closest to the views of totally agree / disagree with	(name)	as he / she says … because he / she thinks … since I firmly believe …

6 Looking at grammar: relative clauses

Grammar

Remember
1 We dislike much **that exists in Cyberspace**.
2 This has brought hope to all **who** are fighting for freedom.
3 These are the people **who / that** Sein Maung writes the *Freedom Newsletter* **with**.
4 This is the room **which / that** they keep the computers **in**.
5 There is something **(which / that)** she can easily do.
6 They attack people **(who / that)** they want to hurt.
7 There is something **which / that** can help Mrs Turner.
8 They attack people **who / that** cannot answer back.

- Mit Relativsätzen können Sie Sätzen notwendige Informationen hinzufügen.
  Beispiel: We dislike much. (+ It exists in Cyberspace.) (1)
- Bei Dingen nimmt man *which / that* (1), bei Personen *who / that* (2).
- Präpositionen kommen gewöhnlich ans Ende des Relativsatzes. (3) (4)
- Wenn *which / who / that* das Objekt des Relativsatzes darstellt, kann man es weglassen. (5) (6)
- Wenn *which / who / that* das Subjekt des Relativsatzes ist, kann man es nicht weglassen. (7) (8)

7 Practising grammar

A Form complete sentences. Use *who, which* or *that*.
1 Mrs Turner / person / ban / computer / house
2 her letter / one / call for / end of the internet
3 Luis Fernandez / Sein Maung / people / support / internet / most strongly
4 Luis Fernandez / also / one / strongly attack / Mrs Turner's ideas
5 *Freedom Newsletter* / website publication / Sein Maung / publish / last three years
6 Diana Stein's points / ones / seem / give / most balanced view / internet
7 she / person / point out / no one can prevent / publication of lies / internet

B Complete the paragraph. Add *which, who* or *that* to the relative clauses where necessary.

It happened many years ago, but I will never, never forget the awful shock ...[1] I had when I lost 14 hours of work from my computer. I was working on a project ...[2] was very urgent, and the people ...[3] I was doing the project for were always asking for the finished work. My main contact at the company was someone ...[4] spent all her time worrying – and worrying me. And so, all ...[5] I had time to do that month was to work, eat a little and sleep! Then came the day of the accident – a day ...[6] I still hate to think about even now! I had started work at 7 am, and I was still working at 9 that night. I was completely buried in the work ...[7] I was doing, and I forgot to save it all day. And it was an old-fashioned machine ...[8] had no automatic 'save' function. Then there was a sudden storm – and a power cut ...[9] blacked out the whole town. The computer screen went dead, and I will never forget the sudden horror ...[10] I felt. Since then, I always save work ...[11] I have done every few minutes. Losing work so stupidly is one thing ...[12] will, I hope, never happen to me again!

8 Writing a comment

⟲ Lernhilfen 4.4, S.148

Write a comment on this question:
Do you think the internet is generally a good thing or a bad thing?

Use ideas from the letters to the newspaper.
Use the following to guide your writing.

Paragraph 1
Introduction
There are arguments on both sides. However, in my opinion, the internet is basically an excellent / a terrible thing for the world.

Paragraph 2
First development (arguments against your opinion)
Of course, there are people who point out many bad / good things about the internet. For example, (example 1). Again, (example 2).

Paragraph 3
Second development (arguments in favour of your view)
On the other hand, though, there are a lot of points in favour of / against the internet. Here are just a few. First of all, (point 1). Secondly, (point 2). Thirdly, (point 3).

Paragraph 4
Conclusion
In conclusion, it seems to me that the internet is ... . Naturally, it can also be used badly / well. However, I feel that on balance its positive / negative aspects outweigh the problems / benefits that it brings.

9 Discussion

How much information should people have to carry around with them? Which of the following is the best situation?

UK/USA

No ID card system in use. US drivers must carry driving licence, but UK drivers need not.

Germany

ID card must be carried at all times. Information includes name, date and place of birth, height, colour of eyes, present address.

Future EU?

There is a possibility of a new EU 'smart card': (a prototype used for immigrants has already been developed in the Netherlands). It could carry everything on an ordinary ID card, plus up to 36 more types of information, including:

details of family – wife/husband, children, parents and where they are • details of personal transport • details of present employment • details of social security payments • education and qualifications • fingerprints • full medical history • membership of any political party • police record • present residential status • religion

If an EU Smart Card arrived, we would all have to carry it. We would have to give correct information for the card, and we would then have to have it with us at all times and show it when asked. If a person did not do any of these things, he or she might lose state benefits such as social security payments. Non-EU residents could lose all rights to residence. So is the Smart Card something we should refuse? Or could it help to make life easier?

www.privacy.org/pi/activities/idcard

10 Speaking: role-play

Work in groups of four. You are in a government 'focus group' to discuss the smart card question. Choose a role from p 138 and try to persuade the group. Vote for or against the smart card system. Then report your vote – and reasons – to the class.

C Further reading

The internet has joined newspapers, radio and TV as yet another way for us to get the latest news.

A Match the jumbled newsflashes to the following dates and times.

13 Feb, 18:00	**14 Feb, 14:45**	**14 Feb, 20:00**	**15 Feb, 10:30**
14 Feb, 13:00	**14 Feb, 16:30**	**15 Feb, 08:00**	
14 Feb, 14:15			

Newsflash! Alpine avalanche chaos

a Desperate rescue work continues into night at Saint Monique, where tourist chalet lies under three metres of snow. Numbers trapped beneath snow unknown, but most visitors believed to have been on ski slopes at time of avalanche.

b Heavy snowfalls across Alps bring fears of avalanches. Authorities have warned skiers to avoid off-piste skiing. Meanwhile, resorts and slopes overcrowded as winter holiday brings record numbers of skiers. 5

c Within two hours of avalanche higher up valley, new avalanche swallows at least one chalet on outskirts of Saint Monique. Rescuers rushing to search for survivors.

d After 17 hours in cold and darkness, newly-arrived English chalet girl Christine Parker pulled from beneath avalanche-crushed walls and roof of holiday chalet at edge of 10 Saint Monique. Employed to cook and keep house for visitors, Christine said, 'They told me this job would be a unique experience. They were right.'

e As darkness falls over Saint Monique valley, rescuers pull one body from snow. Identity not yet known. Search continues for remaining two under floodlights. Extreme care necessary to prevent further snow slides. 15

f First reports of large avalanche shortly after midday on high slopes up valley from popular ski resort of Saint Monique.

g Remaining two bodies of off-piste skiers rescued from beneath avalanche snow. Rescue chief, Jean-Luc Didier stated, 'These people died because they ignored warnings and 20 skied off-piste. All skiers, please! Avoid any more such tragedies.'

h Eye-witness report says 200-metre-wide avalanche started above group of three off-piste skiers, rapidly burying them. Rescuers now rushing to help, but little hope of finding skiers alive. 25

(275 words)

B Work in pairs. Create TV news interviews with rescue chief Jean-Luc Didier and avalanche victim Christine Parker. Include questions about events and their experiences. Include their statements reported above.

Focus

A Which type of driver in the cartoon do you think each speaker is?

1

2

3

My old banger would fail its MOT**, but I can't afford the repairs. I just top up the oil every day and hope I'll keep moving. I know it's polluting, but think of all the other environmental damage from today's traffic! Insurance and car tax? I can't afford those either. Hope the police don't stop me!

I just commute to and from work, and I never do more than 25*. I daren't. My reactions aren't what they were! The rush-hour traffic is terrible these days, too. You get horrible men trying to pass when it's dangerous. They're always having road rage attacks, staring and shouting as they pass!

Time is money for me, so I often break the speed limit getting between jobs. Speeding makes up a bit for hours crawling in motorway tailbacks and stuck in gridlocks all over town. If they spent more of my fuel tax and car tax on transport infrastructure, maybe I wouldn't have to break the law!

* 25 = 25 miles per hour (mph) or 40 (kph)
** MOT = Ministry of Transport test: a test all cars three years and older must take every year

B Discuss these questions.
1 Which driver should be given the title 'Driver from hell'? Say why.
2 What do you think the police should do with each of them?
3 Have you seen any examples of dangerous driving recently? What happened?

www.oneworld.org/guides/energy/front.shtml

Track 21

■ What do the title of the text and the pie chart suggest that the article will be about?

A society of car junkies
by Mary-Anne Singer

Why are we so addicted to cars? A recent UK survey showed that for young women the most important thing was the independence that driving gave them. For many young men there was also the thrill of driving – often fast and dangerously. Generally, driving has given us a flexible, affordable freedom to travel and do things that our ancestors never dreamed of.

The American way to work

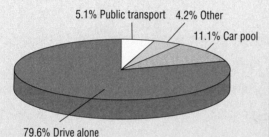

5.1% Public transport 4.2% Other
11.1% Car pool
79.6% Drive alone

Those are the big upsides, but there are huge downsides, too. One is that our freedom to drive is destroying that very freedom. More and more cars are on the roads at rush hour, tailbacks get longer, gridlocks become more frequent and urban journey times grow. There is also environmental damage: cars consume declining fossil fuel resources, and they cause pollution.

Back in the 1970s, America began encouraging people onto buses and trains, or to share car journeys to work[1]. Back then, 25% of commuters were using public transport or car pools. Twenty years later, though, the figure had fallen to 16% and is still falling now. This is despite offers of tax cuts and free travel passes.

If people cannot be encouraged to stop driving, perhaps they can be forced through high petrol prices. Britain has tried this through a high 'carbon' tax[2], and British drivers now pay far more than other Europeans. But they still keep driving. Car numbers are predicted to double between 1997 and 2025. Clearly, new answers to the problems are needed.

On crowding, new electronic guidance systems can help us use our roads more efficiently. They can, for example, suggest less crowded routes. One day, 'telematics' technology may even take over completely and guide groups of driverless cars along the road together.

Alternatives to the traditional engine are also being developed. Clean, quiet electric cars exist, but they are quite expensive and their heavy batteries need frequent recharging. Hybrid cars are better, using a small petrol engine and an electric motor. When the engine is running, the batteries recharge from the car's movement. This improves range, but with two power units these cars are very expensive.

Fuel cell technology is the latest hope, although it was actually invented many years ago. Fuel cells combine hydrogen and oxygen to produce electricity – and water. No oil is used. No polluting gases[3] are produced. Engineers are racing to make fuel cells cheaper, and test vehicles are already on the roads.

Let's say they succeed. What then? Even with miracles from telematics, new roads will still have to be built. And just how much more land do we really want to cover with concrete?

(424 words)

1 A response to the 1970s oil crises, when OPEC (Organization of Petroleum Exporting Countries) members suddenly raised the price of oil dramatically.
2 Called this because of carbon-based emissions from petrol engines.
3 The main problem gas is carbon dioxide (the greenhouse gas most responsible for global warming).

1 Looking at the text

A Say whether the statements are true, false or unclear from the text.
Correct the false ones, and explain why the unclear statements are unclear.

1 The average young woman is as likely to die on the roads as the average young man.
2 The length of time spent on all car journeys is increasing.
3 The average car uses less fuel than in the past.
4 America has offered people financial encouragement to use buses and trains.
5 Governments in Britain and America have succeeded in reducing private transport.
6 If telematics is successful, more new roads will not be needed in the future.

B Copy and complete the following table with information from the text. Add notes on electric, hybrid and fuel cell power units.

Power units	Advantages	Disadvantages
conventional	good range	…
	good performance	…
	affordable	…

C Did you recognize your own area in the text? If so, in what way? If not, why not?

When the text	says that (tailbacks are getting longer), refers to (longer tailbacks),	that reminds me of …
We don't have	any many	of these problems. Perhaps	that's because … the reason is that …

2 Working with words

A Use the prefixes *de-, dis-, in-* and *un-* to make the opposites of these words. Which prefix goes with each group? Use your dictionary if necessary.

dis (i)   *advantage* ▪ *honest* ▪ *like*
de (ii)   *coded* ▪ *contaminated* ▪ *value*
in (iii)   *damaged* ▪ *decided* ▪ *pleasant* ▪ *important*
un (iv)   *expensive* ▪ *flexible* ▪ *frequent*

B Complete the text with words or their opposites from **2A** (making necessary changes). The number in brackets shows you which row the answer comes from.

Day after day, I have to sit in the rush hour traffic, and I really ___ (i)[1] it. In fact, I hate it! It's such an ___ (iii)[2] way for me – and millions of other people – to spend two or three hours every day. As for the trains, there simply aren't enough: they go too ___ (iv)[3] from my little town to London. So I often sit in my car, thinking about the many ___ (i)[4] of working at home as a telecommuter. For example, life would be much more ___ (iv)[5]: I could work when I wanted. And without the cost of travel, life would be a lot less ___ (iv)[6], as well. There must be ___ (i)[7] with telecommuting too, but it's hard to think of any when I'm sitting in a two-mile tailback on the motorway!

3 Culture check: body language and personal space

Crowded public transport means physical contact with others and a loss of personal space – one reason why people love their cars. But different cultures have different feelings about these things, and knowing the differences is very important. The table shows what is acceptable (✔) and what is not (✗) in various cultures.

	firm handshake	touching (other than handshaking)	eye contact	private space		
				40 cm	60 cm	80+ cm
N. Europe	✔	✔	✔	✗	✔	✗
USA	✔	✔	✔	✗	✔	✗
Latin America, S. Europe	✔	✔	✔	✔	✗	✗
Muslim/Arab countries	✗	✗	✔	✔	✗	✗
Asian countries	✔	✗	✗	✗	✗	✔

Work in pairs. Read the situations and then use the table to explain what went wrong. After that, think up similar situations and swap with another pair.

1   Susan Watson from London is talking to Carlos Santos from Mexico City at a party. Carlos seems amusing, friendly and harmless, but Susan feels uncomfortable because he comes very close when talking to her. Carlos is surprised when Susan makes an excuse to leave, and then joins somebody else.

2   When Anita Peters from Manchester first meets her new Japanese agent, Hiro Honda, their eyes rarely meet while they are talking. She thinks that he is pleasant enough, but she wonders if he has the friendly confidence and energy to do a tough selling job. Meanwhile, Hiro Honda thinks Anita is OK, but finds her uncomfortably pushy.

The Oil Crisis of 2015

Track 22

SIMPSON   Good evening. I'm Peter Simpson and this is the 10 o'clock News. Today, it has been announced that Middle East oil supplies will be further reduced, due to the political crisis there. Oil prices are rocketing, and a litre of petrol is now five euros. Unsurprisingly, fierce new protests from business, haulage contractors and consumer groups are being heard across Europe. Meanwhile, there's panic buying at petrol stations everywhere. Later, we'll speak to Signor Luigi Correlli, European Commissioner for Energy. But first I'd like to go over to our energy correspondent, Yasmin Hassan. Yasmin.

HASSAN   Thanks, Peter. Well, I'm here at a busy petrol station in Birmingham. Tonight, there's a queue that stretches half a kilometre down the road. And I'm talking to some of the drivers, starting with Carol Straw here. Excuse me, but does this mean it is time to switch to public transport?

STRAW   I'd take the bus, but I'm a busy mum with things to do on the way to the office. Unless the bus stops at the day-care centre, dry cleaner's and supermarket, I've got no use for it.

HASSAN   Thanks. Next, Winston Thorpe, you commute to work at the airport by car. Why not by train?

THORPE   I'd just rather be in my own space, listening to my music. Not standing next to strangers, smelling what they had for breakfast.

HASSAN   What about a hybrid electric car or a fuel cell car?

THORPE   They're expensive, and they're boring to drive. But if this crisis goes on, I may be forced to change.

HASSAN   Thank you. Now, Dave Sutton, a self-employed truck driver. How has the haulage industry been affected by the crisis?

SUTTON   Disastrously. With rising energy taxes on top of everything else, companies are going bankrupt daily.

HASSAN Shouldn't you get rid of your diesel truck and invest in new fuel cell technology?

SUTTON What? I'm up to my ears in debt. First, cut fuel taxes and prices!

HASSAN Thanks. So that's all from Birmingham. Back to you in London, Peter.

SIMPSON And straight over to Brussels. Signor Correlli, aren't you concerned by that?

CORRELLI Yes, very. But no, taxes can't be cut. Let me explain. Quite apart from the Middle East crisis, global oil production is now falling, and there won't be any more big, new discoveries. New technologies – everything from fuel cells to windpower – must be made as affordable as oil once was. That work – and big improvements in public transport – is being paid for by the taxes.

SIMPSON So, bad news for Dave Sutton.

CORRELLI Not necessarily. We're actually considering whether to subsidize purchases of new-technology vehicles. The faster we can all get away from oil the better.

(434 words)

4 Looking at the text

⊃ Lernhilfen 4.2, S.146

A Answer the questions on the text.
1 What three factors are pushing retail fuel prices higher?
2 What do Yasmin Hassan's three interviewees do, and what effect is the crisis having on each of them?

B Use what you know from the text to say a) who is talking and b) how you know.
1 'Necessary decisions are not always popular with everyone. We have to decide what is best for the Union in the long term, and that certainly means public anger in the short term.'
2 'If I put up my prices to cover my costs, I'll lose customers in the coming months. But if I don't, I'll lose everything in the coming weeks.'
3 'I'd love time off work with the baby, but we need the money. And with the coming economic crisis, I'd never get my job back!'
4 'With prices shooting up, I'm worried that there'll be much less foreign travel this year. That means job cuts for people like me.'

C Give your opinion.
1 If all goes well, where would you like to be and what would you like to be doing by 2015?

By	2015,	I'd like to	be …
	then,	I want to	have …
	that time,	I hope I'll	be …ing …

2 Do you think there could be a world oil crisis – and how might it affect you?

| A crisis like this | might | mean …ing … |
| This sort of crisis | could | make me … |

5 Looking at grammar: the passive

Grammar

Remember

1 No oil **is used**. No polluting gases **are produced**. (simple present)
2 It **was invented** many years ago. (simple past)
3 An announcement **has been made**. (present perfect)
4 Oil supplies **will be reduced**. (will future)
5 Protests **are being heard** across Europe. (present continuous)
6 Taxes **cannot be cut**.
7 How has the haulage industry been affected **by the crisis**?
8 **It** has been announced that oil supplies will be further reduced.

- Die Zeiten des Passiv werden mit der jeweiligen Zeitform von *be* + Partizip Perfekt (3. Form) gebildet. (1)–(5)
- Passivsätze mit modalen Hilfsverben werden mit modalem Hilfsverb + *be* + Partizip Perfekt (3. Form) gebildet. (6)
- Wenn wir den/die Handelnde/n erwähnen wollen, benutzen wir *by* … . (7)
- Wenn unbekannt, selbstverständlich oder unwichtig, wird der *by-agent* weggelassen. (1)–(6)
- Das Passiv wird für formale oder unpersönliche Situationen verwendet. Auch wenn der/die Verursacher/in einer Handlung unwichtig ist, benutzt man das Passiv, oft mit *It*. (8)
- Bildet man einen Passiv- aus einem Aktivsatz, geht man nach folgendem Muster vor:

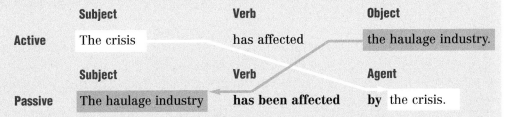

	Subject	Verb	Object
Active	The crisis	has affected	the haulage industry.

	Subject	Verb	Agent
Passive	The haulage industry	**has been affected**	**by** the crisis.

- Wenn ein Aktivsatz zwei Objekte hat, sind zwei verschiedene Passivsätze möglich.
  Brussels will give help to truck drivers.
  Help will be given **to truck drivers** … / **Truck drivers** will be given **help** …

6 Practising grammar

A Rewrite the following in the passive. If appropriate, leave out the agent.

The Council of Ministers has announced the following special actions.
1 We have bought extra oil supplies from non-Middle East producers.
2 Oil companies are shipping this oil to Europe in every available oil tanker.
3 We are increasing the size of EU oil reserves in this way.
4 Last night, we sent a team to discuss diplomatic solutions to the crisis.
5 In the meantime, we must prepare plans for a major emergency.
6 We are now printing fuel ration books all over Europe.
7 We are going to distribute these to all vehicle owners next week.
8 We plan to start rationing at midday on Saturday, 21st May.
9 We will limit car owners to 20 litres of fuel per week.

B Take this chance to study the layout of business letters.
Make the underlined phrases more formal using the passive.

Cargo Fuels Ltd

Great Western Way
Swindon
Wilts SN5 9T2
Telephone 01793 / 878288
Fax 01793 / 8785157
E-mail cargo.fuels@network.uk

2 February 20..

Mr D Sutton
DS Road Haulage Ltd
15 Warbeck Road
Birmingham BR8 5DH

Dear Mr Sutton

Re: Invoice No 175821/DS: third reminder

Although we have sent you[1] two reminders, we have still not received payment[2] of the above overdue invoice.

We have considered your request[3] for further time to pay. However, under our terms of business, customers must pay all bills[4] within thirty days. Regretfully, we can make no exceptions to this rule[5].

If you do not pay the bill[6] within the next ten days, you will force us[7] to take legal steps to recover the money.

In the meantime, you leave us with no alternative[8] but to refuse further fuel supplies until you have paid the overdue amount[9] in full.

Yours sincerely

(Mrs) D West
(Finance Director)

reminder – *Mahnung*, overdue – *überfällig*, terms of business – *Geschäftsbedingungen*, regretfully – *bedauerlicherweise*, exception – *Ausnahme*, take legal steps – *rechtliche Schritte unternehmen*

7 Writing a comment

⟳ Lernhilfen 4.4, S.148

Which interviewee on the 10 o'clock News did you most sympathize with?
Write an e-mail supporting this viewpoint. Use passives where appropriate.

8 Listening

A Henby is an old town with narrow streets and many traffic problems.
Look at the map: what problems do you think there might be? Some of these
words may help you.

> *crossroads* ▪ *junction (T-junction / Y-junction)* ▪ *lane* ▪ *one-way system* ▪
> *pedestrian precinct* ▪ *roadworks* ▪ *(mini-)roundabout* ▪ *(bus / railway)*
> *station* ▪ *traffic lights* ▪ *tailback* ▪ *pedestrianized* ▪ *commuter*

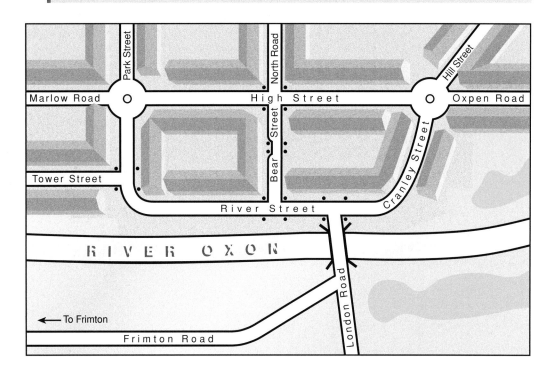

Track 23

B You are on holiday with your family and you have to drive through the town of
Henby. The road is very busy, and you turn on the radio for the traffic news.
Listen to Part 1. Who are the people talking? What problems are mentioned?

C Listen to Part 2. What possible solutions are discussed? The following language
may help you.

(name)	says thinks feels believes	that	…	must be should be could be needs to be ought to be has to be	moved changed widened turned into removed built

9 Speaking

Work in a group. Think about traffic problems in your area. What could be done
about them? Discuss possible solutions and report your ideas to the class.

C Further reading

The freedom of travel and the open road have always been part of the American Dream – and the American way of life, too. (Far more Americans than Europeans move from region to region for work.) This is echoed in the many American 'road' movies, and also in many songs about travelling, moving on and finding something different. A famous one is California Dreaming *by the Mamas & the Papas.*

 Track 24

A Read the lyrics. Try and work out the missing words.

B Turn to the map on the inside back cover and find LA. Where, for example, might the 'dreaming' be happening? Name a possible city. Then listen to the song and check.

California Dreaming
California Dreaming

All the leaves are brown
And the ...[1] is gray
I've been for a walk
On a winter's ...[2]
I'd be safe and warm
...[3] I was in LA.
California dreaming
...[4] such a winter's day.

Stepped into a church
I passed along the ...[5].
Well, I got ...[6] on my knees
And I pretend to pray,
You know the preacher lights the coals,
He knows I'm gonna ...[7].
California dreaming
On such a ... ...[8].

All the ... ...[9] brown
And the ... ...[10].
I've been for a walk
On a winter's day.
...[11] I didn't tell her,
I could leave ...[12].
California dreaming
California dreaming on such a
California dreaming on such a ... ...[13].

C Is long-distance travel, eg holiday travel by air, or shopping trips to other countries, a luxury that the world can no longer afford?

6 Buying and selling

Focus

A Match the selling outlets to the pictures.

> *from a market stall* ■ *at a specialist outlet, small shop* ■ *on the doorstep* ■ *at a supermarket* ■ *on the internet, online* ■ *at a department store* ■ *from a (mail order) catalogue* ■ *at home*

B Now answer these questions.

1 What kinds of outlet are there in your town, neighbourhood or area?
2 Where do you do your own shopping?
3 Do you enjoy shopping, or do you find it boring?
4 Do you decide what you want and then buy it, or do you enjoy window-shopping as well? Do you sometimes buy things on impulse?
5 What's your best/worst buy? Say why.

A People and society

Radio Scotland's Lisa Cameron is talking to Jim Hudson, a retailing consultant from Edinburgh and Ann Gordon, an economist with the Scottish Consumers' Association, about shopping online.

Lisa Let me start with you, Ann. You've always been sceptical about internet shopping, haven't you?

Ann Too true. I've been sceptical about it
5 right from the very start.

Lisa Yes, but I know plenty of people who buy online.

Ann Sure, but are the retailers making any money? Delivery: that's the problem. People are
10 often out during the day so there's nobody to take the goods. And in any case, most people enjoy shopping. They like to get out of the house. I think the whole psychology of internet shopping is wrong. And then there's the problem of credit card security, of
20 course.

Jim I'm sorry, Lisa, but may I break in there?
Lisa Of course. Go ahead.
Jim Well, there are answers to these problems. To start with, you're probably safer
25 using your credit card on the internet than in a normal store now. As for deliveries, if people know the exact delivery time, they'll make sure somebody's at home. And anyhow, if deliveries came in the evening, customers would be at home, of course.
30

Ann Yes, but who wants evening deliveries? People want to relax, watch TV, go out.

Lisa Isn't Ann right, Jim? Will a lot of online shops fail if they don't find an answer to the delivery problem?
35

Jim Yes, they probably will, but not because of delivery problems. Ann's missed the point, frankly. To begin with, you have to distinguish between goods and services. Online banking, for example, is growing at over eight per cent a year.
40 And look at budget airlines. Around 90% of EasyJet's tickets are sold online. And what about downloading music? It's booming.

Ann Oh, come on. I'm talking about goods that have to be delivered by van, Jim.
45

Jim Sure, but even with goods, things just aren't that simple. What about mail order firms, for example? They've always had to deliver goods, Ann. What's new? The internet is just a quick and convenient way of placing orders,
50 that's all. Mail order firms with plenty of regular customers and a good delivery system are doing very well.

Ann Yes? Why have so many internet retailers failed then?
55

Jim Look, these firms don't fail because of your so-called 'delivery problem', right? That's just a red herring. They fail because they are badly run and don't have enough capital. If they had more regular customers and set up efficient
60 delivery systems, they wouldn't have so many problems.

(393 words)

1 Looking at the text

⊃ Lernhilfen 4.2, S.146

Answer the questions on the text.
1 According to Ann, what are the main problems about shopping on the internet?
2 Why does Ann think that 'the whole psychology of internet shopping is wrong'?
3 How does Jim answer Ann's points about deliveries and security?
4 What does Jim mean by saying that Ann's argument is 'just a red herring'?

2 Working with words

A How are the ideas below expressed in the dialogue? They are in the same order.
1 I'd like to ask you a question first, Ann.
2 I've always had my doubts about online retailing.
3 There's nobody at home to accept deliveries.
4 Then there's the difficulty with making safe payments.
5 Do you mind if I interrupt there?
6 It is necessary to make a difference between types of product.
7 The sale of financial services is increasing very fast.
8 It's growing very quickly.
9 Why have so many online retailers gone bankrupt?
10 They collapse because of bad management and shortage of money.

B Find a noun form of these verbs in the introduction and the dialogue. They are in the same order.
1 (to) consult   5 (to) secure
2 (to) shop   6 (to) serve
3 (to) retail   7 (to) order
4 (to) deliver

3 Listening

Track 26

First, read the Hollywood World leaflet below to find out what information to listen for. Then listen to the recorded message and take notes. Finally, complete the leaflet (on a separate piece of paper) with the missing details.

HOLLYWOOD WORLD

Opening Hours

April 1 to ...¹   9 am – ...² pm
...³ to March 31: ...⁴ am – 6 pm

Admission Prices

Adults: $...⁵
Children, 4–14: $...⁶
Children under 4: no ...⁷

Special rates for ... ...⁸ and disabled people: apply for details at the ...⁹ at the ... ...¹⁰ entrance.

Group rates, including school parties: please call Laura ...¹¹ on 213 ...¹², Monday – ...¹³ between 9 am and ...¹⁴ pm.

Free loan of strollers and wheelchairs for a $...¹⁵ deposit.

No dogs are allowed. Free kennels are available at the entrance to the ... ...¹⁶ parking lot.

B People and issues

Track 27

An important part of "consumerism" is the idea that possessing a certain product – or brand – defines who you are. As Marshall Lee, a New York psychologist, says, 'Clothes have always sent messages about what a person may be like. But consumerism goes to absurd and sometimes sick extremes. It doesn't just say "what you may be like", but "who you actually are". It makes a personality statement.' Read on to find out more.

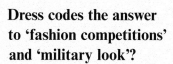

Dress codes the answer to 'fashion competitions' and 'military look'?

Birmingham, Alabama Schools across America say there is a simple answer to the problem of fashion competitions among stu-
5 dents and the use of 'inappropriate and threatening' military-style uniforms in school: dress codes.

The list of banned items at
10 Birmingham's West End High now includes gold chains, cycling pants, fur, revealing shorts and halters, military boots and combat jackets, and ripped jeans.

Robin Wilson, 15, a West Ender who believes in
15 school uniforms, would like to go further. 'If we all wore the same uniform, teachers would spend less time checking the dress code,' he says. But Robin's classmate, Hilary Fields, disagrees. 'Dress codes are repressive,' she says. 'Schools are
20 saying we must conform, and that can't be good in a democracy.'

The new hell of consumerism?

According to the latest UK crime statistics, a big increase in street crime among young people has been caused mainly by a 46% rise in thefts of prepaid mobile phones.
5 Now, the government is thinking of making PIN codes compulsory. But the answer may not be that simple. As Ian Morton, an industry spokesman, pointed out, 'Worried parents often give their very young
10 children mobiles for security reasons. Stealing them is like taking sweets from babies. But if the phone is protected, it's frightening what thieves may do to find out the PIN code.' 'The real trouble,' says Helen
15 Jones, a police psychologist, 'is that people will do almost anything to get a mobile. If you haven't got one, you're nobody. You aren't there.'

I'm very worried that fewer and fewer young people have basic life skills, and schools aren't even aware of the problem.
Many under-25s can't even cook a simple meal
5 or change a halogen bulb, much less mend their clothes or decorate a room. All these people can do is sub-contract their lives out to 'service providers'. This is another terrible result of consumerism. What I find so sad is that the
10 under-25s, who are always talking about freedom of choice and 'doing their own thing', are in fact the real 'unfree'. They are totally dependent. A lot of them will be lost if they become ill or lose their jobs.

(355 words)

Louise Conran

www.ethicalconsumer.org   www.verdant.net

4 Looking at the texts

⊃ Lernhilfen 4.2, S.146

A Answer the questions on the texts.
  1 Summarize the arguments for and against dress codes and/or school uniforms.
  2 What has caused a big rise in street crime in the UK and how could the problem be solved?
  3 Why does Louise Conran describe the under-25s as the real 'unfree'?

B First, read the speech bubbles and the names in the box. Then use the texts, including the introduction, to say a) who is talking and b) how you know.

> *Helen Jones* ▪ *Hilary Fields* ▪ *Ian Morton* ▪ *Louise Conran* ▪ *Robin Wilson* ▪ *Worried parent*

1 Another problem is that advertisers do all they can to persuade young people that mobiles are 'cool'.

2 I get really angry when schools replace cookery and home repair classes with, you've guessed it, yet more IT.

3 If somebody wants to wear a school uniform, fine, but compulsory uniforms are undemocratic.

4 It may sound silly, but our 8-year-old has a mobile. The streets are so unsafe nowadays.

5 PIN codes will not stop people stealing mobiles.

6 Politicians always look for easy answers. In a year's time, we'll be talking about a huge increase in the violent theft of mobiles.

7 By making us wear a uniform, schools are taking away our freedom.

8 With a standard school uniform, you can see immediately who isn't dressed appropriately.

C Give your opinion.
  1 Work in pairs. Look at the list of items that are banned at West End High. Would you change the list by removing, replacing or adding any items? Give reasons.
  2 Do you think that dress codes and/or school uniforms can be called 'repressive' and 'undemocratic'? Say why/why not.

5 Looking at grammar: *if*-sentences types I and II

Grammar

Remember

1 **If** people **know** the delivery time, they **will make** sure somebody is at home.
2 A lot of under-25s **will be** lost if they **become** ill or **lose** their jobs.
3 **If** deliveries **came** in the evening, customers **would be** at home.
4 **If** they **arranged** proper delivery systems, they **would not have** so many problems.
5 **Will** a lot of online shops **fail if** they **don't solve** the delivery problem?

Form

- Ein *if*-Satz besteht aus zwei Teilen: dem *if*-Teil und dem Hauptteil.
- Außer bei Fragen (s. unten) kann der *if*-Teil vor oder nach dem Hauptteil stehen. Steht der *if*-Teil an erster Stelle, wird er von dem Hauptteil durch ein Komma getrennt. (1) (3) (4)
- Bei *if*-Sätzen vom Typ I und Typ II kommen folgende Zeitmuster am häufigsten vor:

Typ I	*If* + simple present + *will* future	(1) (2) (5)
Typ II	*If* + simple past + *would* + Infinitiv	(3) (4)

- Je nach Sinn kann man den *if*-Teil, den Hauptteil oder beide Teile eines *if*-Satzes verneinen. (4) (5)
- Bei Fragen wird nur der Hauptteil umgebildet. (5)

Gebrauch

- Der *if*-Teil drückt eine Bedingung aus, der Hauptteil eine Folge.
- Wir benutzen *if*-Sätze gemäß der Wahrscheinlichkeit der zu erwartenden Folge:

Typ I	Folge sicher bzw. höchst wahrscheinlich.	(1) (2) (5)
Typ II	Folge theoretisch möglich, aber kaum wahrscheinlich.	(3) (4)

6 Practising grammar

A Put the verbs into the correct tense. Look at the examples first.

Examples If all mobiles have PIN codes, violent robbery *will increase* (increase).
Would life be (life/be) easier if we banned mobiles under the age of 14?

1 If retailers concentrate on services, they *will* ... (be able to) deliver online.
2 If goods were delivered at night, people *would* ... (complain) about the noise.
3 *Will* ... (internet shopping/become) more popular if there is no delivery charge?
4 If you ... (look at) the crime figures, you will find that street crime is not increasing.
5 I'm sure that if there *was* ... (be) more security, people would shop online.
6 *Would* ... (the company/have to) close if they banned free downloads?
7 Ann *would* ... (not be) so negative if she looked at all the facts.
8 Online shops won't stay in business if they ... (not solve) the delivery problem. *don't*

B   Complete the sentences. Read the German first to find out which kind of
    if-sentence (I or II) you should use. Look at the example first.

> Example   If we *had* (have) a uniform, teachers *would have* (have) more time to
> teach.
> *(Höchstwahrscheinlich wird die Schule die Kleiderordnung nicht ändern.)*

1. If parents ... (be) more sensible, they ... (not give) young children mobiles.
   (Es ist zweifelhaft, ob Eltern vernünftiger werden.)

2. If the phone companies ... (cooperate), the police ... (be able to) solve the
   problem of theft.
   (Die Firmen werden sicherlich mit der Polizei zusammenarbeiten.)

3. If we ... (introduce) a strict dress code, some students ... (simply + ignore) it.
   (Eine Kleiderordnung wird wahrscheinlich die genannte Folge haben.)

4. Fewer students ... (take) part-time jobs if they ... (not need) so much money
   for clothes and other things.
   (Wahrscheinlich werden Studenten weiterhin Teilzeitjobs nachgehen.)

5. Unemployment ... (rise) if people ... (not consume) more than they need.
   (Wahrscheinlich werden die Leute weiterhin über Bedarf einkaufen.)

6. The under-25s ... (be) less dependent if they ... (learn) life skills at school.
   (Wahrscheinlich werden die Schulen sich nicht ändern.)

7. If internet shops ... (not solve) the delivery problem, a lot of them ... (go) out
   of business.
   (Viele Internethändler werden wegen Lieferproblemen in Konkurs gehen.)

8. Students ... (not be) willing to obey a dress code if we ... (have) one.
   *(Höchstwahrscheinlich werden Studenten nicht bereit sein, eine Kleiderord-
   nung zu akzeptieren.)*

9. If consumerism ... (continue) to grow, we ... (develop) into a society of selfish
   materialists.
   (Der Konsumwahn wird weiterhin anwachsen mit der genannten Folge.)

10. It ... (be) great if people ... (stop) complaining about consumerism and just ...
    (have) a bit of fun.
    (Leute werden sich weiterhin über Konsumwahn beklagen.)

7   Writing: a letter to the editor

⊃ Lernhilfen 4, S.146

Write a letter to the editor giving your opinion on either school uniforms or what can
be done about the theft of mobiles. The ideas in the box below may help you.

School uniforms	Mobile phones
▪ stop competition among pupils	▪ not give mobiles to very young children
▪ ban aggressive/revealing/unsuitable clothes/accessories	▪ protect mobiles with PINs
▪ reduce friction between ... and ...	▪ make the streets safer for young children
▪ create a sense of belonging/identity	▪ punish theft of mobiles severely
▪ be undemocratic/old-fashioned	▪ work against / be critical towards consumerism
▪ suppress individuality / freedom of expression	▪ provide everybody with a mobile
▪ cost money	▪ be cheaper than policing

8 Speaking: an interview

We sell more than just products and services. In fact, we 'sell ourselves' every time we meet somebody new, and particularly at job interviews.

A Work with a partner. Read the leaflet below and say what kind of person Camp Florida is looking for. Compare your results with the rest of your class to produce a 'perfect applicant profile'.

www.aifs.org/camp/

B Role-play a job interview. One of you (the interviewer) works for Camp Florida's Cologne office, the other (the applicant) wants a job. Ask questions based on **A** and answer them honestly. Then swap roles.

What is Camp Florida?

Camp Florida is a job agency that finds suitable young people from all over the world to work in
5 American summer camps for nine weeks. In exchange, they receive free flights, accommodation and no end of fun and life experience.
10 The jobs are hard but rewarding. You'll be working with children, mainly outdoors, organizing sporting activities, teaching basic arts and crafts,
15 and helping those in your care to develop their life skills.

Alternatively, you could be cooking or cleaning for them, or helping run the camp office.
20 Whichever job you choose, you'll get to know America through its children, and they'll learn about your home country through you.

25 Most important of all, you'll have the chance to learn a lot about yourself. Camp Florida will develop your ability to work in a team, increase your
30 self-confidence and personal independence, and enable you to react flexibly to changing situations – qualities that employers are always
35 looking for.

Take a job with us and in return we'll pay your return flight from Germany to the USA, take you to your camp,
40 arrange your work visa, allow you up to six weeks travel in the USA and Canada when your job is over – and pay you generous
45 pocket money as well.

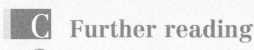

C Further reading

Track 28   **A** Read the text and complete the timeline.

1957
Vance Packard's
*The Hidden
Persuaders* attacks
advertisers

1962
Rachel Carson's
Silent Spring
describes risks of
agri-chemicals

1964
U.S. report proves …

go on.

The consumer revolution

On 11 January 2001, the German government changed its old Federal Ministry of Agriculture into the Federal Ministry for Consumer Protection, Food and Agriculture. In other words, it changed a farmers' lobby into a consumer watchdog. A few months later, a new law was introduced in Germany to force advertisers to tell the factual truth. From now on, '3-litre cars' must be just that and Super Glitzy wonder-toothpaste really does have to make your teeth as white as snow.

These reforms alone show the radical change in attitudes that has taken place over the last 20 years or so. It is a change from a 'take it or leave it' economy controlled by suppliers to a 'What would you like?' economy serving consumers.

Although few people realized it at the time, this 'consumer revolution' probably began in the United States in 1957 with the publication of Vance Packard's attack on advertising, *The Hidden Persuaders*. Another book was Rachel Carson's *Silent Spring* (1962), which described the effect of agri-chemicals on nature and the human food chain. A third publication was the U.S. Surgeon-General's report on smoking that came out in 1964. This proved what tobacco companies had long known, but always denied, ie that smoking causes cancer.

Further milestones on the road to the consumer revolution followed throughout the 1970s. For example, in Britain a new law (1976) gave consumers the right to withdraw from a sales agreement within a period of seven days after signing. This put pushy doorstep salesmen out of business for a start. Another law (1977) gave consumers the right to get their money back in full, even if they had no receipt and had bought the goods in a sale. Yet another important consumer-friendly move was the reform of shopping hours, which began in the UK in 1982. What gave the consumer revolution the final push was the appearance of BSE in the UK in 1984. This development closed a circle, for it was exactly what Rachel Carson had forecast in her book over 20 years earlier.

But what Ms Carson did not forecast was 'economically unreasonable' consumer demands for cheaper and cheaper goods, particularly food, that forced producers to do anything to produce what consumers wanted at a price they were willing to pay. Who really closed the circle? Who protects producers from greedy and unreasonable consumers?

(381 words)

B Give your opinion.
1 What do you think of Germany's law about strictly factual advertising?
2 What is your answer to the two questions at the end of the text?

www.consumer.gov.uk   www.which.net   www.ftc.gov

Focus

A What can you say about the person in the picture, her interests and her life? What time of year is it?

B Items a–g reached her room from all over the world. Match them with descriptions 1–7.
1 designed in Japan, made in Malaysia, and sold to music lovers everywhere
2 grown in Kenya and flown to Britain for processing and packaging
3 grown in the desert in southern Israel in the winter, and flown out by refrigerated plane for sale in northern Europe
4 designed by a German company in the USA, manufactured in Mexico and sold mainly in the USA and Europe for personal transport with fun and nostalgia
5 made from natural plant extracts found only in the Amazon jungle
6 designed by American scientists to share information, now used by hundreds of millions worldwide
7 designed and made in Sweden, for everyone to keep talking to everyone else

C Many producers of goods and services are multinational organizations. Name as many multinationals as you can and say what and where they produce.

Track 29 *Susan Miller (see* Focus*) has benefited greatly from free trade and globalization, but she may also become a victim. Her employer is thinking of moving production to lower-cost eastern Europe. If that happens, she will get reasonable redundancy pay and will probably find another job in her affluent part of the UK. But for Alma Molina, in Mexico, things are tougher.*

www.fairtradefederation.com

Free trade: whose freedom?

Alma knows all about free trade. She lives and works in Mexico's free-trade border zone – described by one commentator as 'a facsimile of hell on earth'. Thanks to California's high
5 taxes and tight air pollution controls, to NAFTA (the North Atlantic Free Trade Area)

and to Mexico's weak controls, over 2,000 large manufacturing operations have moved there in recent years. For these organizations,
10 free trade means the chance to push up profits by pushing down labour costs to rock-bottom levels, while paying few taxes and little attention to the environmental effects of their operations.
15 For Alma free trade also means working with dangerous chemicals without protective clothing. It means skin which is always stinging. And it means the sack for workers who try to organize and get better conditions.

'I went to work for a US company with a 20 plant in Juarez,' says Alma. 'I was one of about 300 workers who make electrical switches and sensors. I earned the Mexican minimum wage of $4.50 for a nine-hour day.

A group of us wanted to improve our 25 working conditions, safety and wages at this company (Clarostate). Six of us began to organize a union. We had meetings every two weeks. But after a few 30 months I was fired because of that.

Shortly after I was fired, I was hired by a General Electric subsidiary (Electro-componentes). At 35 that plant, 1,800 workers make wiring for refrigerators sold in the US. But I had been at GE for just seven days when I was called to the personnel office and shown 40 a list with my name on it. The personnel man did not know how my name had got on the list, but he said he had to fire me anyway.'

Multinationals hold the whip hand. Ex- 45 pensive American workers had already lost the jobs that went to Mexico. Now, if Alma and her colleagues ever succeed in their battle for better pay and conditions, their victory may be hollow. There are plenty more, even 50 poorer, countries that will be happy to offer the multinationals what they want.

(396 words)

⊃ Lernhilfen 4.2, S.146

1 Looking at the text

A Read quickly to find and explain these numbers in the text.

> *2,000* ▪ *300* ▪ *$4.50* ▪ *nine-hour* ▪ *six* ▪ *two weeks* ▪
> *1,800* ▪ *seven days*

B Answer the questions on the text.
  1 Who is Susan Miller, and how has she benefited from global free trade? Give some examples.
  2 The introduction suggests that unemployment is not as hard for someone from Britain as for a Mexican. In what two ways?
  3 What four things make manufacturing in Mexico attractive to many American companies?
  4 Why did Alma lose the first job? And why, apparently, the second one?
  5 If Mexican workers succeed in getting better conditions, why may that victory be an empty one?

C Give your opinion.
  If you worked at Clarostate, and if a new union was started, would you join it or not? What if you had a family to support?

2 Working with words

⊃ Lernhilfen 1.1, S.140

A Copy the table of word families and add words from the text. Use your dictionary, if necessary, to complete the table.

verb	noun	adjective
globalize	1) globe 2) …	…
…	1) product 2) …	productive
…	1) pollutant 2) …	polluting
…	1) … 2) …	manufactured
…	1) … 2) …	organized
…	1) protection 2) …	…

B Complete the following with the correct form of words from **2A**.

Today, we live in a …[1] economy, which means that economic conditions around the world are closely connected. It also means that …[2] can move the …[3] of goods to where they can be …[4] most cheaply and then transported to where they can be sold most expensively. Two huge problems with this …[5] of manufacturing and trade are the loss of 'expensive' jobs in richer countries and the fact that workers in poor countries are not …[6] from poor pay or bad working conditions. Often, there is also little or no environmental …[7] in these poor countries.

C Explain the following in your own words.
1 free trade (line 1)   5 organize (line 19)
2 labour costs (line 11)   6 minimum wage (line 23)
3 rock-bottom levels (lines 11–12) 7 I was fired (line 33)
4 the sack (line 18)   8 hold the whip hand (line 45)

3 Listening

Track 30

A Copy the following. Then listen to the first part of the radio programme and complete the notes.

Name of programme: ...   Today's company focus: ...
Today's country focus: ...   Today's issue: ... versus ...

B Copy the following. Then listen to the interviews and complete the brief notes.

The union wants: 1 ...
                        2 ...
                        3 ...
The company wants: 1 ...
                        2 ...
                        3 ...
The government wants: 1 ...
                        2 ...
                        3 ...

4 Culture check: national stereotypes

With globalization comes the need to understand cultural differences. Cultural awareness today is more important than ever.
But there are also simplistic national stereotypes which can be unhelpful when trying to understand another country and its people.

Look at these stereotypes in the cartoon.

1 Which nationalities has the cartoonist drawn?
2 What is he trying to say about the characters?
3 Do you agree with any of the stereotypes? Explain why (not).

B People and issues

Track 31

Global Watch – winners and losers

Adrian Turnbull

This week we look at how globalization affects different people in different places. There are both losers and winners, as these case studies show.

Sanjay Kara, Section Head, US Datex (India), Ahmadabad, Gujirat

My parents were poor, but they helped me through my college computer studies. If they hadn't done that, I would have ended up in poorly-paid work. Instead, I'm with US Datex. They send large data packages down the line to us when work finishes in ⁵ Chicago, in time for the start of our day here. We process the data and send it back ready for their next day. I know we're paid much less than Americans, but the pay is good by Indian standards. It means I can look after my parents now and help my brother through college too.

Florence Muhindo, wife, mother and subsistence farmer, Katakwi district, Uganda

Last year, government experts helped the men of our village with cheap fertiliser for our new cash ¹⁵ crop, cocoa, and helped build a well out in the cocoa plantation. They said, 'You can sell the cocoa for export and make real money.' ²⁰ Sadly, they didn't help us women, and we're the ones who grow the food everyone actually eats. Well, this year there's been a drought ²⁵ and the cocoa got all the water from the well. And now world cocoa prices have fallen. So there's no money and we're hungry. If the experts had helped us women, at least we might have grown enough to eat.

Jane Barnet, factory worker, Auto-Dubois UK, Near Swindon, UK

They're French, and they set up here to supply ⁴⁵ car parts to manufacturers around here. We've had ups and downs – especially when we lost the Honda contract. I wouldn't have been surprised if they'd closed down then. Anyway, I thought we were OK now, but ⁵⁰ management has just hit everyone with redundancy notices. They say it's too expensive to produce here, and they're going to ship all the equipment to a factory in Poland. ⁵⁵ If I'd known that a month ago, I'd have thought twice about buying my beautiful little Mini. I won't be able to keep up the loan payments if I don't get another job quickly. ⁶⁰

Dr Yukio Suzuki, Culham, near Oxford, UK

If anyone had told me ten years ago about my new life here, I would have laughed. I'm here as part of the worldwide project to develop nuclear fusion, the safe, new energy source that the whole world will one day use. ³⁵
We had a separate project in Japan, but later we joined the Europeans, who were more advanced. The Russians and Americans joined, too. Now it's a massive, 50-year project continuing here and around the world. It's extremely expensive, too. ⁴⁰ If our countries hadn't all combined resources, it would probably have collapsed by now.

(408 words)

5 Looking at the text

⟲ Lernhilfen 4.2, S.146

A Say which of the four profiles best demonstrate these very important things about globalization today and why.

1 The ease with which companies can move production to cheaper countries.
2 The danger of sudden economic disaster when world prices for particular products or cash crops drop.
3 The ease with which goods are transported across great distances.
4 The huge amount of information we can send electronically around the world.
5 The ease with which people can now move around the world.
6 The great increase in international cooperation on large projects.

B Answer the questions on the text.

1 Which people in the magazine article clearly benefit from globalization? In what way is each of them an example of international cooperation?
2 Which people used to benefit from globalization, but not now? What has caused the damage in both cases?

6 Writing a comment

⟲ Lernhilfen 4.4, S.148

Write a comment on this question. Do you think it is always best to buy German?

> *types of product* ▪ *quality* ▪ *attractiveness* ▪ *variety of choice* ▪ *price* ▪ *environmental damage by transport* ▪ *need for competition* ▪ *need for international trade* ▪ *pressures of global competition on German producers*

7 Looking at grammar: the past perfect + *if*-sentences type III

Grammar

Remember

1 I **had been** at GE for just seven days when I was called to the personnel office.
2 **Once** that **had succeeded**, America, Japan and Russia joined in.
3 **If** anyone **had told** me ten years ago about my new life here, I **would have laughed**.
4 **If I'd** (= had) **known** that, **I'd** (= would) **have thought** twice about buying my car.
5 **If** the experts **had helped** us, we **might have grown** enough to eat.

▪ Das **past perfect** wird benutzt, um auszudrücken, dass eine Handlung oder ein Zustand in der Vergangenheit bereits abgeschlossen war, als etwas Neues geschah. Die frühere Handlung wird mit *had* + Partizip Perfekt (3. Form) gebildet, die spätere mit dem **simple past**. (1) (2)

▪ Die Handlungen werden häufig durch Adverbien oder adverbiale Bestimmungen, wie z.B. *as soon as, before, by the time, once, until, when, after* verbunden. In diesem Fall steht gewöhnlich ein Komma zwischen den beiden Sätzen. (2)

▪ Das **past perfect** steht auch in *if*-Sätzen vom Typ III, wenn von einer möglichen Situation in der Vergangenheit die Rede ist – etwas, das nicht geschah. In diesem Fall wird *if* + **past perfect**, *would / could / might have* + Partizip Perfekt verwendet. (3)–(5)

▪ Ein Komma steht nur, wenn der *if*-Satz zuerst kommt. (3)–(5)

8 Practising grammar

A Put the sentences together, using the simple past and the past perfect. Use the time expressions in brackets to join the two clauses and commas between clauses where necessary.

Example Alma worked in terrible conditions for a year. She decided to help start a union. (before)
Alma had worked in terrible conditions for a year before she decided to help start a union.

1 Alma and her colleagues made this decision. Nobody ever took action against the company. (until)
2 Management always made decisions without discussions with workers. Alma and the others acted. (until)
3 Managers knew about the union. It secretly grew to 20% of the work force. (before)
4 Management started holding emergency meetings among themselves. It found out about the union. (once)
5 It received the union's first request for better conditions. It reacted angrily and refused. (as soon as)
6 Alma and the others called their next meeting. The company decided to fire them all. (by the time)

B Poorly qualified, Ranjit Dessai left school to join the local shipyard. But global competition closed it down – and put him on the road to success. Put the sentence parts together to form *if*-sentences type III.

Example Ranjit not be lazy at school / get more qualifications
If Ranjit hadn't been lazy at school, he would have got more qualifications.

1 Ranjit leave school with good qualifications / go to college and study philosophy
2 never go to work in the shipyard / not leave school with so few qualifications
3 not join the shipyard / not be made redundant three years later when it closed
4 be able to keep his job / not retrain as a chef
5 never think of making a business out of Indian food / this not happen
6 and not think of this / probably become a hotel or restaurant chef
Luckily, this was exactly the right time for his new business idea.
7 start an Indian fast-food store years earlier / probably not be popular and successful
8 not be very successful / not be able to develop into a small chain of stores
9 this not be successful / not have the money to expand again and start supplying supermarkets
10 and this never happen / not become a millionaire
But it *did* happen, and he *is* a millionaire!

9 Speaking: role-play

Work in groups of five. You are negotiating fair pay and conditions in Indonesian factories that produce trainers for the American sportswear giant Nike Inc. Four members of the group each take one of the following roles:

- a Nike executive: wants fair conditions but must have extremely low prices – American market is very competitive.
- a Korean factory owner: moved to Indonesia when Korean costs rose; bitter about Nike's high profits; may have to move again to keep contract.
- an Indonesian government official: wants Nike problem dealt with quietly; desperate to keep Nike production in Indonesia.
- an Indonesian factory worker: suffering awful working conditions, but frightened of losing job; wants all to act together for better conditions.
- The fifth person in the group is a mediator from the International Consumers' Association. The mediator should chair the meeting and push for an agreement.

Each negotiator chooses a role card on p 139. Read it carefully and plan your arguments. This language may help you.

> **Asking for information**
> Perhaps you could explain (what) …
> So tell me, (what) …
>
> **Asking leading questions**
> Don't you think … ?
> Shouldn't that mean … ?
>
> **Avoiding answering**
> I don't want to comment on this particular case.
>
> **Stating a strong position**
> That's totally unacceptable.
> I can't accept the recent demands.
>
> **Explaining**
> You see, what you've got to realize is that …
> Perhaps I can put it this way …
> I think it's important to understand that …
>
> **Stating willingness to compromise**
> In the end I'm sure we'll all find a way forward together.
> Everybody must work towards a compromise.
> We must all try to find a way forward together.

10 Writing

⟲ Lernhilfen 4.4, S.148

At the end of the role-play, each group must prepare a press release (100–150 words) stating publicly what has been agreed. Everyone should check carefully to see that it says exactly what you agreed – and of course you must also check the language for correctness. If you prepare your press release on computer, you can print copies to hand out for class discussion.

A Have you ever swapped things that you own with friends? Have you ever helped friends in exchange for their help with other things? Was it successful?

B Read and say: a) what Bobbins, Pigs and Strouds are and b) who the people in the photos are, and what they do.

C Would you ever think about joining a group like this? What goods or services could you trade?

Track 32

HOW A PIZZA BECOMES A POT

Not everybody accepts life in a globalized world of trade. In fact, many do the opposite and try to keep their trade within a small
5 community. In Britain, tens of thousands of people do this by swapping goods
10 and services locally. These groups – 'local exchange trading systems' (LETS) – use tokens that members exchange for work. In Manchester they call them Bobbins; in Scunthorpe they use Pigs; in Stroud
15 they are simply Strouds.

■ Such tokens cover the cost of members' time and skills, but not the cost of outside raw materials, which have to be bought normally. This means payment is often a mixture of cash and
20 tokens.

■ How does it work? Take this example from the small town of Stroud. Maggie Mills, who owns a restaurant, accepts 50% Strouds from her cus-tomers. These include Alice Friend, a therapist who also charges half cash and half Strouds. 25 Tim Wilcox is a handyman, who often goes to Mrs Friend for help, and he pays her as much as he can in Strouds. In turn, he is building a house extension for John Rhodes, a gardener, who will pay half the bill in Strouds. He has plenty of 30 Strouds because he accepts them from several customers. Sophia Hughes, a potter, recently paid him 30% in Strouds for cutting her hedge.

Ms Hughes herself was recently paid in Strouds for 35 pots that Mrs Mills uses in her restaurant.

■ 'The scheme has been a wonderful success,' Ms Hughes reports. 'It is great 40 when you are on a low income or ill, as you can afford services you would never normally be able to pay for.' ■

a Stroud cheque

Stroud LETS
The British School, Slad Road,
STROUD, GL5 1QW

Date 29th January 2002
A/C No. 375
To Matthew Williams
Amount in Words $20
Twenty Strouds
A/C No. 71
From Sophia Hughes
Signature Sophia Hughes

(277 words)

Wasting the world

Focus

There are four main categories of waste:

Recyclable waste	Bio-degradable waste	Non-degradable waste	Special waste
can be collected, reprocessed and used again.	is made of natural material that, in time, simply rots away.	does not rot. It is disposed of by incineration, in landfill sites or at sea.	is toxic and must be disposed of separately.

Look at the photos and answer these questions.

1 Which categories do you think the waste shown in the photos belongs to? Say why.
2 Which kinds of waste do you produce?
3 How do you dispose of your waste?
4 Is the illegal dumping of rubbish a problem in your area? Which kinds of waste are disposed of in this way? What could you do about it?

A People and society

  'Techno-waste' is a relatively new kind of waste made up of electrical equipment such as TVs, computer hardware and fridges. Although techno-waste is only a small percentage of total waste, a lot of it is very toxic and therefore difficult to dispose of safely.

Industry playing down techno-waste problem, conference told

by ALISON FOX in Amsterdam

Brian Webster of Waste Watch, a British environmental lobbyist, said at a conference on waste disposal here last night that the disposal of hazardous techno-
5 waste was fast becoming 'the hottest issue' in the EU.

He told delegates that although industry said that 'only 2%' of the roughly 2000 million tons of waste produced in the EU
10 each year was techno-waste, this use of percentages played down the problem. In fact, this 'only 2%' translated into approximately 40 million tons of sometimes very toxic waste that was extremely
15 difficult and expensive to dispose of safely.

He pointed out that for that reason, organized crime had already turned to the illegal disposal of toxic waste as a
20 highly profitable business – and one that was certainly easier than people smuggling because governments often turned a blind eye to it.

Mr Webster went on to tell delegates that
25 in the UK, 'the place he knew best', just under 45% of domestic technical waste was made up of large household equipment like fridges, cookers and dishwashers, many of which were in perfect working order. People 'with more money 30 than sense' were replacing equipment long before the end of its service life, he said.

A further 30% was computer hardware, again much of it in good order, that 35 contained a cocktail of toxic metals such as mercury, lead and cadmium. Add to that the 2 million TVs and the 635 million cadmium and lithium batteries that the British threw away each year, and 40 you were faced with a big problem, he continued.

Unsurprisingly, Mr Webster saw the spread of digital technology as 'more of a curse than a blessing'. While he agreed 45 that a new generation of TVs and mobile phones, for example, would create jobs and might even be more environmentally friendly, he wondered how we would dispose of the old equipment it replaced. 50

(317 words)

1 Looking at the text

Answer the questions on the text.

1 What role do these figures play in Brian Webster's talk?

> *2%* ▪ *2000 million tons* ▪ *45%* ▪ *30%* ▪ *2 million* ▪ *635 million*

2 According to Mr Webster, why is techno-waste 'fast becoming the hottest issue in the EU'?

3 What could consumers do to reduce the problem of techno-waste?

4 Explain Mr Webster's attitude to the spread of digital technology.

2 Working with words

⟳ Lernhilfen 1.2, S.142

A Explain what these expressions from the text mean.
1 the hottest issue (lines 5–6)
2 play down a problem (line 11)
3 turn a blind eye to sth (lines 22–23)
4 service life (line 32)
5 more of a curse than a blessing (lines 44–45)

B Complete the reader's letter with words and expressions from the box.

> car manufacturers ▪ cover ▪ create ▪ disposing ▪ economic disaster ▪
> household equipment ▪ materials ▪ models ▪ plastics ▪ replacing ▪
> savings ▪ service life ▪ solutions ▪ taken apart ▪ toxic waste

Sir or Madam – I agree with much of what Brian Webster of Waste Watch says about the problem of …[1] of techno-waste (your report, 15 May), but unfortunately he did not offer any …[2] to it. Or does he expect people to stop …[3] their electrical equipment with the latest …[4], which would probably be an …[5]?

Next year, …[6] must take back their cars when they have reached the end of their …[7]. The old cars will then be …[8], and many materials – …[9], for example – will be recycled. …[10] will be disposed of safely. According to the experts, …[11] made by recycling …[12] in this way will more than …[13] the cost of the take-back system. And, of course, it will also …[14] jobs. Why can't we do the same with …[15], TVs and computer hardware?

Jane Harper, Liverpool

3 Listening

Track 34

You are going to hear about Germany's unusual waste problem.
Work with a partner. First, read the assignments, then listen and take notes. Finally, do the assignments.

A All these statements are wrong. Correct them.
1 Germany is producing too much waste.
2 Household rubbish increased enormously during the 1990s.
3 Germans have taken little notice of anti-waste campaigns.
4 Most German waste is disposed of in landfill sites.
5 Very little is done to recycle waste.
6 A Belgian factory was forced to send its waste to Düsseldorf's new incinerator.

B Complete the sentences with detailed information from the report.
1 North Rhine Westphalia is importing waste from …[1] by …[2] to keep its incinerators in business.
2 Total German waste production fell by …[1]% during the …[2].
3 The production of household rubbish has fallen by …[1]% since 1990, when it stood at …[2] million tons.
4 A lot of waste is changed into …[1] and …[2], for example.
5 Incinerators burn non-recyclable waste and use the …[1] to generate …[2].
6 Stora once sold its waste to a …-…[1] for $…[2] a ton; now it can sell it for $…[3] a ton.

B People and issues

Track 35

This press report is about water shortages caused by mass tourism. It centres on the resort of Benidorm in southern Spain, the driest region in Europe.

As Benidorm grows, local farmers are left high and dry

THE SPANISH resort of Benidorm is like a concrete forest on a narrow strip of land between the Mediterranean and the mountains, its high-rise hotels blocking out the sun like
5 trees. While the town has a resident population of about 50,000, in the summer this figure rises to more than 320,000.

To house the visitors, there are 132 hotels and four more, one of them the tallest in Europe, are
10 under construction. Twelve further hotels and caravan parks are planned, which will bring the town's summer population to around 550,000, or well over ten times its resident population.

Like a real forest, the concrete forest of Benidorm
15 needs fresh water to live and grow: water for showers and toilets in thousands of hotel rooms, water for hundreds of bars and kitchens, water for around 30,000 swimming pools.

But water is scarce, and it is getting scarcer as
20 the concrete trees of Benidorm push their way up into the sky. With very little rainfall, the town has to get its water from underground. Wells that were once just 15 metres deep, are now six times that depth. And as the level of the ground water
25 drops, seawater replaces it, contaminating wells with salt, and destroying farmland and livestock.

Experts say that the water crisis caused by mass tourism is one of the world's most explosive issues, and – because tourism is not only the biggest industry on earth, but also its fastest
30 growing – it is a problem that can only get worse. Some even see water shortages as a possible cause of future wars.

Since 1960, the number of tourists travelling abroad has risen nearly ten times, from around
35 70 million arrivals a year to 670 million in 2000. And this number is continuing to grow at about 4.5%, or 30 million arrivals, per year based on the figure for the year 2000.

To neutral observers, Spain – which is both
40 Europe's most popular tourist destination and its driest country – is heading for a major disaster. But Spanish authorities, afraid of a drop in tourist earnings, deny that there is a problem at all. When asked about the crisis in farming around
45 Benidorm, the town's mayor, Vicente Pérez Devesa, said that there was plenty of water for

Tourist arrivals in millions

Year	Arrivals (millions)
1950	25
1960	70
1970	150
1980	300
1990	450
2000	670

everybody and stories about shortages were nothing more than 'media exaggeration'. And Pedro Pastor Rosello, a water official from Denia,
50 agreed. He told journalists to listen to the facts and not to take any notice of 'scare stories' spread by the 'prophets of doom'.

(434 words)

A Answer the questions on the text.
  1 Why does the writer compare Benidorm to a forest?
  2 What effect does mass tourism have on Benidorm?
  3 What is the cause of the water shortage in dry regions like southern Spain?
  4 Why do the Spanish authorities deny that there is a water crisis at all?

B Describe the chart.

  The chart shows … in … from … to … . In 1950, arrivals stood at … .
  By 1960, this … . Ten years later, …

C Summarize the text.
  Pick information out of the text to show that the report is not just a 'scare story'.

D Give your opinion.
  Would you be willing to holiday at home to help save the world's water?

5 Looking at grammar: indirect speech

Grammar

Remember

1 'The disposal of hazardous techno-waste is becoming a big problem.'
  → He said (that) the disposal of techno-waste **was becoming** a big problem.
2 'Organized crime has already turned to the illegal disposal of toxic waste as a highly profitable business.'
  → He pointed out (that) organized crime **had** already **turned** to the illegal disposal of toxic waste as a highly profitable business.
3 'How will we dispose of the old equipment?'
  → He wondered/wanted to know **how we would dispose** of the old equipment.
4 'Can you offer a solution to the problem, Mr Webster?'
  → She asked Mr Webster **if/whether he could offer** a solution to the problem.
5 'Listen to the facts and don't take any notice of 'scare stories'.
  → He told us **to listen** to the facts and **not to take** any notice of 'scare stories'.

Aussagen

■ Möchten wir den Inhalt eines Gespräches oder Vortrages wiedergeben, benutzen wir die indirekte Rede. (1)–(5)
■ Steht das einleitende Verb im **simple past**, z.B. *said, mentioned, pointed out,* dann ändern sich die Zeiten in der indirekten Rede wie folgt:

direkte Rede	indirekte Rede	
present	past	(1)
past	past perfect	
present perfect	past perfect	(2)
will-future	*would*	(3)

■ Die Modalverben ändern sich wie folgt:
  can/may/have to   could/might/had to (4)

- Zeit- und Ortsangaben müssen dem Sinn entsprechend geändert werden:

today	*that day*
tomorrow	*the next/following day*
yesterday	*the day before/the previous day*
this week/these weeks/...	*that week/those weeks/...*
next week/month/...	*the following week/month/...*
last week/month/...	*the week/... before/the previous week/...*
now/here	*then/there*

- Personalpronomen müssen dem Sinn entsprechend ebenfalls geändert werden. (4)

Fragen

- Bei Fragen mit Fragewort (3) wird dieses übernommen. Beachten Sie die veränderte Satzstellung.
- Bei Fragen ohne Fragewort (4) benutzen wir *if/whether* (ob), um zu zeigen, dass es sich um eine Frage handelt.

Bitten und Aufforderungen

- Indirekte Bitten und Aufforderungen (5) werden durch *asked* (bitten) bzw. *told* (sagen) eingeleitet.

! **Beachten Sie:** Die Verben *ask* und *tell* haben immer ein Objekt. Daher muss die angesprochene Person erwähnt werden.

- Das Verb erscheint als *to* + Infinitiv. Bei verneinten Sätzen setzen wir *not* unmittelbar vor *to*. (5)

6 Practising grammar

A Clare Connors works for Irish Water Technology (IWT), and you are her assistant. You have taken several messages for Clare. Use indirect statements to give her the messages.

Example Uli Klein: 'I'll phone you as soon as I land, OK?'
→ *Mr Klein said / rang to say (that) he would phone us as soon as he landed.*

1 Hotel: 'We're sorry but we'll have to put Mr Klein in a double room and we'll charge you for a single.'
2 Ted Grant: 'IWT has won a prize for its new filter system. I'm sure this will lead to lots of orders.'
3 Mike: 'I know Clare will be angry, but I have to stay off work for at least another two weeks.'
4 Mrs Gregg: 'It's nearly the end of July and I'm still waiting for Clare's business expenses for May and June. I must have them as soon as she gets back or the Accounts Department may not pay them.'
5 Uli Schneider: 'I'm afraid I won't be able to have dinner with Ms Connors next Thursday after all. I'm seeing a colleague from the university at 8.00. Perhaps we could have a drink before then – 7.00, say.'
6 Printer: 'The new catalogue won't be ready before the end of next week. We're going to have to delay printing because they delivered the wrong paper.'

B A group of school-leavers from a Dublin school is asking Clare about her company and the water industry. Report the questions for the school magazine.
Use a name or *somebody/someone + asked / wanted to know / wondered*.

Examples   When was the company founded?
   → *Somebody asked when the company had been founded.*
   Do you enjoy your work?
   → *Diana wanted to know if/whether Ms Connors enjoyed her work.*

1   How many people work for IWT?
2   Does your company export any of its products?
3   Do you train school-leavers like us?
4   What qualifications must you have to become a trainee?
5   Has IWT taken over a big water company in France?
6   Where does Dublin's water come from?
7   Is it true that we will have to pay much more for water soon?
8   Who actually owns IWT? Does it belong to the government?

C Eve Miller is a waste disposal adviser. This is what she said to members of a youth club. Report what she said using *advised us / asked us / told us (not) to … .*

Example   'Never replace things that are in good working order.'
   → *Ms Miller told us never to replace things that were in good working order.*

1   Don't buy products with outer packaging, or leave the packaging in the shop.

2   If you have a garden, make a compost heap for food remains.

3   Always use returnable glass bottles rather than cans.

4   Go to the recycling container on your way to work or the shops. Don't make special journeys.

5   Sort your rubbish into recyclable materials, compostible materials and the rest.

6   Don't put hazardous waste like batteries into the dustbin.

7   Only buy a new TV at a shop that is willing to take back your old one.

8   Always ask yourself this question: 'Do I really need this?'

7 Listening

Track 36 The airport announcement that you are about to hear tells passengers a) that their flight has been delayed, b) that some passengers will now miss their connecting flights and c) what arrangements have been made for them.

A First, read the assignments so that you know what to listen for. Then listen to the announcement, taking notes as you do so. Finally, do the assignments.

B Some passengers come to the information desk with questions. Tell them what to do.
1 'Excuse me, please. Where do I get a new JAL ticket for the Singapore-Tokyo leg?'
2 'This is outrageous. How long are we going to be delayed this time?'
3 'What? Such a long delay and no refreshments? Why did I pay business class?'
4 'Did I hear right? Am I going to miss my connecting flight to Brisbane? What's the story now?'
5 'Somebody's just told me BA flight 763 is delayed. What time is take-off now?'

8 Speaking: giving a talk

⟳ Lernhilfen 5, S.150

Work with a partner or in small groups. Prepare and give a talk on the water crisis and its causes, effects and a possible solution. Use information from this unit, adding any information you may have from other sources and from the media.

www.envirolink.org   www.keeper.org   ww.foe.co.uk

9 Writing: a report

⟳ Lernhilfen 4, S.146

In the UK, there are about 28 million cars and light vans at present in use.
Each year, just over two million new vehicles replace just under two million old ones.
(This difference is causing a net increase in vehicle ownership of about 50,000
vehicles per year, in spite of very high fuel costs and current low investment in roads.)

A Look at the pie-chart to see the extent of the problem – and why the EU is trying to force car manufacturers to provide a free take-back service to stop people dumping their old cars in fields and on the side of the road.

B Use the information in the pie-chart to write a report for a school magazine about disposing of cars at the end of their service life.

Think about:
– Which materials can be recycled?
– Which must be disposed of as 'unusable waste'?
– Which materials are toxic?
– Who should pay the costs?
– Your own view.

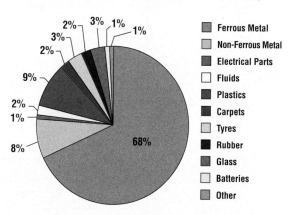

Materials used in cars: percentage of total weight

Ferrous Metal
Non-Ferrous Metal
Electrical Parts
Fluids
Plastics
Carpets
Tyres
Rubber
Glass
Batteries
Other

Are you an eco-warrior or a litter-bug?

Are you an eco-warrior, a litter-bug or something in between? Find out by answering this questionnaire. Answer each question with Yes or No and then look at the table to work out your score.

1 Do you use your motorbike, scooter or car, even when you could easily walk, take a bus or go by bike?

2 Do you often eat from throw-away plastic plates, use throw-away plastic cutlery or drink from throw-away metal cans?

3 Do you think it is right to return to 'natural' farming methods as quickly as possible, even if this means higher prices and some job losses?

4 Do you always sort your rubbish and use recycling containers?

5 Do you sometimes buy electrical equipment with throw-away batteries when you could have the same equipment with rechargeable batteries or mains power?

6 You see somebody dumping an old TV in a field. Would you tell the person to stop what he or she is doing?

7 You're out with friends and everybody is having a great time. Then somebody drops a drinks can in the street. Would you tell him or her to pick it up, even if this could spoil the fun?

8 Do you use stand-by switches on TVs and VCRs or leave lights on when you could easily switch them all off?

9 Your brother wants to buy a used car. He could buy a small modern car or a fantastic old BMW that drinks petrol and has not got a catalytic converter. Your brother asks you what you think. Would you say, 'Buy the BMW. If you don't, somebody else will'?

10 Do you secretly find all this talk about global warming and other ecological issues a bit boring and even exaggerated?

Finding out your score

Question	1	2	3	4	5	6	7	8	9	10
Yes	0	0	3	2	0	3	2	0	0	0
No	3	2	0	1	2	0	1	2	3	2

What your score says about you

0–3 You seem to be a very selfish person who doesn't care about anybody or anything as long as you're having an easy time. You're also too stupid to see that you're making holes in the bottom of your own boat.

4–7 You're doing your bit to destroy the earth, though you at least seem to understand that this is wrong. You must take ecological issues more seriously and do more to protect the earth for future generations.

8–12 You're beginning to do something to protect the earth but you could easily do very much more. Still, at least you understand how important protecting the environment is – as long as it doesn't cause you too much trouble, of course.

13–16 This is a good score. You're like most sensible people. You understand that there is a problem and you are doing your bit to help to solve it. But are you brave enough to speak out when you see somebody else behaving stupidly or selfishly?

17–21 Terrific! You've got the message loud and clear, and you're brave enough to pass it on to other people as well. If all her children were like you, Mother Earth would have nothing to worry about.

22–24 Hey, come on! Is this the real 'you'? If not, go back and do the test again to find out your true score. If it is, you could have problems. Do you prefer trees to people? Are you sure you're getting the most out of life?

Focus

A Match the crimes to the pictures below. Choose from the following types of crime. Describe each picture.

> *armed robbery* ▪ *assault* ▪ *burglary* ▪ *computer crime* ▪ *credit card fraud* ▪ *drug-taking* ▪ *drug-trafficking* ▪ *drunk driving* ▪ *hijacking* ▪ *industrial espionage* ▪ *kidnapping* ▪ *manslaughter* ▪ *mugging* ▪ *murder* ▪ *rape* ▪ *shoplifting* ▪ *smuggling (cigarettes, people, etc)* ▪ *theft (bicycle, car, mobile phone, etc)* ▪ *vandalism*

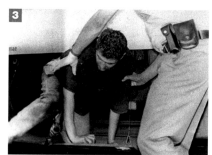

B Are any of the sorts of crime listed above a big problem where you live? Are there other common sorts of law-breaking? Give examples.

Track 37

The rise, fall and rise of
American crime

Serious crime in the USA began rising rapidly in the 1960s towards a terrible peak in 1993. New York alone had over 2,000 murders a year. Much crime, from mugging to murder, was
5 drug-related, and the police appeared almost powerless. Society seemed close to collapse.

Since then, crime rates have apparently fallen by 40% or more. In one recent year, murder was down by eight per cent nationally, and rape fell
10 by five per cent. At 10% and 11%, the declines in car theft and robbery were even greater. 'Our communities are now the safest they have been for a generation,' the President recently declared.

Modern security technology has helped make
15 much crime more difficult. Movement-sensitive lighting, burglar alarms and closed-circuit TV (CCTV) all make crime against property harder. Electronic locks have reduced car theft similarly.

What gets most of the publicity is hardline
20 policing, though. 'Zero-tolerance' policies in cities such as New York and Los Angeles mean immediate tough action against offenders. Another (baseball) catchphrase – 'Three strikes and you're out' – means an automatic prison
25 sentence after three offences. The American public likes this.

But do these results mean dramatic improvement? Not really. For a start, two million Americans are now in jail, and this cannot be good. Then again, tough police action often
30 focuses on young, ethnic urban males, especially blacks. Naturally, racial tension increases.

This leads to differences between actual crime and reported crime. When certain social groups are treated harshly by heavy-handed police, they
35 tend not to report crimes or request police help. This has probably helped 'reduce' crime considerably.

Furthermore, 'modern' crimes such as computer crime, credit card fraud
40 and, among the wealthy, tax evasion, are actually increasing fast. Among the young, mobile phone theft is rocketing – and so too is shoplifting.

Around 23 million Americans have
45 shoplifted, and this costs retailers $12 billion yearly. This forces up prices, and so the average family pays an annual 'shoplifting tax' of $800.

Teenagers are the largest group of shoplifters,
50 and their main targets are not basics like food, but non-essentials – often fashion goods. Why do they do it? The chart offers an explanation:

Why teenagers shoplift

To resell the product: **14%**
For the thrill: **5%**
Other: **2%**
I couldn't afford it: **28%**
I didn't want to pay for it: **25%**
To impress my friends: **26%**

over half steal because they want more than they can – or want to – afford. America's epidemic of
55 'serious' crime may be under control, but its epidemic of consumerism and consumer-related crime is not. And, actually, this is very serious, too.

(402 words)

1   Looking at the text

↻ Lernhilfen 4.2, S.146

A   Read quickly to find and explain these numbers in the text.

> over 2,000 ▪ 40% ▪ 10% and 11% ▪ two million ▪ 23 million ▪
> $800 ▪ over half

B   Summarize points from the text which support the following statements.
- America has largely succeeded in dealing with its crime crisis.
- American society has not really repaired itself.

C   Give your opinion.
How well or badly do you think the police deal with crime in your area?

2   Working with words

A   Explain the following in your own words.
1. hardline policing (lines 19–20)
2. helped 'reduce' crime [referring to the use of inverted commas] (lines 37–38)
3. is rocketing (line 43)
4. shoplifting tax (line 49)

B   Find opposites of the following in the text.
1. easier (2 opposites)   3. rural   5. traditional
2. delayed   4. gentle   6. the poor

C   Use pairs of words from **2B** to complete the following.
1. Crime is not found just in cities. It is a … problem as well as an … one.
2. With few police in country areas, … responses to urgent calls are common and … action is often not possible.
3. Surprisingly, there are more crime victims among …, who already have so little, than among … .
4. … crime such as computer fraud requires hi-tech police work, but … methods of community policing remain very important.

3   Listening

Track 38

Seventeen-year-old Carrie – not her real name – was a once-only shoplifter.
It was totally pointless since she needs nothing. She lives in a comfortable Seattle suburb with her wealthy parents. She wants her story to be told as a warning to others. Listen and make brief notes on the main points. Retell her story in your own words.

Main points:
- What happened at the start of the day:
- Lisa's part in what happened next: (two points)
- Things stolen: (two things)
- How caught:
- What actions security guards/police took: (three things)
- Punishment by parents:
- Other punishments: (two points)

Track 39

Murder madness: what would you have done?

by Cathy Mendoza, a student counselor at Mid-West High, Oklahoma

HEATH HIGH in Paducah, Kentucky; Heritage High in Conyers, Georgia, Columbine High near Denver, Colorado.
5 These are some of the most infamous names in a long line of school massacres. Did these killings really have to happen?

And must they go on happe-
10 ning?
Last year alone over 6,000 students were expelled for brin-ging guns to school – and those were just the ones who were
15 caught. Therefore, one way of preventing at least some of the massacres would be to change this country's gun laws and make weapons harder to get.
20 But even after years of cam-paigning, activists have not succee-ded in bringing change. The fact
25 is, most Americans prefer to keep their guns.
The parents of the three girls shot
30 dead by Michael Carneal at Heath High looked in another direction. They believed that
35 their daughters died partly because other people knew about the danger but did nothing. As a result, they recently sued
40 around 50 students who, they claimed, let the tragedy happen.
Many admitted hearing Carneal talk about his grotes-que ideas. For example, Jeremy
45 T Ellis, who knew Carneal from the school band, said, 'He told
50 me once or twice that it would be cool to run down the halls
55 shooting peo-ple. And he told me once it would be cool to go to prison. ... You look back and see all these things that were sort of warning
60 signs, but you didn't really rea-lize it at the time.'
William J Alonso was another one. Carneal showed him his guns the Saturday before the
65 killings. Alonso failed to men-tion seeing them to anybody because Carneal's action 'didn't seem too out of place'.
On the morning of the mur-
70 ders, Toby Nace saw Carneal putting earplugs in and then pulling a gun out of his bak-kpack. But he did nothing because 'I didn't want to get my
75 friend into trouble'.
Scott Poland, president of the National Association of School Psychologists says, 'Many stu-dents just don't believe that
80 serious violence could happen in their school. Others don't want to tell on their friends. And then there are those who fear retaliation.'
85 Nevertheless, says Professor Dewey Cornell, who has studied juvenile crime for many years, 'You need to act. I have talked to a number of kids in jail who
90 wish one of their friends had done something.'
So were Carneal's fellow students really partly to blame? The judge trying the case finally
95 decided not, and she dismissed the lawsuit. Many of them, though, will not stop asking themselves that question for the rest of their lives. And here is
100 another question. Would you or I have acted any differently from those Heath High kids?

(439 words)

4 Looking at the text

⟳ Lernhilfen 4.2, S.146

A Briefly state in your own words the (main) point made by each of these people.

> *Jeremy T Ellis* ▪ *William J Alonso* ▪ *Toby Nace* ▪ *Scott Poland* ▪
> *Professor Dewey Cornell*

B Answer the following questions.
1 How might the parents' lawyer have explained their views to the court at the start of the lawsuit?
2 At the end, how might the judge have explained her reasons for dismissing the case?

5 Looking at grammar: verb + infinitive / verb + *-ing*

Grammar

Remember
1 I didn't **want to get** my friend into trouble.
2 Many **admitted hearing** Carneal talk.
3 Most Americans **prefer keeping / to keep** their guns.
4 Most Americans **would prefer to keep** their guns.
5 Crime **began rising / to rise** rapidly in the 1960s.
6 Many will not **stop asking** themselves that question.

- Der Infinitiv folgt auf Verben wie *agree, appear, dare, decide, fail, learn, manage, offer, pretend, promise, refuse, seem, tend, threaten, want*. (1)
- Die *-ing*-Form folgt auf Verben wie *admit, avoid, can't bear/stand, dislike, enjoy, finish, imagine, keep, practise, suggest*. (2)
- Auf *like, love, hate* und *prefer* können beide Formen folgen. (3) Auf *would like, would love, would hate* und *would prefer* folgt allerdings immer der Infinitiv. (4)
- Auf *begin, continue, intend* und *start* können auch beide Formen folgen (5) – es sei denn, diese Verben stehen in einer Verlaufsform. In dem Fall kann nur der Infinitiv stehen.
- Auf einige andere Verben können ebenfalls beide Formen folgen, allerdings mit einem Bedeutungsunterschied. (6) Vergleichen Sie folgende Sätze:
  I **remember being** here years ago. (*Ich erinnere mich ...*)
  I must **remember to call** Tom. (*Ich muss daran denken ...*)
  You'd better **stop doing** that! (*unterlassen*)
  You'd better **stop to have** a break. (*unterbrechen*)
  I'll **try walking** to work instead of driving. (*Ich werde es probieren ...*)
  I'll **try to finish** by 5 pm. (*Ich gebe mir Mühe ...*)
- Auf eine Präposition folgt meistens eine *-ing*-Form, wie z.B. bei *accuse sb of, agree with, argue for/against, congratulate sb on, decide against, dream of, feel like, prevent sb from, stop sb from, succeed in, thank sb for, think about/of, warn sb against.*
  Worried activists have not **succeeded in bringing** change.
- Auf Ausdrücke, die aus einem Nomen/Adjektiv + Präposition bestehen, folgt auch oft eine *-ing*-Form:
  They have had no **success in bringing** change.
  They have not been **successful in bringing** change.

6 Practising grammar

A Complete the following news report, choosing pairs of verbs from the list.

> *enjoy/show* ▪ *fail/take* ▪ *intend/do* ▪ *keep/tell* ▪ *remember/hear* ▪
> *stop from/kill* ▪ *start/serve* ▪ ~~*succeed in/bring*~~ ▪ *think of/tell* ▪
> *want/punish*

The parents of the three murdered students at Heath High, Paducah, finally
succeeded in bringing[1] their lawsuit to court this morning. They ... the law
...[2] approximately 50 people who apparently knew what Michael Carneal
might do but ...[3] any action to ... him ...[4] the three girls and wounding five
others. Carneal himself has now ...[5] a prison sentence of 15–20 years and
was not in court.

It seems that Carneal ...[6] other students what he ...[7], and he even ...[8] his
guns to people. One of the 50 on trial freely admits that he ...[9] Carneal talk
about running through the school halls killing people. However, he never
...[10] a teacher or other adults about it because he simply did not believe
Carneal meant what he was saying.

B Complete the sentences, putting the verbs in brackets in the correct forms.

For many years, the police ...[1] (fail / halt) the rise in crime in Newham,
London's poorest area. Whatever they did, crime just ...[2] (keep / rise).
Local people ...[3] (avoid / walk) through certain parts of the area at
night. In fact, people ...[4] (refuse / live) in Newham at all if
possible. Fortunately, today that ...[5] (seem / be) about to
change.

About two years ago, the local council and the police
...[6] (decide / install) CCTV cameras everywhere. The
police also ...[7] (suggest / use) new software that could
recognize the faces of the 100 worst criminals in the
area. As a first step, they ...[8] (agree / put up) cameras
along the main road. They did this and then ...[9] (continue / put up)
more cameras until most of Newham was under the eye of a camera.
Crime figures immediately ...[10] (begin / fall) and they ...[11] (not stop / fall)
ever since. For example, the cameras ...[12] (succeed in / reduce) car theft
and burglaries by 39% each in the last year.

When local people were recently asked if they ...[13] (dislike / live) with the
cameras everywhere, over 90% said that they ...[14] (not mind / have) them at
all. In fact, many locals are so pleased that they ... the police ...[15] (would
like / set up) even more cameras around Newham.

7 Writing a comment

⟳ Lernhilfen 4.4, S.148

Write about either of the following:
- If you think a crime may be committed, do you think you should definitely call the
  police? What if this might put you in danger?
- After the shocking Erfurt killings in April 2002 should we now feel that German
  schools are no safer than those in America?

8 Speaking

Work with a partner and decide on a punishment for each of these crimes. (Feel free *not* to choose the possible punishments listed below.) Report your decisions to the class, and compare them with other people's verdicts.

The crimes ...

Karen Lee (15)
Stole 75-year-old senior citizen's savings (£500); stole for drugs – third offence; victim still in hospital weeks later after heart attack.

Luke Parry (17)
Kicked a police officer during a demonstration that was trying to stop a rail shipment of nuclear waste.

Andrea Silvestrini (53)
Tried to steal £5,000 diamond necklace while on holiday; well-known Brussels politician, due to return to Italy tomorrow.

Spike Moreno (42)
Head of a family of five and with no criminal record so far; fascinated by all things military; caught in unauthorized possession of various firearms, including a submachine gun found in car boot.

Rosie Wilson (29)
Stole children's winter clothing; living only on social security following divorce; single mother with three small children.

Barry West (36)
Stole expensive car, knifing and seriously injuring owner who tried to stop him; history of car theft and violence.

... and the punishments

- Let the person off with a warning.
- Require the offender to do community service (stating hours per week and for how long).
- Fine him/her (saying how much – up to £3,000).
- Give a suspended prison sentence (stating for how long), and put the offender on probation for that period.
- Sentence the offender to prison (or detention centre if under 18) for up to six months.

---

minor/major breach of the law ▪ *trivial/serious offence* ▪ *previous offence(s)* ▪ *first-time/repeat offender* ▪ *(not) deserve ... because of mitigating circumstances / due to sb's previous record* ▪ *verdict* ▪ *sentence sb to* ▪ *light/heavy/severe sentence/punishment* ▪ *effective deterrent* ▪ *deter sb from repeating the offence* ▪ *be lenient/tolerant/tough* ▪ *make an example of sb*

We've obviously got to take age / the previous offences / ... into account.
In view of ... and ..., I suggest that we ...
We decided/agreed to sentence (name) to ... because we felt that ...
Unfortunately, we couldn't agree on a verdict. I think ..., but ... recommends ...

Just like everybody else, criminals sometimes make mistakes. Read the following to find the two true stories that match the cartoons.

1   In fact, the glue was so good that the police had to cut the floor around Sergio in order to take him to the police station.

2   For this particular project, he decided that wearing an ancient suit of steel armour would give him his best chance of success.

3   One day, though, he realized that he could greatly improve his quality of life if he missed out the retail sector and went straight to the producer – the local glue factory.

4   Being the owner of several suits of armour, the dealer realized that a moving one was unusual, so he knocked it over and, after it had rolled loudly to the foot of the stairs, dropped an antique cupboard across it.

5   On the night of 4th November 1933, a Parisian burglar showed the world how not to rob the home of an antique dealer.

6   When he finally woke up, he found that he was completely stuck to the floor by the excellent glue, and he was still there when people arrived for work and found him on Monday morning.

7   One Saturday evening, he managed to break into the factory and, before collecting future supplies, began enjoying the product at its freshest and best by leaning over the side of a huge bath of it.

8   Unfortunately for the burglar, the antique cupboard badly damaged the ancient armour, and it took the police 24 hours to get him out.

9   Sergio de Sa was a glue-sniffing addict who, for years, had stolen glue in small amounts from local shops to support his habit.

10   He managed to break into the house, but he soon found that the armour was worryingly noisy when everything else was so quiet in the dead of night.

11   Not surprisingly, he was soon overwhelmed by the strong fumes and collapsed onto the floor, knocking over a large quantity of glue as he did so.

12   Of course, the dealer woke up, got up, went out of his bedroom and there he saw a suit of armour climbing the stairs towards him.

Focus

Read the speech bubbles and then answer the questions.

> Being a member of a minority isn't all bad. I mean, look at Whites in South Africa – or aristocrats, come to that.

> Peter's missed the point. A member of a minority is somebody discriminated against because of their race, sex, lifestyle and so on. It's got nothing to do with numbers.

Kavita

Peter

> I think quotas are the only answer. Everybody knows there's a glass ceiling stopping ethnic minorities from getting decent jobs or into politics.

Harry

Tony

> I sometimes think the only people who aren't members of a minority are able-bodied white men under 50 with a job.

Jodie

> I don't think affirmative action is the answer because it's discriminatory, too. You can't correct one wrong with another, can you?

Sally

> I agree with Tony – quotas for women politicians, for example. If I'm elected, I want it to be because of me, not just because I'm a woman.

1. How many members of minorities can you identify among the speakers? Why?
2. Which speaker do you agree with most? Why?
3. Do you agree with Kavita that Peter has missed the point?
4. Do you agree with Tony or Harry about quotas? Why?
5. Do you feel that you are a member of a minority? Say why/why not.

This extract from the Western Evening News *shows what can happen when the quota system is used to choose electoral candidates.*

Court challenge against quotas

Bristol, Tuesday John Carr, 39, the disappointed Labour candidate for North Bristol, is planning to challenge the quota system in the courts. Speaking to reporters at his home in Clifton last night, Mr Carr said: "I was not chosen because I'm white. I have nothing against the successful candidate, Grant Summers, and I'm certainly not racist or a bad loser. But Mr Summers was chosen because of his colour. The fact is that he is not better qualified or more likely to win the election than myself. This is unfair and illegal because it discriminates against whites." When asked about

(98 words)

Two letters to the editor

These two letters to the editor react to John Carr's complaint about the quota system. In the end, the question comes down to whether the quota system is 'automatic' or not.

Sir or Madam – I was very interested to read your report in today's *Western Evening News* on John Carr's plan to go to court about the quota system. Whatever you may think of positive discrimination to help disadvantaged minorities – and that is what quotas are – in my opinion Mr Carr has a good chance of winning the argument. Surely the selection committee in Bristol North must know that 'automatic selection' has been found 'discriminatory' by the European Court of Human Rights in Strasbourg? European human rights law says that everybody is equal and any form of discrimination, positive or not, is illegal. In the North Bristol case, if Mr Carr and Mr Summers are really completely equal except for their colour, then the only legal way of choosing between them is by 'random selection', by tossing a coin, for example.

Helen Budd, Portishead

(140 words)

Sir or Madam – Quotas are not as illegal as Helen Budd (Letters, 23 April) thinks. In fact, they were brought in to get rid of the real form of 'automatic selection' that has always given white men an unfair advantage. Since their introduction, quotas have been used in Germany and Scandinavia not only to help women to get their fair share of parliamentary seats, but also top jobs in the civil service, the police and schools, for example. Anyhow, it is a mistake to think that quotas are 'automatic'. To begin with, people from ethnic and other minorities, including women, still have to compete against other members of their minority. And, secondly, they are selected strictly according to their presence in society at large. This seems to me to be completely fair, and the only way to break the hold of middle-class white males on our public life.

Mike Davis, Filton

(145 words)

1 Looking at the texts

⤴ Lernhilfen 4.2, S.146

Answer the questions on the texts.

1 Why is John Carr going to court?
2 Explain why Helen Budd thinks the selection committee has made a mistake.
3 Why does Mike Davis think that quotas are not the same as automatic selection?
4 What do you think of quotas as an answer to unfair discrimination?

2 Working with words

A Fill in the missing prepositions without looking at the texts again.
1 John Carr explained ...[1] journalists that he is talking ...[2] his lawyers ...[3] fighting the quota system ...[4] the courts.
2 Helen Budd thinks that Mr Carr has a good chance ...[1] winning if he decides to go ...[2] court because automatic selection has been found illegal ...[3] the European Court ...[4] Human Rights ...[5] Strasbourg.
3 The court says that if people are really equal except ...[1] their sex, say, then the only legal way ...[2] choosing between them is ...[3] random selection.
4 Mike Davis writes that quotas were brought ...[1] as an answer ...[2] legal objections ...[3] automatic selection.
5 Quotas are used ...[1] Germany to give women their fair share ...[2] seats ...[3] parliaments and jobs ...[4] the civil service.

B Complete the sentences with adjectives from the texts.
1 *Automatic* selection because of who you are is illegal, but it still often happens.
2 'Affirmative action' is another name for ... discrimination.
3 A ... seat is a seat in a parliament.
4 By '... life' we mean the life of the nation that everybody should be allowed to take part in.
5 In Africa and Asia, whites are an ... minority.
6 Members of ... minorities are unfairly discriminated against because of their colour, religion, sex or lifestyle.
7 People who work for the government are often members of the ... service.
8 We call basic rights that everybody has '... rights'.

3 Listening

Track 41

Ann and Mark are talking about women in higher positions at work.

A First, read the questions below to find out what to listen for. Then listen to the dialogue and take notes. Finally, answer the questions.
1 What does Ann say in answer to Mark's argument that women do not have enough talent to get to the top?
2 Why does Ann think that men do not want women to get top jobs?
3 According to Mark, why do so few women apply for top jobs?
4 In Ann's opinion, why have some political parties and firms introduced quotas to help women?
5 Why is Mark glad that his own mother did not go out to work?
6 What is Ann's answer to the problem of women going out to work?

B Who do you most agree with, Mark or Ann? Say why/why not.

www.oneworld.net/themes/topic/

Track 42

In spite of the fact that the Aborigines take little part in the life and prosperity of Australia, their art and culture is used by both the government and companies to sell the country to foreign visitors. Although this earns Australia billions of 'tourist dollars', the Aborigines get very little benefit from them.

'Noble savages' sell Australia

Aborigines are 17 times more likely to be arrested and, on average, their life expectancy is 12 years less than other Australians. Most Aborigines spend their lives just sitting around. Having no work, they are completely
5 dependent on government handouts. But despite this grim reality, Aborigines play a central role in selling Australia to the rest of the world.

Look, for example,
10 at the 2000 Olympics. No event was complete without an Aborigine dance troupe in traditional body paint,
15 while at the opening ceremony the Olympic flame was lit by an Aborigine, Cathy Freeman.

20 But Aborigines feel that such displays are just cynical window dressing which has nothing to do with
25 the awful reality of their lives. Sol Bellear, an Aborigine leader, said: "Many people have a romanticized idea of Aborigines because of the way Australia sells us. We are sick of the noble savage image." He said that while Aborigines were used
30 to sell Australia to foreigners, they were never used in domestic advertisements.

Linda Burney, head of the New South Wales Department of Aboriginal Affairs, said: "I get very angry when I see car companies using didgeridoo music in their ads.
35 Do these companies employ Aborigine people? Where's the payback?"

During the run-up to the Sydney Olympics, Qantas, Australia's national airline, brought out an ad with a beaming 10-year-old Aborigine girl and the slogan "The
40 Spirit of Australia". The girl, Carol Napangardi, now 18, has two children, and lives in a simple one-room shack

in the deserts of Western Australia. She shares it with her husband, more than a dozen in-laws and six dogs.

While Ms Napangardi says she was glad of the
45 A$4,000 (€2,135) that Qantas paid her, the contrast

between the joy of the photo and her life now could hardly be greater.

Qantas says that it has had a special employment programme for Aborigines since 1988, but 13 years later
50 Aborigines still make up less than one per cent of its workforce. And while tourists spend about A$95 million (€52 m) a year on didgeri-
55 doos, boomerangs and dot paintings, almost none of this money finds its way to the Aborigines.

60 Mr Bellear said: "You never see an Aborigine serving in a souvenir shop. You know, a lot of
65 this stuff is made in Taiwan or Korea. There are even un-
scrupulous traders up in Queensland who employ English backpackers to produce didgeridoos and dot
70 paintings."

(Adapted from *The Sunday Telegraph*, London, 17 September 2000)

(379 words)

www.aboriginenews.com   www.aboriginalart.com.au

4 Looking at the text

⤴ Lernhilfen 4.2, S.146

Answer the questions in complete sentences.

1　How does the situation of Aborigines differ from that of other Australians?
2　Why were the Aborigines angry about the publicity for the Sydney Olympics?
3　Explain Sol Bellear's statement 'We are sick of the noble savage image' (lines 28–29).
4　What evidence can you find in the text to support the opinion that 'many people have a romanticized idea of Aborigines'?
5　What do you think could be done to give Aborigines a fair deal and to improve their life situation?

5 Looking at grammar: participle structures

Grammar

Remember

1　There is a 'glass ceiling' **stopping** women from getting the top jobs.
   There is a glass ceiling **that/which is stopping** …
2　A minority is a group **discriminated** against because of race, for example.
   A minority is a group **that/which is discriminated** against …
3　**Having** no work, the Aborigines are dependent on handouts.
   Because/As they have no work, the Aborigines …
4　(When) **Asked** about her photo, Carol said she had been glad of the money.
   When she was asked about her photo, Carol …

- Das Partizip hat zwei Formen: das Partizip Präsens (-*ing*-Form) und das Partizip Perfekt (3. Form).
- Ist das Subjekt eines Relativsatzes auch das Subjekt des Hauptsatzes, können wir Relativsätze mit Hilfe eines Partizips verkürzen. Bei Aktivsätzen benutzen wir das Partizip Präsens (1) und bei Passivsätzen das Partizip Perfekt (2).
- Genau wie bei der Verkürzung von Relativsätzen ist es nur dann möglich, Adverbialsätze zu verkürzen, wenn das gleiche Subjekt im Haupt- und Nebensatz vorkommt. Auch in diesem Fall benutzen wir bei Aktivsätzen das Partizip Präsens (3) und bei Passivsätzen das Partizip Perfekt (4).

6 Practising grammar

A　Shorten the sentences by replacing the adverbial clauses with present or past participles.

1　Josh says that because he is black, he won't get a flat in this part of town.
2　If racial groups are mixed, they learn to understand each other.
3　When children are treated well, they behave well.
4　When this program has been installed, it will run a diagnostic test.
5　When Mr Carr was asked about quotas, he became very angry.
6　After the government had changed the law, it forced companies to employ more disabled people.
7　Jack quickly forgot his friends after he had been promoted to sales manager.
8　While I agree that women are equal, I can't ignore the biological differences.
9　It's stupid to criticize people before you know all the facts.
10　Barbara was offered the job, so now of course she should get it.

B Shorten the sentences by replacing the relative clauses.

1 Cathy Freeman is the athlete that was given the honour of lighting the Olympic flame.
2 The Aborigine that was arrested by the police died in prison.
3 The journalists who were questioning the minister were not very respectful.
4 The little girl who is laughing in the ad is Carol Napangardi.
5 The video about minorities that was shown at school was great.
6 We only invest in firms that employ more than ten Aborigines.

7 Speaking: a group discussion

Work in groups. Read the information box and the speech bubbles, and then brainstorm 'positive discrimination'. Are you in favour of it, against it, or somewhere in between? Organize your ideas, with reasons, and hold a group discussion. Take notes of what other groups say and make a statement about the opinion of your class as a whole.

> ▶ **Positive discrimination**
> ▶ The idea of positive discrimination or 'PD' comes from the USA. Its
> ▶ original aim was to give members of ethnic minorities, particularly
> ▶ blacks, a fair deal when competing against whites for work, education,
> ▶ housing and health care. Since then, however, it has been extended to
> ▶ other unfairly disadvantaged minorities, particularly to women.

My name's Josh Adams. As a black person myself, I wish I could say that PD has had a positive effect. But I'm afraid I can't. Blacks still make up most of America's poor, and their situation is getting worse. I hate to say it, but I think this has a lot to do with how blacks see themselves. And PD is partly to blame by telling blacks that they can't get through life without special help. It makes being black a disability.

My name's Helen Brown from York. Of course I think that everybody should be treated equally, but how can you do this by law? Often you just replace one injustice with another. That's the problem with quotas.

Good afternoon. My name's Jane Scott. Of course you can pass laws against some kinds of discrimination. For example, wheelchair-users are discriminated against every time they go out. They can't use buses and trains, and they can't even get into a lot of public buildings because there are just steps and no ramps. I don't care what you call it, but parliament should force people by law to do something for the disabled.

Hi. My name's Nick King. I think some of your callers have missed the point. Aren't they talking about prejudice? Of course you can't do anything about prejudice by law, but you can certainly do a lot about the effect of prejudice, which is discrimination. For example, you can force the police and schools to hire more blacks and Asians, can't you?

www.debatabase.org/details.asp?topicID=40

8 Writing: analyzing statistics

A Study the table and complete the text with the missing information.

Share of total hours (as %) spent per week on ...

| | HOUSEWORK | | CHILD CARE | | PAID WORK | |
	women	men	women	men	women	men
Canada	64	36	84	16	37	63
Germany	79	21	71	29	33	67
Italy	75	25	80	20	27	73
Japan	90	10	87	13	33	67
Russia	63	37	73	27	44	56
UK	72	28	77	23	35	65
USA	63	37	71	29	37	63

The figures in the table show that women still do most of their work at home, while men do most of theirs outside the home. For example, even in ...[1] and the USA, the countries in which men spend the highest percentage of their time looking after children, men still spend well over twice as much time on ...[2]. In Canada and ...[3] with 16% and ...%[4] – the lowest scorers for men – ...[5] continue to be almost entirely responsible for child care. This also applies to Japanese women when it comes to doing the ...[6]. There, men only spend ...%[7] of their time helping in the house, which is by far the lowest percentage among the ...[8] countries compared in the ...[9]. This seems particularly unfair, as Japanese women also do as much ...[10] outside the home as ...[11] women do.

B What is your own opinion of the figures for Germany? Do you think the division of work in German households is a) fair and satisfactory, b) not really fair, but acceptable or c) totally unfair and unacceptable? Give reasons for your opinion.

- *most men still leave the house to do paid work*
- *some women do a job as well as housework and being responsible for child care*
- *psychologists say young children need their mothers more than their fathers, but children need their fathers more and more as they get older*
- *simple justice says there should be a 50/50 partnership in the family*
- *women have as much right to their own lives as men*
- *in our culture, men leave the home to work, and women stay at home to care for the family*
- *realistically, this is simply the way things are*
- *...*

www.statistik-bund.de   www.europa.eu.int

Track 43

Read the press report and then answer these questions.

1 Do you agree with the charities for the homeless and the police in their condemnation of 'rough sleeper holidays'? Say why/why not.
2 Would you go on a holiday like this? Say why/why not.
3 What other 'exotic holidays' of this kind can you think of, for example a week on an oil-rig? Collect ideas and report back to the class explaining why you think your suggestions would be exotic and fun.

Dutch firm offers sleeping rough holidays in London

It almost seems like a bargain. For £300 (€486), tourists will have the chance to stay in some of London's most exclusive areas, Piccadilly, Shaftesbury Avenue, Oxford Street and others.
5 Usually a four-day trip would cost far more, but costs are low as holidaymakers will be sleeping on the streets.

Charities for the homeless have condemned the plan and police have warned that Dutch holiday-
10 makers trying life as a vagrant could end up in jail.

Under the scheme, called 'Live Like a Tramp in London', a Dutch firm, Kamstra Travel, plans to spread 50 tourists around London and then leave
15 them to look after themselves for four days. Each will be given a sleeping bag and the choice of either a musical instrument or sketch pad and pencil with which they will have to try to survive. They will get some of the comforts of a real
20 holiday only on their last night. Then they will be taken to a good hotel and given a meal.

Lodewyk Brondyk of Kamstra said: 'The idea is to give people a taste of life on the streets of London. We hope it will be a life-changing
25 experience for them.'

But the idea that 'rough sleeper holidays' can be fun has outraged London's charities for the homeless and the police. A spokesman for the Rough Sleepers Unit said: 'The streets are an
30 extremely dangerous and unpleasant place in

which to sleep and definitely not a holiday destination.'

Jim Hinton, a spokesman for Scotland Yard, said: 'Any company offering "homeless holidays" is trivializing the very real suffering which the 35 young people that we see are going through. No one chooses to be homeless; they end up on the streets because they have nowhere else to go.'

He warned bogus tramps that they could find themselves with a roof over their heads after all. 40 He said: 'We act firmly with beggars who abuse the generosity of Londoners and visitors by pretending to be homeless ... and the Vagrancy Act of 1966 provides us with the power of arrest.' 45

(Adapted from *The Guardian*, London, 27 August 2001)

(337 words)

Focus

The photos show recent work in genetic modification (GM) where changes have been made to the natural combination of genes that make up the genetic codes of plants and animals. (These codes are the instructions that decide all aspects of every living thing – its size, its health, its colour, everything.)

A Match the following areas of GM work with photos a–d.

    1 preventing hereditary
       (*erblich*) diseases

    2 cloning

    3 improving food crops
    4 replacing body parts

B How do you feel about these particular
    experiments?

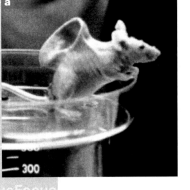

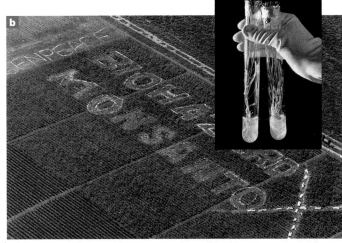

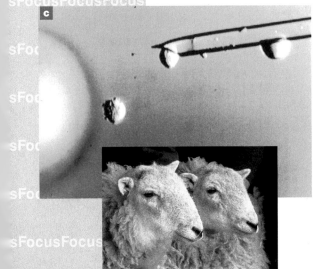

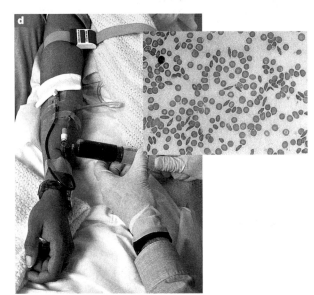

A People and society

Track 44 *With GM, are we now playing God? And is there a danger of creating uncontrollable monster plants, animals and even human beings? We must soon answer these questions, and many more. But first, here are some of the facts.*

GM – friend or foe?

1 GM and world hunger

It is estimated that by 2050 the world population will be about 11 billion – nearly double today's total. And the
5 food supply is not keeping up. Pests and diseases destroy crops as they grow. Every year, the world also loses farmland to erosion, to deserts, and to cities and roads. Malnutrition and
10 starvation are now major and fast-growing problems.

Enter GM: the upside ...

Using GM technology, scientists are creating crops that resist diseases and
15 pests and produce better yields. This means more food from the same land. Science is also making more land usable: there are new crops that can grow in deserts and on salty land.
20 Again, new crops with extra nutritional properties are appearing. For example, a new kind of rice has genes from peas that add vitamin A, and this could save the two million children that vitamin A
25 deficiency kills every year.

... and the downside

About a quarter of Europeans suffer from allergies – often food allergies. By slightly changing plant properties,
30 we may drastically increase such allergies. Therefore, in trying to fight hunger, we may in fact create food that many people cannot eat!

2 The environment

Life forms exist in a complex balance. Change one 35
thing and many others can be affected – often disastrously. For example, mink farms were once set up in Britain to produce fur for women's coats. Some mink escaped, and these brutal killers have now destroyed most other animals along many 40
rivers. Could GM plants do something similar?

Enter GM, the upside ...

Farmers have long used hundreds of farm chemicals. These protect crops, but poison far more than just unwanted insects and weeds. However, 45
GM corn, for example, now produces chemicals for itself that attack its attackers. Result: far fewer poisonous chemicals in the environment.

... and the downside

Many mainstream scientists fear GM crops will 50
breed with natural plants, spreading their powerful new genes into the wild and perhaps producing powerful mutant 'superweeds'. These could become uncontrollable, taking over the wild and farmland alike. If this sounds like science fiction, consider 55
a tropical marine weed which apparently mutated (naturally) in research laboratories near Marseilles, and then recently escaped into the sea. Having rapidly spread to dozens of areas around the Mediterranean, it is killing all other plant life. And 60
because it is toxic to almost all plant-eating marine life, the food chain is now collapsing, the sea is dying, and the process is out of control. For GM activists in Britain, Germany, Canada and elsewhere the only response is to destroy the new crops in 65
the fields where they grow.

(435 words)

1 Looking at the text

⊃ Lernhilfen 4.2, S.146

A Read quickly to find and explain these numbers in the text.

> *11 billion* ▪ *two million* ▪ *a quarter* ▪ *hundreds* ▪ *dozens*

B Summarize in two paragraphs the advantages and disadvantages of GM.

C Give your opinion.
How do you now feel about GM food? Should further development be encouraged, controlled, or simply stopped? *Could* it be stopped?

2 Working with words

⊃ Lernhilfe 1.2, S.142

A Explain the following in your own words.
1 playing God (introduction)
2 better yields (line 15)
3 (to) fight hunger (lines 31–32)
4 toxic (line 61)
5 the food chain (line 62)
6 activist (line 64)

B Copy and complete the table of word families. Add words from the text (which appear in the order of the table). Use your dictionary, if necessary.

Verb	Noun	Adjective
...	creation	...
...	...	populated/populous
...	destruction	...
...	...	eroded
...	...	starved/starving
...	...	resistant (to)
...	...	protected/protective
...	poison	...
...	mutant/mutation	...
live	...	...

C Complete the following using words from **2B** above. Sometimes you have to make grammatical changes.
1 With little rain south of the Sahara, there is little food. Millions of animals have already ... to death, and people are now facing ..., too.
2 Scientists have already ... various GM crops, and they are working hard on the ... of suitable crops for use in Africa.
3 For example, there is a new type of sweet potato which has strong ... to dry conditions and is also ... to most pests.
4 However, scientists are worried about introducing new GM plants that could ... into new types of plants – ... that might resist all types of farm chemicals.
5 The fear is that such super-plants might take over everything. This could lead to the ... of other plant species, and would most certainly ... people's belief in GM crops.
6 The future is very uncertain. GM food could help billions of people ... better, healthier ... . But GM could also have the opposite effect.

B People and issues

Track 45

In 2000, scientists completed a huge project in genetics: they produced a complete description of the human genetic code. This opens up enormous medical possibilities – and moral questions. Future News (The Sunday Times, 2000) *takes a look ahead.*

Harry's son makes history

16.10.2013 Baby Stephen, born yesterday to Harry and Sophie West, is the first child with changes to his genetic blueprint made soon after his conception. Without these
5 changes, he would have developed diabetes.

'Before Harry and I got married, we had a genetic test,' said Sophie. 'It showed that I carry a gene responsible for diabetes.'

Stephen was conceived outside the womb
10 and after three days, when the embryo consisted of only eight cells, the defective gene was replaced.

Critics of genetic engineering are worried about the implications. 'Nobody wants
15 children to suffer terrible diseases,' said Marilyn Hardwick of the Bioethics Movement, 'but where will this end?'

DNA lesson

21.12.2017 ■
FORCE 2020 now requires DNA scans for all new pupils. The

5 company, which last year started running all state nursery schools, says this is 'practical and sensible'.
10 A company director said, 'Every new-born child now gets a card with its DNA printout. The information it contains on aptitude 15 will help greatly when deciding each child's best learning method.'

The controversial DNA card will also be 20 searched for genes indicating future anti-social behaviour such as violence or alcoholism. 25

Opponents say that FORCE 2020's plan clearly undermines civil liberties and they will challenge the company 30 in court. ■

Playing with nature's plan

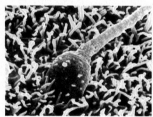

30.11.2020 Designer babies are being produced in Cuban fertility clinics, according to new reports.

Couples are paying $100,000
5 to have fertilized eggs given top-quality genes.

'Our children need the best possible start in life,' explains Pamela Lofts of Miami. 'And
10 none of my embryos had genes for high intelligence ... so we've had them put in. Then there's the gene for that greeny-grey eye colour I just love. We've had that put in too.' 15

'But,' says Professor Peter Greenspoon of Guy's Hospital, London, 'this playing with life is dangerous and wrong.'

Clinic director Dr Raul 20 Ibarra disagrees. 'All our work is carefully researched and safe. And it's no more wrong than paying extra for good schooling. We're just extending 25 the idea. Kids who look good get on better.'

Critics fear we are heading towards a genetically divided society: those who can afford 30 improvement and those who can't.

The damage done

15.04.2022 **'Why did you make me live?'** These extraordinary words rang out across a silent courtroom today at the opening of a trial that is gripping America.
5 David Peters is suing his parents for not having a genetic test at the time of his conception. This would have shown that he had a rare disease – adrenoleukodystrophy.
10 'My client's nervous system is collapsing,' said David's lawyer. 'And this suffering was caused by his parents' neglect.'

If David wins, his parents will face multi-million dollar damages.

(447 words)

3 Looking at the texts

A Answer the questions on the texts.
1 What important difference is there between the actions of Stephen's and David's parents?
2 In what fundamental way do the actions of Stephen's doctors differ from those of Dr Raul Ibarra's team?
3 Why might children of the poor in 'a genetically divided society' be treated differently by FORCE 2020 from children of rich people like Pamela Lofts?

B Use what you know from the text to say a) who is talking, b) about what and c) who to. Give reasons.
1 'Of course, it's expensive to change your child's genes – especially the ones for intelligence. But think of the wonderful results we offer you and think of the children you will have!'
2 'If our scientists find the possibility of anti-social behaviour, it is of course your job to try to stop it developing in your day-to-day work with the child. But, naturally, we will also have to tell the police and the social services.'
3 'I'm so glad you had that test done and got them to treat me so I'd be safe from it for the rest of my life.'
4 'No, it wasn't because we didn't care about him. We didn't do the test simply because we didn't believe in it. After all, my wife would never have ended the pregnancy, whatever the result.'

4 Looking at grammar: problems with verbs

Grammar

Remember

! **Simple present, present continuous und present perfect** ⮎ S. 9, 10, 47
1 **Every year,** the world **loses** farmland.
2 The food chain **is now collapsing**.
3 Farmers **have** long **used** farm chemicals.

! **Simple past und present perfect** ⮎ S. 13, 47
1 Some mink **escaped a few years ago**.
2 They **have now destroyed** most other animals.

! *If*-Sätze ⮎ S. 83, 92
1 **If** David **wins,** his parents **will face** multi-million dollar damages.
2 **If** scientists **stopped** work on GM, the world **would face** starvation.
3 **If** Harry and Sophie **had not had** the test, they **would not have known** about the diabetes gene.

! **Das Passiv** ⮎ S. 74
It is estimated that the population will be 11 billion.

Ebenso: *It is (sometimes/often/generally) said/thought/claimed/believed/ assumed/imagined that ...*

Vergleichen Sie den Gebrauch des Aktivs im Deutschen:
Man sagt/meint, dass ...

5 Practising grammar

A Put the verbs in brackets into the correct form.

1 The world's population ... (multiply) four times in the 20th century, and it ... (still + grow) rapidly today.

2 If that population explosion ...(happen) a century earlier, millions ... (starve) because food production ... (be) much less advanced in those days.

3 Today, GM ... (appear) to offer a way of feeding the huge future population, but if we ... (take) the GM route, we ... (face) serious dangers.

4 Apparently, a mutant marine weed ... (escape) from a French laboratory into the sea a few years ago. Since then, it ... (spread) uncontrollably, so that whole areas of the Mediterranean ... (now + die).

5 The report ... (suggest) that if GM 'superweeds' ... (develop) in the wild, they ... (can get) out of control in the same sort of way.

B Finish translating the sentences into English.

1 Ich kenne Tom Snow, seit wir gemeinsam in der Schule waren.
I ...Tom Snow ... at school together.

2 Er ist gerade nach Cambridge umgezogen.
He ... to Cambridge.

3 Dort arbeitet er für eine große Pharmafirma.
He ... pharmaceutical company there.

4 Im Moment ist er Mitglied einer Gruppe, die menschliche Gene untersucht.
... he is a member of a group ... human genes.

5 Das finde ich merkwürdig, da Tom immer gegen die Genforschung war.
... strange because ... genetic research.

6 Aber jetzt sagt er, dass sie der Schlüssel zu medizinischem Fortschritt sei.
But now he says that ... to medical progress.

7 Seine Firma war vor kurzem in den Nachrichten und es heißt, dass die Forschungsgruppe vor einem großen Durchbruch stehe.
His company ... in the news recently, and ... the research team is about to make a big breakthrough.

8 Er hat mich gerade eingeladen ihn in seinem Labor zu besuchen.
He ... in his laboratory.

9 Natürlich gehe ich hin, da ich vielleicht nie wieder solch eine Chance bekommen werde.
Of course ... because perhaps ... such a chance again.

10 Wenn ich mir die Zeit für den Besuch nicht nehmen würde, täte es mir bestimmt Leid.
If I ... the time to visit, I'm sure I would be sorry.

6 Listening

Track 46

A Copy the following. Then listen to Part A of the radio programme and complete the notes.

Name of programme: ...   Today's issue: ...   Phone number: ...

B Listen to Part B. Write a brief note of each caller's view.

Example   Caller 1: *Positive. Feels essential due to fast world population growth.*

7 Writing: a letter to the editor

⟳ Lernhilfen 4.4, S.148

Read these extracts from letters to the editor. Decide what you agree / disagree / partly agree with, and then write a further letter to the newspaper with your own views.

You may find these words and expressions useful.

> *It seems to me that …*
> *I totally agree/disagree with … when he/she says that …*
> *I agree with … up to a point / to some extent. However, …*
> *On the one hand, … . On the other, …*
> *The thing/point/issue that we must remember / never forget is that …*

(from Colin Sharpe)

We will soon be able to get rid of bad genes and keep only those that are good.
I predict that our grandchildren will all be intelligent, good-looking, disease-free and socially useful people. Human beings will at last be superhuman! This must be the way forward for the human race.

(from Anne-Marie Larkin)

I was horrified to read Colin Sharpe's recent letter. What would happen to embryos that were not all 'good'? Would they just have to die? Which of us would be allowed to live? Who is going to make such decisions?

Start like this.

> *Dear Sir/Madam*
>
> *I refer to the recent letters from Colin Sharpe and Anne-Marie Larkin on the issue of genetic engineering.*
> *It seems to me that …*

8 Speaking: a class presentation

⟳ Lernhilfen 5, S.150

1 Work with a partner. Decide on an aspect of genetic engineering that has been in the news recently, eg a new development and protests against it, and prepare a presentation.
2 Think about scientific, political and social aspects, as appropriate.
3 The following websites may be useful.

www.foe.co.uk   www.truefoodnow.org

C Further reading

Scientists have already cloned sheep and cows. Should there be human clones too, or is it wrong? Or, again, do you agree with American animal cloning expert, Mark Westhusin? 'I've never met a human worth cloning!' To find out what people think, TIME/CNN carried out the following survey with 1,015 adult Americans on 7–8 February 2001 ('Not sures' omitted).

A Which majority answers do you agree/disagree with? Why?

B Do any of the majority views surprise you? Why?

- **Is it a good or bad idea to clone animals such as sheep?**
  Good idea 29% Bad idea 67%

- **Is it a good idea to clone human beings?**
  Good idea 7% Bad idea 90%

  The 914 people who think human cloning is a bad idea were asked this follow-up question:

  What is the main reason you are against cloning humans?
  Religious beliefs 34%
  Interferes with human
    distinctiveness/individuality 22%
  Used for questionable purposes
    like breeding a superior race 22%
  The technology is dangerous 14%

- **Is it against God's will to clone humans?**
  Yes 69% No 23%

- **Would a clone of a dead person have his or her same personality?**
  Yes 10% No 74%

- **If you had a chance, would you clone yourself?**
  Yes 5% No 93%

- **Do the following justify creating a human clone?**

	Yes	No
To produce clones whose vital organs can be used to save others	28%	68%
To save the life of the person being cloned	21%	74%
To help infertile couples have children	20%	76%
To allow parents to have a twin child later	10%	88%
To allow parents to create a clone of a child that they have lost	10%	88%
To allow gay couples to have children	10%	86%
To create genetically superior people	6%	92%

- **When will it be possible to create a human clone?**
  In the next:

10 years	45%
20 years	23%
50+ years	10%
Never	15%

Focus

A   Work in pairs or teams. Choose the right answer by noting the letter –
a, **b** or **c** – on a piece of paper.

B   When you have finished, check your answers against the key on p 139.

A quiz about the EU

1 Where was the treaty signed that set up what has become the EU?

a   Brussels
b   Paris
c   Rome

2 How many countries founded the old European Economic Community, now the EU?

a   5
b   6
c   7

3 When did the European Community change its name to the 'European Union'?

a   1986
b   1992
c   1995

4 On 1 January of which year were euro coins and banknotes introduced?

a   1999
b   2001
c   2002

5 How many countries introduced euro coins and banknotes right from the beginning?

a   9
b   10
c   12

6 Where is the European Central Bank?

a   Amsterdam
b   Frankfurt
c   London

7 Which city is often called 'the capital of the EU'?

a   Berlin
b   Brussels
c   Rome

8 Who wrote the music to what has become the European anthem?

a   Beethoven
b   Elgar
c   Verdi

A People and society

Track 47 *According to opinion polls, few EU citizens are particularly interested in the European single market or in its currency, the euro. But need it be like that? David Owen, an economist with a German investment bank in London, says 'No, it needn't – if only ...'.*

Just a crazy dream?

IT IS 2015. The USA has been in recession for four years after the Wall Street crash of 2011. Frankfurt is now the world's financial centre, and the euro its reserve currency.

5 Growth in the euro zone has averaged 4.8% for the last five years. Unemployment has fallen to 3%. Only the planned immigration of

skilled workers from Asia, Eastern Europe and, yes, America is keeping the machines running 10 and the shops full.

Welcome to the United States of Europe, the new global economic superpower with a population of over 450 million people stretching from Finland in the north to Cyprus in the 15 south, and from Ireland in the west to Ukraine in the east.

Does this all sound like a crazy dream? Perhaps, but according to Mr Owen the EU and its citizens could make it come true.

20 David Owen has analyzed trade flows (see chart) within Europe, and he says that the

dream need not be so crazy after all. But only if Europeans are willing to change the habits of a lifetime in two ways.

First, they must give up the idea of 'national 25 economies' that produce everything from coal to cola. Instead, they must go over to regional specialization, as in the USA. There, most planes are built in Seattle and most cars in Detroit; 30 most fruit is grown in California and most wheat in the Mid-West.

For Europe, this means that if the Germans can 35 make better cars at lower cost than anybody else, the French better wine and the British better pharmaceut- icals, then it makes sense 40 for Germany to make the EU's cars, France its wine and the UK its drugs.

Of course, giving up national economies and 45 local industries will be extremely painful, particularly if you are making cars in Birmingham, wine in Baden or drugs in Leverkusen. But, according to Mr Owen, it's the only way to go. 50

And it will also mean agreeing to his second big change: a highly mobile workforce that is fluent in the EU's *lingua franca*, English, and is willing to move to where the jobs are at a wage decided by the market. 55

Are you fluent in English? Would you move to, say, Italy? Would you accept a lower wage for a secure job? Or would you prefer to be unemployed at Hotel Mama in your home town? 60

www.europa.eu.int

(382 words)

1 Looking at the text

⟳ Lernhilfen 4.2, S.146

A Answer the questions on the text.
1 Why can the United States of Europe claim to be 'a global economic superpower'?
2 What does David Owen mean by 'regional specialization'? Give examples.
3 Compare the life situation of somebody living and working in the EU today with Mr Owen's idea of the future.

B Give your opinion.
Work in small groups. Answer the questions in the final paragraph and compare your results with other groups.

2 Working with words

⟳ Lernhilfen 1.2, S.142

A Find expressions in the text (and introduction) to complete these sentences.
1 ... are used to find out what people think.
2 You can trade and work wherever you like in a ... .
3 ... help companies find the capital they need to grow.
4 London and Frankfurt are both ... with stock exchanges and a lot of banks.
5 A ... is a strong currency like the US dollar used in international trade.
6 The parts of the EU that use the euro are called the '...'.
7 We call the economy of a single country its '...'.
8 In Baden, for example, the production of wine is a ... .

B Explain these expressions from the text.
1 (to) be in recession (line 1)
2 planned immigration (line 7)
3 skilled workers (line 8)
4 a crazy dream (line 17)
5 trade flows (line 20)
6 mobile workforce (line 52)
7 a secure job (line 58)
8 Hotel Mama (line 59)

3 Listening

Track 48

In this radio interview, Lisa Kaiser, a German expert on EU consumer affairs, is talking to Peter Bond of the British Standards Institute about introducing standardized plugs (*Stecker*) and sockets (*Steckdosen*) throughout the EU.

Complete the sentences with details from the interview.
1 The EU began discussions on a standard European ... in ... .
2 Brussels gave up the idea in ... because some countries were not willing to give up '... ... ...'.
3 There is already a standard plug for small appliances like ... and ... that you can use everywhere except in the ... .
4 This standard plug is a flat ...-... plastic plug that is connected to the ... ... at the ... .
5 It would cost ... ... million euros to convert to a standard European plug for heavy appliances in ... alone.
6 In the whole of the ..., the cost would be ... times the German amount.
7 Conversion would take at least ... years.
8 Conversion would also create 600,000 tons of ... and ... waste.

B People and issues

Track 49   *In January 2001, America's Microsoft Corporation brought out its new dictionary of International, ie American, English. That really says it all. It is the massive economic, political and cultural power of the USA that has put English where it is today. But read the report below to find out what this could mean in the EU.*

English is still on the march

Britons are lazy about languages because English is the EU's *lingua franca*

IS ENGLISH becoming the European Union's *lingua franca*? A survey of the language skills of 16,000 EU citizens says that it is well on the way to becoming just that. Perhaps more surpris-
5 ingly, the survey also suggests that more and more (non-British or Irish) Europeans accept the idea that all Europeans should learn English.

Over 40% of respondents 'claimed to speak' English as a foreign language. Add to that the
10 almost 16% of the EU's citizens who speak English as a native language, and you already have over half the population of the EU.

The unstoppable march of English is often said to anger non-native English-speakers across
15 Europe, particularly the French and, increas-
ingly, the Germans and others as well. However, the survey seems to show that this anti-English opposition may be much exaggerated by a loud minority of 'linguistic nationalists'.

In fact, about 69% of respondents agreed with 20 the statement that 'everybody should speak English' – including 66% of the French. This is only slightly less than the number for the UK itself.

The rise of English within the EU may be good 25 news for those who dream of a truly united Europe. They have always had to fight against the argument that political integration, as well as labour mobility within the single 30 market, is impracticable because of the lack of a single European language.

But those in favour of a united Europe should not celebrate too 35 soon. Even now, nearly half of all EU citizens still speak no language other than their own, though many of these are native speakers of English. 40 More threatening to federalist dreams are the words 'claimed to speak'. As any personnel manager will tell you, people are nothing if not optimistic about their 45 knowledge of a foreign language – until they actually have to use it.

Everyone in the EU should be able to speak English: % saying 'yes'

Chart showing percentages by country: Netherlands, Luxemburg, Sweden, Greece, Italy, Ireland, Denmark, UK, Belgium, EU 15, Germany, France, Portugal, Austria, Spain, Finland

(320 words)

4 Looking at the text

A Answer the questions on the text.

1 Pick out evidence from the report to show that English is becoming Europe's international language.

2 Why are 'linguistic nationalists' likely to be disappointed by the findings of the survey?

3 Why should people who dream of a united Europe be in two minds about the survey?

4 Why does the writer mention the experience of personnel managers at the end of the report?

B Give your opinion.
Do you agree with the statement 'everybody should speak English'?
Give reasons.

5 Looking at grammar: problem plurals

Grammar

Remember

1 Be careful. **This crossroads is** dangerous. – I know. There **are** several dangerous **crossroads** around here.

2 **People are** optimistic about their knowledge of a foreign language.

3 **Those jeans are** far too expensive. Here **are some** cheaper **ones**.

4 Have you got **a pair of scissors**, please?

■ Die meisten Nomen, die im Singular auf -*s* enden, bleiben im Plural unverändert. (1) Weitere Beispiele sind *headquarters*, *means* (Mittel), *series*, *species*, *works* (Werk). Ausnahmen sind etwa *news* oder *United States*, die zwar auch wie Singularformen behandelt werden, aber keinen Plural bilden.

! Einige Nomen, die nicht auf -*s* enden, bleiben ebenfalls im Plural unverändert. Am wichtigsten sind *aircraft* (und andere Fahrzeuge die auf -*craft* enden), *Chinese* (und andere Nationalitäten, die auf -*ese* enden), *fish* und *sheep*.

■ Einige Nomen, die meist aber nicht nur auf -*s* enden, haben keine Singularform. Diese Nomen werden immer im Plural benutzt. (2) Am wichtigsten sind *cattle* (Rinder), *clothes*, *contents*, *customs* (Zoll), *goods*, *manners* (Benehmen), *outskirts* (Stadtrand), *people*, *police*, *premises* (Gebäude, Gelände), *savings*, *stairs*, *steps* (Treppen) und *thanks*.

■ Kleidung und Werkzeuge, die aus zwei Teilen bestehen, werden immer im Plural benutzt. (3) Am wichtigsten sind *bathing trunks*, *binoculars* (Fernglas), *glasses* (Brille), *jeans*, *leggings*, *pants* (! AE Hosen, BE Unterhosen), *pliers* (Zange), *pyjamas*, *scales* (Waage), *scissors*, *shorts*, *tights* (Strumpfhose), *trousers*. Wollen Sie diese Nomen im Singular benutzen, fügen Sie *a pair of* zu. (4)

■ Einige Nomen bezeichnen unbestimmte Mengen und sind daher nicht zählbar. Dazu gehören z.B. *advice*, *equipment*, *evidence*, *information*, *knowledge*, *news* und *work*. Alle diese Wörter haben keine Pluralformen; in Verbindung mit *a bit/piece of* kann man sie jedoch wie zählbare Nomen verwenden.

6 Practising grammar

Where necessary, choose the correct verb and complete the sentences with the English equivalent of the German nouns.

1 It's often true that 'no ... is/are good news'. (*Nachricht*)
2 These/This ... was/were made in Jena. (*Fernglas*)
3 ... is/are returning to the Rhine because the water is cleaner now. (*Fisch*)
4 You can't get contact lenses or a ... free any longer. (*Brille*)
5 Your ... is/are covered in oil. Don't sit down, please. (*Hose*)
6 How many ... is/are coming to the party? (*Leute*)
7 The ... is/are questioning two pupils about the fire. (*Polizei*)
8 Today only a few British ... has/have BSE. (*Rindvieh*)
9 The ... of London is/are not very attractive. (*Stadtrand*)
10 Which is the cheapest ..., high-speed trains or ...? (*Verkehrsmittel, Flugzeug*)
11 There is/are a big steel ... at the end of our street. (*Werk*)
12 You need a bigger ... to pull out that nail. (*Zange*)

7 Speaking: giving a talk

⟳ Lernhilfen 5, S.150

Work in small groups. Prepare and give a talk on the problem of banning or limiting the use of drinks cans in the EU. Find arguments for and against the idea, and give your own opinion. The information in the box below may give you some ideas.

In Denmark, beer in cans is banned. In Sweden, cans are allowed, but they carry a high deposit of 50 cents per can. Now Germany is planning to introduce the Swedish model as well.

In 1997 the European Commission ordered Denmark to lift its ban on cans. Brussels is also looking into the Swedish and German system as well. One British producer of mineral water is threatening to take Germany to court if it goes ahead with its plan to allow the sale of mineral water only in returnable glass or light plastic bottles. The British producer has the support of the European Commission, and could win in court.

Why?

The commission argues that Denmark is definitely breaking EU competition law and Sweden and Germany almost certainly are. It says that foreign drinks producers – like the British mineral water company – cannot be expected to transport their products to these three countries only in bottles, and then to collect the empty bottles again for reuse. This would increase their costs so much that, in effect, domestic drinks producers would have an unfair advantage. Hindering free competition in this way is forbidden in a number of EU treaties, which Denmark, Germany and Sweden have all agreed to.

Writing: a chronological review

Use information from the timeline to write a review of the development of the EU. You do not need to use all the information in the timeline; add any information or opinions of your own. Work with a partner if you wish.

1957
B, D, F, I, L and NL set up European Economic Community (EEC).

1968
'The 6' abolish all import duties.

1973
DK, GB, IRL, join EEC; 'the 6' now 'the 9'.

1979
Citizens of 'the 9' elect members to European Parliament for first time.

1981
GR joins; 'the 9' becomes 'the 10'.

1986
E and P join, making 'the 10' 'the 12'. EEC drops 'Economic' to become European Community (EC).

1990
German reunification makes the former GDR part of the EC.

1992
EC becomes European Union (EU). EU decides to introduce the euro (Maastricht Treaty).

1993
B, D, E, F, GR, I, L, NL, P abolish internal frontiers at Schengen.

1995
A, SF and S join; 'the 12' now 'the 15'.

1998
EU begins negotiations with 6 applicants, incl. CZ, H and PL.

1999
The euro becomes the currency of exchange in 11 EU countries (euro zone).

2000
EU begins negotiations with 6 further applicants, incl. BG, R and SK.

2001
IRL refuses to agree to Nice Treaty, thus threatening expansion of the EU.

2002
Euro coins and notes replace national currencies in the 12 euro zone countries.

???

A	Austria	**GB**	United Kingdom	**NL**	The Netherlands
B	Belgium	**GDR**	German Democratic Republic	**P**	Portugal
BG	Bulgaria			**PL**	Poland
CZ	Czech Republic	**GR**	Greece	**R**	Romania
D	Germany	**H**	Hungary	**S**	Sweden
DK	Denmark	**I**	Italy	**SF**	Finland
E	Spain	**IRL**	Ireland	**SK**	Slovakia
F	France	**L**	Luxembourg		

C   Further reading

Who decides, and how?

First, read the information in the infobox and then the opinions in the bubbles. Who do you agree/disagree with most? Say why.

By 2015 the EU could have 25 members. Although nobody really knows what this will mean, one thing is already certain. As the 'Brussels cake' is divided up between more and more countries, all countries will get less than they once did or, in the case of new members, than they were hoping for. And then there is perhaps the biggest problem of all: who decides what happens in the EU, and how? Should, for example, the present national veto be replaced by simple majority voting on all decisions that affect the whole of the EU? Or should the European Parliament be given more power than national parliaments?

Kati Böhme, Essen

Well, I don't necessarily want a United States of Europe, but we must at least have real majority voting so that individual countries can't veto anything they don't like. It's ridiculous that Ireland, say, can stop everybody else from doing what they want.

Anna Riedl, Graz

Does it matter what a small country like Austria thinks? We all know that France, Germany, Italy and the UK get together and do whatever they want. Until we have equal voting for all countries, I'm not really interested.

I'm for a United States of Europe with a constitution. Give all power to an elected European parliament with an elected president and a professional European civil service responsible to it. In the USE, the UK would be like one of the bigger German Länder, Baden-Württemberg or North Rhine-Westphalia, say.

Ben Snow, London

Odile Duval, Lyon

Why change things at all? The EU should only decide things like external tariffs that can't be decided lower down. I'm fed up with unelected foreign bureaucrats in Brussels telling France what to do.

Whatever happens, all decisions must be made by everybody in the EU, not by the heads of national governments meeting in secret. You can't decide what's best for the whole of the EU by quarrelling about national interests. That's just stupid. Give power to the people, I say. If that means a USE, okay.

Ruud Maas, Utrecht

Mario Rossi, Milan

The USA has got 50 states, some of them very small. So what? It works fine. Of course it's possible to set up a USE with half that number of states and English as its official language. It's just a matter of political will, that's all.

Anhang

Partner pages

Unit 4

Role-play, S. 66

Beatrix Andriessen, Home Affairs official, the Netherlands

You support the smart card.

Reasons: all this information about us is on computers anyway; makes administration (*Verwaltung*) much easier to have it all in one place; makes cheating (*betrügen*) the welfare system (*Sozialsystem*) much less easy (eg making false old-style ID cards); saves the tax payers' money.

Petra Beckmann, human rights activist, Germany

You hate the idea.

Reasons: against the Constitution (*Verfassung*) of Germany – people not allowed to store all these types of information for no real reason; it would be like taking away people's clothing, leaving them naked (*nackt*); this is not acceptable.

Mafuz Osman, political refugee, Sudan

You accept the smart card.

Reasons: small price to pay in return for political asylum in Belgium; nothing to hide; glad to have everything on one card, and therefore no language problems whenever you have to get help, eg with housing; OK if system catches false asylum seekers (*Asylsuchende*) – that is good for the smaller number of real asylum seekers like yourself.

Dietrich Lascelles, Alsace, France

You do not trust the smart card.

Reasons: you know what people are really like – although you hope for the best from people, life has taught you to expect the worst; you know information is power; history shows what can happen when the government gets too much power over individuals.

Nike executive

Nike has to spend millions on product development and marketing. (You pay leading sports stars around $20 m every year to promote eg trainers.) Profits last year were $200 m, but these could quickly fall in this competitive market. Production costs must be kept down. This is why production moved from the USA first to S Korea (wages $2.00 per hour), then to Indonesia ($0.15 per hour), and now even to China ($0.10 per hour). Working conditions in these factories are not very good. Nike does not inspect them often.

Korean factory owner

You produced Nike trainers in Korea until labour costs rose too high. You then moved to Indonesia where production is cheaper and where taxes are also low. Even so, Nike pushes down prices all the time, and you have to agree. Nike can choose from many other low-cost countries in SE Asia. This means you only make $1.50 profit on a $90.00 pair of trainers. You are bitter as you know Nike makes big profits. There is little money to improve factory conditions or to raise wages. But why invest too much in Indonesia? Political conditions are unstable, and you may have to move production to another country soon.

Indonesian government official

The government has borrowed billions of dollars for Indonesia's infrastructure. This money must be paid back. This takes up to 35% of the country's export earnings. To keep paying, you have to keep attracting foreign manufacturers. This means low wages, a quiet workforce without free unions or strikes, low taxes for companies and few checks and controls on their operations. Your government cannot spend very much money on health, education and social security. The Nike problem *must* be dealt with quietly and quickly. If not, Nike may move away and this might mean that other foreign investors choose not to come to Indonesia.

Indonesian factory worker

You work 12 hours a day 6 days a week, sometimes even longer when you have to do overtime. You live cheaply and sleep in a large room with 30 other women. But you do not have very much extra money to send back to your family. At work, the heat is terrible, the smell of glue (*Klebstoff*) makes you feel ill, and the machinery is loud and dangerous. (Friends have lost fingers and hands.) If you get ill or pregnant, you lose your job. The government-controlled union does little to help you. Sometimes there are inspections, but then you have to clean up the factory, wear clean clothes – and keep quiet. You are afraid of losing your job but you hope that if you all strike together, you will win better conditions. You know that Nike's payments to top sports stars – about $20 m – is what Nike pays all the workers in all Nike factories in SE Asia.

Unit 12 (answer key)

1 c	Rome	3 b	1992	5 c	12	7 b	Brussels
2 b	6	4 c	2002	6 b	Frankfurt	8 a	Beethoven

Lernhilfen

▮1 Keine Angst vor unbekannten Wörtern

In der Oberstufe beschäftigen Sie sich häufig mit englischen Originaltexten. Wenn Sie bei unbekannten Wörtern immer gleich zum Wörterbuch greifen, kann das Lesen zu einer langsamen und mühseligen Angelegenheit werden. Was tun? Zum Glück gibt es andere Möglichkeiten. Denken Sie nach: **Benutzen Sie zuerst den Kopf, dann das Wörterbuch.**

Wenn Sie auf ein unbekanntes Wort stoßen, das für das Verständnis des Textes wirklich wichtig ist, gibt es diverse Anhaltspunkte, mit denen Sie sich die Wortbedeutung selber erschließen können.

a **Internationale Wörter** (z.B. *microchip, jeans, marketing, chat*)
b **Englische Wörter, die deutschen ähneln** (z.B. *transatlantic, combined, politics*)
c **Von bekannten Wörtern abgeleitete Wörter** (z.B. *indescribable* von dem Verb *to describe* + Vorsilbe *in-* + Nachsilbe *-able*, *unbroken* von dem Verb *to break* + Vorsilbe *un-*)

1.1 Wortbildung

Hier eine Übersicht über die Bildung solcher zusammengesetzer Wörter:

Vorsilben
Einige Vorsilben geben dem Wort eine entgegengesetzte Bedeutung.

Vorsilbe	Bedeutung	Beispiel		
anti-	against	clockwise	→	anticlockwise
dis-	opposite	agree	→	disagree
il-	opposite	legal	→	illegal
im-	opposite	possible	→	impossible
in-	opposite	expensive	→	inexpensive
ir-	opposite	regular	→	irregular
un-	opposite	happiness	→	unhappiness
mis-	wrongly	understand	→	misunderstand

Andere Vorsilben wiederum erweitern die Bedeutung eines Wortes.

be-	make or treat like	friend	→	befriend
co-	with, together	operate	→	cooperate
inter-	between, together, from one to another	national	→	international
micro-	very small	chip	→	microchip
super-	above, over, more than, very efficient	man	→	superman
re-	again	paint	→	repaint
trans-	across, beyond, into another state or place	form	→	transform

Nachsilben

Nachsilben verändern eine Wortart, z.B. wird aus einem Verb ein Nomen.
Einige Wörter verfügen über eine große Vielfalt grammatischer Formen, z.B.:

Verb	Nomen (Person)	Nomen (Sache/Abstraktum)	Adjektiv	Adverb
'organize	'organizer	organi'zation	organi'zational	organi'zationally

Mit dem Wechsel der Wortart kann sich auch die Betonung des Wortes ändern:
'organize/organi'zation.

Die meisten Wörter verfügen nur über wenige Formen, können jedoch durch unterschiedliche Nachsilben vielfach verändert werden. Hier einige der gebräuchlichsten Formen:

Verb	+	Nachsilbe	→	Nomen
paint		-er		painter
act		-or		actor
express		-ion		expression
invite		-(a)tion		invitation
feel		-ing		feeling
govern		-ment		government

Verb/Nomen	+	Nachsilbe	→	Adjektiv
fashion		-able		fashionable
sense		-ible		sensible
nation		-al		national
beauty		-ful		beautiful
care		-ing		caring
act		-ive		active
talk		-ative		talkative
week		-ly		weekly
hunger		-y		hungry

Adjektiv/Nomen	+	Nachsilbe	→	Verb
active		-ate		activate
wide		-en		widen
solid		-ify		solidify
standard		-ize		standardize

Adjektiv	+	Nachsilbe	→	Nomen
stupid		-ity		stupidity
tired		-ness		tiredness

Adjektiv	+	Nachsilbe	→	Adverb
helpful		-ly		helpfully
environment		-ally		environmentally

1.2 Wörter aus dem Kontext erschließen

- Keine Angst vor unbekannten Wörtern. **Lesen Sie einfach weiter!** Eine Erklärung, ein Beispiel oder ein Synonym folgen häufig wenige Zeilen weiter.
- Ist Ihnen ein Wort unbekannt, ignorieren Sie dieses und lesen Sie den Text zunächst zu Ende. Danach und bei genauerer Betrachtung des Satzes, in dem das Wort steht, schließen sich Verständnislücken meist von selbst.
- Für das generelle Verständnis reicht häufig eine annähernde Kenntnis des Wortes aus.

Sehen wir uns das anhand eines Beispiels einmal genauer an. In der folgenden Äußerung gibt es zwei Wörter, die Sie vermutlich nicht kennen.

*Business is bad at the moment and we don't expect it to **rally** for at least a year. All the signals are very **inauspicious**, I'm afraid.*

Mit *rally* ist hier natürlich keine Autorally gemeint. Was kann dieses Wort bedeuten?
- Der Zusammenhang sagt Ihnen, dass es um die derzeit schlechte wirtschaftliche Lage geht. *Rally* hat hier also vermutlich etwas mit der wirtschaftlichen Lage zu tun.
- Die Erwartungen für die Zukunft im zweiten Satzteil scheinen der momentanen Situation nicht zu widersprechen: Es gibt keinen Ausdruck wie *but*, der die Aussicht auf eine Verbesserung nahe legen könnte. Man kann schlussfolgern: Wenigstens ein Jahr lang wird sich an der schlechten Lage nichts ändern.
- Wenn man mit diesen Überlegungen im Hinterkopf den Satz zu übersetzen versucht, ergibt sich eine Lücke, die sich leicht aus dem Zusammenhang schließen lässt: „Das Geschäft läuft schlecht im Moment, und wir erwarten für den Zeitraum von mindestens einem Jahr auch nicht, dass es" – hier passt nur etwas wie „besser laufen" oder „sich verbessern".

Nun zu *inauspicious*. Der Zusammenhang ist mittlerweile klar – was also kann das Wort bedeuten?
- Der Ausdruck *I'm afraid* drückt Bedauern über die Situation aus. Jetzt geht es um die Signale für die wirtschaftliche Entwicklung.
- Diese Signale werden mit einer Verneinung beschrieben – die Vorsilbe *in-* meint immer das Gegenteil von etwas. Wenn das Gegenteil von etwas bedauert wird, ist dieses „Etwas" also sicher etwas Positives – und *inauspicious* das Gegenteil davon: „Die Signale verheißen leider alle nichts Gutes".

2 Neue Wörter sammeln und lernen

Sie müssen nicht jedes neue Wort lernen. **Seien Sie wählerisch!** Helfen Sie Ihrem Gedächtnis, indem Sie neue Wörter nach Kategorien und Wortgruppen ordnen. Je besser die Einteilung, desto leichter ist das spätere Abrufen. **Gehen Sie systematisch vor!**

2.1 Wortfamilien

- Es empfiehlt sich verschiedene Formen eines Wortes zu sammeln. Nachsilben bestimmen häufig die grammatische Form, Vorsilben verändern die Bedeutung eines Wortes und zusammengesetzte Ausdrücke, die Formen des Wortes enthalten, runden die Wortfamilie ab.

– Wortfamilien lassen sich z.B. auf Karteikarten sammeln.
   Vorteil: Leicht transportabel und handhabbar, außerdem unbegrenzt erweiterbar, um neue Wörter und Informationen aufzunehmen.
– Ein Eintrag in einer Wortkartei (oder im Computer) könnte folgendermaßen angelegt sein:

Advertise

verb	noun	noun	noun
'advertise	(person, company)	(thing)	(abstract)
(regular)	'advertiser	advert/ad/	'advertising
		ad'vertisement	

expressions

advertise (a car) for sale

classified ad (in newspaper)

full page ad (in newspaper)

advertise for (new) staff

2.2 Wortkombinationen

Ein Wort zu wissen reicht meistens nicht aus. Man sollte auch lernen, mit welchen anderen Wörtern es zusammen gebraucht wird. Daher bietet es sich auch an, Wortkombinationen, also Wortgruppen und zusammengesetzte Ausdrücke, die ein Schlüsselwort enthalten, zu sammeln. Dazu gehören **zusammengesetzte Verben**, **feststehende Begriffspaare** und **Zusammensetzungen aus Verb und Nomen**.

Zusammengesetzte Verben
Die Bedeutung von zusammengesetzten Verben ist nicht immer offensichtlich und muss daher gelernt werden. Einige dieser Verben ziehen ein Objekt nach sich, andere wiederum nicht. Für diese Ausdrücke eignen sich Wortlisten am besten:

Verb	Bedeutung	Beispiel
set (sb/sth) back	slow down a plan or action	Money problems set the work back by six months.
set off	start a journey	We set off for the airport at 7 am.
set (sth) up	make something ready for use	We set the new tent up in the garden.

Feststehende Begriffspaare
Es ist hilfreich feststehende Begriffspaare zu kennen, z.B. *exercise machine, sewing machine* und *washing machine*.
Begriffspaare können wie folgt gesammelt werden:

exercise
sewing —— machine   Oder so: traffic —— accident / lights / jam
washing

Zusammensetzungen aus Verb und Nomen

Verben gehen oft mit Nomen eine feste Verbindung ein. Da diese Verbindungen sich oft vom Deutschen unterscheiden, ist es sinnvoll z.B. nicht nur *love*, sondern gleichzeitig *to fall in love* zu lernen. Oder wenn man zusammen mit dem Begriff *photo* auch die Verbindung *to take a photo* lernt, vermeidet man Fehler wie ~~I made a photo of the house~~.

2.3 Thematische Wortgruppen

Wörter und Ausdrücke zu einem Thema lassen sich in Form von **Wortfeldern** (Listen, in denen alle Worte zu einem bestimmten Thema gesammelt werden) oder **Wortnetzen** sammeln. Mit einem Wortnetz lässt sich ein Wortfeld visuell in sinnverwandte Untergruppen gliedern, indem man in der Mitte einer Seite mit dem Oberbegriff beginnt, z.B. *sporting activities*, und das Netz spinnwebenartig zu den Rändern hin erweitert. Vorteile: Die Wörter werden sinnvoll in Untergruppen gegliedert, die optische Darstellung erleichtert das Lernen und das Netz lässt sich leicht erweitern, was Spaß macht. Hier das Wortfeld *sporting activities* in Form eines Wortnetzes.

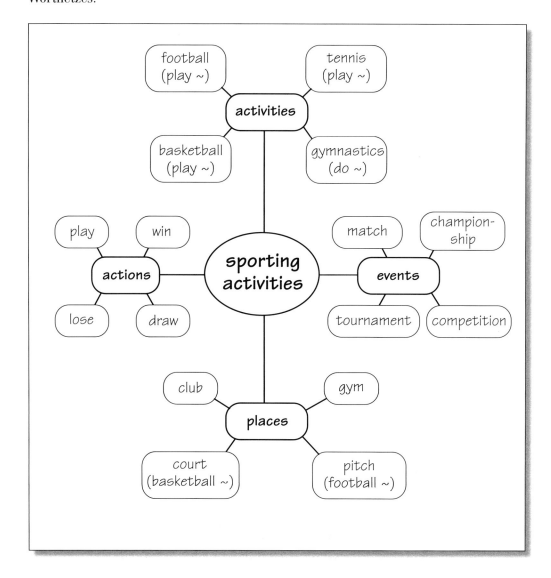

3 Effektives Lesen

Für eine **effektive Lesetrategie** ist es wichtig zu wissen, worauf geachtet werden soll: besondere Fakten oder Zahlen, ein allgemeines Textverständnis oder ein detailliertes Verständnis bestimmter Passagen oder des ganzen Textes. Worauf es zu achten gilt, wird meist durch Fragen oder Aufgabenstellungen vorgegeben, sodass diese zunächst gelesen werden sollten. Wählen Sie eine Lesetechnik, die Sie möglichst schnell ans vorgegebene Ziel bringt.

3.1 Erst einen Überblick über den Text verschaffen

- Um sich mit dem Thema vertraut zu machen, sehen Sie sich vor dem Lesen die Überschriften, die Bilder oder Grafiken an. Ein sorgfältiger Blick auf die Aufgabenstellungen ist für ein allgemeines Erfassen des Textes ebenso hilfreich.
- Ist ein **Vorspann** vorhanden, lesen Sie diesen sorgfältig. Meist bringt er das Thema oder Anliegen des Textes auf den Punkt.
- Lesen Sie nun den Text **zügig** durch, ohne sich zu lange an Einzelheiten aufzuhalten. Lesen Sie bei kleineren Verständnisproblemen einfach weiter! Die Bedeutung der meisten Wörter erschließt sich in der Regel einige Zeilen weiter. Konzentrieren Sie sich beim Lesen a) auf die **Schlüsselwörter** (diese, meist Nomen und Verben, sind die sinntragenden Elemente eines Textes) und b) auf die **Struktur** des Textes, d.h. auf die einführende These, gefolgt von Argumenten und Belegen und die abschließende Zusammenfassung, in der alle wesentlichen Punkte aufgegriffen werden. Meist beginnen die einzelnen Passagen mit einem Schlüsselsatz, dem Argumente und Belege logisch folgen. Beachten Sie Konjunktionen wie *however*, *moreover*, *although*.

3.2 Schnelles Herausfiltern von Informationen

- Halten Sie Ausschau nach der Art von Informationen, die Sie suchen. Optisch stechen Zahlen besonders gut heraus, ebenso wie Personennamen, Orte und Organisationen, die mit einem Großbuchstaben beginnen.
- Bewegen Sie die Augen zügig von oben nach unten über den Text. Versuchen Sie dabei alles, was Sie im Moment nicht benötigen, außer Acht zu lassen.

3.3 Detailverständnis

- Verschaffen Sie sich einen Überblick über den Text, um zu wissen, worum es geht.
- Sehen Sie sich dann die Fragen und Aufgabenstellungen genau an. Daran erkennen Sie, worauf es beim Lesen zu achten gilt.
- Lesen Sie nun den Text Satz für Satz im Detail. Sollten Sie Wörter, Redewendungen oder gar ganze Sätze nicht verstehen, ist dies kein Grund zur Sorge. **Lesen Sie einfach weiter** und kommen Sie später darauf zurück.
- Wenn Sie den Text durchgelesen haben, klären Sie möglichst viele unbekannte Wörter mithilfe der Techniken für das Verstehen von neuen Wörtern (S. 140–142).
- Schlagen Sie nur die Wörter nach, deren exakte Bedeutung Sie wissen müssen und bei denen Sie durch Überlegen und Schlussfolgern nicht weiterkommen.
- Nachdem Sie die Bedeutung der sinntragenden Wörter geklärt haben, lesen Sie den Text für ein zusammenhängendes Verständnis ein drittes Mal durch. Beantworten Sie dann die Fragen oder führen Sie die Aufgabenstellungen aus.

4 Kleine Schreibwerkstatt: Wie man Fragen zum Text beantwortet und Zusammenfassungen und Aufsätze schreibt

4.1 Der erste Schritt: Die Zielsetzung klären

– Wenn es um eine Textaufgabe oder eine Zusammenfassung geht: Vergewissern Sie sich, dass Sie den Text verstanden haben.
– Lesen Sie die Frage (bzw. das Aufsatzthema) gründlich durch. Lassen Sie sich immer von der Frage leiten: **Worauf zielt diese Frage genau ab?** (Dies ist nicht immer einfach. Für die Antwort müssen Sie möglicherweise über den gesamten Text verstreute Informationen zusammentragen oder gar „zwischen den Zeilen" lesen, um zu erfassen, was der/die Lehrer/in genau wissen will.) Bei Aufsatzthemen sollten Sie im Auge behalten, dass jedes Thema in der einen oder anderen Weise begrenzt ist. Schließen Sie Unwesentliches oder Nebensächliches aus, da Sie sonst das Thema verfehlen.

Hier ein Beispiel für ein Aufsatzthema. Die Begriffe, die das Thema eingrenzen, sind unterstrichen.

> ie, not the whole town   ie, not modern   ie, but not for eg buses or taxis
>
> The <u>centres</u> of <u>historical</u> towns should be closed to <u>private vehicles</u>
>
> ie, not just during parts of the day
> <u>at all times</u>.

4.2 Fragen zum Text beantworten

Wenn Sie das Gefühl haben, den Text verstanden zu haben, und sich über die Zielsetzung im Klaren sind, können Sie damit beginnen sich **Notizen** zu machen. Die Schwierigkeit beim Anfertigen von Notizen besteht darin, eine kurze, präzise Liste anzulegen, anstatt ganze Sätze oder gar Absätze aus dem Text herauszuschreiben. Die folgenden Schritte helfen Ihnen dabei, Notizen anzulegen, die Ihnen danach, wenn Sie selber etwas schreiben müssen, eine wirkliche Hilfe sind.

– Fassen Sie die **wesentlichen Unterthemen** des Textes zusammen, die Sie auch als Überschriften nutzen können. Achten Sie darauf, nach den Überschriften ausreichend Platz für die Stichpunkte freizulassen.

Hier ein Beispiel für Überschriften aus einem Text über Energie:

fossil fuels			renewables		
types	advantages	disadvantages	types	advantages	disadvantages

– Konkret ergeben Ihre Notizen eine Liste von **Schlüssel-** bzw. **Stichwörtern**, meist Nomen und Verben sowie manchmal auch Adjektiven. Konzentrieren Sie sich darauf und ignorieren Sie den Rest.
– Suchen Sie nun **Signale** im Text wie Hervorhebungen, Wiederholungen und bedeutungstragende Adjektive und Adverbien wie *absolutely*, *unbelievable*, *amazing*, *massive* usw. Dies alles sind Signale dafür, was der/die Verfasser/in für wichtig hält.
– Prüfen Sie, ob Sie alle Informationen zusammengestellt haben, die Sie brauchen. Diese können über den gesamten Text verstreut sein.

Wenn Ihre Notizen vollständig sind, können Sie mit der Beantwortung der Frage beginnen.

– Achten Sie darauf, nur Informationen für die Antwort zu verwenden, die zu dieser und nicht etwa zu einer späteren Frage gehören. Arbeiten Sie **nur** die im Text enthaltenen Informationen heraus und verwenden Sie nur Informationen, die Sie für eine klare und präzise Antwort benötigen.
– Benutzen Sie die **Zeitform** der Fragestellung. In der Regel ist dies das Simple Present.
– Der erste Satz ist oft der schwierigste. Um diese Hürde elegant zu nehmen, greifen Sie zuerst einmal die Formulierung der Frage in Ihrem ersten Satz auf. Versuchen Sie sich dann schrittweise von dieser Formulierung zu entfernen. Hier ein Beispiel, wie Sie Wörter, Ausdrücke und grammatische Strukturen ändern können.

Frage: *Why does the writer think that violent crime in the USA has declined to a great extent in recent years?*

Entwurf 1: *The writer thinks that violent crime in the USA has declined to a great extent in recent years because …*

Synonym   Änderung der grammatischen Struktur

Entwurf 2: *The writer believes that crime involving violence has recently been reduced greatly because …*

Synonym; Aktiv → Passiv   Synonym

Bevor Sie die Reinschrift erstellen, überprüfen Sie Ihre Antwort auf mögliche Fehler (vgl. 4.5).

4.3 Einen Text zusammenfassen

Obgleich Sie in der Abschlussprüfung meist keine Zusammenfassung schreiben müssen, hilft diese Fähigkeit, die Konzentration auf den wesentlichen Gedankengang in einem Text zu lenken. Darüber hinaus wird in der Oberstufe immer wieder von Ihnen verlangt, kürzere oder längere Texte zusammenzufassen.

Auch hier müssen alle Unklarheiten im Vorfeld beseitigt werden. Jetzt können Sie mit der Vorbereitung der Zusammenfassung beginnen.

– Lesen Sie den Text noch einmal Absatz für Absatz und filtern Sie in jedem den zentralen Satz heraus. Achten Sie auf alles, was wesentlich ist.
– Wenn Ihnen das Buch gehört, können Sie all die wesentlichen Sätze, Satzteile, Wörter oder Wortgruppen unterstreichen oder markieren und die unwesentlichen einklammern.
  Folgendes wird vermutlich in Klammern stehen:
  ▪ **Beispiele** (*For instance, …*)
  ▪ **Wiederholungen** (*In other words, …*)
  ▪ **Anekdoten** und **Exkurse** (*By the way, …*)
  ▪ **Zitate**, die eine Ausführung veranschaulichen oder einen Beweis stützen sollen;
  ▪ **Stilmittel** wie Vergleiche (*The effect of these changes on society was like a major earthquake.* Stattdessen könnte man sagen: *These changes had a major effect on society.*).

- Gehen Sie noch mal alle Textteile durch, die Sie markiert haben. Vergewissern Sie sich, das Sie **alles Wesentliche berücksichtigt** und alles Unwesentliche weggelassen haben.
- Bilden Sie nun aus dem Kern des Textes, den Sie abstrahiert haben, Ihre Zusammenfassung.
- Schreiben Sie Ihren Text möglichst in eigenen Worten. Achten Sie darauf, dass die Gedankengänge und Sätze **logisch verknüpft** sind. Verwenden Sie hierfür Konjunktionen wie *however*, *moreover*, *although*.
- Eine gute Zusammenfassung entspricht, je nach gedanklicher Dichte des Textes, etwa einem Drittel der Länge des Originaltextes.

Überprüfen Sie jetzt Ihre Zusammenfassung auf mögliche Fehler (vgl. 4.5).

4.4 Einen Aufsatz schreiben

In der Oberstufe müssen Sie sich oft schriftlich mit einem Thema auseinander setzen. Dies kann ein kürzerer Text (wie eine Notiz) oder ein längerer Text (wie ein Aufsatz) sein. Letzterer ist ein fortlaufender Sachtext, in dem Sie Ihre persönliche Meinung äußern.

Die hierfür relevante Aufsatzform ist der argumentative Sachtext. In diesem legt der/die Verfasser/in seine/ihre Meinung für oder gegen etwas dar. Aus diesem Grund ist die Überschrift meist als provokative These formuliert, zu der eine eigene Meinung geäußert werden soll.

Hier einige hilfreiche Tipps zum Verfassen eines Sachtextes:
- Verlieren Sie in keiner Phase das Aufsatzthema aus den Augen (vgl. 4.1).
- Schreiben Sie zuerst Ihre Sicht der Dinge auf Konzeptpapier. Machen Sie sich keine Sorgen, wenn Sie Ihren Standpunkt noch nicht genau festlegen, da Sie ihn später noch ändern können.
- Sammeln Sie nun Argumente **für** und **gegen** die These. Die Argumente stammen aus den Texten, die Sie zu diesem Thema gelesen haben, und entspringen Ihrer eigenen Vorstellungskraft. Machen Sie ein „Brainstorming" und schreiben Sie die Argumente in der Reihenfolge auf, wie Sie Ihnen einfallen. Hierfür ist ein **Gedankengerüst** sehr hilfreich. Dieses nimmt zunächst etwas mehr Zeit in Anspruch, lässt Sie später aber viel effektiver arbeiten.

Ein **Gedankengerüst** gleicht im Grunde einem Wortnetz (vgl. 2.3), wobei der Schwerpunkt der **Inhalt** und nicht die Bedeutung der Wörter ist. Auf der folgenden Seite finden Sie ein Beispiel für ein Gedankengerüst für das in Abschnitt 4.1 erwähnte Aufsatzthema:

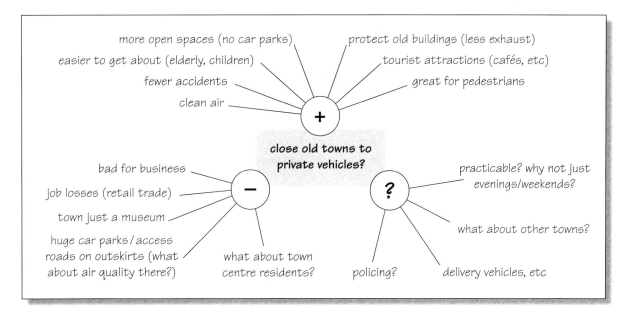

– Schreiben Sie nun einen ersten Entwurf Ihres Aufsatzes auf Konzeptpapier. Folgen Sie dabei dem unten skizzierten Aufbau. Bleiben Sie konsequent beim Thema. (Hier erweist sich ein gutes Gedankengerüst bereits als wertvolle Hilfe.)

Einleitung	Darstellung des Problems sowie Ihres Standpunkts
Hauptteil	Argumente pro/kontra, Belege
Schlussteil	Zusammenfassung der Hauptargumente für Ihren Standpunkt und kurze Schlussfolgerung

– Vergegenwärtigen Sie sich nochmals die Themenstellung und lesen Sie Ihren Entwurf durch, um sich zu vergewissern, dass Sie beim Thema bleiben. Dies kann in jedem Arbeitsstadium gemacht werden.
– Sehen Sie Ihren Entwurf sorgfältig auf sprachliche Fehler und stilistisch ungeschickte Wendungen durch (vgl. 4.5).
– Wenn Sie mit Ihrem Entwurf zufrieden sind, fertigen Sie die Reinschrift an. Halten Sie einen breiten Rand und Platz zwischen den Zeilen für die Korrekturen frei.

4.5   Wichtig: Die Fehlerkontrolle

Bevor Sie von Ihrer Antwort/Zusammenfassung bzw. Ihrem Aufsatz die Reinschrift erstellen, überprüfen Sie Ihren Text auf:
- **Rechtschreibung**
- **Wortstellung**
- **Gebrauch von Artikeln und Präpositionen**
- **Wahl der Zeitformen** (verwenden Sie die Zeitform des Originaltextes – meist das Simple Present)
- **Zeichensetzung** (oft werden zu viele Kommas gesetzt, z.B. vor Nebensätzen mit *because* oder *that*)
- **Stil** (etwa ob Ihre Antwort Wiederholungen oder lange direkte Zitate enthält).

5 Ein Referat halten

Wecken Sie das Interesse der Zuhörer, indem Sie Ihr Referat mit einer provokativen These, einer rhetorischen Frage oder einer kurzen Anekdote beginnen. Seien Sie vorsichtig mit Witzen in der Fremdsprache, da der Schuss auch nach hinten losgehen und betretenes Schweigen folgen könnte.

– Bereiten Sie **visuelle Hilfsmittel** zur Veranschaulichung der Ergebnisse vor. Gestalten Sie optische Anreize, wie Diagramme auf Folie für den Overheadprojektor, möglichst eindrucksvoll und setzen Sie diese wirkungsvoll ein. All das bringt Abwechslung in Ihren Vortrag und fesselt das Interesse der Zuhörer.
– Strukturieren Sie Ihre Gedanken in **logischen Schritten**, damit Sie nicht vom Thema abschweifen.
– Referate, die in der Schule gehalten werden, sind meist wie eine Erörterung über ein Thema aufgebaut, d.h. eine These, also Ihre Meinung, wird mit **Beweisen** gestützt.

Referate über **unstrittige** Themen wie die Kontrolle des Treibhauseffektes oder das Verbot von Kinderpornographie werden in drei Teile gegliedert:

Einleitung	Darlegung des Themas und Ihres Standpunkts
Hauptteil	Beweise, um Ihre Argumente zu stützen
Schlussteil	Hauptargumente für Ihre Meinung und Schlussfolgerung

Sollten Sie über ein **kontroverses** Thema sprechen, wie z.B. die Aufhebung des Ladenschlussgesetzes in Deutschland, können Sie Ihr Referat wie folgt gliedern:

Einführung	Lösungsvorschlag für das Problem – **äußern Sie noch nicht Ihre Meinung**
Hauptteil I	Argumente **gegen** den Vorschlag (*cons*)
Hauptteil II	Argumente **für** den Vorschlag (*pros*)
Schlussfolgerung	Äußern Sie Ihre Meinung mit einer kurzen Begründung

– Verwenden Sie **kurze Sätze** mit maximal neun oder zehn Wörtern.
– **Bleiben Sie beim Thema.** Schweifen Sie nicht ab und wiederholen Sie sich nicht.
– **Heben** Sie Ihre Hauptargumente oder Beweise **hervor.**
– Versuchen Sie nicht witzig zu sein und **behandeln Sie ein ernstes Thema nicht leichtfertig.**

Wenn Sie das Referat halten, beachten Sie folgende Punkte:
– Haben zwei oder mehr Partner die Ergebnisse erarbeitet, sollte der Vortrag inhaltlich schlüssig von allen dargeboten werden. Für zwei Partner könnte die Aufteilung wie folgt aussehen:
  – Partner 1 Einführung
  – Partner 2 Präsentation der Ergebnisse
  – Partner 1 Schlussfolgerung
– **Lesen Sie das Referat nicht vom Blatt ab** und lernen Sie auch nicht auswendig. Lesen Sie Ihr Referat mehrmals, bevor Sie es halten und verwenden Sie einen **Stichwortzettel** (Schlüsselwörter, Hauptgedanken) als Gedächtnisstütze. (Machen Sie es wie Fernsehmoderatoren.)

- **Schauen Sie Ihre Zuhörer an**, aber nicht immer nur eine Person. Gute Redner lassen den Blick während des Sprechens langsam von einer Seite zur anderen schweifen.
- **Stehen Sie nicht wie eine Salzsäule**, wandern Sie aber auch nicht zu viel herum. Seien Sie entspannt und selbstbewusst – stellen Sie sich vor zu einem Freund zu sprechen.
- **Variieren Sie die Lautstärke der Stimme** gemäß den Argumenten, mit denen Sie überzeugen wollen. Heben Sie wichtige Punkte hervor, indem Sie lauter und langsamer sprechen. Werden Sie jedoch nicht zu laut. Stellen Sie sich wiederum vor zu einem Freund zu sprechen.
- Unterstreichen Sie wichtige Punkte mit **Gesten**, vermeiden Sie aber theatralisches Gestikulieren.

6 Wie besorge ich mir Informationen aus dem Internet?

Die schnellste Methode zur Recherche ist sicherlich das Internet. Doch der Umgang mit der Masse an Informationen, die einem begegnet, ist nicht immer einfach.

6.1 Suchmaschinen

Es ist angesichts tausender von Seiten, die in der einen oder anderen Weise mit einem bestimmten Thema zu tun haben, unmöglich ohne eine gute Suchmaschine an relevante Informationen zu kommen. Bei vielen Suchmaschinen können Sie die Funktion **Erweiterte Suche** bzw. **Suchoptionen** benutzen, um festzulegen, dass die eingegebenen Wörter unbedingt vorkommen müssen (in der Regel durch + oder **AND** bzw. **UND**) oder nicht vorkommen sollen (meistens durch – oder **NOT** bzw. **NICHT**). Häufig werden getrennte Wörter jedoch schon automatisch wie UND-Verknüpfungen behandelt. Gängige Suchmaschinen sind z.B.:

www.altavista.de   www.fireball.de   www.google.de
www.lycos.de   www.web.de   www.yahoo.de

Meistens bekommen Sie die amerikanische Version einer Internetseite, wenn Sie die Länderkennung **de** durch **com** ersetzen. Für die britische Version geben Sie stattdessen **co.uk** ein.
Australien und Neuseeland haben ihre eigene, sehr empfehlenswerte Suchmaschine: www.anzwers.com.au

6.2 Auswahl empfehlenswerter Internetseiten

Auch wenn es unmöglich ist, eine repräsentative Auswahl von Internetseiten mit allgemeinen Informationen aufzulisten, können Ihnen die folgenden vielleicht weiterhelfen. Die meisten von ihnen sind auf Englisch und beziehen sich vorwiegend auf die englischsprachige Welt.

- Die Quelle für **Zahlen, Daten und Fakten** über Länder:
  www.cia.gov/cia/publications/factbook/ (Das jährliche Statistik-Handbuch des CIA.)

– Allgemeine **Enzyklopädien**:
www.encarta.com (Die Microsoft Encarta; wenn Sie auf „Reference" gehen, können Sie nach einzelnen Begriffen suchen.)
www.encyclopedia.com
www.britannica.com (Die Online-Ausgabe der berühmten Encyclopaedia Britannica, der Enzyklopädie schlechthin – wer sich die gedruckte Ausgabe in einer Bibliothek ansehen möchte, wird aus dem Stöbern so schnell nicht herauskommen.)

– Das A–Z zu **Computer und Internet**: www.networds.de

– Das Kompendium von **Wissenschaft und Technik**: www.howstuffworks.com
(Wie funktioniert was in der Welt? Hier finden Sie die ultimativen Antworten.)

– Für Informationen und Berichte zu aktuellen Themen, die für das Fach Englisch relevant sind, sind englischsprachige **Medien**, vor allem die **Presse**, ein guter Einstieg. Alle wichtigen Medien sind im Internet vertreten, auch wenn der Zugang zum Archiv manchmal eine Registrierung erfordert oder gar kostenpflichtig ist.

– Zum Thema **Großbritannien** ist www.bbc.co.uk eine unschätzbare Quelle. Hier, auf der Seite des riesigen britischen öffentlich-rechtlichen Medienunternehmens BBC, finden Sie eine Fülle von Nachrichten und Hintergrundberichten zu allen britischen Themen in gut verständlicher Sprache. Eine andere, wenn auch sprachlich oft anspruchsvollere Quelle, sind britische Zeitungen, vor allem:
www.guardianunlimited.co.uk   www.independent.co.uk

– Von den **amerikanischen** Medien sind vor allem zu empfehlen:
www.iht.com   www.time.com
Aktuelle Nachrichten finden Sie auch unter www.cnn.com.

– Eine gute Übersicht über Zeitungen, die ein eigenes Online-Angebot haben, finden Sie bei Yahoo in der Rubrik „Nachrichten und Medien". (yahoo.de für deutsche Zeitungen, yahoo.co.uk für englische, yahoo.com für amerikanische. Dort heißt die entsprechende Rubrik „News & Media".)

– Zuverlässige **Fakten und Informationen über englischsprachige Länder** erhalten Sie auf den Seiten der jeweiligen Regierungen:

Australien	www.fed.gov.au
Großbritannien	www.ukonline.gov.uk
Indien	www.nic.in
Irland	www.irlgov.ie
Kanada	www.canada.gc.ca
Neuseeland	www.govt.nz
Südafrika	www.gov.za
USA	www.usinfo.state.gov www.firstgov.gov

– Schließlich seien noch die Seiten folgender internationaler Organisationen empfohlen:

Commonwealth	www.thecommonwealth.org
EU	www.europa.eu.int
United Nations	www.un.org

Und jetzt viel Spaß beim Stöbern!

Hörverständnistexte

Unit 1 ▪ Exercise 4

page 35

PRESENTER   Well, now, let's start with a basic question. How do adverts actually work?

MARCUS   Oh, in lots of different ways. Some advertising promotes the brand and keeps the brand name – Coca-Cola or whatever – at the front of our minds. Then again, some advertising aims to promote a particular product and maybe a special offer.

PRESENTER   Something like this magazine insert for CDs and cassettes perhaps?

MARCUS   Yes, this is a very good example, and this sort of advertising often uses a special formula: AIDA – A-I-D-A.

PRESENTER   AIDA? What does that stand for?

MARCUS   Well, A stands for 'attract *attention'*. And you see, the leaflet's bright colours attract our attention immediately as it falls out of the magazine.

PRESENTER   Yes, I see. And, er … what does 'I' stand for?

MARCUS   That's for 'arouse *interest'*. We immediately see in large print the words 'Take 6. Pay for 1.', and, of course, our interest is aroused.

PRESENTER   And 'D'?

MARCUS   That stands for 'create *desire'*. The ad does that as we read further and see all … all the many different CD titles that we can choose.

PRESENTER   And so … that brings us to the last letter: 'A'.

MARCUS   That means 'make *action* easy'. And look here it is. Here's a card for us to fill in, cut out and send off in order to get our six CDs. And look, there's no need for a stamp. It's freepost – pre-paid. So … what could be easier than that?

PRESENTER   Yes, I see what you mean. Very good. Well, er … moving on from there, I'd like to ask you about recent changes in the world of advertising. In the news, we've been hearing a lot …

Unit 2 ▪ Exercise 3

page 44

Part 1

FRAU KAUFMANN   So, it's Frau Fischer, isn't it? Barbara Fischer. Thank you for coming this morning.

FRAU FISCHER   OK. No problem.

FRAU KAUFMANN   Er, let's begin by talking about you a little bit. I see from your application that you're 27. And you've had some work experience.

FRAU FISCHER   Yeah. A bit.

FRAU KAUFMANN   Could you say a little more about that? Where was it?

FRAU FISCHER   Here and there. At a pub. Then an Italian place. It's there in my application.

FRAU KAUFMANN   Er … yes. Café Milano.

FRAU FISCHER   Yeah, whatever.

FRAU KAUFMANN   Mm. Can you speak Italian?

FRAU FISCHER   A bit. I lived in Italy for a year.

FRAU KAUFMANN   And do you have any other foreign languages apart from English?

FRAU FISCHER   French. I lived in France for five years.

FRAU KAUFMANN   So is French your first foreign language?

FRAU FISCHER   I suppose. And I've got some English from school. No escape from that!

FRAU KAUFMANN   I see. Well, tell me, do you actually like this sort of work – serving in a café?

FRAU FISCHER   It pays the bills.

FRAU KAUFMANN   Does that mean that you would work Saturday and Sunday?

Frau Fischer   No, just Saturday. I couldn't stand working *all* weekend.

FRAU KAUFMANN   So do you think you would be right for Café Charisma?

FRAU FISCHER   No problem. I can do this sort of work in my sleep.

FRAU KAUFMANN   Well, er, thank you. Have you got any questions you would like to ask?

FRAU FISCHER   Just one thing. I'd like to know a bit more about the pay.

FRAU KAUFMANN   All right. Well, the starting pay is …

Part 2

FRAU KAUFMANN   Ah, you're Herr Schneider, aren't you?

HERR SCHNEIDER   Yes, that's right. Stefan Schneider.

FRAU KAUFMANN   Now I see that you haven't had much work experience so far.

HERR SCHNEIDER   Yes, that's right. I'm only seventeen, so I'm just getting started really. But I've been doing a Saturday afternoon job at Pizza Hut for the last six months. That's been mainly clearing tables, though, so I'm interested in moving on to something better.

FRAU KAUFMANN   Good, yes. But I see that you're still at school, so can you really give up time for a weekend job?

HERR SCHNEIDER   Well, I can work all day on Saturday. But I'm afraid that's all I can do this year. I need Sunday to do school work and to spend a bit of time with friends and family. Am I right in thinking that working just on Saturdays would be all right?

FRAU KAUFMANN   Yes, as the advert says, we're happy to take the right people for just one day at the weekend. Now, I'd like to move on to talk about languages.

HERR SCHNEIDER   Well, I've got German, of course, and English … and a little bit of French. For me, one of the good things about this job is the chance to use my English – and perhaps improve it a bit.

FRAU KAUFMANN   Well, of course, it is the foreign language that most people can speak, so ... OK, we'd prefer more languages, but it needn't be a big problem. One last thing: do you have any questions?

HERR SCHNEIDER   Yes, there are one or two things I'd like to ask about. First, I wonder how soon you could tell me if you want me, and how soon I would start? You see, I feel I ought to give Pizza Hut some warning, so that they can look for someone else. The sooner I could tell them the better.

FRAU KAUFMANN   Sure, I fully understand. Well, thank you for coming in today. You'll hear from us shortly.

HERR SCHNEIDER   And thank you for the chance of an interview. I'll look forward to hearing from you.

FRAU KAUFMANN   Right. In fact, we'll let you know by ...

Unit 3 ▪ Exercise 4

page 53

DAVE S   Before you decide to join, Ann, perhaps you'd like a look around the Centre with me.

ANN R   I'd love to have a quick look around.

DAVE S   Well, here we are in the reception area. If you could come this way, let's start with a look at the bar restaurant – through these double doors in front of us. It's a good place for a light lunch with your friends after you finish your game of tennis or whatever. And you can continue to watch the tennis through those great big windows – there are three tennis courts altogether.

ANN R   Ah, yes. Great for the summer. And where do those other double doors across reception lead to?

DAVE S   Through there is the main gym. We use that for all sorts of things – badminton, basketball, aerobics. All sorts.

ANN R   And what's around the corner and along the corridor?

DAVE S   Let's go and look. This way ...

ANN R   By the way, how much does it cost for members here?

DAVE S   Well, basic membership for individuals is £250 a year.

ANN R   Mm, not too bad.

DAVE S   I'll give you all the details back at the office. ... So, now to our left is another entrance to the bar restaurant. And now if we turn right, we go down past the men's and women's changing rooms to our left and to our right is another entrance to the main gym ... and now at the end of the corridor we have the pool room. There's only one pool table, I'm afraid, and it's always busy. You have to book well ahead.

ANN R   Well, it's not my game. It seems to be more popular with boys, doesn't it?

DAVE S   That's right. Now, we need to turn right and go straight along here to the next thing. Now right again, and there's a sauna straight ahead.

ANN R   Ah, a sauna. I like a good sauna.

DAVE S   And on the right, there's a solarium. A lot of people use that to get a little bit brown before they go on holiday.

ANN R   Very useful.

DAVE S   And through the third door here, on the left, we come to the swimming pool.

ANN R   Oh, nice. If you don't mind me asking, how big is the pool?

DAVE S   It's a full Olympic-size pool, and in fact there are often swimming championships here. Now, let's walk along the side of the pool to the other entrance. And you can see there's a class from a local school over there. They're practising for their life-saving certificates ...
And here we are at the other entrance. Let's go out and turn sharp right.

ANN R   Ah, squash courts!

DAVE S   Yes. Here as you can see, we've got two squash courts. It's a fast game. Do you play?

ANN R   No, but I'd like to learn.

DAVE S   And if we go back now, and go in here next to the squash courts, we've got the fitness training room. As you can see, it has got all the latest exercise machines.

ANN R   So many of them.

DAVE S   Yes, there's something for everyone here.

ANN R   Good, well I'll certainly use them.

DAVE S   And you can have the help of a personal fitness trainer who will be able to help design a training programme just for you.

ANN R   Excellent.

DAVE S   Well, good, now let's go back along the corridor to reception.

ANN R   Well, thanks very much for showing me round.

DAVE S   You're very welcome. What do you think? Would you like to join?

ANN R   Yes, I certainly think you've got everything here that I need – and what's more, I can't wait to get started!

Unit 4 ▪ Exercise 3

page 62

Part 1

HELGA   Guten Morgen, Handysystem. Wie kann ich Ihnen helfen?

MR HALL   Hello. I'm sorry, but is it all right if I speak English?

HELGA   Yes, certainly, please go ahead. How can I help you?

MR HALL   Thank you. Well, you see, I want to buy one of the mobile phones you're advertising at the moment.

HELGA   Yes, certainly. Which one? Could you give me the code?

MR HALL   That's it. I'm sorry, but I'm not sure which I should buy. I saw three different models advertised on that cable TV shopping programme – you know, *Shop on Air* – but I didn't have time to note down the details. Do you think you could go through them with me?

HELGA   Yes, of course. We've got several models on offer at the moment, and I think they're the ones you saw on TV.

MR HALL   I expect you're right. What were they again?

HELGA   Well, first there's the Nexus 321. And then there's the Star TR2. And finally there's the Laser 101.

MR HALL   Right, well could you possibly explain what's different about each of them? The different features.

Part 2

HELGA   Yes, of course. What particular features were you thinking of?

MR HALL   Well, now, I want something that lasts a long time before the battery runs out.

HELGA   They're all quite similar from that point of view. The Nexus gives you 250 minutes of talktime, the Star lasts 240 minutes, and the Laser is a little better – 260 minutes.

MR HALL   And it needs to be easy to use.

HELGA   They've all got voice-activated dialling. You say the number and the phone dials it for you. And if the name is in the memory, you can just say that and it'll dial too.

MR HALL   That's great. So they're all about the same so far.

HELGA   Yes, but there's a difference in the memories of the three phones. The Laser can hold up to 99 names and numbers, while the Nexus holds 290 and the Star a fantastic 500!

MR HALL   But that's far too many for me. I would only ever call my family and a few friends and one or two people at work.

HELGA   I see. And what about internet access? The Nexus and the Star offer you that.

MR HALL   Nice, but not necessary for me. Er ... perhaps you could tell me about text messaging. Can any of them do that?

HELGA   Oh, yes, they've all got it.

MR HALL   Oh, that's very useful. But now, I wonder if you could tell me something about the cost of these machines?

HELGA   Certainly. The Star and Laser models are both pay-as-you-go models. But with the Star, you pay 75 cents per minute for the first five minutes each day, any time of the day or night, and after that it's just fifteen cents per minute. On the other hand, with the Laser, you pay 30 cents per minute at peak time, but only 10 cents per minute at off-peak time – in the evening and at the weekend.

MR HALL   And that's all I have to pay? No fixed monthly charges?

HELGA   Yes, that's right with those two, the Star and the Laser. But with the Nexus, there's a 12-month contract, which costs €45 a month, and that gives you 10 hours of free calls each month.

MR HALL   Yes, but you see, I'll only use the phone a few times a month – just short calls in emergencies – when I'm going to be late for a meeting or a party. That sort of thing. I really only want to pay for the time that I use – and the cheaper the better.

Part 3

HELGA   Well, now, let me just run over the order details quickly.

MR HALL   Yes, of course.

HELGA   You're going take the Laser 101, Code M4565 – at €139.99.

MR HALL   Yes, that's right.

HELGA   And now, may I take your details – name, address and so on?

MR HALL   Yes, of course. My name is Hall. Stephen Hall.

HELGA   Yes, Mr Hall. Is that Stephen with a p-h?

MR HALL   That's right. And my address is Sonnenweg 21, D-58455, Witten.

HELGA   Sonnenweg 21, D-58455, Witten. And your phone number?

MR HALL   0-2-3-0-2—1-8-9—7-0-6.

HELGA   0-2-3-0-2—1-8-9—7-0-6. OK ... and let me give you an order reference number. Perhaps you could make a note of it just in case there's any problem and you need to quote it.

MR HALL   Yes, certainly.

HELGA   It's P-W-V-7-1-3-9-double 0-S-H.

MR HALL   P-W-V-7-1-3-9-double 0-S-H. Right, I've got that.

HELGA   Now, how would you like to pay for this, Mr Hall? By credit card?

MR HALL   Yes, please. By Visa. The number is 4929 712 345 605.

HELGA   Thank you. And one more little thing. May I ask, how did you first find out about our products?

MR HALL   Oh, well, the first time I heard about your products was on that shopping programme on TV. The one which I told you about.

HELGA   Oh, I see, Well, that's fine, Mr Hall. Thank you very much. I hope you and your family get a lot of fun out of your new mobile phone ...

Unit 5 ▪ Exercise 8

page 76

Part 1

JIM   ... and yes, on the town council, we're doing everything we can to improve our local hospital service here in Henby.

TONY   Good. Our listeners will be very pleased to hear that. And if any of you out there would like to speak to Councillor Jim Esplin, do please give us a call on 01491 321456. Now, time for Liz Kent with the latest update on the traffic news. Liz.

LIZ   Thank you, Tony. Well, it's bad news again with the morning rush hour in Henby. There's a long tailback on Frimton Road leading towards the Y-junction just before the bridge into town. What's more, the traffic lights at the junction of Tower Street with River Street are broken and that's causing more trouble. And then, on top of that, there's been an accident at the crossroads on the High Street. It seems that the centre of Henby is one great big traffic jam. So … all you drivers out there, avoid Henby for the next hour or two if you can…

Part 2

TONY Thanks, Liz. Now, Henby Councillor Jim Esplin, thanks for staying with us.

JIM My pleasure.

TONY Before we continue the discussion about the hospital and start taking calls, let's just talk about Henby's traffic problems. From what Liz was saying, it's terrible there this morning – even worse than usual.

JIM Yes, it's really bad, and it makes me angry and frustrated. My party has been trying to bring in changes for years, but we don't control the council, and the people who do don't like change.

TONY What sorts of change?

JIM Well, for a start, something should be done about the Y-junction where Frimton Road joins London Road just before the bridge into town.

TONY I'm sure you're right. Liz, as our traffic news reporter, what do you think?

LIZ Well, that Y-junction … I think a big roundabout should be built there to ease the traffic problems.

JIM But roundabouts cost a lot and they take up a lot of space. We'd have to knock down some buildings around the junction. So I believe that some traffic lights ought to be put there.

TONY Sounds sensible, but is it enough? Personally, I've always thought that another bridge over the river needs to be built.

JIM Great idea, but it would take a lot of time and money, and there would be environmental problems too.

TONY What other ideas have you got?

JIM Well, Bear Street is a real problem. Half of it is very narrow, with enough room for just one lane, so a lot of us on the Council say that it needs to be pedestrianized.

LIZ Good idea! And that means the traffic lights at the junction with River Street could be removed.

TONY Great. That would let traffic move much faster along the High Street. And with the pedestrian precinct, the heart of the town would be given back to people to walk around freely.

JIM Yes, and we believe that the roads in the centre of town could be turned into a one-way system.

LIZ Yes, that would be much better. Can you explain?

JIM Yes, sure. The idea is that from the Marlow Road/Park Street roundabout the traffic goes along River Street, then into Cranley Street and up to the Oxpen Road roundabout and turns left along High Street. Most commuters driving to the station come across the London Road bridge and driving in that direction gives the fastest possible access to the station,

which is a little way down the Oxpen Road, as you know. And one more thing: we think that the bus station ought to be moved next to the railway station.

TONY Yes, it would become easier for people to travel to and from Henby by train and then change to the buses for local transport – out to Frimton, for example. It should mean fewer people coming to Henby by car – and that could only be a good thing!

Unit 6 ▪ Exercise 3

page 80

This is a recorded message. Thank you for calling Hollywood World.

We are open every day of the year except Christmas Day.

Our opening hours are 9 am to 10 pm from the first of April to the thirty-first of October, and from 10 am to 6 pm during the winter months: November to March.

Our admission charges are $15 for adults and $8 for children aged 4 to 14. There is no charge for children under 4. We have special rates for senior citizens and disabled people. Please ask for details at the information desk at the Hollywood Parkway entrance.

We also have generous group rates for parties of 12 people or more, and special rates for school groups. Please call Laura Snow on two-one-three six-nine-two eight-six-three-three Monday to Friday between 9 am and 4 pm for details.

You can borrow strollers and wheelchairs at the main entrance free of charge for a deposit of $5. Please understand that no dogs are allowed in the park. However, free kennels are available at the Oscar Avenue parking lot entrance.

Unit 7 ▪ Exercise 3

page 90

Part 1

PRESENTER Good morning, and welcome to this week's edition of Worldwide Watchdog, the programme which looks at global issues that affect ordinary people – here and all around the world.

Today, Worldwide Watchdog's country focus is Mexico. More exactly, we want to look at one of the many manufacturing operations that have grown up on the Mexican border with the USA. They are there to use cheap local labour and to trade freely into Mexico's rich northern neighbour under the free trade conditions of NAFTA. And of course, most of these organizations are owned by American companies or have other close links. Recently, there have been growing signs that local people are unhappy with their poor pay and conditions, and to find out more today we are going to focus on one company, Clarostate. They produce electrical switches and sensors. Our reporter Matt Hunter went to talk to some of the people involved in the struggle there between the company and its workforce over the issue of profits versus pay and conditions for the workers.

Part 2 The Interviews

MATT HUNTER Hello, I'm Matt Hunter, and first I have with me a union organizer, Signora Maria-Rosa Fuentes. Signora Fuentes, your new union is planning a strike against the company – the first that there has ever been. Perhaps you could explain the situation to our listeners.

SIGNORA FUENTES Yes, it's quite simple, really. For a long time, the company has been forcing absolutely terrible conditions on us. We can't accept this. A strike is the only answer.

MATT HUNTER Don't you think it'll be very bad for you if you fail?

SIGNORA FUENTES Yes, it'll be very bad for us – as it was for people who tried before. They lost their jobs, and then they were blacklisted by other companies and couldn't get new work. But, hey, I don't want to talk about failing. I want to talk about succeeding! And this time we have a lot of members, and a lot of supporters in other companies around here.

MATT HUNTER Fine. So tell me, what are you demanding from the company?

SIGNORA FUENTES Three things. First, we must have better wages. We work very long days and yet we only get a small part of what American workers get – just five kilometres over there to the north. We have families to feed too!

MATT HUNTER And secondly?

SIGNORA FUENTES Secondly, we need safe working conditions. Our skin stings all the time from the dangerous chemicals in the factory. We'd like all the companies here to clean up the whole environment, but we'll start just with the factory environment.

MATT HUNTER So ... safe working conditions. What else?

SIGNORA FUENTES Job protection. Up to now, when orders are down, the company has fired people without discussion and without redundancy pay. That's totally unacceptable, and it has got to stop. We must have proper job protection.

MATT HUNTER Thank you Signora Fuentes.

MATT HUNTER Now let's talk to Esteban Navarro, Chief Executive Officer. Signor Navarro, what's your point of view on all of this?

SIGNOR NAVARRO I'm a reasonable man, but we must all live in the real world, and everyone else must be reasonable too. Of course, I want the best for my workers, but I can't accept the recent demands.

MATT HUNTER But don't you think that their demands are fair?

SIGNOR NAVARRO No. You see, what you've got to realize is that the world doesn't owe us a living. That means several things. First, we've got to produce high-quality products.

MATT HUNTER Mm ... high-quality products. Shouldn't that mean high-quality pay and conditions, too?

SIGNOR NAVARRO It means fair pay and conditions for this part of the world. Remember, to keep the business here, we have to have very competitive labour costs.

MATT HUNTER So, in other words, you want low labour costs.

SIGNOR NAVARRO Yes, it's essential in order to make sure our American owners are satisfied with their investment here. If our costs start rising, the owners will soon start looking for a cheaper part of the world and move production there.

MATT HUNTER So you need to keep the American owners happy.

SIGNOR NAVARRO Yes, and in the end I'm sure we will all agree on a fair deal.

MATT HUNTER Finally, I have with me Doctor Antonio Aznar, Minister of Finance and Credit. Dr Aznar, I think you know all about the problems at Clarostate. What's the government's view of it all?

DR AZNAR Well, I don't want to comment on a particular case. That's for the company and its workforce to sort out.

MATT HUNTER But what's the government's general policy on foreign investment in industry here in Mexico?

DR AZNAR The first thing to say is that we must do everything possible to attract foreign investors to this country.

MATT HUNTER So you want foreign investment.

DR AZNAR Yes, it's essential for the long-term development of our economy for us to become a fully-developed economy like our powerful neighbour to the north.

MATT HUNTER So you're aiming at a developed economy.

DR AZNAR Of course. This will be for the good of all our people.

MATT HUNTER But what about the good of your people now? Shouldn't you do more to protect them from big business? There are millions of workers out there who are living very hard lives!

DR AZNAR Their lives are not as hard as their parents' and grandparents' were. We must be patient. And at Clarostate, everybody must work towards a compromise. We must all try to find something fair for both sides. If we want to keep the international investment, we must have industrial peace in this country.

MATT HUNTER So ... industrial peace, then.

Unit 8 ▪ Exercise 3

page 98

This may be surprising to American listeners, but Germany doesn't have too *much* waste, but far too *little*. Now, the state of North Rhine Westphalia is importing waste from Italy by train to keep its incinerators in business. As crazy as this may sound to American ears, German statistics show an amazing decrease in all types of waste. During the 1990s, total German waste production fell by over 16%, while America's grew by nearly 27%. Household garbage, which stood at 43.3 million tons in 1990, has fallen by a massive 56%. Since the late 1980s, endless advertising campaigns have asked Germans to sort and recycle their garbage. And they have done just that. A whole new industry has grown up to convert waste into plastics and fertilizers, for example. High-temperature incinerators have been built at huge cost to burn waste that cannot be recycled safely and to use the heat to generate electricity. The result? A big boom in waste.

The shortage of this new cheap raw material has led to some pretty crazy situations – for example, importing waste from Italy is just one. In 1996, the city of Düsseldorf told Stora, a local paper-maker, to stop selling its waste to a Belgian cement factory for $162 a ton – instead they should send it to the city's brand-new incinerator at a cost of $324 a ton.

Unit 8 ▪ Exercise 7

page 103

Here is an important announcement for passengers flying on British Airways flight BA 763 to Singapore due to take off at 10.25. Owing to a technical problem the flight will be delayed for at least two and a half hours. This flight will now take off at 13.15.

Passengers planning to continue their journey from Singapore to Brisbane or Sydney on Qantas connecting flight QU 894 will now land too late for this flight. Will these passengers please go to the Qantas information desk in Terminal 3 for details of alternative flights.

Arrangements have been made for passengers flying from Singapore to Bangkok, Hong Kong and Tokyo to transfer to Japan Airlines flight JAL 443 in Singapore. Would these passengers please go to the British Airways information desk in the main entrance hall in Terminal 2 to collect their revised travel documents.

Refreshments will be served in the business class lounge in Terminal 3 from 11 o'clock. We are sorry that this service is not available to tourist class passengers.

Unit 9 ▪ Exercise 3

page 107

That Monday was the worst day of my life. My boyfriend Damian broke up with me after eight months together. He treated me really badly. I was very upset. Angry too. Anyway, I told Lisa, a girl in my Math class, and she suggested we forget about the rest of school and go on down to the mall.

At first we just walked round. Then I bought a T-shirt on special offer. After that, when we stopped and looked at more T-shirts, Lisa started taking things and dropping them into my bag – a couple of shirts and a pair of earrings, too. I knew it was bad, but I just didn't care. I was so unhappy.

I started to get a bit worried then, but Lisa said, 'Come on, it's easy,' and she dropped another T-shirt in the bag. And I thought, 'Well, why not?' and I did the same. I knew it wasn't right but it was exciting at the same time.

Then we started walking away, talking and laughing on our way out to my car in the parking lot. But I was thinking too. I was thinking, 'How am I going to explain all this shopping to Mom?'

Then it happened. A lady from the store came up to me and said, 'I'd like to see what you've got in that bag.' There was a security guard with her. A minute later, I was in handcuffs, and the two of them were leading me back into the mall. I looked back. Lisa was still standing there. She'd said nothing, done nothing. Now she turned away to leave me and go. I knew I'd never, ever speak to her again.

In the security office, they took photos of everything in the bag. They took my purse and went through everything in that, too. They said they were going to prosecute me and I'd be sent to prison.

Later a cop came and started questioning me, and I cried the whole way through. I was so worried and frightened. They said they'd call my parents. What was I going to say to them? What was going to happen to me?

Back home, Dad knew immediately that something was wrong, and I had to tell him everything. He was really shocked. Then Mom got home, and I had to go through it all again. They discussed it for hours while I just lay on my bed crying and thinking how stupid and wrong I'd been.

In the end, they took away the keys to my car for a month. Now I have to go to school by bus.

The store said they'd prosecute me and take me to court, but in the end they didn't. They just wanted a $100 fine, which I paid. And I had to see a counselor with some other kids who'd been caught shoplifting, too. Some of them were laughing about stealing and the counselor even laughed with them, and I found myself saying, 'What's funny about this?'

I'm trying hard to win back my parents' trust again, but I don't know when things will ever be the same as they used to be between us. And I can never forget about what happened either. I just wish that day could be taken out of my life. But it never can.

Unit 10 ■ Exercise 3

page 115

MARK   There's a woman at work who's always talking nonsense about a 'glass ceiling' that's stopping her getting a top job.

ANN   Well, I don't think that's nonsense. There really is a glass ceiling like that, isn't there?

MARK   Oh, come on! Only women talk about a 'glass ceiling', don't they? They just want to explain their own lack of success.

ANN   Why are there so few women in top jobs then? You tell me, Mark.

MARK   Look, talented people always get to the top, right? What about Margaret Thatcher and Hillary Clinton, for example?

ANN   Well, that's my whole point. They're famous because they are so rare. And it can't be because of lack of talent, Mark. Women do better at university than men do. I think men are simply afraid of losing their privileges.

MARK   Oh, come off it, will you? Companies who *do* try to hire women for top jobs get hardly any applicants. Most women aren't interested. They want more from life than just work. You know, making a nest, having children.

ANN   Really! Men always say that because they don't want to care for children themselves. That's why some political parties and even firms have introduced quotas to help women overcome male prejudice.

MARK   Rubbish. Anyhow, women really are better carers. I'm glad my mum stayed at home and looked after me.

ANN   Look, Mark, of course people are better at some things than others. That's fine. But women think there must be more to life than housework and looking after children, just as most men want more from life than cleaning the car. What's wrong with a partnership, for heaven's sake?

Unit 11 ■ Exercise 6

page 126

Part A

KIRSTY WALKER   Welcome back to Worldwide Watchdog. I'm Kirsty Walker, and we're going back to the issue that we started to discuss here on Worldwide Watchdog before the break: Cloning, Good or Bad? And now it's time to open the phone lines to your calls. This is your chance to say what you think. So do pick up the phone and call us now on 020 930 7463. That's 020 930 7463. We want to hear from you on today's issue: Cloning, Good or Bad?

Part B

KIRSTY WALKER   And ... yes .. we have our first caller. Hello?

DAVID CLARKE   Hello, Kirsty, this is David Clarke from Manchester.

KIRSTY WALKER   Hello, David. What's your view on GM then?

DAVID CLARKE   It's very simple and practical really. I think we really need GM food. Without GM, we soon won't be able to feed ourselves. The world population passed six billion at the end of the last century and by 2070 it'll be around eleven billion. In other words, we have to have GM because of the world population explosion.

KIRSTY WALKER   So ... a very positive view. Thank you, David. And our second caller is ...

ANN MCDONALD   Ann McDonald, from Glasgow. Hi, Kirsty.

KIRSTY WALKER   Hi, Ann. So what's your opinion on this issue?

ANN MCDONALD   Well, I've got to disagree with your previous caller. We really don't need GM. We produce more than enough food to feed the world. The trouble is that we give millions of tons of crops to animals and then we eat the animals. That's very inefficient. We need to eat the corn ourselves. That would be much more efficient. In other words, if we all eat less meat, we can feed more people.

KIRSTY WALKER   So you're against GM, and you feel we can feed the world if more of us become vegetarian.

ANN MCDONALD   That's right.

KIRSTY WALKER   Thanks, Ann. And now to our third caller, who is ...?

MANJIT SINGH   Manjit Singh, from Bradford.

KIRSTY WALKER   Hello, Manjit. What's your view?

MANJIT SINGH   Well, I'm worried that we just don't know enough about what we're doing with these new types of plants. We're mixing up genes in unnatural ways, and how do we know these new plants are safe to eat? I think we should stop GM – at least until we've done far more research.

KIRSTY WALKER   So you're against GM food until you know for sure it's safe.

MANJIT SINGH   That's right, Kirsty.

KIRSTY WALKER   Right, thank you, Manjit – and on to our next caller. Hello?

CARRIE LARSEN   Hi, this is Carrie Larsen, from Wisconsin.

KIRSTY WALKER   Ah, an American view. Welcome to the show.

CARRIE LARSEN   Thanks, Kirsty. Now I'm a farmer out there in the mid-west, and I can tell you we've been using GM for years. Our corn is GM and so's pretty much everything else. It's allowed us to raise production and quality. And GM food isn't hurting anybody. So what I'm saying is this: your previous caller is far too worried. GM is fine. It's fine for farmers, and it's fine for consumers.

KIRSTY WALKER   Well, a very positive view: GM food is here already, and it's good, and it's safe. Thank you, Carrie. And there's just time for one more caller, who is ...?

PETER ROBERTS   Peter Roberts, from London.

KIRSTY WALKER   Welcome to the show, Peter. What's your view?

PETER ROBERTS   I've got to say that I think we're playing with fire when we create new plants using GM technology – plants that can be protected against disease and pests and chemicals. The danger is that these new plants will spread their genes into the wild, breeding with wild plants and producing superweeds. Weeds that we can't kill and we can't stop. They could take over the whole world.

KIRSTY WALKER   So you feel that there's a danger of superweeds that can't be stopped or controlled.

PETER ROBERTS   That's absolutely right. So we should stop GM before we create a Frankenstein's monster of the plant world that can't be stopped.

KIRSTY WALKER   Well, that's all we have time for now. Clearly, there are lots of strong views on both sides, and it's an issue that isn't going to disappear. I expect we'll come back to it in a future programme. And so, on to a report now on ...

Unit 12   Exercise 3

page 131

LISA KAISER   Mr Bond, at the moment almost every country in the EU has its own plug. But when the EU tried to get agreement on a standard European plug in 1990, it was a flop. They had to give up the idea in 1996 because several countries refused to give up 'their special plug'. Is that really the best the EU can do?

PETER BOND   Well, I'd welcome a standard plug. I'd certainly be willing to give up the British design. It really is out of date.

LISA KAISER   What went wrong then?

PETER BOND   Well, to begin with, it is simply not true that there is no standard European plug. Unfortunately, you cannot use this 'Euro-plug' in the UK because of our three-pin sockets, but it is standard almost everywhere else. It's used for small appliances like radios and hairdryers.

LISA KAISER   Oh, yes. That's a flat two-pin plastic plug that is already joined to the end of the power cable at the factory, isn't it?

PETER BOND   Exactly. The problem was to find a plug for big appliances like washing-machines. Of course, exporters of these appliances wanted a standard plug as well because fitting different plugs means higher production costs.

LISA KAISER   Sure, but such costs are always just passed on to the consumer anyway, aren't they?

PETER BOND   Well, yes, true.

LISA KAISER   Mmm. But if it's possible to have a standard plug for small appliances, what's the problem with bigger ones?

PETER BOND   Well, heavier plugs are much more complicated than lighter ones and of course cost more. And there's another problem – the cost of conversion. You know these costs in Germany alone would be about fifteen thousand million euros. In the whole of the EU it would be eight times that.

LISA KAISER   Good heavens. So much? Those really are huge numbers.

PETER BOND   True, and you haven't finished yet. Conversion would take at least ten years, during which time consumers would have to use expensive adapters. In addition, conversion would create over 600,000 tons of non-recyclable plastic and metal, which would also cost a huge amount to dispose of.

LISA KAISER   Yes, well, I see what you mean. So travellers in the EU will have to go on filling their suitcases with adapters, is that right?

PETER BOND   Not unless they're going to or coming from the UK, and even then they only need one. Or do you take a washing-machine on holiday with you?!

Grundwortschatz

Diese Liste enthält ca. 1.050 Grundwörter, die in *New Focus on Success* als bekannt vorausgesetzt werden. Nicht aufgeführt, jedoch vorausgesetzt sind Strukturwörter und einige sehr elementare Wörter, wie einfache Präpositionen, Pronomen, Farben, Zahlen, Tagen, Jahreszeiten und genaue Entsprechungen, wie z.B. *hotel, restaurant*.

AE = amerikanisches Englisch
BE = britisches Englisch

A

a bit of ein wenig, etwas
able fähig, in der Lage
about über, etwa, um
abroad im/ins Ausland
accident Zufall, Unfall
a couple of ein paar
across (hin)über, (quer) durch
address Adresse
adult Erwachsene/r
advantage Vorteil
to afford sich leisten (können)
afraid of ängstlich vor
after nach, nachdem
afternoon Nachmittag
again wieder
ago vor
to agree zustimmen, sich einigen
air Luft
airport Flughafen
a little ein wenig, ein bisschen
alive lebend, lebendig
all alle, alles
to allow erlauben, gestatten, zulassen
all right in Ordnung, (schon) gut
almost fast, beinahe
alone allein(e)
along entlang, weiter, vorwärts
a lot viel, sehr
already schon, bereits
also auch, außerdem
always immer
amazing erstaunlich
American amerikanisch; Amerikaner/in
angry böse, zornig, ärgerlich
animal Tier
another noch eine/r/s, ein/e andere/r/s

to answer; answer (be)antworten; Antwort, Lösung
any irgendetwas, irgendwelche
anybody jemand, jeder
anything etwas, alles
anyway jedenfalls
anywhere irgendwo(hin)
to argue (sich) streiten
argument Streit, Argument
around herum, ungefähr
to arrange verabreden, organisieren, vorbereiten
to arrive ankommen
art Kunst
article Artikel, Gegenstand
as wie, als, da
to ask fragen, bitten
assistant Assistent/in
at in, an, bei, auf
at first zuerst, anfangs
at home zu Hause
at least wenigstens, mindestens
at the moment im Augenblick
author Autor/in
automatic automatisch
available erhältlich, lieferbar
away weg, entfernt
awful furchtbar, schrecklich

B

back zurück; Rücken
bad, worse, worst schlecht, schlechter, am schlechtesten
bag Tasche, Tüte, Beutel
band (Musik-)Kapelle, Band
bar Bar, Riegel
bath Bad, Badewanne
battery Batterie
to be sein
beach Strand

beautiful schön
beauty Schönheit
because weil
because of wegen
to become werden
bed Bett
bedroom Schlafzimmer
beef Rindfleisch
beer Bier
before vor(her), bevor
to begin anfangen, beginnen
beginning Anfang, Beginn
behind hinter, hinten
to believe glauben
to belong to (dazu) gehören
between zwischen
big groß, kräftig
bike Fahrrad, Rad
bill Rechnung
birth Geburt
boat Boot, Schiff
body Körper
to book; book buchen, bestellen; Buch
boot Stiefel, Kofferraum
boring langweilig
born geboren
to borrow (sich etw) borgen, leihen
boss Chef/in
both beide
bottle Flasche
bottom Boden
box Kiste, Schachtel, Karton
boy Junge
boyfriend Freund
brave mutig, tapfer
bread Brot
to break (zer)brechen
breakfast Frühstück
bridge Brücke
to bring (mit)bringen, holen
broken kaputt

brother Bruder
to build (auf)bauen
building Gebäude
burger bar Hamburgerlokal
to burn (ver)brennen
bus (Linien-)Bus
business Geschäft(e), Unternehmen
bus stop Bushaltestelle
busy beschäftigt, besetzt
but aber, sondern
to buy kaufen

C

cable Kabel
cake Kuchen
to call; call (an)rufen, nennen; Anruf
camera Kamera
camp Lager
can dürfen, können
car Auto
card Karte
care Sorge, Pflege
to care about sich kümmern um
carpet Teppich
to carry tragen
case Fall, Koffer
cash Bargeld
cassette Kassette
catalogue Katalog
to catch fangen
certainly sicherlich, gewiss, bestimmt
chance Gelegenheit
to change; change (sich) ändern; (Ver-)Änderung
character Charakter
to chat; chat sich unterhalten; Unterhaltung
cheap billig
to check; check (über)prüfen; Überprüfung
cheese Käse

chemical chemisch;
  Chemikalie
chicken Huhn, Hähnchen
child, children Kind,
  Kinder
chips Pommes frites
chocolate Schokolade
to choose (aus)wählen,
  aussuchen
Christmas Weihnachten
church Kirche
cigarette Zigarette
cinema Kino
class (Schul-)Klasse
classmate Klassen-
  kamerad/in
to clean; clean reinigen;
  sauber
clear klar, deutlich
to click; click klicken;
  Klicken
clinic Klinik
close nah(e)
to close schließen
clothes Kleidung, Kleider
clothing Bekleidung
coat Mantel
coffee Kaffee
coffee shop Café, Kaffee-
  haus
cold kalt; Erkältung
college (Berufs-)Fach-
  schule, Fachhochschule
colour Farbe
to come kommen
common verbreitet, normal
to complete; complete ver-
  vollständigen; vollständig
computer program
  Computerprogramm
condition Bedingung
conflict Konflikt
congratulations Glück-
  wünsche
contents Inhalt
to continue fortsetzen,
  weitergehen
to control; control kontrollieren, beherrschen;
  Kontrolle
conversation Unterhaltung
to cook; cook kochen;
  Koch
to copy; copy kopieren;
  Kopie
corner Ecke
to correct; correct berich-
  tigen; richtig
to cost; cost kosten; Kosten
could konnte/n, könnte/n
country Land, Staat

course Kurs
to cover (be)decken
crazy verrückt
credit card Kreditkarte
crime Verbrechen
crisis Krise
crowd Menschenmenge
to cry; cry schreien,
  weinen; Schrei
culture Kultur
cupboard Schrank
customer Kunde, Kundin
to cut; cut schneiden;
  Schnitt

D
daily täglich
danger Gefahr
dangerous gefährlich
data Daten
date Datum, Termin
day Tag
dead tot; Tote/r
dear liebe/r
to decide (sich) entscheiden
decision Entscheidung
deep tief
to describe beschreiben
description Beschreibung
desk (Schreib-)Tisch
detail Einzelheit
dialogue Dialog
dictionary Wörterbuch
to die sterben
difference Unterschied
different verschieden
difficult schwer, schwierig
dinner (Abend-)Essen
direct gerade, unmittelbar
dirt Schmutz
dirty schmutzig
disappear verschwinden
disk Diskette
distance Entfernung
do tun, machen
document Dokument
dog Hund
door Tür
double doppelt
double room Doppel-
  zimmer
to doubt; doubt zweifeln;
  Zweifel
to dream; dream träumen;
  Traum
to dress; dress (sich)
  anziehen; Kleid
to drink; drink trinken;
  Getränk
to drive fahren

driver Fahrer/in
drugs Drogen
to dry trocknen

E
each jede/r/s
ear Ohr
early früh
to earn verdienen
earth Erde
east Osten
easy einfach, leicht
to eat essen
education Erziehung,
  Bildung
eg z.B.
egg Ei
electric elektrisch
electricity Elektrizität
else andere/r/s
empty leer
end Ende
English englisch
to enjoy genießen
enough genug
to enter eingeben, betreten
entrance Eingang
environment Umwelt
European europäisch;
  Europäer/in
even sogar
evening Abend
ever je(mals)
every jede/r/s
everybody jede/r, jeder-
  mann
everyone jede/r/s, alle
everything alles
everywhere überall
exactly genau
example Beispiel
excellent ausgezeichnet
except außer
except for abgesehen von
exchange student
  Austauschstudent/in
exciting aufregend
excuse me Entschuldigung
exercise Übung
expensive teuer
to experience; experience
  erfahren; Erfahrung
expert sachkundig; Fach-
  mann/frau
to explain erklären
to express ausdrücken
eye Auge

F
face Gesicht
to fall (hin)fallen

false falsch
family Familie
famous berühmt
fantastic fantastisch
far weit (entfernt)
farm Bauernhof
farmer Bauer, Bäuerin
fashion Mode
fast schnell
fat fett; Fett
father Vater
favourite liebste/r/s
to feed füttern
to feel (sich) fühlen
feeling Gefühl
female weiblich
few wenige
field Feld, Bereich
to fight; fight kämpfen;
  Kampf
to fill füllen
final endgültig
to find finden, suchen
to find out herausfinden
fine gut, fein; Geldstrafe
finger Finger
to finish beenden,
  aufhören
fire Feuer
firm fest; Firma
first erste/r/s; zuerst
to fish; fish angeln; Fisch
to fix befestigen
flat flach; Wohnung
flexible flexibel
floor Etage; (Fuß-)Boden
to fly fliegen
to follow folgen
food Essen, Lebensmittel
football Fußball
to forbid verbieten
foreign ausländisch,
  fremd
forever (für) immer
for example zum Beispiel
to forget vergessen
to form; form bilden,
  formen; Form, Formular
for sale zu verkaufen
free frei, gratis
friend Freund/in
friendly freundlich
frightened of verängstigt
  über
front Vorderseite
fruit Obst, Frucht
full voll
fun Spaß
funny komisch
furniture Möbel(stücke)
future zunkünftig; Zukunft

G

game Spiel, Partie
garden Garten
gardener Gärtner/in
German deutsch
to get holen, bekommen, werden
to get home heimkommen
to get to know kennen lernen
girl Mädchen
girlfriend Freundin
to give geben
to give up aufgeben
glass Glas
glasses Brille
to go gehen
God Gott
gold Gold
good, better, best gut, besser, am besten
good-looking gut aussehend
Good luck Viel Glück
grandchildren Enkel
grandfather Großvater
grandmother Großmutter
grandparents Großeltern
great groß(artig)
to greet (be)grüßen
ground gemahlen; Boden, Erde
group Gruppe
grow wachsen
grow up aufwachsen
guess (er)raten
guest Gast
gun (Schuss-)Waffe

H

habit Gewohnheit
half halb; Hälfte
hall Flur, Halle
hand Hand
to happen passieren, geschehen
happy glücklich
hard schwer, hart
to hate hassen
head Kopf
health Gesundheit
healthy gesund
to hear hören
heart Herz
heat Hitze, Wärme
heavy schwer
to help; help helfen; Hilfe
helpful hilfreich, nützlich
here hier
to hide verstecken, verbergen
high hoch

history Geschichte
to hit schlagen
hockey Hockey
to hold halten
hole Loch
holiday Ferien, Urlaub
home Heim, Haus
home town Heimatort
homework, do ~ Hausaufgaben machen
honest ehrlich
to hope; hope hoffen; Hoffnung
horrible schrecklich
horror Entsetzen
horse Pferd
hospital Krankenhaus
hot heiß
hotel room Hotelzimmer
hour Stunde
house Haus
housewife Hausfrau
how wie
however jedoch, aber
human menschlich; Mensch
hunger Hunger
hungry hungrig
to hurry (up) sich beeilen
to hurt (sich) wehtun
husband (Ehe-)Mann

I

idea Idee
if wenn, ob
to ignore ignorieren
ill krank
illness Krankheit
to imagine sich vorstellen
important wichtig
impossible unmöglich
to improve verbessern
in case falls
incorrect falsch
indoor Hallen-
to inform informieren
information Auskunft, Information(en)
in front of vor
in order to um zu
in private privat
insect Insekt
inside innerhalb
instruction Anweisung
intelligent intelligent
to interest; interest interessieren; Interesse
interesting interessant
international international
to introduce vorstellen, einführen
to invite einladen

J

jacket Jacke
job Arbeit, Arbeitsplatz
to joke; joke Witze machen; Witz
joy Freude
juice Saft
just nur, gerade, genau

K

to keep (be)halten
key Schlüssel
to kick treten
to kill töten
kilo Kilo
kilometre Kilometer
kind nett, großzügig
kitchen Küche
knee Knie
knife Messer
to know kennen, wissen

L

lady Dame
to land; land landen; Land
language Sprache
large groß
last letzte/r/s
last night gestern Abend
late spät
later später
to laugh lachen
lazy faul
lead führen
leader Führer/in
leaf Blatt
to learn lernen
leave (ver)lassen
leg Bein
less weniger
to let erlauben, (zu)lassen
letter Buchstabe, Brief
level eben; Niveau
to lie liegen, lügen
life Leben
lifestyle Lebensstil
to lift heben
light hell, leicht
to like mögen, gern haben
limit Grenze, Frist
line Linie, Reihe
to list; list auflisten; Liste
to listen hören
to listen to zuhören
little klein, wenig
litre Liter
to live wohnen, leben
local hiesig
to lock abschließen
long lang
to look; look schauen, blicken; Blick

to look after aufpassen auf, sorgen für
to look at ansehen
to look for suchen nach
lorry Lastwagen
to lose verlieren
loser Verlierer/in
lost verloren
lots viel
lots of viel(e)
loud laut
lounge Warteraum
to love; love lieben; Liebe
luxury Luxus

M

machine Maschine, Gerät
mad verrückt
madam gnädige Frau
magazine Zeitschrift
mail Post
main Haupt-
main road Hauptstraße
majority Mehrheit
to make machen
to make sure sicherstellen
male männlich
man, men Mann, Männer
many viele
map Stadtplan, Landkarte
market Markt
married verheiratet
may dürfen, können
maybe vielleicht
meal Mahlzeit
to mean bedeuten, meinen
meaning Bedeutung, Sinn
meat Fleisch
media Medien
to meet treffen, kennen lernen
meeting Versammlung, Besprechung, Treffen
member Mitglied
menu Speisekarte
message Nachricht
method Methode
metre Meter
middle Mitte
milk Milch
millionaire Millionär/in
to mind etw dagegen haben
mineral water Mineralwasser
minimum Minimum
minister Minister/in
minute Minute
to miss verpassen, vermissen
mistake Fehler
to mix mischen

mixed gemischt
mobile phone Handy
model Modell
modern modern
mom (AE) Mama
money Geld
month Monat
more mehr
morning Morgen
most am meisten, die meisten
mother Mutter
motorbike Motorrad
mountain (größerer) Berg
to move (sich) bewegen, umziehen
movie (Spiel-)Film
Mr Herr
much viel
mum, mummy (BE) Mama
to murder; murder ermorden; Mord
museum Museum
music Musik
must müssen

N

to name nennen; Name
national national, landesweit
nationality Staatsangehörigkeit
natural natürlich
nature Natur
near nahe
nearly beinahe, fast
necessary nötig, notwendig
to need brauchen; Bedarf
negative negativ
neighbour Nachbar/in
neighbourhood Nachbarschaft
neither ... nor weder ... noch
net netto
never nie(mals)
new neu
news Neuigkeit(en), Nachricht(en)
newspaper Zeitung
next nächste/r/s, danach
nice schön, nett
night Nacht
nobody niemand
noise Lärm
normal gewöhnlich, üblich
north Norden, Nord-
note; to note beachten, notieren; Notiz
nothing nichts

to notice; notice bemerken; Bekanntmachung
now nun, jetzt
nowadays heutzutage
nowhere nirgends
number Nummer

O

of course natürlich, selbstverständlich
to offer; offer anbieten; Angebot
office Büro
often oft, häufig
oil Öl
old alt
old-fashioned altmodisch
once einmal
only nur; einzig
to open; open (sich) öffnen; offen, auf
opinion Meinung
opposite gegenüber (von); Gegenteil
or oder
to organize organisieren
other andere/r/s
outdoor im Freien
outside außerhalb, draußen
over über; zu Ende, vorbei
over there da drüben
to own; own besitzen; eigene/r/s

P

packet Packung
page Seite
painful schmerzhaft
pair Paar
pants (BE) Unterhosen
pants (AE) Hose(n)
paper Papier, Zeitung
parents Eltern
parliament Parlament
part Teil, Rolle
party Partei, Party
to pass bestehen, vorbeigehen (an)
passenger Passagier/in
passport Reisepass
past Vergangenheit
patient Patient/in
to pay; pay (be)zahlen; Bezahlung
PC PC, Personalcomputer
pea Erbse
pencil Bleistift
perfect perfekt, ideal
perhaps vielleicht

period Zeitabschnitt
person, people Mensch(en), Leute
to phone; phone anrufen; Telefon
phone call Anruf
physical körperlich
physics Physik
to pick auswählen
to pick up aufheben, aufnehmen
picture Bild, Gemälde
piece Stück
pity Mitleid
place Stelle, Platz, Ort
to plan; plan planen; Plan, Konzept
plane Flugzeug
plant Werk; Pflanze
plastic plastisch; Plastik, Kunststoff
plate Teller
to play; play spielen; Stück
to please; please gefallen, zufrieden stellen; bitte
pleased erfreut, zufrieden
pm nachmittags
pocket Tasche
point Punkt, Spitze
police Polizei
police station Polizeiwache
polite höflich
political politisch
politician Politiker/in
politics Politik
poor arm, schlecht
popular beliebt
population Bevölkerung
pork Schweinefleisch
positive positiv
possible möglich
post Post
potato Kartoffel
power Kraft, Macht
to prefer vorziehen
pregnant schwanger
to prepare (sich) vorbereiten, zubereiten
present gegenwärtig; Geschenk
pretty hübsch
price (Kauf-)Preis
to print drucken
printer Drucker/in
private privat, persönlich
prize Preis (als Gewinn)
pro (da)für
probably wahrscheinlich
problem Problem
to produce produzieren
product Produkt, Erzeugnis

programme Programm
project Projekt
to promise; promise versprechen; Versprechen
to protect (be)schützen
protest Protest
to prove beweisen
pub Kneipe
public öffentlich; Öffentlichkeit
public transport öffentlicher Nahverkehr
to pull ziehen
pupil Schüler/in
to push drängen, schieben
to put setzen, stellen, legen
pyjamas Schlafanzug

Q

quick(ly) schnell
question Frage
quiet ruhig
quite ziemlich

R

race Rasse, Rennen
racist rassistisch; Rassist
railway (Eisen-)Bahn
to rain; rain regnen; Regen
to reach erreichen
reaction Reaktion
to read lesen
ready fertig, bereit
real wirklich
to realize merken
really wirklich, tatsächlich
reason Vernunft, Grund
record Aufzeichnung, Rekord
to recover sich erholen
to recycle wieder verwerten
regular regelmäßig
to relax (sich) entspannen
religion Religion
to remember sich erinnern
to repair; repair reparieren; Reparatur
to repeat wiederholen
to reply; reply antworten; Antwort
to report; report berichten; Bericht
reporter Reporter/in
to reserve reservieren
responsible verantwortlich
to rest; rest sich ausruhen; Pause; Rest
result Ergebnis
rice Reis
rich reich

to ride, ride fahren; Fahrt
right rechts, richtig; Recht
right, to be ~ Recht haben
to ring anrufen, klingeln
to rise (an)steigen
risk Risiko
river Fluss
road (Land-)Straße
roof Dach
room Zimmer, Raum, Platz
rubbish Abfall, Müll
to rule; rule herrschen;
  Vorschrift, Regel
run laufen, rennen
rush eilen

S
sad traurig
safe sicher
salad Salat
sale (Schluss-)Verkauf
salt Salz
same der-, die-, dasselbe
sandwich belegtes Brot
to save sparen, sichern
to say sagen
scene Szene
school Schule
science Wissenschaft
scientist Wissenschaftler/in
scissors Schere
score Punkt(estand)
screen Bildschirm
sea Meer, (die) See
seat (Sitz-)Platz
to see sehen
to seem (er)scheinen
to sell verkaufen
to send senden
sentence Satz
serious ernst
to set setzen, stellen
sex Geschlecht
ship Schiff
shirt Hemd
shock Schock
to shoot (er)schießen
to shop; shop einkaufen;
  Laden, Geschäft
shorts Shorts
should sollte/n
to shout; shout rufen,
  schreien; Ruf, Schrei
to show zeigen
shower Dusche
sick krank, übel
side Seite
to sign; sign unterschrei-
  ben; Zeichen, Schild
silent still, stumm
silly dumm

simple einfach
simply einfach
single ledig, alleinstehend,
  einzeln
sister Schwester
to sit sitzen
to sit down sich setzen
situation Lage
size Größe
skin Haut
sky Himmel
to sleep; sleep schlafen;
  Schlaf
small klein
smart schick, flott
to smell riechen
to smile; smile lächeln;
  Lächeln
to smoke; smoke rauchen;
  Rauch
to snow; snow schneien;
  Schnee
so deshalb, so
soap Seife
social sozial, gesellschaft-
  lich
society Gesellschaft
some einige, etwas
somebody jemand
something etwas
sometimes manchmal
somewhere irgendwo
son Sohn
song Lied
soon bald
sorry traurig
to sound; sound klingen;
  Geräusch
south Süden, Süd-
space Raum, Platz
spare time Freizeit
to speak sprechen
special besondere/r/s
to spend ausgeben, ver-
  bringen
sport Sport(art)
spring Frühling
stairs Treppe
stamp Briefmarke
to stand stehen
to start; start starten,
  beginnen; Start, Anfang
state Zustand; Staat
station Bahnhof
to stay; stay bleiben;
  Aufenthalt
to steal stehlen
step Schritt, Stufe
stereotype Stereotyp
still (immer) noch
stone Stein

to stop; stop anhalten; Halt
to store; store (AE) spei-
  chern, lagern; Laden,
  Geschäft
storm Gewitter, Sturm
story Erzählung,
  Geschichte
strange seltsam
stranger Fremde/r
street Straße
strict streng
strong stark
studies Studium
to study; study lernen,
  studieren; Studie
stupid dumm
style Stil
subject (Schul-)Fach
success Erfolg
successful erfolgreich
such solche/r/s
such as wie zum Beispiel
suddenly plötzlich
sugar Zucker
suitcase Koffer
summary Zusammen-
  fassung
summer Sommer
sun Sonne
supermarket Supermarkt
to suppose annehmen, ver-
  muten
sure sicher
surprise Überraschung
sweet süß; Bonbon
to swim schwimmen
swimming pool Schwimm-
  bad
to switch off ausschalten
system System

T
table Tisch
to take nehmen, dauern
to take part in teilnehmen
  an
to take photos of fotogra-
  fieren
to take place stattfinden
to take the bus mit dem
  Bus fahren
to talk; talk sprechen,
  reden; Rede, Referat
tall groß, lang
to taste; taste schmecken,
  kosten; Geschmack
tattoo Tätowierung
to teach unterrichten,
  lehren
teacher Lehrer/in
technical technisch

teenage Teenager-
to tell sagen, erzählen
temperature Temperatur
terrible schrecklich,
  fürchterlich
than als
thanks danke; Dank
that dass; das; jene/r/s
their ihr/e
then dann
there da, dort
these diese
thin dünn
thing Sache, Ding
to think denken
this dies, diese/r/s
those jene
through durch
tidy ordentlich
time Zeit
tiny winzig, klein
tired müde
title Titel
today heute
together zusammen
toilet Toilette
tomorrow morgen
too auch
tooth (pl. teeth) Zahn
toothpaste Zahnpasta
top oben; obere; beste/r/s;
  Spitze
topic Thema
total (ins)gesamt; Gesamt-
  betrag
to touch; touch berühren;
  Berührung
tough zäh, robust
tourist Tourist/in
town Stadt
town centre Stadtzentrum
traffic (Straßen-)Verkehr
traffic lights (Verkehrs-)
  Ampel
to train; train ausbilden,
  trainieren; Zug
trainers Turnschuhe
train station Bahnhof
translate übersetzen
tree Baum
trip Ausflug, Reise
trousers (BE) Hose(n)
truck (AE) Last(kraft)wagen
true richtig, wahr
truth Wahrheit
to try versuchen
to turn drehen, abbiegen
to turn on ein-, anschalten
TV programme Fernseh-
  sendung
twin Zwilling

U

uncomfortable unbequem
underground U-Bahn, unterirdisch
to understand verstehen
unfair ungerecht
unfortunately leider
unhappy unglücklich
uniform Uniform
university Universität
unless wenn nicht, es sei denn
until bis
upstairs (nach) oben
to use; use benutzen, verwenden; Gebrauch
useful nützlich
usual gewöhnlich
usually meistens

V

vacation (AE) Urlaub, Ferien
vegetable Gemüse
vegetarian vegetarisch; Vegetarier/in
very sehr
view Sicht, Ausblick
village Dorf
visa Visum
to visit; visit besuchen; Besuch
visitor Besucher/in
vitamin Vitamin
voice Stimme

W

to wait warten
to wake up aufwecken
to walk; walk (zu Fuß) gehen; Spaziergang
wall Wand, Mauer
to want wollen
war Krieg
warm warm
to warn warnen
to wash (sich) waschen
to watch; watch beobachten, anschauen; (Armband-)Uhr
water Wasser
way Weg, Art (und Weise)

weak schwach
wealthy reich
week Woche
weekend Wochenende
to welcome willkommen heißen
well gut
well-known sehr bekannt
west Westen, West-
what was, welche/r/s
what else was sonst (noch)
when als, wann
where wo
whether ob
which welche/r/s
while während
whisper flüstern; Geflüster
whole ganz
why warum
wide breit
wife (Ehe-)Frau
will werde(n)
to win gewinnen
window Fenster
wine Wein
winner Gewinner/in

winter Winter
to wish; wish wünschen; Wunsch
with mit
woman, women Frau, Frauen
wonderful wundervoll
word Wort
to work; work funktionieren, arbeiten; Arbeit
worker Arbeiter/in
world Welt
to worry sich Sorgen machen
worth wert
would würde(n)
to write schreiben
wrong falsch

Y

year Jahr
yesterday gestern
yet schon
yoghurt Joghurt
young jung
youth club Jugendklub

Chronologisches Wörterverzeichnis

Dieses Wörterverzeichnis enthält alle Wörter in *New Focus on Success* in der Reihenfolge ihrer Erscheinung. Nicht aufgeführt sind die Wörter aus der Grundwortschatzliste. Die Wörter der *Further Reading*-Seiten werden in den darauf folgenden Units nicht vorausgesetzt.
Wörter, die in den Hörverständnisübungen vorkommen, sind mit einem CD-Symbol gekennzeichnet.
Wörter aus den *Partner pages* sind mit einem Partnersymbol markiert.

REFRESHER COURSE

Unit A ▪ Blue Sky

6

travel agency ['trævl ˌeɪdʒənsi]	Reisebüro
company ['kʌmpəni]	Unternehmen, Firma
to specialize in ['speʃəlaɪz ɪn]	sich spezialisieren auf
exotic [ɪg'zɒtɪk]	exotisch
adventure [əd'ventʃə]	Abenteuer
to backpack ['bækbæk]	als Rucksacktourist reisen
to canoe [kə'nuː]	mit dem Kanu fahren
full-time [ˌfʊl 'taɪm]	Ganztags-
staff [stɑːf]	Angestellte, Personal
to include [ɪn'kluːd]	enthalten, einbeziehen
to manage ['mænɪdʒ]	leiten
employee [ɪm'plɔɪiː]	Angestellte/r
to call at ['kɔːl ət]	vorbeischauen bei
to go well [ˌgəʊ 'wel]	gut gehen
to take up [ˌteɪk 'ʌp]	beanspruchen
at present [ət 'preznt]	zurzeit, derzeit
to advertise ['ædvətaɪz]	inserieren, werben (für)
(web)site [saɪt]	Website
as well [əz 'wel]	auch (noch), ebenfalls
huge [hjuːdʒ]	riesig
amount [ə'maʊnt]	Menge, Ausmaß
seldom ['seldəm]	selten
meanwhile ['miːnwaɪl]	inzwischen
above [ə'bʌv]	über
to take a break [ˌteɪk ə 'breɪk]	eine Pause machen
misunderstanding [ˌmɪsʌndə'stændɪŋ]	Missverständnis
although [ɔːl'ðəʊ]	obwohl
to quarrel ['kwɒrəl]	streiten
unusual [ʌn'juːʒʊəl]	ungewöhnlich
similar ['sɪmələ]	ähnlich
difficulty ['dɪfɪkəlti]	Schwierigkeit
particularly [pə'tɪkjələli]	besonders
IT [aɪ 'tiː]	Informationstechnologie
to install [ɪn'stɔːl]	installieren, einrichten
button ['bʌtn]	Taste, Knopf
to expect [ɪk'spekt]	erwarten
unemployed [ˌʌnɪm'plɔɪd]	arbeitslos, ohne Beschäftigung
specialist ['speʃəlɪst]	Fachmann/frau
to boom [buːm]	boomen

7

well-paid [ˌwel'peɪd]	gut bezahlt

economy [ɪ'kɒnəmi]	Wirtschaft
lively ['laɪvli]	lebendig, lebhaft
to pass by [ˌpɑːs 'baɪ]	vorübergehen
to put into practice [ˌpʊt ɪntə 'præktɪs]	in die Praxis umsetzen
creative [kri'eɪtɪv]	kreativ, schöpferisch
fluent ['fluːənt]	fließend
maybe ['meɪbi]	vielleicht
major ['meɪdʒə]	größer, wichtig
under pressure ['preʃə]	unter Druck
qualification [ˌkwɒlɪfɪ'keɪʃn]	Qualifikation, Fähigkeit
creativity [ˌkriːeɪ'tɪvəti]	Kreativität
currently ['kʌrəntli]	momentan
software engineer [ˌsɒftweə ˌendʒɪ'nɪə]	Softwareentwickler/in
website designer [ˌwebsaɪt dɪ'zaɪnə]	Webdesigner, Internet-programmierer/in
ideally [aɪ'diːəli]	idealerweise
BSc degree [ˌbiː es 'siː dɪ'griː]	(Universitäts-)Abschluss als Bachelor of Science
at least [ət 'liːst]	mindestens
CV [ˌsiː 'viː]	Lebenslauf
plain text [pleɪn 'tekst]	nur Text
attachment [ə'tætʃmənt]	Anlage
initial [ɪ'nɪʃl]	Initiale(n)
file name ['faɪl neɪm]	Name der Datei
statement ['steɪtmənt]	Aussage
budget ['bʌdʒɪt]	preisgünstig
to accept [ək'sept]	akzeptieren
applicant ['æplɪkənt]	Bewerber/in
practical ['præktɪkl]	praktisch

8

order ['ɔːdə]	Reihenfolge
to employ [ɪm'plɔɪ]	beschäftigen
to practise ['præktɪs]	(ein)üben
to qualify ['kwɒlɪfaɪ]	(sich) qualifizieren
to create [kri'eɪt]	bilden, erstellen
to design [dɪ'zaɪn]	entwerfen, konstruieren
ad [æd]	Anzeige
disability [ˌdɪsə'bɪləti]	Behinderung
home worker ['həʊmwɜːkə]	Heimarbeiter/in
application [ˌæplɪ'keɪʃn]	Bewerbung
Ms [mɪz]	Frau/Fräulein
to suit [suːt]	passen, recht sein
wheelchair ['wiːltʃeə]	Rollstuhl
user ['juːzə]	Benutzer/in
obvious ['ɒbviəs]	offensichtlich
to get about [ˌget ə'baʊt]	herumkommen
for this reason [fə ðɪs 'riːzn]	aus diesem Grund

since [sɪns]	seit	
temporary ['temprəri]	vorübergehend, zeitlich befristet	
secure [sɪ'kjuə]	sicher, fest	
With best regards [wɪð ˌbest rɪ'gɑːdz]	Viele Grüße	

9

rarely ['reəli]	selten
hardly ever [ˌhɑːdli 'evə]	fast nie
occasionally [ə'keɪʒənəli]	gelegentlich
generally ['dʒenrəli]	im Allgemeinen
normally ['nɔːməli]	normalerweise
regularly ['regjələli]	regelmäßig
checklist ['tʃek lɪst]	Checkliste
either ['aɪðə]	entweder
to supply [sə'plaɪ]	liefern
final destination [ˌfaɪnl ˌdestɪ'neɪʃn]	Zielort
to provide [prə'vaɪd]	bieten, sorgen für
leaflet ['liːflət]	Broschüre, Prospekt
careful ['keəfl]	sorgfältig
accommodation [əˌkɒmə'deɪʃn]	Unterkunft
baggage ['bægɪdʒ]	Gepäck
insurance [ɪn'ʃuərəns]	Versicherung
to guarantee [ˌgærən'tiː]	garantieren
currency ['kʌrənsi]	Währung
to hire ['haɪə]	einstellen
guide [gaɪd]	Führer/in
instructor [ɪn'strʌktə]	Lehrer/in, Ausbilder/in
equipment [ɪ'kwɪpmənt]	Ausrüstung

10

to underline [ˌʌndə'laɪn]	unterstreichen
bracket ['brækɪt]	Klammer
flight [flaɪt]	Flug
to attract [ə'trækt]	anziehen
to dislike [dɪs'laɪk]	nicht mögen

11

on one's own [ɒn wʌnz 'əun]	allein
to calm down [ˌkɑːm 'daun]	(sich) beruhigen
to discuss [dɪ'skʌs]	besprechen, erörtern
to get on with [ˌget ɒn wɪð]	vorankommen mit
to deal with [ˌdiːl wɪð]	sich befassen mit
instead [ɪn'sted]	stattdessen
several ['sevrəl]	einige, mehrere
luck [lʌk]	Glück
to complain [kəm'pleɪn]	(sich) beschweren
leisure time ['leʒə taɪm]	Freizeit
working week [ˌwɜːkɪŋ 'wiːk]	Arbeitswoche
to make up for [ˌmeɪk ʌp fə]	wettmachen, ausgleichen
during ['djuərɪŋ]	während
far-off ['fɑːrɒf]	weit entfernt, entlegen
to slow down [ˌsləu 'daun]	nachlassen
shortage ['ʃɔːtɪdʒ]	Mangel
economist [ɪ'kɒnəmɪst]	Wirtschaftswissenschaftler/in
government ['gʌvənmənt]	Regierung
citizen ['sɪtɪzn]	(Staats-)Bürger/in
newcomer ['njuːkʌmə]	Neuling

Unit B ▪ Where's my money?

12

wilderness ['wɪldənəs]	Wildnis
disappointment [ˌdɪsə'pɔɪntmənt]	Enttäuschung
complaint [kəm'pleɪnt]	Beschwerde
Ltd ['lɪmɪtɪd]	(Gesellschaft) mit beschränkter Haftung, GmbH
sir [sɜː]	mein Herr
madam ['mædəm]	gnädige Frau
satisfied ['sætɪsfaɪd]	zufrieden
trouble ['trʌbl]	Schwierigkeit, Ärger
pleasant ['pleznt]	angenehm, nett
edge [edʒ]	Rand
in fact [ɪn 'fækt]	tatsächlich
freeway ['friːweɪ]	Autobahn
past [pɑːst]	vorbei (an)
to take off [ˌteɪk 'ɒf]	abheben, starten
comfortable ['kʌmftəbl]	bequem
van [væn]	Transporter
rusty ['rʌsti]	rostig
minibus ['mɪnibʌs]	Kleinbus
to collect [kə'lekt]	abholen
to load [ləud]	(be)laden
civilization [ˌsɪvəlaɪ'zeɪʃn]	Zivilisation
solitude ['sɒlɪtjuːd]	Einsamkeit
crowded ['kraudɪd]	überfüllt
responsibility [rɪˌspɒnsə'bɪləti]	Verantwortung
to advise [əd'vaɪz]	raten
to contact ['kɒntækt]	sich wenden an
refund ['riːfʌnd]	Rückzahlung, (Rück-)Erstattung
to enclose [ɪn'kləuz]	beilegen, beifügen
Yours faithfully [jɔːz 'feɪθfəli]	Mit freundlichen Grüßen, Hochachtungsvoll
encl [ɪŋkl]	Anlage

13

overnight [ˌəuvə'naɪt]	Übernachtungs-
nasty ['nɑːsti]	unangenehm
to react to [ri'ækt tə]	reagieren auf
synonym ['sɪnənɪm]	Synonym
to speed [spiːd]	(zu) schnell fahren
loneliness ['ləunlinəs]	Einsamkeit
to claim [kleɪm]	(als) Schadensersatz fordern
error ['erə]	Fehler, Irrtum

14

recession [rɪ'seʃn]	Rezession, Wirtschaftsflaute
package holiday ['pækɪdʒ hɒlədeɪ]	Pauschalreise
critic ['krɪtɪk]	Kritiker/in
without [wɪ'ðaut]	ohne
to join [dʒɔɪn]	eintreten (in)
volunteer [ˌvɒlən'tɪə]	Freiwillige/r
straight [streɪt]	direkt
themselves [ðəm'selvz]	(sie) selbst
element ['elɪmənt]	Element

noisy ['nɔɪzi]	laut	
agent ['eɪdʒənt]	Vertreter/in	

15

display [dɪ'spleɪ]	Anzeige
solitaire [ˌsɒlɪ'teə]	Patience
resort [rɪ'zɔ:t]	Ferien-, Urlaubsort
to point out [ˌpɔɪnt 'aʊt]	hinweisen auf

16

to apply to [ə'plaɪ tə]	gelten für, zutreffen auf
subjective [səb'dʒektɪv]	subjektiv
immediately [ɪ'mi:dɪətli]	sofort, umgehend

Unit C ▪ A gap year

17

gap year ['gæp jɪə]	ein Jahr Pause
school-leaver [ˌsku:l'li:və]	Schulabgänger/in
nurse [nɜ:s]	Krankenschwester, -pfleger/in
basics ['beɪsɪks]	das Wesentliche
financially [faɪ'nænʃəli]	finanziell
to run out [ˌrʌn 'aʊt]	ausgehen, zu Ende gehen
choice [tʃɔɪs]	Wahl, Auswahl
architecture ['ɑ:kɪtektʃə]	Architektur
on the other hand	andererseits
[ɒn ði 'ʌðə hænd]	

18

standard ['stændəd]	Niveau
comfort ['kʌmfət]	Komfort, Bequemlichkeit
basic ['beɪsɪk]	einfach, schlicht
transport ['trænspɔ:t]	Verkehr(smittel)
policy ['pɒləsi]	(Firmen-)Politik
experienced [ɪk'spɪərɪənst]	erfahren
otherwise ['ʌðəwaɪz]	sonst
to fetch [fetʃ]	holen
role [rəʊl]	Rolle
to serve [sɜ:v]	bedienen
architect ['ɑ:kɪtekt]	Architekt/in
to succeed in [sək'si:d ɪn]	Erfolg haben mit
technical ['teknɪkl]	technisch
muslim ['mʊzlɪm]	moslemisch
emperor ['empərə]	Kaiser
dome [dəʊm]	Kuppel
pure [pjʊə]	rein, pur, echt
marble ['mɑ:bl]	Marmor
to decorate ['dekəreɪt]	schmücken
advanced [əd'vɑ:nst]	fortgeschritten

19

rather than ['rɑ:ðə ðən]	anstelle von, anstatt
individual [ˌɪndɪ'vɪdʒuəl]	einzeln, individuell
furious ['fjʊərɪəs]	wütend
to set up [ˌset 'ʌp]	einrichten
to begin with [tə bɪ'gɪn wɪð]	zunächst, um es voraus-
	zuschicken
personal ['pɜ:sənl]	persönlich
to deliver [dɪ'lɪvə]	abliefern

20

bonus ['bəʊnəs]	Zulage
powerful ['paʊəfl]	leistungsstark
programmer ['prəʊgræmə]	Programmierer/in
definitely ['defɪnətli]	bestimmt
press [pres]	Presse
to retire [rɪ'taɪə]	in den Ruhestand gehen
owner ['əʊnə]	Besitzer/in
salary ['sæləri]	Gehalt, Lohn
reception [rɪ'sepʃn]	Empfang
to launch [lɔ:ntʃ]	starten, einführen
plenty of ['plenti əv]	viele

Unit D ▪ Honesty is best

21

to fry [fraɪ]	(in der Sonne) grillen
specialist ['speʃəlɪst]	Spezialist/in
branch [brɑ:ntʃ]	Filiale, Zweigstelle
nationwide ['neɪʃnwaɪd]	landesweit
award-winning	preisgekrönt
[ə'wɔ:d wɪnɪŋ]	
to select [sɪ'lekt]	auswählen
to trust [trʌst]	vertrauen
passport to paradise	Pass ins Paradies
[ˌpɑ:spɔ:t tə 'pærədaɪs]	
hell [hel]	Hölle
hype [haɪp]	Rummel, Reklame
spokesperson ['spəʊkspɜ:sn]	Sprecher/in
flood [flʌd]	Flut
highly ['haɪli]	äußerst
critical ['krɪtɪkl]	kritisch
disappointed [ˌdɪsə'pɔɪntɪd]	enttäuscht
holidaymaker	Urlauber/in
['hɒlədeɪmeɪkə]	
to mislead [ˌmɪs'li:d]	irreführen
motorway ['məʊtəweɪ]	Autobahn
overcrowded [ˌəʊvə'kraʊdɪd]	überfüllt
destination [ˌdestɪ'neɪʃn]	Reiseziel
to disagree [ˌdɪsə'gri:]	anderer Meinung sein,
	widersprechen
support [sə'pɔ:t]	Unterstützung
completely [kəm'pli:tli]	völlig
in their hands	in ihren Händen
[ɪn ðeə 'hændz]	
in a way [ɪn ə 'weɪ]	in gewisser Weise
producer [prə'dju:sə]	Produzent/in
to treat [tri:t]	behandeln
co-owner ['kəʊ əʊnə]	Mitbesitzer/in
worried ['wʌrid]	besorgt, beunruhigt
publicity [pʌb'lɪsəti]	Publicity, Werbung
to add [æd]	hinzufügen

22

objective [əb'dʒektɪv]	objektiv
dissatisfied [dɪs'sætɪsfaɪd]	unzufrieden
definition [ˌdefɪ'nɪʃn]	Definition
expression [ɪk'spreʃn]	Ausdruck
expectation [ˌekspek'teɪʃn]	Erwartung
to cross [krɒs]	überqueren

border ['bɔːdə] Grenze
journey ['dʒɜːni] Reise, Fahrt
foolish ['fuːlɪʃ] dumm, töricht
exaggeration [ɪɡˌzædʒə'reɪʃn] Übertreibung

23

to beware of [bɪ'weər əv] aufpassen auf, Vorsicht
vor
thief [θiːf] Dieb/in
mainly ['meɪnli] hauptsächlich, vor allem
separate ['seprət] getrennt
security [sɪ'kjʊərəti] Sicherheit
site [saɪt] Ort
to clean out [ˌkliːn 'aʊt] leeren
valuables ['væljuəblz] Wertgegenstände
jewellery ['dʒuːəlri] Schmuck(stücke)
receptionist [rɪ'sepʃənɪst] Empfangsdame, -chef

24

to remain [rɪ'meɪn] bleiben
column ['kɒləm] Spalte
finally ['faɪnəli] zum Schluss
further ['fɜːðə] weitere/r/s

25

reasonable ['riːznəbl] vernünftig
to have to do with zu tun haben mit
[hæv tə 'duː wɪð]
region ['riːdʒən] Gebiet, Gegend
by air [baɪ 'eə] mit dem Flugzeug
nonsense ['nɒnsns] Unsinn
intention [ɪn'tenʃn] Absicht
to avoid [ə'vɔɪd] vermeiden
unfortunate [ʌn'fɔːtʃənət] unglücklich
broadcast ['brɔːdkɑːst] übertragen, senden
consumer [kən'sjuːmə] Verbraucher/in
frank [fræŋk] offen, aufrichtig
dishonest [dɪs'ɒnɪst] unehrlich

Unit E ▪ Let's celebrate!

26

to celebrate ['selɪbreɪt] feiern
journalist ['dʒɜːnəlɪst] Journalist/in
at all [ət 'ɔːl] überhaupt
advice [əd'vaɪs] Ratschlag, (guter) Rat
gate-crasher ['geɪtkræʃə] ungebetener Gast
unofficial [ˌʌnə'fɪʃl] inoffiziell
good heavens [gʊd 'hevnz] ach du meine Güte
videotape ['vɪdiəʊteɪp] Videokassette
glad [glæd] froh
in all [ɪn 'ɔːl] insgesamt, alles in allem
set buffet [set 'bʊfeɪ] kaltes Büfett
variety [və'raɪəti] Auswahl
might [maɪt] könnte
poultry ['pəʊltri] Geflügel
selection [sɪ'lekʃn] Auswahl, Angebot
soft drink [ˌsɒft 'drɪŋk] alkoholfreies Getränk
spirits ['spɪrɪts] Spirituosen

27

likely ['laɪkli] wahrscheinlich
according to [ə'kɔːdɪŋ tə] laut, nach
uninvited [ˌʌnɪn'vaɪtɪd] nicht (ein)geladen
to replace [rɪ'pleɪs] ersetzen, austauschen
to attend [ə'tend] teilnehmen an
commercial [kə'mɜːʃl] Geschäfts-, gewerblich
loaf [ləʊf] Laib
slice [slaɪs] Scheibe
tin [tɪn] Dose
luggage ['lʌɡɪdʒ] Gepäck
hardware ['hɑːdweə] Hardware, Geräte
evidence ['evɪdəns] Beweis(mittel)

28

police officer [pə'liːs ˌɒfɪsə] Polizeibeamter/beamtin
on their way [ɒn ðeə 'weɪ] unterwegs
suitable ['suːtəbl] geeignet, passend
industry ['ɪndəstri] Industrie, Gewerbe
paint [peɪnt] Farbe
petrol ['petrəl] Benzin
robbery ['rɒbəri] Raub
these days [ðiːz 'deɪz] heutzutage
to damage ['dæmɪdʒ] beschädigen
to injure ['ɪndʒə] verletzen
to put on [ˌpʊt 'ɒn] anziehen

29

parking space ['pɑːkɪŋ speɪs] Parkplatz, -lücke
appointment [ə'pɔɪntmənt] Termin, Verabredung
to lend [lend] leihen
fitness centre ['fɪtnəs sentə] Fitnessstudio
weight [weɪt] Gewicht
apartment [ə'pɑːtmənt] Wohnung
to share [ʃeə] (sich) teilen
umbrella [ʌm'brelə] (Regen-)Schirm
management ['mænɪdʒmənt] Verwaltung

30

figure ['fɪɡə] Zahl
competitor [kəm'petɪtə] Konkurrent/in, Wettbewer-
ber/in
invitation [ˌɪnvɪ'teɪʃn] Einladung
recently ['riːsntli] in letzter Zeit, vor kurzem
to fill up [ˌfɪl 'ʌp] füllen, auftanken

31

freedom ['friːdəm] Freiheit
sauce [sɔːs] Soße
white wine [ˌwaɪt 'waɪn] Weißwein
each other [iːtʃ 'ʌðə] einander
relationship [rɪ'leɪʃnʃɪp] Beziehung, Verhältnis
to give sb a ring [ɡɪv ə 'rɪŋ] jdn. anrufen
food shop ['fuːd ʃɒp] Lebensmittelladen
shopping mall ['ʃɒpɪŋ mæl] Einkaufszentrum
understanding Verständnis
[ˌʌndə'stændɪŋ]

Unit 1 ▪ Advertising and us

32

advertisement [əd'vɜ:tɪsmənt]	Reklame, Werbung, Anzeige
sort [sɔ:t]	Art, Sorte, Typ
brochure ['brəʊʃə]	Broschüre, Prospekt
classified ad [ˌklæsɪfaɪd 'æd]	Kleinanzeige
neon sign [ˌni:ɒn 'saɪn]	Neonreklame
sponsorship ['spɒnsəʃɪp]	Sponsorentum
controversial [ˌkɒntrə'vɜ:ʃl]	kontrovers, umstritten
daring ['deərɪŋ]	kühn, wagemutig
erotic [ɪ'rɒtɪk]	erotisch
hard-hitting ['hɑ:dhɪtɪŋ]	zur Sache gehend
sentimental [ˌsentɪ'mentl]	gefühlsmäßig, sentimental
shocking ['ʃɒkɪŋ]	schrecklich, schockierend
to aim to do ['eɪm tə du:]	beabsichtigen zu tun
to persuade [pə'sweɪd]	überzeugen, überreden
to promote [prə'məʊt]	anpreisen

33

to break into ['breɪk ɪntə]	„einsteigen" in
league [li:g]	Liga
fortunately ['fɔ:tʃənətli]	glücklicherweise
summer job ['sʌmə dʒɒb]	(Sommer-)Ferienjob
production [prə'dʌkʃn]	Produktion
to put together [ˌpʊt tə'geðə]	zusammenstellen
deal [di:l]	Geschäft, Abkommen
lucky ['lʌki]	glücklich
career [kə'rɪə]	Karriere, Beruf
to apply for [ə'plaɪ fə]	sich bewerben um
various ['veəriəs]	verschiedene
account manager [ə'kaʊnt ˌmænɪdʒə]	Kundenbetreuer/in
client ['klaɪənt]	Kunde, Kundin
of one's own [əv wʌnz 'əʊn]	eigen
for the first time [fə ðə fɜ:st 'taɪm]	zum ersten Mal
to work on ['wɜ:k ɒn]	arbeiten an
launch [lɔ:ntʃ]	Start(kampagne)
terrifying ['terɪfaɪɪŋ]	erschreckend
so far [ˌsəʊ 'fɑ:]	bis jetzt
general ['dʒenrəl]	allgemein
especially [ɪ'speʃəli]	besonders
to develop [dɪ'veləp]	entwickeln
image ['ɪmɪdʒ]	Image, Bild
campaign [kæm'peɪn]	Kampagne
media planner [ˌmi:diə 'plænə]	Medienplaner
burst [bɜ:st]	„Salve"
magazine [ˌmægə'zi:n]	Zeitschrift, Magazin
actual ['æktʃuəl]	tatsächlich *(adjectiv)*

34

apart from [ə'pɑ:t frəm]	außer, abgesehen von
paragraph ['pærəgrɑ:f]	Absatz, Abschnitt
heading ['hedɪŋ]	Überschrift
progress ['prəʊgres]	Fortschritt/e
to take charge of [teɪk 'tʃɑ:dʒ əv]	übernehmen

search [sɜ:tʃ]	Suche
media planning [ˌmi:diə 'plænɪŋ]	Medienplanung *medium/media*
enjoyable [ɪn'dʒɔɪəbl]	angenehm
at a guess [ət ə 'ges]	schätzungsweise
due to ['dju: tə]	wegen, aufgrund von, dank
to be good at sth [bi 'gʊd ət]	etw. gut können
to match [mætʃ]	zuordnen
agreement [ə'gri:mənt]	Vertrag, Vereinbarung
fortunate ['fɔ:tʃənət]	glücklich (Umstände)
rapid ['ræpɪd] *rappid*	schnell, rasch
to expand [ɪk'spænd]	expandieren
to rewrite [ˌri:'raɪt]	umschreiben

35

form of address [fɔ:m əv ə'dres]	Anrede(form)
to suggest [sə'dʒest]	vorschlagen
first name ['fɜ:st neɪm]	Vorname
to take a seat [teɪk ə 'si:t]	Platz nehmen
to manage to ['mænɪdʒ]	(es) schaffen
informal [ɪn'fɔ:ml]	ungezwungen, informell
formal ['fɔ:ml]	formell, förmlich
junior ['dʒu:niə]	untergeordnet
senior ['si:niə]	vorgesetzt, leitend
nothing like ['nʌθɪŋ laɪk]	nicht zu vergleichen mit
closeness ['kləʊsnəs]	Nähe *(close – somebody lang)*
formula ['fɔ:mjələ]	Formel
one [wʌn]	eins, man
co-founder ['kəʊfaʊndə]	Mitbegründer/in
co-director [ˌkəʊdə'rektə]	Vorstandskollege/kollegin
to stand for ['stænd fə]	stehen für

actually ['æktʃuəli]	eigentlich, tatsächlich *(adverb)*
brand [brænd]	Marke, Typ
whatever [wɒt'evə]	was auch immer
then again [ðən ə'gen]	dann wiederum
special offer [ˌspeʃl 'ɒfə]	Sonderangebot
insert ['ɪnsɜ:t]	Ein-, Beilage
attention [ə'tenʃn]	Aufmerksamkeit
bright [braɪt]	leuchtend, hell
to arouse [ə'raʊz]	wecken
desire [dɪ'zaɪə]	Wunsch
action ['ækʃn]	Aktion, Handlung
to fill in [ˌfɪl 'ɪn]	ausfüllen
to send off [ˌsend 'ɒf]	abschicken *(off – etwas weg)*
freepost ['fri:pəʊst]	Porto zahlt Empfänger
pre-paid [ˌpri:'peɪd]	vorher bezahlt
to move on [ˌmu:v 'ɒn]	weitergehen
recent ['ri:snt]	letzte, jüngst
feature ['fi:tʃə]	Merkmal, Kennzeichen, Eigenschaft

36

panel of experts [ˌpænl əv 'ekspɜ:ts]	Expertenrunde
youth [ju:θ]	Jugend
conference ['kɒnfərəns]	Konferenz, Tagung
to justify ['dʒʌstɪfaɪ]	rechtfertigen
advertisers ['ædvətaɪzəz]	Werbeleute

task [tɑːsk]		Aufgabe
to trivialize ['trɪvɪəlaɪz]		trivial machen
dumb (AE) [dʌm]		dumm, doof
to turn into ['tɜːn ɪntə]		verwandeln in, machen zu
sex object ['seks ˌɒbdʒɪkt]		Sexobjekt
to upset [ˌʌp'set]		verwirren, aufregen
in fact [ɪn 'fækt]		tatsächlich
elegant ['elɪgənt]		elegant
ordinary ['ɔːdnri]		gewöhnlich, normal
leopard ['lepəd]		Leopard
elegance ['elɪgəns]		Eleganz
to take on [ˌteɪk 'ɒn]		annehmen
quality ['kwɒləti]		Qualität, Eigenschaft
business empire [ˌbɪznəs 'empaɪə]		Wirtschaftsimperium
in charge [ɪn 'tʃɑːdʒ]		in leitender Position
hard sell [ˌhɑːd 'sel]		aggressives Verkaufsverhalten
sophisticated [sə'fɪstɪkeɪtɪd]		raffiniert, differenziert
subtle ['sʌtl]		raffiniert, subtil
to ban [bæn]		verbieten
to increase [ɪn'kriːs]		erhöhen
competition [ˌkɒmpə'tɪʃn]		Wettbewerb
to force [fɔːs]		zwingen
what's more [wɒts 'mɔː]		zudem
manufacturer [ˌmænju'fæktʃərə]		Hersteller/in, Produzent/in
goods [gʊdz]		Ware(n)
loads [ləʊdz]		jede Menge
global ['gləʊbl]		global
resource [rɪ'sɔːs]		Mittel, Reserve
wasteful ['weɪstfl]		verschwenderisch
vital ['vaɪtl]		(lebens)wichtig, wesentlich
sale [seɪl]		Verkauf
to collapse [kə'læps]		zusammenbrechen
tax [tæks]		Steuer
to get rid of [get 'rɪd əv]		beseitigen, abschaffen
the Middle Ages [ðə ˌmɪdl 'eɪdʒɪz]		das Mittelalter

37

unclear [ˌʌn'klɪə]		unklar
director [də'rektə]		Direktor/in, Geschäftsführer/in
to reduce [rɪ'djuːs]		reduzieren, verringern
waste [weɪst]		Abfall, Müll
realistic [ˌriːə'lɪstɪk]		realistisch
alternative [ɔːl'tɜːnətɪv]		Alternative
to mention ['menʃn]		erwähnen
totally ['təʊtəli]		völlig
partly ['pɑːtli]		teilweise
personally ['pɜːsənəli]		persönlich
to exaggerate [ɪg'zædʒəreɪt]		übertreiben
one-sided [ˌwʌn'saɪdɪd]		einseitig
packaging ['pækɪdʒɪŋ]		Verpackung
anti-drugs campaign [ˌænti'drʌgz kæm'peɪn]		Kampagne gegen Drogen
approach [ə'prəʊtʃ]		Ansatz

38

to decrease [dɪ'kriːs]		abnehmen
sharp [ʃɑːp]		stark
steady ['stedi]		gleichmäßig

gradually ['grædʒʊəli]		allmählich
previous ['priːvɪəs]		vorhergehend

39

fairly ['feəli]		ziemlich
to move to ['muːv tə]		umziehen nach
target audience [ˌtɑːgɪt 'ɔːdɪəns]		Zielgruppe

Unit 1 Further reading

40

skill [skɪl]		Fertigkeit, Fähigkeit
courier ['kʊriə]		Kurier
accounts [ə'kaʊnts]		Buchhaltung
internet access [ˌɪntənet 'ækses]		Internetzugang
graphics ['græfɪks]		Grafik
art department ['ɑːt dɪ'pɑːtmənt]		Kunstabteilung
facility [fə'sɪləti]		Vor-, Einrichtung
action group ['ækʃn gruːp]		Aktionsgruppe
newsletter ['njuːzletə]		Rundschreiben, Informationsblatt
word processing ['wɜːd ˌprəʊsesɪŋ]		Textverarbeitung
delighted [dɪ'laɪtɪd]		(sehr) erfreut
down-to-earth [ˌdaʊn tu 'ɜːθ]		pragmatisch
computing [kəm'pjuːtɪŋ]		Computer-
enemy ['enəmi]		Feind
to concentrate on ['kɒnsntreɪt ɒn]		sich konzentrieren auf
to put to use [pʊt tə 'juːs]		einsetzen, gebrauchen
keyboarding ['kiːbɔːdɪŋ]		Texteingabe, -erfassung
accounting [ə'kaʊntɪŋ]		Rechnungswesen, (Bilanz-)Buchhaltung
to keep an eye on [kiːp ən 'aɪ ɒn]		ein (wachsames) Auge haben auf
income ['ɪnkʌm]		Einkommen
expenditure [ɪk'spendɪtʃə]		Ausgabe(n), (Un-)Kosten
preparation [ˌprepə'reɪʃn]		Vorbereitung
quarterly ['kwɔːtəli]		vierteljährlich
annual ['ænjʊəl]		jährlich
to open up [ˌəʊpən 'ʌp]		öffnen, erschließen
potential [pə'tenʃl]		Potenzial
intensive [ɪn'tensɪv]		intensiv
reduction [rɪ'dʌkʃn]		Ermäßigung
senior citizen [ˌsiːniə 'sɪtɪzn]		Senior/in

Unit 2 ▪ Earning a living

41

to earn a living [ˌɜːn ə 'lɪvɪŋ]		den Lebensunterhalt verdienen
waitress ['weɪtrɪs]		Kellnerin, Serviererin
farm worker ['fɑːmwɜːkə]		Landarbeiter/in
call centre operator [ˌkɔːl sentə 'ɒpəreɪtə]		Telefonist/in in einem Callcenter
carer ['keərə]		Pfleger/in

technician [tek'nɪʃn]	Techniker/in	
clerk [klɑ:k]	Angestellte/r, Kaufmann/frau	
shop assistant ['ʃɒp ə,sɪstənt]	Verkäufer/in	
insecure [,ɪnsɪ'kjʊə]	unsicher	
stressful ['stresfl]	sehr anstrengend, stressig	
stress-free ['stresfri:]	stressfrei	
at all times [ət ɔ:l 'taɪmz]	jederzeit	
independent [,ɪndɪ'pendənt]	unabhängig	
to gain [geɪn]	gewinnen	
colleague ['kɒli:g]	Kollege, Kollegin	
irregular [ɪ'regjələ]	unregelmäßig	
unsocial [,ʌn'səʊʃl]	unsozial	
traditional [trə'dɪʃənl]	traditionell	

42

counselor (AE) ['kaʊnsələ]	Berater/in
to seek [si:k]	suchen
part-time [,pɑ:'taɪm]	Teilzeit-, Halbtags-
counter ['kaʊntə]	Ladentisch
junior year (AE) ['dʒu:niə jɪə]	vorletztes Schuljahr
high school (AE) ['haɪ sku:l]	Oberschule, Gymnasium
a third [ə 'θɜ:d]	ein Drittel
statistics [stə'tɪstɪks]	Statistiken, statistische Angaben
teen (AE) [ti:n]	Teenager, Jugendliche/r
to go for it [tə 'gəʊ fər ɪt]	es machen
satisfaction [,sætɪs'fækʃn]	Befriedigung, Zufriedenheit
to consider [kən'sɪdə]	nachdenken über
to be on top of sth [ɒn 'tɒp əv]	etw. im Griff haben
schoolwork ['sku:lwɜ:k]	Schularbeiten
grade (AE) [greɪd]	Note
to affect [ə'fekt]	beeinflussen
domestic chores [də,mestɪk 'tʃɔ:z]	Arbeit im Haushalt
bad-tempered [,bæd'tempəd]	schlecht gelaunt
extra-curricular [,ekstrə kə'rɪkjʊlə]	außerlehrplanmäßig
activity [æk'tɪvəti]	Aktivität, Tätigkeit
to get a kick out of [get ə 'kɪk aʊt əv]	Spaß an etw. haben
opening ['əʊpnɪŋ]	offene Stelle
to look out for [,lʊk 'aʊt fə]	achten auf, suchen nach
storefront (AE) ['stɔ: frʌnt]	Ladenfront
job board ['dʒɒb bɔ:d]	Brett mit Stellenanzeigen
job center (AE) ['dʒɒb sentə]	Arbeitsamt
scared [skeəd]	verstört, ängstlich
form [fɔ:m]	Formular
social security [,səʊʃl sɪ'kjʊərəti]	Sozialversicherung
reference ['refərəns]	Referenz
resumé (AE) ['rezjumeɪ]	Lebenslauf
to make an impression [meɪk ən ɪm'preʃn]	einen Eindruck machen
dress code ['dres kəʊd]	Kleiderordnung
even so ['i:vn səʊ]	trotzdem
neat [ni:t]	ordentlich, sauber
to cover up [,kʌvər 'ʌp]	bedecken
to take out [,teɪk 'aʊt]	herausnehmen
nose ring ['nəʊz rɪŋ]	Nasenring
to stand out from [,stænd 'aʊt frəm]	sich abheben von

enthusiasm [ɪn'θju:ziæzəm]	Begeisterung
math (AE) [mæθ]	Mathe(matik)
aptitude ['æptɪtju:d]	Eignung

43

to have in common [həv ɪn 'kɒmən]	gemeinsam haben
in addition to [ɪn ə'dɪʃn tə]	zusätzlich zu
area ['eəriə]	Bereich
employer [ɪm'plɔɪə]	Arbeitgeber/in, Unternehmer/in
network ['netwɜ:k]	Netz(werk)
benefit ['benɪfɪt]	zusätzliche Leistung
academic [,ækə'demɪk]	akademisch
hourly rate [,aʊli 'reɪt]	Stundenlohn
overtime ['əʊvətaɪm]	Überstunden
paper qualifications [,peɪpə ,kwɒlɪfɪ'keɪʃnz]	Zeugnisse
permanent ['pɜ:mənənt]	ständig, dauerhaft
wages [weɪdʒɪz]	Lohn

44

exam certificate [ɪg,zæm sə'tɪfɪkət]	Abschlusszeugnis
available [ə'veɪləbl]	verfügbar
people skills ['pi:pl skɪlz]	Fähigkeiten im Umgang mit Menschen
attitude ['ætɪtju:d]	Einstellung, Haltung
charisma [kə'rɪzmə]	Charisma
waiter ['weɪtə]	Kellner
employment [ɪm'plɔɪmənt]	Beschäftigung
appearance [ə'pɪərəns]	Auftreten, äußere Erscheinung
communicator [kə'mju:nɪkeɪtə]	jd., der gut mit Leuten umgehen kann
essential [ɪ'senʃl]	(unbedingt) erforderlich

Part 1

escape [ɪ'skeɪp]	Entkommen

Part 2

though [ðəʊ]	jedoch
to wonder ['wʌndə]	sich fragen
ought [ɔ:t]	sollte/n
shortly ['ʃɔ:tli]	in Kürze
to look forward to [,lʊk 'fɔ:wəd tə]	sich freuen auf
factory ['fæktəri]	Fabrik
section head ['sekʃn hed]	Abteilungsleiter/in
to shake [ʃeɪk]	schütteln
neither ['naɪðə]	keiner

45

mission ['mɪʃn]	Auftrag, Mission
affair [ə'feə]	Angelegenheit
correspondent [,kɒrə'spɒndənt]	Korrespondent/in
to juggle ['dʒʌgl]	miteinander vereinbaren
workplace ['wɜ:kpleɪs]	Arbeitsplatz
exhausted [ɪg'zɔ:stɪd]	erschöpft
increasing [ɪn'kri:sɪŋ]	zunehmend

guilty ['gɪlti]	schuldig
playschool ['pleɪskuːl]	Kindertagesstätte
constantly ['kɒnstəntli]	ständig
to rely on [rɪ'laɪ ɒn]	sich verlassen auf
heavily ['hevɪli]	stark
nanny ['næni]	Kindermädchen
housework ['haʊswɜːk]	Hausarbeit(en)
to bring up [ˌbrɪŋ 'ʌp]	aufziehen
properly ['prɒpəli]	richtig, korrekt
human being	Mensch
[ˌhjuːmən 'biːɪŋ]	
retreat [rɪ'triːt]	sich zurückziehen

46

original [ə'rɪdʒənl]	Original
to raise [reɪz]	aufziehen
to concentrate on	sich konzentrieren auf
['kɒnsntreɪt ɒn]	
homemaker ['həʊmmeɪkə]	Hausfrau
to fail [feɪl]	scheitern, versagen
position [pə'zɪʃn]	Lage
no longer [nəʊ 'lɒŋgə]	nicht mehr
stage [steɪdʒ]	Phase, Stadium
to conclude [kən'kluːd]	(ab)schließen

47

accessory [ək'sesəri]	Accessoire
allowance [ə'laʊəns]	finanzielle Unterstützung
shift [ʃɪft]	Schicht

48

to refer to [rɪ'fɜː tə]	sich beziehen auf
brief [briːf]	kurz
former ['fɔːmə]	ehemalig, früher
to act as ['ækt əz]	dienen als
to cut a long story short	um es kurz zu machen
[tə kʌt ə lɒŋ ˌstɔːri 'ʃɔːt]	

Unit 2 Further reading

49

return air ticket	Hin- und Rückflugticket
[rɪˌtɜːn 'eə tɪkɪt]	
to enjoy oneself	sich amüsieren, Spaß haben
[ɪn'dʒɔɪ wʌnself]	
agricultural [ˌægrɪ'kʌltʃərəl]	landwirtschaftlich
cattle ['kætl]	Rinder, Vieh
sheep [ʃiːp]	Schaf
crocodile ['krɒkədaɪl]	Krokodil
throughout [θruː'aʊt]	überall (in)
fee [fiː]	Gebühr
peace [piːs]	Frieden
workcamp ['wɜːkkæmp]	Arbeitscamp
childcare ['tʃaɪldkeə]	Kinderbetreuung
urban ['ɜːbən]	städtisch, Stadt-
Aboriginal [ˌæbə'rɪdʒənl]	(austral.) Ureinwohner/in
community [kə'mjuːnəti]	Gemeinde
primary school	Grundschule
['praɪməri skuːl]	
willing ['wɪlɪŋ]	arbeitswillig
organic [ɔː'gænɪk]	ökologisch

non-profitmaking	gemeinnützig
[ˌnɒn'prɒfɪtmeɪkɪŋ]	
approx [ə'prɒksɪmətli]	ungefähr, etwa
cultural ['kʌltʃərəl]	kulturell, Kultur-
exchange [ɪks'tʃeɪndʒ]	Austausch
farmwork ['fɑːmwɜːk]	Landarbeit
typing ['taɪpɪŋ]	Maschineschreiben
maintenance ['meɪntənəns]	Pflege
sleeping bag ['sliːpɪŋbæg]	Schlafsack
fare [feə]	Fahrgeld
membership ['membəʃɪp]	Mitgliedschaft

Unit 3 ▪ Fitness and food

50

type [taɪp]	Art, Typ, Sorte
absolutely ['æbsəluːtli]	absolut, völlig
balanced ['bælənst]	ausgeglichen, ausgewogen
mixture ['mɪkstʃə]	Mischung
protein ['prəʊtiːn]	Protein
carbohydrates	Kohlenhydrate
[ˌkɑːbəʊ'haɪdreɪts]	
cereals ['sɪəriəlz]	Getreideflocken, Cornflakes
dairy products	Milchprodukte
['deəri prɒdʌkts]	
to work out [ˌwɜːk 'aʊt]	ausarbeiten, sich ausdenken
calories ['kæləriz]	Kalorien

51

unfit [ʌn'fɪt]	nicht fit
sports and leisure centre	Sport- und Freizeitzentrum
[ˌspɔːts ənd 'leʒə sentə]	
in their teens [ɪn ðeə 'tiːnz]	zwischen 13 und 19
matter ['mætə]	Sache, Angelegenheit
episode ['epɪsəʊd]	Episode
to join in [ˌdʒɔɪn 'ɪn]	mitmachen
flight of stairs [flaɪt əv 'steəz]	Treppe
out of breath [aʊt əf 'breθ]	außer Atem
overweight [ˌəʊvə'weɪt]	übergewichtig
vigorous ['vɪgərəs]	kräftig, kraftvoll
by the way [baɪ ðə 'weɪ]	übrigens, nebenbei
average ['ævərɪdʒ]	durchschnittlich
heart rate ['hɑːt reɪt]	Herzschlag
oxygen ['ɒksɪdʒən]	Sauerstoff
muscle ['mʌsl]	Muskel
to relieve [rɪ'liːv]	lindern
extreme [ɪk'striːm]	extrem
long-distance running	Langstreckenlauf
[ˌlɒŋ'dɪstəns rʌnɪŋ]	
to get around [ˌget ə'raʊnd]	sich bewegen
to get off [ˌget 'ɒf]	aussteigen
lunch hour ['lʌntʃ aʊə]	Mittagspause
to do a good turn	etwas Gutes tun
[duː ə gʊd 'tɜːn]	
out of shape [aʊt əf 'ʃeɪp]	übergewichtig
to store up [ˌstɔːr 'ʌp]	ansammeln
long-term [ˌlɒŋ'tɜːm]	langfristig
lack of ['læk əv]	Mangel an, Fehlen von
to contribute to	beitragen zu
[kən'trɪbjuːt tə]	

to lead to ['li:d tə]	führen zu	
heart disease ['hɑ:t dɪzi:z]	Herzkrankheit	
osteoporosis [ˌɒstiəʊpəˈrəʊsɪs]	Osteoporose, Knochenschwund	
diabetes [ˌdaɪəˈbiːtiːz]	Zuckerkrankheit, Diabetes	

52

PE (= physical exercise) [ˌpiː ˈiː]	Sport(unterricht)
to keep to [ˈkiːp tə]	sich halten an
to my mind [tə ˈmaɪ maɪnd]	meiner Meinung nach
to take in [ˌteɪk ˈɪn]	zu sich nehmen
energetic [ˌenəˈdʒetɪk]	kraftvoll, energisch
elastic [ɪˈlæstɪk]	elastisch
movement [ˈmuːvmənt]	Bewegung
energy [ˈenədʒi]	Energie
to take away [ˌteɪk əˈweɪ]	wegnehmen
guy [gaɪ]	Kerl, Typ
to weigh [weɪ]	wiegen
the other day [ði ˌʌðə ˈdeɪ]	vor ein paar Tagen
gym [dʒɪm]	Sportstudio, Fitnessraum

53

indirect [ˌɪndəˈrekt]	indirekt
to get into shape [get ɪntə ˈʃeɪp]	in Form kommen
to draw [drɔː]	zeichnen
route [ruːt]	Route, Strecke
changing room [ˈtʃeɪndʒɪŋ ruːm]	Umkleideraum
sauna [ˈsɔːnə]	Sauna
solarium [səˈleəriəm]	Solarium
squash court [ˈskwɒʃ kɔːt]	Squashplatz
tennis court [ˈtenɪs kɔːt]	Tennisplatz

altogether [ˌɔːltəˈgeðə]	insgesamt
corridor [ˈkɒrɪdɔː]	Gang, Korridor
pool table [ˈpuːl teɪbl]	Poolbillardtisch
ahead [əˈhed]	nach vorne, voraus
Olympic-size [əˈlɪmpɪksaɪz]	in Olympia-Größe
championship [ˈtʃæmpiənʃɪp]	Meisterschaft
life-saving [ˈlaɪfseɪvɪŋ]	Lebensrettungs-
certificate [səˈtɪfɪkət]	Zeugnis, Urkunde
latest [ˈleɪtɪst]	neueste/r/s

54

issue [ˈɪʃuː]	aktuelle Frage
anchorman [ˈæŋkəmæn]	Fernsehmoderator
studio audience [ˈstjuːdiəʊ ɔːdiəns]	Studiogäste, -publikum
catering manager [ˈkeɪtərɪŋ mænɪdʒə]	Gastronom/in
scandal [ˈskændl]	Skandal
BSE [ˌbiː es ˈiː]	BSE
Creuzfeldt-Jakob Disease [ˌkrɔɪtsfelt ˈjækɒb dɪzi:z]	Creutzfeldt-Jakob-Krankheit
farming [ˈfɑːmɪŋ]	Landwirtschaft
factory farming [ˈfæktəri fɑːmɪŋ]	industrielle Landwirtschaft
cost-cutting [ˈkɒstkʌtɪŋ]	kostensenkend
mass [mæs]	Masse
habitat [ˈhæbɪtæt]	Lebensraum

to destroy [dɪˈstrɔɪ]	zerstören, vernichten
farmland [ˈfɑːmlænd]	landwirtschaftlich genutzte Fläche
cruel [kruːəl]	grausam
unnatural [ʌnˈnætʃrəl]	unnatürlich
livestock [ˈlaɪvstɒk]	Vieh
source [sɔːs]	Quelle
so-called [ˌsəʊˈkɔːld]	so genannt
MP [ˌem ˈpiː]	Parlamentsmitglied
to blame [bleɪm]	die Schuld geben
to demand [dɪˈmɑːnd]	fordern
rock-bottom price [ˌrɒkˈbɒtəm praɪs]	Niedrigstpreis
to undercut [ˌʌndəˈkʌt]	unterbieten
low [ləʊ]	niedrig
to make profit [meɪk ˈprɒfɪt]	Gewinn machen
to suffer [ˈsʌfə]	leiden
terrible [ˈterəbl]	schrecklich, furchtbar
to insist on [ɪnˈsɪst ɒn]	bestehen auf
to switch to [ˈswɪtʃ tə]	sich umstellen auf

55

to go along with [ˌgəʊ əˈlɒŋ wɪð]	einverstanden sein mit
poisonous [ˈpɔɪzənəs]	giftig

56

health club [ˈhelθ klʌb]	Fitnessklub
to do well [ˌduː ˈwel]	gut gehen
to pay back [ˌpeɪ ˈbæk]	zurückzahlen
pet store [ˈpet stɔː]	Zoohandlung
to get up [ˌget ˈʌp]	aufstehen
to turn over [ˌtɜːn ˈəʊvə]	sich umdrehen
to get used to [get ˈjuːst tə]	sich gewöhnen an
tour [tʊə]	Rundgang

57

department store [dɪˈpɑːtmənt stɔː]	Kauf-, Warenhaus
pentathlon event [penˈtæθlən ɪvent]	Fünfkampf
athletics [æθˈletɪks]	Leichtathletik
fencing [ˈfensɪŋ]	Fechten
suggestion [səˈdʒestʃən]	Vorschlag

Unit 3 Further reading

58

rate [reɪt]	abschneiden
safety [ˈseɪfti]	Sicherheit
to apply to [əˈplaɪ tə]	gelten für, zutreffen auf
to act [ækt]	sich verhalten, handeln
commentary [ˈkɒməntri]	Kommentar
cutting board [ˈkʌtɪŋ bɔːd]	Schneidebrett
raw [rɔː]	roh
dish [dɪʃ]	(flache) Schale
hamburger patty (AE) [ˈhæmbɜːgə pæti]	Fleischklops
to come into contact with [ˌkʌm ɪntə ˈkɒntækt wɪð]	in Kontakt kommen mit
soapy [ˈsəʊpi]	seifig

bowl [bəʊl]	Schale, Schüssel	wristwatch ['rɪstwɒtʃ]	Armbanduhr
worktop ['wɜːktɒp]	Arbeitsplatte	receiver [rɪ'siːvə]	Empfänger
bacteria [bæk'tɪəriə]	Bakterien	sour ['saʊə]	sauer
leftovers ['leftəʊvəz]	Reste	hybrid car ['haɪbrɪd kɑː]	Auto mit Benzin- und
room temperature	Raumtemperatur		Elektroantrieb
[ruːm 'temprətʃə]		to tap into [tæp 'ɪntə]	eingeben
stomach ache ['stʌmək eɪk]	Magenschmerzen	Global Positioning Satellite	Navigationssatellit
hit and miss [ˌhɪt ənd 'mɪs]	russisches Roulette	[ˌgləʊbl pəˌzɪʃnɪŋ 'sætəlaɪt]	
terrific [tə'rɪfɪk]	großartig, phantastisch	overhead ['əʊvəhed]	darüber
bacteria buster	Bakterienschreck	delay [dɪ'leɪ]	Stau
[bæk'tɪəriə bʌstə]		roadworks ['rəʊdwɜːks]	Straßenbauarbeiten
food-borne illness	durch Nahrung übertragene	windscreen ['wɪndskriːn]	Windschutzscheibe
[ˌfʊdbɔːn 'ɪlnəs]	Krankheit	to sense [sens]	wahrnehmen
surface ['sɜːfɪs]	Arbeitsfläche	laser sensor ['leɪzə sensə]	Lasersensor
to contaminate	verseuchen	vehicle number	Kfz-Kennzeichen
[kən'tæmɪneɪt]		['viːəkl nʌmbə]	
veggie (vegetable) ['vedʒi]	Gemüse	to charge [tʃɑːdʒ]	belasten
apart [ə'pɑːt]	getrennt	radar ['reɪdɑː]	Radar
utensil [juːtensl]	Gerät	to detect [dɪ'tekt]	entdecken
to prevent [prɪ'vent]	verhindern, verhüten	lane [leɪn]	(Fahr-)Spur
spread [spred]	Verbreitung	to watch out [ˌwɒtʃ 'aʊt]	aufpassen
ground beef (AE)	Rinderhack	to pull back [ˌpʊl 'bæk]	zurücksteuern
[graʊnd 'biːf]		payment ['peɪmənt]	Zahlung
internal [ɪn'tɜːnl]	innere	project consultant	Projektberater/in
thermometer [θə'mɒmɪtə]	Thermometer	[ˌprɒdʒekt kən'sʌltənt]	
fridge [frɪdʒ]	Kühlschrank	to insert [ɪn'sɜːt]	einführen
adapt [ə'dæpt]	adaptieren	smart card ['smɑːt kɑːd]	Kreditkarte
		laser beam ['leɪzə biːm]	Laserstrahl
		iris ['aɪrɪs]	Iris

Unit 4 ▪ Can't stop communicating!

		identification	Identifizierung
59		[aɪˌdentɪfɪ'keɪʃn]	
to communicate	kommunizieren	transaction [træn'zækʃn]	Überweisung
[kə'mjuːnɪkeɪt]		via ['vaɪə]	über
cartoonist [kɑː'tuːnɪst]	Karikaturist/in	profile ['prəʊfaɪl]	Porträt, Beschreibung,
communications	Kommunikation	memory ['meməri]	Gedächtnis, Speicher
[kəˌmjuːnɪ'keɪʃnz]		miniature ['mɪnətʃə]	Miniatur-
to appear [ə'pɪə]	scheinen	transmitter [træns'mɪtə]	Sender
		breath analyser	Atemprüfgerät
60		[breθ 'ænəlaɪzə]	
futurologist [ˌfjuːtʃə'rɒlədʒɪst]	Futurologe/-login	prototype ['prəʊtətaɪp]	Prototyp
technology [tek'nɒlədʒi]	Technik, Technologie	invention [ɪn'venʃn]	Erfindung
vision ['vɪʒn]	Vision	laboratory [lə'bɒrətri]	Labor(atorium)
seashore ['siːʃɔː]	Strand, Meeresufer		
common sense	gesunder Menschenverstand	61	
[ˌkɒmən 'sens]		to break down [ˌbreɪk'daʊn]	zusammenbrechen
link [lɪŋk]	Verbindung	development [dɪ'veləpmənt]	Entwicklung
magic ['mædʒɪk]	magisch, Zauber	believable [bɪ'liːvəbl]	glaubhaft
mirror ['mɪrə]	Spiegel	sensitive ['sensətɪv]	empfindlich, sensibel
worldwide ['wɜːldwaɪd]	weltweit	informative [ɪn'fɔːmətɪv]	informativ
electronic [ˌɪlek'trɒnɪk]	elektronisch	apparent [ə'pærənt]	anscheinend
brain [breɪn]	Gehirn	to endanger [ɪn'deɪndʒə]	gefährden
knowledge ['nɒlɪdʒ]	Wissen	to fantasize ['fæntəsaɪz]	sich erträumen
coffee pot ['kɒfi pɒt]	Kaffeekanne	fantasy ['fæntəsi]	Fantasie
coffee table ['kɒfi teɪbl]	Couchtisch	fantastic [fæn'tæstɪk]	fantastisch
to print out [ˌprɪnt 'aʊt]	ausdrucken	to invent [ɪn'vent]	erfinden
personalized ['pɜːsənəlaɪzd]	personalisiert, individuell	inventive [ɪn'ventɪv]	erfinderisch
	gestaltet	out of control	außer Kontrolle
edition [ɪ'dɪʃn]	Ausgabe	[ˌaʊt əv kən'trəʊl]	
to scan [skæn]	scannen, einlesen, erfassen	to go mad [gəʊ 'mæd]	durchdrehen
to announce [ə'naʊns]	verkünden	delivery service	Lieferservice
		[dɪ'lɪvəri sɜːvɪs]	

62

telephone sales ['telɪfəʊn seɪlz]	Telefonverkauf
warehouse ['weəhaʊs]	Lager(haus)
talk time ['tɔːk taɪm]	Sprechzeit
to dial ['daɪəl]	wählen
voice-activated ['vɔɪs æktɪveɪtɪd]	sprachgesteuert
contract ['kɒntrækt]	Vertrag
pay as you go [ˌpeɪ əz ju 'gəʊ]	Zahlung nach Verbrauch
peak [piːk]	Spitze(nzeit)

Part 1

to note down [ˌnəʊt 'daʊn]	aufschreiben, notieren
on offer [ɒn 'ɒfə]	im Angebot

Part 2

point of view [ˌpɔɪnt əv 'vjuː]	Standpunkt
text messaging [tekst 'mesɪdʒɪŋ]	SMS schicken
monthly ['mʌnθli]	monatlich
emergency [ɪ'mɜːdʒənsi]	Notfall

Part 3

to run over [ˌrʌn 'əʊvə]	durchgehen
reference number ['refərəns nʌmbə]	Bestellnummer
to make a note of [meɪk ə 'nəʊt əv]	sich notieren
to quote [kwəʊt]	angeben
rude [ruːd]	unhöflich
politeness [pə'laɪtnəs]	Höflichkeit
indirectness [ˌɪndə'rektnəs]	Indirektheit
absurd [əb'sɜːd]	absurd
request [rɪ'kwest]	Bitte

63

editor ['edɪtə]	Redakteur/in, Herausgeber/in
comment on ['kɒment ɒn]	Kommentar zu
educational [ˌedʒu'keɪʃənl]	Ausbildungs-, erzieherisch
purpose ['pɜːpəs]	Zweck
to access ['ækses]	zugreifen auf
to contain [kən'teɪn]	enthalten
pornographic [ˌpɔːnə'græfɪk]	pornographisch
to corrupt [kə'rʌpt]	korrumpieren
horrified ['hɒrɪfaɪd]	entsetzt
free speech [friː 'spiːtʃ]	Meinungsfreiheit
to exist [ɪg'zɪst]	existieren
Internet Service Provider [ˌɪntənet 'sɜːvɪs prəvaɪdə]	Internetprovider
to prevent [prɪ'vent]	verhindern, verhüten
political refugee [pəˌlɪtɪkl ˌrefju'dʒiː]	politischer Flüchtling
correspondence [ˌkɒrɪ'spɒndəns]	Korrespondenz
with fascination [wɪð ˌfæsɪ'neɪʃn]	fasziniert
to struggle ['strʌgl]	kämpfen
military ruler ['mɪlətri ruːlə]	Militärmachthaber
exile ['eksaɪl]	Exil
to publish ['pʌblɪʃ]	veröffentlichen

censor ['sensə]	Zensor/in
to tear out [ˌteər 'aʊt]	herausreißen
to jam [dʒæm]	stören
dictator [dɪk'teɪtə]	Diktator/in
truthful ['truːθfl]	wahrhaftig
victim ['vɪktɪm]	Opfer
to take sb to court [teɪk tə 'kɔːt]	gegen jdn. gerichtlich vorgehen, jdn. verklagen
phone line ['fəʊn laɪn]	Telefonleitung
to put out a message [ˌpʊt 'aʊt ə 'mesɪdʒ]	eine Nachricht verbreiten
conspiracy theory [kən'spɪrəsi θɪəri]	Verschwörungstheorie
to attack [ə'tæk]	angreifen
to answer back [ˌɑːnsə 'bæk]	antworten, reagieren
propaganda [ˌprɒpə'gændə]	Propaganda
killing ['kɪlɪŋ]	Tötung, Mord

64

to depend on [dɪ'pend ɒn]	angewiesen sein auf, abhängen von
unwelcome [ʌn'welkəm]	nicht willkommen
firm [fɜːm]	fest
to call for ['kɔːl fə]	verlangen
publication [ˌpʌblɪ'keɪʃn]	Veröffentlichung, Verbreitung

65

urgent ['ɜːdʒənt]	dringend, eilig
to bury ['beri]	begraben
automatic save function [ˌɔːtə'mætɪk 'seɪv fʌŋkʃn]	automatische Speicherfunktion
sudden ['sʌdn]	plötzlich
power cut ['paʊə kʌt]	Stromausfall
to black out [ˌblæk 'aʊt]	verdunkeln
computer screen [kəm'pjuːtə skriːn]	Computerbildschirm
basically ['beɪsɪkli]	im Grunde
conclusion [kən'kluːʒn]	(Schluss-)Folgerung
on balance [ɒn 'bæləns]	alles in allem
aspect ['æspekt]	Aspekt, Seite
to outweigh [ˌaʊt'weɪ]	überwiegen

66

to carry around [ˌkæri ə'raʊnd]	herumtragen
ID card [aɪ 'diː kɑːd]	Personalausweis
driving licence ['draɪvɪŋˌlaɪsns]	Führerschein
height [haɪt]	Höhe, Größe
possibility [ˌpɒsə'bɪləti]	Möglichkeit
immigrant ['ɪmɪgrənt]	Einwanderer, Einwanderin
up to ['ʌp tə]	bis zu
social security payment [ˌsəʊʃl sɪ'kjʊərəti peɪmənt]	Sozialhilfezahlung
fingerprint ['fɪŋgəprɪnt]	Fingerabdruck
medical ['medɪkl]	medizinisch
membership ['membəʃɪp]	Mitgliedschaft
police record [pə'liːs rekɔːd]	Polizeibericht
residential [rezɪˌdenʃl]	den Aufenthalt betreffend
state benefit [ˌsteɪt 'benɪfɪt]	staatliche Unterstützung
resident ['rezɪdənt]	Einwohner/in

right to ['raɪt tə]	Berechtigung zu	
residence ['rezɪdəns]	Wohnsitz	
to refuse [rɪ'fjuːz]	ablehnen	
focus group ['fəʊkəs gruːp]	Fachgruppe	
vote [vəʊt]	Wahl	

138

Home Affairs [həʊm ə'feəz]	Innenministerium
official [ə'fɪʃl]	Beamter/Beamtin
human rights [ˌhjuːmən 'raɪts]	Menschenrechte
activist ['æktɪvɪst]	Aktivist/in
in return for [ɪn rɪ'tɜːn fə]	als Gegenleistung für
asylum [ə'saɪləm]	Asyl
whenever [wen'evə]	immer wenn
housing ['haʊzɪŋ]	Unterbringung, -kunft

Unit 4 Further reading

67

to jumble ['dʒʌmbl]	vermischen
newsflash ['njuːz flæʃ]	Kurzmeldungen
Alpine ['ælpaɪn]	alpin
avalanche ['ævəlɑːnʃ]	Lawine
chaos ['keɪɒs]	Chaos
desperate ['despərət]	verzweifelt
rescue work ['reskjuː wɜːk]	Rettungsarbeit(en)
chalet ['ʃæleɪ]	Landhaus
to trap [træp]	fangen
beneath [bɪ'niːθ]	unter
unknown [ˌʌn'nəʊn]	unbekannt
ski slope ['skiː sləʊp]	Skihang
snowfall ['snəʊfɔːl]	Schneefall
fear [fɪə]	Angst, Furcht
authorities [ɔː'θɒrətiz]	Behörden
skier ['skiːə]	Skiläufer/in
off-piste skiing	Skilaufen abseits der Pisten
[ˌɒf'piːst skiːɪŋ]	
within [wɪ'ðɪn]	innerhalb (von)
valley ['væli]	Tal
swallow ['swɒləʊ]	verschlucken
outskirts ['aʊtskɜːts]	Außengebiete, Stadtrand
rescuer ['reskjuːə]	Retter
survivor [sə'vaɪvə]	Überlebende/r
darkness ['dɑːknəs]	Dunkelheit
chalet girl ['ʃæleɪ gɜːl]	Hausmädchen
to pull from ['pʊl frəm]	herausziehen aus
to crush [krʌʃ]	zerquetschen, zerdrücken
to keep house [kiːp 'haʊs]	den Haushalt führen
unique [ju'niːk]	einzigartig
identity [aɪ'dentəti]	Identität
floodlight ['flʌdlaɪt]	Flutlicht
snow slide ['snəʊ slaɪd]	Schneeabgang
midday [ˌmɪd'deɪ]	Mittag
chief [tʃiːf]	Leiter
tragedy ['trædʒədi]	Tragödie
eye-witness ['aɪwɪtnəs]	Augenzeuge/zeugin
victim ['vɪktɪm]	Opfer

Unit 5 ▪ Which road to the future?

68

cartoon [kɑː'tuːn]	Karikatur
old banger [əʊld 'bæŋə]	alte Klapperkiste
to top up [ˌtɒp 'ʌp]	auffüllen
pollute [pə'luːt]	(die Umwelt) verschmutzen
environmental	Umwelt-
[ɪnˌvaɪrən'mentl]	
to commute [kə'mjuːt]	pendeln
to dare [deə]	(es) wagen, sich trauen
rush-hour traffic	Berufsverkehr
[ˌrʌʃaʊə 'træfɪk]	
road rage attack	Angriff wütender Autofahrer
[ˌrəʊd reɪdʒ ə'tæk]	
to stare [steə]	starren
speed [spiːd]	Geschwindigkeit
to crawl [krɔːl]	kriechen
tailback ['teɪlbæk]	Rückstau
stuck [stʌk]	eingeklemmt
gridlock ['grɪdlɒk]	Verkehrsinfarkt
fuel ['fjuːəl]	Kraftstoff, Benzin
infrastructure ['ɪnfrəstrʌktʃə]	Infrastruktur
law [lɔː]	Gesetz
ministry of transport	Verkehrsministerium
[ˌmɪnɪstri əv 'trænspɔːt]	

69

pie chart ['paɪ tʃɑːt]	Kreisdiagramm
junkie ['dʒʌŋki]	Süchtige/r
addicted to [ə'dɪktɪd tə]	süchtig nach, abhängig von
survey ['sɜːveɪ]	(Meinungs-)Umfrage, Untersuchung
independence [ˌɪndɪ'pendəns]	Unabhängigkeit
affordable [ə'fɔːdəbl]	erschwinglich
ancestor ['ænsestə]	Vorfahr
car pool ['kɑː puːl]	Fahrgemeinschaft
upside ['ʌpsaɪd]	Vorzug
downside ['daʊnsaɪd]	Nachteil
frequent ['friːkwənt]	häufig
urban ['ɜːbən]	städtisch
to consume [kən'sjuːm]	verbrauchen
to decline [dɪ'klaɪn]	abnehmen
fossil ['fɒsl]	fossil
pollution [pə'luːʃn]	(Umwelt-)Verschmutzung
to encourage [ɪn'kʌrɪdʒ]	motivieren, auffordern
commuter [kə'mjuːtə]	Pendler/in
despite [dɪ'spaɪt]	trotz
tax cut ['tæks kʌt]	Steuersenkung
travel pass ['trævl pɑːs]	Fahrausweis
carbon ['kɑːbən]	Kohlenstoff
to predict [prɪ'dɪkt]	vorhersagen
crowding ['kraʊdɪŋ]	dichter Verkehr
electronic guidance system	elektronisches
[ˌɪlek'trɒnɪk 'gaɪdəns sɪstəm]	Navigationssystem
efficiently [ɪ'fɪʃntli]	wirksam
telematics ['telimætɪks]	Fernsteuerung
to take over [ˌteɪk 'əʊvə]	übernehmen
driverless ['draɪvələs]	führerlos
engine ['endʒɪn]	Motor
to recharge [ˌriː'tʃɑːdʒ]	aufladen

motor ['məʊtə]	Motor	
to improve [ɪm'pruːv]	verbessern	
range [reɪndʒ]	Radius	
power unit ['paʊə juːnɪt]	Antriebsaggregat	
fuel cell ['fjuːəl sel]	Brennstoffzelle	
to combine [kəm'baɪn]	verbinden, kombinieren	
hydrogen ['haɪdrədʒən]	Wasserstoff	
gas [gæs]	Gas	
engineer [ˌendʒɪ'nɪə]	Ingenieur/in, Techniker/in	
vehicle ['viːəkl]	Fahrzeug	
miracle ['mɪrəkl]	Wunder	
concrete ['kɒŋkriːt]	Beton	
response [rɪ'spɒns]	Reaktion, Antwort	
organization [ˌɔːgənaɪ'zeɪʃn]	Organisation	
petroleum [pə'trəʊliəm]	Petroleum	
to export [ɪk'spɔːt]	ausführen, exportieren	
to raise [reɪz]	erhöhen	
dramatic [drə'mætɪk]	dramatisch	
carbon-based ['kɑːbənbeɪst]	durch Kohlenstoff verursacht	
emission [ɪ'mɪʃn]	Emission	
carbon dioxide	Kohlendioxid	
[ˌkɑːbən daɪ'ɒksaɪd]		
greenhouse gas	Treibhausgas	
[ˌgriːnhaʊs 'gæs]		
global warming	Erderwärmung, Erwärmung	
[ˌgləʊbl 'wɔːmɪŋ]	der Erdatmosphäre	

70

encouragement	Unterstützung	
[ɪn'kʌrɪdʒmənt]		
conventional [kən'venʃənl]	herkömmlich, konventionell	
performance [pə'fɔːməns]	Leistung(en)	
to remind [rɪ'maɪnd]	(jdn. an etw.) erinnern	
to value ['væljuː]	(ab)schätzen	
telecommuter [ˌtelikə'mjuːtə]	Telearbeiter/in	

71

personal space	Diskretionsabstand	
[ˌpɜːsənl 'speɪs]		
loss [lɒs]	Verlust	
handshake ['hændʃeɪk]	Händedruck	
eye contact ['aɪ kɒntækt]	Blickkontakt	
to swap [swɒp]	tauschen	
amusing [ə'mjuːzɪŋ]	lustig, amüsant	
harmless ['hɑːmləs]	harmlos	
confidence ['kɒnfɪdəns]	Selbstvertrauen	
uncomfortable [ʌn'kʌmftəbl]	ungemütlich	
pushy ['pʊʃi]	sich vordrängend	

72

to rocket ['rɒkɪt]	kräftig steigen	
unsurprisingly	erwartungsgemäß	
[ˌʌnsə'praɪzɪŋli]		
fierce [fɪəs]	heftig	
haulage contractor	Transportunternehmen	
[ˌhɔːlɪdʒ kən'træktə]		
panic ['pænɪk]	Panik	
petrol station ['petrəl steɪʃn]	Tankstelle	
commissioner [kə'mɪʃnə]	Kommissar	
queue [kjuː]	(Warte-)Schlange	
to stretch [stretʃ]	sich (er)strecken	

day-care centre	Kindertagesstätte	
['deɪ keə sentə]		
dry-cleaner's [ˌdraɪ'kliːnəz]	chemische Reinigung	
self-employed	selbstständig	
[ˌself ɪm'plɔɪd]		
truck driver (AE)	Lkw-Fahrer/in	
['trʌk draɪvə]		
haulage industry	Transportgewerbe	
['hɔːlɪdʒ ɪndəstri]		
disastrous [dɪ'zɑːstrəs]	katastrophal	
to go bankrupt	Konkurs machen	
[gəʊ 'bæŋkrʌpt]		

73

to invest [ɪn'vest]	investieren	
debt [det]	Schuld(en)	
concerned [kən'sɜːnd]	betroffen	
global ['gləʊbl]	global, Welt-	
discovery [dɪ'skʌvəri]	Entdeckung	
windpower ['wɪndpaʊə]	Windkraft	
improvement [ɪm'pruːvmənt]	Verbesserung	
to subsidize ['sʌbsɪdaɪz]	subventionieren	
to get away from	wegkommen von	
[ˌget ə'weɪ frəm]		
factor ['fæktə]	Faktor	
retail ['riːteɪl]	Einzelhandels-	
interviewee [ˌɪntəvjuː'iː]	Interviewpartner/in, Befragte/r	
effect [ɪ'fekt]	(Aus-)Wirkung, Einfluss	
Union ['juːniən]	(Europäische) Union	
in the long term	auf Dauer	
[ɪn ðə lɒŋ 'tɜːm]		
anger ['æŋgə]	Zorn, Ärger	
in the short term	kurzfristig, auf kurze Sicht	
[ɪn ðə ʃɔːt 'tɜːm]		
economic [ˌiːkə'nɒmɪk]	wirtschaftlich	
to shoot up [ʃuːt 'ʌp]	in die Höhe schießen	
foreign travel [ˌfɒrən 'trævl]	Auslandsreisen	
job cut ['dʒɒb kʌt]	Stellenkürzung	

74

appropriate [ə'prəʊpriət]	passend	
oil tanker ['ɔɪl tæŋkə]	Öltanker	
diplomatic [ˌdɪplə'mætɪk]	diplomatisch	
in the meantime	in der Zwischenzeit	
[ɪn ðə 'miːntaɪm]		
to print [prɪnt]	drucken	
ration book ['ræʃn bʊk]	Bezugscheine	
to distribute [dɪ'strɪbjuːt]	verteilen	
to ration ['ræʃn]	rationieren	

75

layout ['leɪaʊt]	Layout, Anordnung	
phrase [freɪz]	(Rede-)Wendung, Ausdruck	
Re [ˌɑːr 'iː]	Betr., Betrifft	
invoice ['ɪnvɔɪs]	Rechnung	
No ['nʌmbə]	Nr.	
to receive [rɪ'siːv]	erhalten	
in full [ɪn 'fʊl]	vollständig	
Yours sincerely [jɔːz sɪn'sɪəli]	Mit freundlichen Grüßen	
to sympathize ['sɪmpəθaɪz]	sympathisieren	
viewpoint ['vjuːpɔɪnt]	Standpunkt	

narrow ['næɹəʊ] — eng, schmal
crossroads ['kɹɒsɹəʊdz] — Kreuzung
junction ['dʒʌŋkʃn] — (Straßen-)Kreuzung
T-junction ['tiː dʒʌŋkʃn] — (Kreuzung mit) Rechts- und Linksabbieger
Y-junction ['waɪ dʒʌŋkʃn] — Gabelung
one-way system [ˌwʌnweɪ 'sɪstəm] — System von Einbahn-straßen
pedestrian precinct [pɪˌdestɹiən 'priːsɪŋkt] — Fußgängerzone
mini-roundabout [ˌmɪni 'ɹaʊndəbaʊt] — kleiner Kreisel
pedestrianized [pɪ'destɹiənaɪzd] — für Fußgänger/in

Part 1

council ['kaʊnsl] — Gemeinderat
councillor ['kaʊnsələ] — Ratsmitglied
to give sb a call [gɪv ə 'kɔːl] — jdn. anrufen
update [ˌʌp'deɪt] — letzter Stand
towards [tə'wɔːdz] — auf ... zu, in Richtung auf
on top of that [ɒn 'tɒp əv ðæt] — darüber hinaus
high street ['haɪ striːt] — Hauptgeschäftsstraße
traffic jam ['tɹæfɪk dʒæm] — Verkehrsstau

Part 2

pleasure ['pleʒə] — Vergnügen, Freude
frustrated [fɹʌ'streɪtɪd] — frustriert
for a start [fər ə 'stɑːt] — zunächst einmal
to ease [iːz] — lindern
to take up space [ˌteɪk 'ʌp speɪs] — Platz beanspruchen
to knock down [ˌnɒk 'daʊn] — abreißen
sensible ['sensəbl] — vernünftig
to walk around [ˌwɔːk ə'ɹaʊnd] — herumlaufen
freely ['friːli] — frei, ungestört

to widen ['waɪdn] — erweitern, verbreitern
to remove [ɹɪ'muːv] — entfernen, beseitigen

Unit 5 Further reading

to echo ['ekəʊ] — wieder aufnehmen
lyrics ['lɪɹɪks] — (Lied-)Text
missing ['mɪsɪŋ] — fehlend
to pretend [pɹɪ'tend] — vorgeben, so tun als ob
to pray [pɹeɪ] — beten
preacher ['priːtʃə] — Prediger/in
coal [kəʊl] — Kohle
gonna ['gɒnə] — = going to
long-distance travel [ˌlɒŋ'dɪstəns tɹævl] — Fernverkehr

Unit 6 ▪ Buying and selling

outlet ['aʊtlet] — Verkaufsstelle
market stall ['mɑːkɪt stɔːl] — Marktstand
on the doorstep [ɒn ðə 'dɔːstep] — an der Haustür
mail order catalogue [meɪl'ɔːdə kætəlɒg] — Versandhauskatalog
window-shopping [wɪndəʊʃɒpɪŋ] — Schaufensterbummel
on impulse [ɒn 'ɪmpʌls] — spontan

retailing consultant [ˌriːteɪlɪŋ kən'sʌltənt] — Einzelhandelsberater/in
association [əˌsəʊsi'eɪʃn] — Verband
sceptical ['skeptɪkl] — skeptisch
retailer ['riːteɪlə] — Einzelhändler/in
in any case [ɪn 'eni keɪs] — jedenfalls
psychology [saɪ'kɒlədʒi] — Psychologie
to break in [ˌbreɪk 'ɪn] — unterbrechen
to start with [tə 'stɑːt wɪð] — zunächst
anyhow ['enihaʊ] — jedenfalls, sowieso
to distinguish [dɪ'stɪŋgwɪʃ] — unterscheiden
online banking ['ɒnlaɪn bæŋkɪŋ] — Online-Banking
airline ['eəlaɪn] — Fluggesellschaft
come on [ˌkʌm 'ɒn] — komm (schon)
convenient [kən'viːniənt] — bequem
to place orders [pleɪs 'ɔːdəz] — Bestellungen aufgeben
red herring [ˌred 'herɪŋ] — Ablenkungsmanöver, falsche Fährte
capital ['kæpɪtl] — Kapital

to interrupt [ˌɪntə'ɹʌpt] — unterbrechen
opening hours ['əʊpənɪŋ aʊəz] — Öffnungszeiten
admission [əd'mɪʃn] — Eintritt
rate [reɪt] — Tarif
disabled [dɪs'eɪbld] — (körper)behindert
school party ['skuːl pɑːti] — Schulklasse
loan [ləʊn] — Verleih
stroller (AE) ['strəʊlə] — Buggy, Sportwagen
wheelchair ['wiːltʃeə] — Rollstuhl
deposit [dɪ'pɒzɪt] — Kaution
kennel ['kenl] — Hundehütte
parking lot (AE) ['pɑːkɪŋ lɒt] — Parkplatz

Christmas Day [ˌkrɪsməs 'deɪ] — 1. Weihnachtsfeiertag
senior citizen [ˌsiːniə 'sɪtɪzn] — ältere/r Mitbürger/in, Senior/in

consumerism [kən'sjuːmərɪzəm] — Konsumdenken
to possess [pə'zes] — besitzen
to define [dɪ'faɪn] — definieren, bestimmen
psychologist [saɪ'kɒlədʒɪst] — Psychologe/Psychologin
to go to extremes [gəʊ tu ɪk'striːmz] — bis zum Äußersten gehen
sick [sɪk] — krank

personality [ˌpɜːsəˈnæləti]	Persönlichkeit	
military [ˈmɪlətri]	militärisch	
among [əˈmʌŋ]	unter	
inappropriate [ˌɪnəˈprəʊpriət]	unpassend	
threatening [ˈθretnɪŋ]	bedrohlich	
uniform [ˈjuːnɪfɔːm]	Uniform	
item [ˈaɪtəm]	Artikel, Gegenstand	
gold chain [ˌɡəʊld ˈtʃeɪn]	Goldkette	
cycling pants (AE) [ˈsaɪklɪŋ pænts]	Radfahrhosen	
fur [fɜː]	Pelz	
to reveal [rɪˈviːl]	enthüllen, zeigen	
halter [ˈhɔːltə]	Träger	
combat jacket [ˈkɒmbæt dʒækɪt]	Kampfanzug	
to rip [rɪp]	(zer)reißen	
repressive [rɪˈpresɪv]	repressiv	
to conform [kənˈfɔːm]	entsprechen	
democracy [dɪˈmɒkrəsi]	Demokratie	
street crime [ˈstriːt kraɪm]	Straßenkriminalität	
theft [θeft]	Diebstahl	
mobile (phone) [ˈməʊbaɪl]	Handy	
PIN code [ˈpɪn kəʊd]	PIN-Nummer	
compulsory [kəmˈpʌlsəri]	obligatorisch	
spokesman [ˈspəʊksmən]	Sprecher	
fewer and fewer [ˌfjuːə ənd ˈfjuːə]	immer weniger	
life skills [ˈlaɪf skɪlz]	Alltagsfertigkeiten	
aware of [əˈweər əv]	bewusst	
halogen bulb [ˈhælədʒən bʌlb]	Halogenlampe	
to mend [mend]	ausbessern	
to sub-contract [ˌsʌbkənˈtrækt]	weitervergeben	
service provider [ˈsɜːvɪs prəvaɪdə]	Dienstleister	
unfree [ʌnˈfriː]	Unfreie/r	
dependent (on) [dɪˈpendənt]	abhängig (von)	

82

cookery [ˈkʊkəri]	Kochen
home repair [ˌhəʊm rɪˈpeə]	Haushaltsreparatur
undemocratic [ˌʌndeməˈkrætɪk]	undemokratisch
unsafe [ʌnˈseɪf]	unsicher
violent [ˈvaɪələnt]	gewalttätig
unhealthy [ʌnˈhelθi]	ungesund

83

crime figures [ˈkraɪm fɪɡəz]	Kriminalitätsstatistik

84

to cooperate [kəʊˈɒpəreɪt]	zusammenarbeiten
unemployment [ˌʌnɪmˈplɔɪmənt]	Arbeitslosigkeit
willing [ˈwɪlɪŋ]	gewillt (sein)
to obey [əˈbeɪ]	gehorchen, befolgen
aggressive [əˈgresɪv]	aggressiv
unsuitable [ʌnˈsuːtəbl]	ungeeignet, unpassend
friction [ˈfrɪkʃn]	Reibung
identity [aɪˈdentəti]	Identität
to suppress [səˈpres]	unterdrücken

individuality [ˌɪndɪˌvɪdʒuˈæləti]	Individualität
to punish [ˈpʌnɪʃ]	bestrafen
severe [sɪˈvɪə]	streng, hart
to provide with [prəˈvaɪd wɪð]	versorgen mit
policing [pəˈliːsɪŋ]	Einsatz von Polizeikräften

85

based on [ˈbeɪst ɒn]	basierend auf
summer camp [ˈsʌmə kæmp]	Sommerlager
in exchange [ɪn ɪksˈtʃeɪndʒ]	zum Ausgleich
rewarding [rɪˈwɔːdɪŋ]	lohnend
outdoors [ˌaʊtˈdɔːz]	im Freien
arts and crafts [ˌɑːts ənd ˈkrɑːfts]	Kunsthandwerk
home country [ˌhəʊm ˈkʌntri]	Heimatland
ability [əˈbɪləti]	Fähigkeit, Können
self-confidence [ˌself ˈkɒnfɪdəns]	Selbstsicherheit, -vertrauen
to enable [ɪˈneɪbl]	befähigen
in return (for sth.) [ɪn rɪˈtɜːn]	als Gegenleistung (für etw.)
return flight [rɪˌtɜːn ˈflaɪt]	Rückflug
work visa [wɜːk ˈviːzə]	Arbeitserlaubnis
generous [ˈdʒenərəs]	großzügig
pocket money [ˈpɒkɪt mʌni]	Taschengeld

Unit 6 Further Reading

86

timeline [ˈtaɪmlaɪn]	Zeitachse
agri-chemical [ˌægriˈkemɪkl]	Agrarchemikalie
revolution [ˌrevəˈluːʃn]	Revolution
Federal Ministry of Agriculture [ˌfedərəl ˈmɪnɪstri əv ˈægrɪkʌltʃə]	Bundeslandwirtschaftsministerium
Federal Ministry for Consumer Protection, Food and Agriculture [ˌfedərəl ˈmɪnɪstri fɔː kənˈsjuːmə prəˌtekʃn, fuːd ənd ˈægrɪkʌltʃə]	Bundesministerium für Verbraucherschutz, Ernährung und Landwirtschaft
in other words [ɪn ˈʌðə wɜːdz]	anders ausgedrückt
farmers' lobby [ˌfɑːməz ˈlɒbi]	Bauernlobby
consumer watchdog [kənˌsjuːmə ˈwɒtʃdɒg]	Verbraucherschutzorganisation
factual [ˈfæktʃuəl]	sachlich
glitzy [ˈglɪtsi]	strahlend
reform [rɪˈfɔːm]	Reform
radical [ˈrædɪkl]	radikal
supplier [səˈplaɪə]	Anbieter/in, Lieferant/in
to realize [ˈrɪəlaɪz]	erkennen
food chain [ˈfuːd tʃeɪn]	Nahrungskette
Surgeon-General (AE) [ˌsɜːdʒən ˈdʒenrəl]	Oberster Amtsarzt der USA
to come out [ˌkʌm ˈaʊt]	erscheinen
tobacco company [təˈbækəʊ kʌmpəni]	Tabakfirma
to deny [dɪˈnaɪ]	abstreiten
ie [ˌaɪ ˈiː]	d.h.

cancer ['kænsə]	Krebs
milestone ['maɪlstəʊn]	Meilenstein
throughout [θruː'aʊt]	die ganze Zeit über
to withdraw from [wɪð'drɔː frəm]	zurücktreten von
sales agreement ['seɪlz əgriːmənt]	Kaufvertrag
to put out of business [ˌpʊt aʊt əf 'bɪznəs]	arbeitslos machen
doorstep salesman [ˌdɔːstep 'seɪlzmən]	Vertreter an der Haustür
receipt [rɪ'siːt]	Quittung, Beleg
consumer-friendly [kən'sjuːmə frendli]	verbraucherfreundlich
to close a circle [ˌkləʊz ə 'sɜːkl]	einen Kreis schließen
to forecast ['fɔːkɑːst]	vorhersagen
unreasonable [ʌn'riːznəbl]	unvernünftig
greedy ['griːdi]	gierig

Unit 7 ▪ Big business – little people

87

to process ['prəʊses]	(weiter)verarbeiten
desert ['dezət]	Wüste
to fly out [ˌflaɪ 'aʊt]	ausfliegen
to refrigerate [rɪ'frɪdʒəreɪt]	kühlen
to manufacture [ˌmænju'fæktʃə]	herstellen, produzieren
nostalgia [nɒ'stældʒə]	Nostalgie
plant extract [ˌplɑːnt 'ekstrækt]	Pflanzenauszug
jungle ['dʒʌŋgl]	Dschungel, Urwald
multinational [ˌmʌlti'næʃnəl]	multinational

88

free trade [ˌfriː 'treɪd]	Freihandel
globalization [ˌgləʊbəlaɪ'zeɪʃn]	Globalisierung
lower-cost ['ləʊə kɒst]	Niedriglohn-
redundancy pay [rɪ'dʌndənsi peɪ]	Arbeitslosengeld
affluent ['æfluənt]	wohlhabend
border zone ['bɔːdə zəʊn]	Grenzbereich
commentator ['kɒmənteɪtə]	Kommentator/in
facsimile [fæk'sɪməli]	Nachbildung
tight [taɪt]	streng
air pollution [ˌeə pə'luːʃn]	Luftverschmutzung
North Atlantic Free Trade Area [ˌnɔːθ ət'læntɪk ˌfriː treɪd 'eəriə]	Nordatlantische Freihandelszone
manufacturing operation [ˌmænju'fæktʃərɪŋ ˌɒpə'reɪʃn]	Produktionsvorhaben
profit ['prɒfɪt]	Profit, Gewinn
labour costs ['leɪbə kɒsts]	Lohnkosten
protective clothing [prə,tektɪv 'kləʊðɪŋ]	Schutzkleidung
to sting [stɪŋ]	brennen
the sack [ðə 'sæk]	die Entlassung

switch [swɪtʃ]	Schalter
sensor ['sensə]	Sensor
subsidiary [səb'sɪdiəri]	Tochtergesellschaft
wiring ['waɪərɪŋ]	Verkabelung
refrigerator [rɪ'frɪdʒəreɪtə]	Kühlschrank
personnel [ˌpɜːsə'nel]	Personal
to hold the whip hand [həʊld ðə 'wɪp hænd]	das Sagen haben
battle ['bætl]	Kampf
victory ['vɪktəri]	Sieg
hollow ['hɒləʊ]	hohl

89

attractive [ə'træktɪv]	attraktiv, anziehend
pollutant [pə'luːtənt]	Schadstoff
connect [kə'nekt]	(miteinander) verbinden

90

versus ['vɜːsəs]	gegen(über)

Part 1

involved in [ɪn'vɒlvd ɪn]	beteiligt an
workforce ['wɜːkfɔːs]	Belegschaft

Part 2

strike [straɪk]	Streik
to blacklist ['blæklɪst]	auf eine schwarze Liste setzen
chief executive officer [ˌtʃiːf ɪg'zekjətɪv ɒfɪsə]	geschäftsführende/r Direktor/in
competitive [kəm'petətɪv]	konkurrenzfähig
investment [ɪn'vestmənt]	Investition
finance ['faɪnæns]	Finanz(en)
credit ['kredɪt]	Kredit
to sort out [ˌsɔːt 'aʊt]	klären, lösen
compromise ['kɒmprəmaɪz]	Kompromiss
peace [piːs]	Frieden, Ruhe
awareness [ə'weənəs]	Bewusstsein
simplistic [sɪm'plɪstɪk]	(zu) stark vereinfachend
unhelpful [ˌʌn'helpfl]	nicht hilfreich, irreführend

91

case study ['keɪs stʌdi]	Fallstudie
to end up [ˌend 'ʌp]	enden, landen
data package [ˌdeɪtə 'pækɪdʒ]	Datenpaket
subsistence farmer [səb'sɪstəns fɑːmə]	nur für den eigenen Lebensunterhalt anbauender Landwirt
district ['dɪstrɪkt]	(Verwaltungs-)Bezirk
fertiliser ['fɜːtəlaɪzə]	Dünger
crop [krɒp]	Ernte
cocoa ['kəʊkəʊ]	Kakao
plantation [plæn'teɪʃn]	Plantage
drought [draʊt]	Dürre(periode)
nuclear fusion [ˌnjuːkliə 'fjuːʒn]	Kernfusion
energy source ['enədʒi sɔːs]	Energiequelle
massive ['mæsɪv]	riesig

92

to demonstrate ['demənstreɪt]	demonstrieren, vorstellen
disaster [dɪ'zɑːstə]	Katastrophe, Unglück

to drop [drɒp]	fallen	
cooperation [kəʊˌɒpə'reɪʃn]	Zusammenarbeit	
attractiveness [ə'træktɪvnəs]	Attraktivität	

93

to take action [teɪk 'ækʃn]	Schritte unternehmen
secret ['siːkrɪt]	geheim, heimlich
to hold a meeting	eine Sitzung abhalten
[həʊld ə 'miːtɪŋ]	
shipyard ['ʃɪpjɑːd]	Schiffswerft
philosophy [fɪ'lɒsəfi]	Philosophie
to retrain [ˌriː'treɪn]	sich umschulen lassen
chef [ʃef]	Küchenchef
fast-food store (AE)	Imbissladen
[ˌfɑːst 'fuːd stɔː]	
chain [tʃeɪn]	Kette

94

to negotiate [nɪ'gəʊʃieɪt]	aushandeln
sportswear ['spɔːtsweə]	Sportkleidung
giant ['dʒaɪənt]	Riese
Inc [ɪŋk]	Kapitalgesellschaft
executive [ɪg'zekjətɪv]	Manager/in
government official	Regierungsbeamter/beamtin
['gʌvənmənt əfɪʃl]	
desperate ['despərət]	verzweifelt (versuchend)
mediator ['miːdieɪtə]	Vermittler/in
to chair [tʃeə]	leiten

139

leading ['liːdɪŋ]	führend
to inspect [ɪn'spekt]	kontrollieren, überprüfen
to invest [ɪn'vest]	investieren
unstable [ʌn'steɪbl]	instabil
billion ['bɪliən]	Milliarde
export earnings	Exporteinkünfte
[ˌekspɔːt 'ɜːnɪŋz]	
machinery [mə'ʃiːnəri]	Maschinen
inspection [ɪn'spekʃn]	Kontrolle, Inspektion
to clean up [ˌkliːn 'ʌp]	sauber machen, aufräumen
willingness ['wɪlɪŋnəs]	Bereitschaft, Bereitwilligkeit
press release ['pres rɪliːs]	Pressemitteilung
correctness [kə'rektnəs]	Richtigkeit
to hand out [ˌhænd 'aʊt]	austeilen, verteilen

Unit 7 Further reading

95

pot [pɒt]	Topf
community [kə'mjuːnəti]	Gemeinde
exchange [ɪks'tʃeɪndʒ]	Tausch
token ['təʊkən]	Marke, Chip
to cover the cost of	die Kosten decken von
[ˌkʌvə ðə 'kɒst əv]	
raw material [ˌrɔː mə'tɪəriəl]	Rohstoff(e)
therapist ['θerəpɪst]	Therapeut/in
handyman ['hændimæn]	Heimwerker
in turn [ɪn 'tɜːn]	als Gegenleistung
house extension	Hausanbau
[ˌhaʊs ɪk'stenʃn]	

potter ['pɒtə]	Töpfer/in
hedge [hedʒ]	Hecke
scheme [skiːm]	Programm, Projekt
income ['ɪnkʌm]	Einkommen

Unit 8 ▪ Wasting the world

96

category ['kætəgəri]	Kategorie, Klasse
recyclable [ˌriː'saɪkləbl]	wiederverwertbar, recycelbar
to reprocess [ˌriː'prəʊses]	wiederverarbeiten
bio-degradable	biologisch abbaubar
[ˌbaɪəʊdɪ'greɪdəbl]	
in time [ɪn 'taɪm]	rechtzeitig, mit der Zeit
to rot away [rɒt ə'weɪ]	verrotten
non-degradable	nicht abbaubar
[ˌnɒndɪ'greɪdəbl]	
to dispose of [dɪ'spəʊz əv]	beseitigen, entsorgen
incineration [ɪnˌsɪnə'reɪʃn]	Verbrennung
landfill site ['lændfɪl saɪt]	Deponie
toxic ['tɒksɪk]	giftig, toxisch
separately ['seprətli]	getrennt
illegal [ɪ'liːgl]	illegal
to dump [dʌmp]	abladen, verklappen

97

techno-waste ['teknəʊweɪst]	Elektronikschrott
relative ['relətɪv]	relativ
made up of [ˌmeɪd 'ʌp əv]	bestehend aus
fridge [frɪdʒ]	Kühlschrank
percentage [pə'sentɪdʒ]	Prozentsatz
to play down [ˌpleɪ 'daʊn]	herunterspielen
lobbyist ['lɒbiɪst]	Lobbyist/in
waste disposal	Abfallbeseitigung, Müllent-
['weɪst dɪspəʊzl]	sorgung
hazardous ['hæzədəs]	risikoreich, gefährlich
delegate ['delɪgət]	Delegierte/r
roughly ['rʌfli]	ungefähr
ton [tʌn]	Tonne
to translate into	hinauslaufen auf
[træns'leɪt ɪntə]	
approximate [ə'prɒksɪmət]	ungefähr
organized crime	organisierte Kriminalität
['ɔːgənaɪzd kraɪm]	
profitable ['prɒfɪtəbl]	Gewinn bringend
to smuggle ['smʌgl]	schmuggeln
to turn a blind eye	ein Auge zudrücken
[tɜːn ə blaɪnd 'aɪ]	
domestic [də'mestɪk]	Haus-
household equipment	Haushaltsgeräte
[ˌhaʊshəʊld ɪ'kwɪpmənt]	
cooker ['kʊkə]	Herd
dishwasher ['dɪʃwɒʃə]	Geschirrspüler
order ['ɔːdə]	Zustand
metal ['metl]	Metall
mercury ['mɜːkjəri]	Quecksilber
lead [led]	Blei
cadmium ['kædmiəm]	Cadmium
lithium ['lɪθiəm]	Lithium
to throw away [ˌθrəʊ ə'weɪ]	wegwerfen

to be faced with ['feɪst wɪð]	konfrontiert mit	
digital ['dɪdʒɪtl]	digital	
curse [kɜ:s]	Fluch	
blessing ['blesɪŋ]	Segen	
generation [,dʒenə'reɪʃn]	Generation	

98

savings ['seɪvɪŋz]	Ersparnisse
to take apart [,teɪk ə'pɑ:t]	auseinander nehmen, demontieren
enormous [ɪ'nɔ:məs]	enorm, gewaltig
to take notice of [teɪk 'nəʊtɪs əv]	beachten
incinerator [ɪn'sɪnəreɪtə]	Verbrennungsanlage
to import [ɪm'pɔ:t]	einführen, importieren
by [baɪ]	um
non-recyclable [,nɒn,ri:'saɪkləbl]	nicht wiederverwertbar
to generate ['dʒenəreɪt]	erzeugen

garbage ['gɑ:bɪdʒ]	Müll, Abfall
to convert into [kən'vɜ:t ɪntə]	umwandeln in
paper-maker ['peɪpəmeɪkə]	Papierhersteller
cement [sɪ'ment]	Zement
brand-new [,brænd'nju:]	nagelneu

99

mass tourism [,mæs 'tʊərɪzəm]	Massentourismus
to centre on ['sentə ɒn]	sich konzentrieren auf
high and dry [haɪ ən 'draɪ]	auf dem Trockenen
forest ['fɒrɪst]	Wald
strip [strɪp]	Streifen
high-rise ['haɪraɪz]	Hochhaus-
to block out [,blɒk 'aʊt]	verdunkeln
resident population [,rezɪdənt ,pɒpju'leɪʃn]	Wohnbevölkerung
house [haʊz]	unterbringen
under construction [,ʌndə kən'strʌkʃn]	im Bau
caravan park ['kærəvæn pɑ:k]	Campingplatz für Wohnwagen
fresh [freʃ]	frisch
scarce [skeəs]	knapp
rainfall ['reɪnfɔ:l]	Niederschlag
depth [depθ]	Tiefe
ground water ['graʊndwɔ:tə]	Grundwasser
seawater ['si:wɔ:tə]	Meerwasser
explosive [ɪk'spləʊsɪv]	explosiv
arrival [ə'raɪvl]	Ankunft
neutral ['nju:trəl]	neutral
observer [əb'zɜ:və]	Beobachter/in
to head for ['hed fə]	zusteuern auf
authorities [ɔ:'θɒrətiz]	Behörden
earnings ['ɜ:nɪŋz]	Einkünfte
mayor [meə]	Bürgermeister/in
official [ə'fɪʃl]	Beamter/Beamtin
scare story ['skeə stɔ:ri]	Horrorgeschichte
prophet ['prɒfɪt]	Prophet/in
doom [du:m]	(Welt-)Untergang

101

to take a message [,teɪk ə 'mesɪdʒ]	eine Nachricht entgegennehmen
to land [lænd]	landen
to stay off work [,steɪ 'ɒf wɜ:k]	der Arbeit fernbleiben
expenses [ɪk'spensɪz]	Spesen, Unkosten, Ausgaben
accounts department [ə'kaʊnts dɪpɑ:tmənt]	Buchhaltung
after all [,ɑ:ftər 'ɔ:l]	schließlich doch

102

to found [faʊnd]	gründen
adviser [əd'vaɪzə]	Berater/in
outer packaging [,aʊtə 'pækɪdʒɪŋ]	äußere Verpackung
compost heap ['kɒmpɒst hi:p]	Komposthaufen
remains [rɪ'meɪnz]	(Über-)Reste
returnable [rɪ'tɜ:nəbl]	Mehrweg-
container [kən'teɪnə]	Container
compostible ['kɒmpɒstəbl]	kompostierbar
dustbin ['dʌstbɪn]	Mülltonne

103

announcement [ə'naʊnsmənt]	Durchsage
connecting flight [kə,nektɪŋ 'flaɪt]	Anschlussflug
to make arrangements [meɪk ə'reɪndʒmənts]	Vorkehrungen treffen
information desk [ɪnfə'meɪʃn desk]	Informationsschalter, Auskunft
leg [leg]	Strecke
outrageous [aʊt'reɪdʒəs]	empörend
refreshments [rɪ'freʃmənts]	Erfrischungen
What's the story now? [,wɒts ðə 'stɔ:ri naʊ]	Wie geht's jetzt weiter?

owing to ['əʊɪŋ tə]	wegen, aufgrund
to transfer [træns'fɜ:]	umsteigen
terminal ['tɜ:mɪnl]	Abfertigungsgebäude
main entrance hall [,meɪn 'entrəns hɔ:l]	Haupteingangshalle
to revise [rɪ'vaɪz]	überarbeiten
travel documents ['trævl dɒkjuments]	Reisedokumente
tourist class ['tʊərɪst klɑ:s]	Touristenklasse

net [net]	netto
ownership ['əʊnəʃɪp]	Besitz
in spite of [ɪn 'spaɪt əv]	trotz
extent [ɪk'stent]	(Aus-)Maß, Umfang
unusable [ʌn'ju:zəbl]	nicht zu gebrauchen
ferrous ['ferəs]	eisenhaltig
non-ferrous [,nɒn 'ferəs]	nicht eisenhaltig
fluid ['flu:ɪd]	Flüssigkeit
tyre ['taɪə]	Reifen
rubber ['rʌbə]	Gummi

104

eco-warrior [ˌiːkəʊ 'wɒriə]	Umweltaktivist
litter-bug ['lɪtəbʌg]	Umweltverschandler
questionnaire [ˌkwestʃə'neə]	Fragebogen
scooter ['skuːtə]	(Motor-)Roller
cutlery ['kʌtləri]	Besteck
job loss ['dʒɒb lɒs]	Arbeitsplatzverlust
rechargeable battery	aufladbare Batterie
[ˌriːˈtʃɑːdʒəbl 'bætəri]	
mains power ['meɪnz paʊə]	Stromnetz
drinks can ['drɪŋks kæn]	Getränkedose
to spoil [spɔɪl]	verderben
stand-by switch	Bereitschaftsschalter
[ˌstændbaɪ 'swɪtʃ]	
VCR (AE) [ˌviː siː 'ɑː]	Videorekorder
used [juːzd]	gebraucht
catalytic converter	Katalysator
[ˌkætə,lɪtɪk kən'vɜːtə]	
ecological [ˌiːkə'lɒdʒɪkl]	ökologisch
selfish ['selfɪʃ]	egoistisch, selbstsüchtig
to do your bit [du jɔː 'bɪt]	seinen Beitrag leisten
to take seriously	ernst nehmen
[teɪk 'sɪəriəsli]	
to speak out [ˌspiːk 'aʊt]	aussprechen, seine Meinung sagen
to behave [bɪ'heɪv]	sich verhalten, sich benehmen
terrific [tə'rɪfɪk]	großartig, phantastisch
to get the message	es begreifen
[ˌget ðə 'mesɪdʒ]	
to pass on [ˌpɑːs 'ɒn]	weitergeben, -leiten
Mother Earth [ˌmʌðər 'ɜːθ]	Mutter Erde
to get the most out of	den größten Nutzen ziehen aus
[get ðə 'məʊst aʊt əv]	

Unit 9 ▪ Zero tolerance?

105

zero tolerance	Null-Toleranz
[ˌzɪərəʊ 'tɒlərəns]	
armed robbery [ˌɑːmd 'rɒbəri]	bewaffneter Raubüberfall
assault [ə'sɔːlt]	(tätlicher) Angriff
burglary ['bɜːgləri]	Einbruch
credit card fraud	Kreditkartenbetrug
['kredɪt kɑːd frɔːd]	
drug-taking ['drʌg teɪkɪŋ]	Drogenkonsum
drug-trafficking	Drogenhandel
[ˌdrʌg 'træfɪkɪŋ]	
drunk driving	Trunkenheit am Steuer
[ˌdrʌŋk 'draɪvɪŋ]	
hijacking ['haɪdʒækɪŋ]	(Flugzeug-)Entführung
industrial espionage	Industriespionage
[ɪnˌdʌstriəl 'espiənɑːʒ]	
kidnapping ['kɪdnæpɪŋ]	Entführung
manslaughter ['mænslɔːtə]	Totschlag
mugging ['mʌgɪŋ]	Straßenraub
rape [reɪp]	Vergewaltigung
shoplifting ['ʃɒplɪftɪŋ]	Ladendiebstahl
vandalism ['vændəlɪzəm]	Vandalismus
law-breaking ['lɔːbreɪkɪŋ]	Gesetzesbruch

106

drug-related ['drʌg rɪleɪtɪd]	im Zusammenhang mit Drogen
powerless ['paʊələs]	machtlos
crime rate ['kraɪm reɪt]	Verbrechensrate
president ['prezɪdənt]	Präsident/in
movement-sensitive lighting	Außenbeleuchtung mit Bewegungsmelder
[ˌmuːvmənt 'sensɪtɪv laɪtɪŋ]	
burglar alarm	Alarmanlage
['bɜːglər əlɑːm]	
closed-circuit TV (CCTV)	Kameraüberwachung
[ˌkləʊzd sɜːkɪt ˌtiː 'viː]	
property ['prɒpəti]	Eigentum
hardline ['hɑːdlaɪn]	hart durchgreifend
offender [ə'fendə]	Straftäter/in
catchphrase ['kætʃfreɪz]	Motto
prison sentence	Haft-, Gefängnisstrafe
['prɪzn sentəns]	
offence [ə'fens]	Straftat, Vergehen
jail [dʒeɪl]	Gefängnis
to focus on ['fəʊkəs ɒn]	sich konzentrieren auf
ethnic ['eθnɪk]	ethnisch
racial tension [ˌreɪʃl 'tenʃn]	Rassenunruhen
harsh [hɑːʃ]	hart, streng
heavy-handed [ˌhevi-'hændɪd]	scharf vorgehend
considerably [kən'sɪdərəbli]	beträchtlich
tax evasion ['tæks ɪveɪʒn]	Steuerhinterziehung
annual ['ænjuəl]	jährlich
target ['tɑːgɪt]	Ziel
non-essentials [ˌnɒn ɪ'senʃlz]	nicht notwendige Dinge
epidemic [ˌepɪ'demɪk]	Epidemie
consumer-related	konsumbedingt
[kən'sjuːmə rɪleɪtɪd]	
to resell [ˌriː'sel]	wieder verkaufen
thrill [θrɪl]	Kitzel, Gefühl
to impress [ɪm'pres]	beeindrucken, imponieren

107

rural ['rʊərəl]	ländlich
gentle ['dʒentl]	sanft, leicht
hi-tech [ˌhaɪ'tek]	Spitzentechnik
community policing	Polizeiarbeit auf der Straße
[kəˌmjuːnəti pə'liːsɪŋ]	
once-only [ˌwʌn 'əʊnli]	einmalig
pointless ['pɔɪntləs]	sinnlos
suburb ['sʌbɜːb]	Vorort, Außenbezirk
guard [gɑːd]	Wache
punishment ['pʌnɪʃmənt]	Strafe
to break up with	Schluss machen mit
[ˌbreɪk 'ʌp wɪð]	
mall (AE) [mɔːl]	(Einkaufs-)Passage
a pair of earrings	ein Paar Ohrringe
[ə peər əv 'ɪərɪŋz]	
to come up to [ˌkʌm 'ʌp tə]	zukommen auf
handcuff ['hændkʌf]	Handschelle
purse (AE) [pɜːs]	Handtasche
to prosecute ['prɒsɪkjuːt]	strafrechtlich belangen
cop (AE) [kɒp]	Polizist
shocked [ʃɒkt]	schockiert
to win back [ˌwɪn 'bæk]	zurückgewinnen

108

infamous ['ɪnfəməs]	berüchtigt
massacre ['mæsəkə]	Massaker
to expel [ɪk'spel]	ausweisen
weapon ['wepən]	Waffe
to sue [su:]	verklagen, (gerichtlich) belangen
tragedy ['trædʒədi]	Tragödie
to admit [əd'mɪt]	zugeben, gestehen
grotesque [grəʊ'tesk]	grotesk
prison ['prɪzn]	Gefängnis
out of place [aʊt əv 'pleɪs]	ungewöhnlich
earplug ['ɪəplʌg]	Ohrstöpsel
violence ['vaɪələns]	Gewalt
to tell on sb ['tel ɒn]	jdn. verpetzen
to fear [fɪə]	(be)fürchten, Angst haben vor
retaliation [rɪˌtæli'eɪʃn]	Vergeltung
juvenile ['dʒu:vənaɪl]	Jugend-
to be to blame [bi tə 'bleɪm]	schuld sein, verantwortlich sein
to try a case [traɪ ə 'keɪs]	einen Fall behandeln
to dismiss [dɪs'mɪs]	einstellen
lawsuit ['lɔ:su:t]	Verfahren

109

to congratulate sb on [kən'grætʃuleɪt ɒn]	jdm. gratulieren zu
to feel like ['fi:l laɪk]	Lust haben auf

110

to intend [ɪn'tend]	beabsichtigen, vorhaben
to wound [wu:nd]	verwunden
to recognize ['rekəgnaɪz]	erkennen
to commit a crime [kəˌmɪt ə 'kraɪm]	ein Verbrechen begehen
to put sb in danger [pʊt ɪn 'deɪndʒə]	jdn. in Gefahr bringen

111

to decide on [dɪ'saɪd ɒn]	sich entscheiden für
verdict ['vɜ:dɪkt]	Urteil
heart attack ['hɑ:t ətæk]	Herzinfarkt, -anfall
demonstration [ˌdemən'streɪʃn]	Demonstration, Vorführung
rail shipment ['reɪl ʃɪpmənt]	Bahntransport
nuclear waste [ˌnju:kliə 'weɪst]	Atommüll
diamond necklace [ˌdaɪəmənd 'nekləs]	Diamantenkollier
criminal record ['krɪmɪnl rekɔ:d]	Strafakte
to fascinate ['fæsɪneɪt]	faszinieren
unauthorized possession [ˌʌnɔ:θəraɪzd pə'zeʃn]	unbefugter Besitz
firearm ['faɪərɑ:m]	Feuerwaffe
submachine gun [ˌsʌbmə'ʃi:n gʌn]	Maschinenpistole
car boot ['kɑ: bu:t]	Kofferraum
to live on social security [lɪv ɒn ˌsəʊʃl sɪ'kjʊərəti]	von Sozialhilfe leben
divorce [dɪ'vɔ:s]	Scheidung

single mother [ˌsɪŋgl 'mʌðə]	allein erziehende Mutter
to knife [naɪf]	mit einem Messer verletzen
to let so off [ˌlet 'ɒf]	jdn. laufen lassen
community service [kə'mju:nəti sɜ:vɪs]	gemeinnützige Arbeit
to suspend [sə'spend]	aussetzen
to put on probation [ˌpʊt ɒn prə'beɪʃn]	auf Bewährung entlassen
minor ['maɪnə]	unbedeutend, klein
breach of the law [ˌbri:tʃ əv ðə 'lɔ:]	Gesetzesbruch
trivial ['trɪviəl]	trivial, geringfügig
to deserve [dɪ'zɜ:v]	verdienen
mitigating circumstances [ˌmɪtɪgeɪtɪŋ 'sɜ:kəmstənsɪz]	mildernde Umstände
deterrent [dɪ'terənt]	Abschreckung
to deter sb from [dɪ'tɜ: frəm]	jdn. abhalten von
lenient ['li:niənt]	milde
tolerant ['tɒlərənt]	tolerant
to take into account [ˌteɪk ɪntu ə'kaʊnt]	in Betracht ziehen, berücksichtigen
in view of [ɪn 'vju: əv]	angesichts
to recommend [ˌrekə'mend]	empfehlen

Unit 9 Further reading

112

ancient ['eɪnʃənt]	(sehr) alt, historisch
suit of armour [su:t əv 'ɑ:mə]	Rüstung
steel [sti:l]	Stahl
to miss out [ˌmɪs 'aʊt]	auslassen, überspringen
retail sector ['ri:teɪl sektə]	Einzelhandelsbereich
dealer ['di:lə]	Händler/in
to knock over [ˌnɒk 'əʊvə]	niederschlagen
to roll [rəʊl]	rollen
foot of the stairs [ˌfʊt əv ðə 'steəz]	unteres Ende der Treppe
antique [æn'ti:k]	antik
burglar ['bɜ:glə]	Einbrecher/in
to rob [rɒb]	ausrauben
to stick to ['stɪk tə]	festkleben an
supplies [sə'plaɪz]	Vorräte
to lean over ['li:n əʊvə]	sich lehnen über
glue-sniffing addict [ˌglu:snɪfɪŋ 'ædɪkt]	klebstoffschnüffelnde/r Süchtige/r
to support a habit [səˌpɔ:t ə 'hæbɪt]	seine Sucht befriedigen
worryingly ['wʌriɪŋli]	beängstigend
in the dead of night [ɪn ðə ˌded əv 'naɪt]	mitten in der Nacht
overwhelmed [ˌəʊvə'welmd]	überwältigt
fumes [fju:mz]	Dämpfe, Abgase
quantity ['kwɒntəti]	Menge, Quantität
to climb [klaɪm]	ersteigen

Unit 10 ▪ Minorities

113

minority [maɪ'nɒrəti] — Minderheit
quota ['kwəʊtə] — Quote
glass ceiling [ˌglɑːs 'siːlɪŋ] — unsichtbare Beförderungs-sperre
ethnic ['eθnɪk] — ethnisch
decent ['diːsnt] — anständig
to discriminate against [dɪ'skrɪmɪneɪt əgenst] — diskriminieren
able-bodied [ˌeɪbl'bɒdɪd] — nicht behindert
affirmative [ə'fɜːmətɪv] — zustimmend, bejahend
discriminatory [dɪ'skrɪmɪnətəri] — diskriminierend
wrong [rɒŋ] — Unrecht
to elect [ɪ'lekt] — wählen
to identify [aɪ'dentɪfaɪ] — erkennen, identifizieren

114

extract ['ekstrækt] — Auszug
electoral candidate [ɪˌlektərəl 'kændɪdət] — Wahlkandidat/in
challenge ['tʃælɪndʒ] — Anfechtung, Ablehnung
Labour (Party) ['leɪbə pɑːti] — Labour Party
candidate ['kændɪdət] — Bewerber/in, Kandidat/in
to react to [ri'ækt tə] — reagieren auf
to come down to [ˌkʌm 'daʊn tə] — darauf hinauslaufen
positive discrimination [ˌpɒzətɪv dɪˌskrɪmɪ'neɪʃn] — positive Diskriminierung
disadvantaged [ˌdɪsəd'vɑːntɪdʒd] — benachteiligt
surely ['ʃʊəli] — sicherlich
selection committee [sɪˌlekʃn kə'mɪti] — Wahlausschuss
European Court of Human Rights [jʊərə'piːən kɔːt əv ˌhjuːmən 'raɪts] — Europäischer Gerichtshof für Menschenrechte
equal ['iːkwəl] — gleich
legal ['liːgl] — gesetzlich, juristisch, legal
random selection [ˌrændəm sɪ'lekʃn] — Zufallsprinzip
to toss a coin [tɒs ə 'kɔɪn] — eine Münze werfen
parliamentary seat [ˌpɑːlə'mentri siːt] — Parlamentssitz
civil service [ˌsɪvl 'sɜːvɪs] — öffentlicher Dienst
to compete against [kəm'piːt əgenst] — konkurrieren mit
presence ['prezns] — Anwesenheit
at large [ət 'lɑːdʒ] — als Ganzes
hold on [ˌhəʊld 'ɒn] — Vormachtstellung in

115

nation ['neɪʃn] — Nation
talent ['tælənt] — Talent, Begabung

rare [reə] — selten
privilege ['prɪvəlɪdʒ] — Privileg
come off it [ˌkʌm 'ɒf ɪt] — hör auf (damit)
to care for ['keə fə] — versorgen, sorgen für
to overcome [ˌəʊvə'kʌm] — überwinden
partnership ['pɑːtnəʃɪp] — Partnerschaft
for heaven's sake [fə hevnz 'seɪk] — um Himmels willen

116

Aborigine [ˌæbə'rɪdʒəni] — (austral.) Ureinwohner/in
prosperity [prɒ'sperəti] — Wohlstand
noble ['nəʊbl] — edel
savage ['sævɪdʒ] — Wilde/r
to arrest [ə'rest] — verhaften
on average [ɒn 'ævərɪdʒ] — im Durchschnitt, durch-schnittlich
life expectancy ['laɪf ɪspektənsi] — Lebenserwartung
government handout [ˌgʌvənmənt 'hændaʊt] — staatliche Unterstützung
grim [grɪm] — schlimm
reality [ri'æləti] — Wirklichkeit
central ['sentrəl] — zentral
Olympics [ə'lɪmpɪks] — Olympische Spiele
dance troupe ['dɑːns truːp] — Tanzgruppe
body paint ['bɒdi peɪnt] — Körperbemalung
opening ceremony [ˌəʊpnɪŋ 'serəməni] — Eröffnungszeremonie
Olympic flame [əˌlɪmpɪk 'fleɪm] — olympisches Feuer
cynical ['sɪnɪkl] — zynisch
window dressing ['wɪndəʊ dresɪŋ] — Schau, Augenwischerei
romanticized [rəʊ'mæntɪsaɪzd] — romantisiert
to be sick of [bi 'sɪk əv] — (etwas) satt haben
didgeridoo [ˌdɪdʒəri'duː] — Didgeridoo (Holzblasinstru-ment)
run-up ['rʌnʌp] — Vorlauf
airline ['eəlaɪn] — Fluggesellschaft
to bring out [ˌbrɪŋ 'aʊt] — herausbringen
to beam [biːm] — strahlen
shack [ʃæk] — Hütte, Schuppen
dozen ['dʌzn] — Dutzend
in-law ['ɪn lɔː] — angeheiratete/r Verwandte/r
to contrast ['kɒntrɑːst] — Gegensatz, Kontrast
to make up [ˌmeɪk 'ʌp] — bilden
boomerang ['buːməræŋ] — Bumerang
dot painting ['dɒt peɪntɪŋ] — pointilistisches Gemälde
souvenir shop [ˌsuːvə'nɪə ʃɒp] — Souvenirladen
unscrupulous [ʌn'skruːpjʊləs] — skrupellos
trader ['treɪdə] — Händler/in
backpacker ['bækpækə] — Rucksacktourist/in

117

to differ from ['dɪfə frəm] — sich unterscheiden von
diagnostic [ˌdaɪəg'nɒstɪk] — diagnostisch
sales manager ['seɪlz mænɪdʒə] — Verkaufsleiter/in
biological [ˌbaɪə'lɒdʒɪkl] — biologisch
to criticize ['krɪtɪsaɪz] — kritisieren

athlete ['æθli:t] — (Leicht-)Athlet/in, Sportler/in
honour ['ɒnə] — Ehre
respectful [rɪ'spektfl] — ehrfürchtig
health care ['helθ keə] — Gesundheitsfürsorge
injustice [ɪn'dʒʌstɪs] — Ungerechtigkeit
to pass laws [pɑːs 'lɔːz] — Gesetze verabschieden
ramp [ræmp] — Rampe
prejudice ['predʒudɪs] — Vorurteil

to analyze ['ænəlaɪz] — analysieren
entire [ɪn'taɪə] — ganz, vollständig
division [dɪ'vɪʒn] — Teilung
household ['haʊshəʊld] — Haushalt
satisfactory [,sætɪs'fæktəri] — befriedigend

Unit 10 Further reading

charity ['tʃærəti] — Wohltätigkeitsorganisation
homeless ['həʊmləs] — obdachlos
condemnation [,kɒndem'neɪʃn] — Verurteilung
to sleep rough [sliːp 'rʌf] — im Freien schlafen
oil-rig ['ɔɪlrɪg] — Bohrinsel, Ölplattform
bargain ['bɑːgɪn] — günstiges Angebot, Schnäppchen
exclusive [ɪk'skluːsɪv] — exklusiv
to condemn [kən'dem] — verurteilen
vagrant ['veɪgrənt] — Obdachlose/r
tramp [træmp] — Tramp
musical instrument [,mjuːzɪkl 'ɪnstrəmənt] — Musikinstrument
sketch pad ['sketʃ pæd] — Skizzenblock
to survive [sə'vaɪv] — überleben
life-changing ['laɪf tʃeɪndʒɪŋ] — lebensverändernd
outrage ['aʊtreɪdʒ] — verletzen, schockieren, entrüsten
unpleasant [ʌn'pleznt] — unangenehm
Scotland Yard [,skɒtlənd 'jɑːd] — die Londoner Polizei
to trivialize ['trɪvɪəlaɪz] — trivialisieren
bogus ['bəʊgəs] — falsch, unecht
roof over one's head [,ruːf əʊvə wʌnz 'hed] — Dach über dem Kopf
beggar ['begə] — Bettler/in
to abuse [ə'bjuːz] — missbrauchen
generosity [,dʒenə'rɒsəti] — Großzügigkeit
to pretend [prɪ'tend] — vorgeben, so tun als ob
Vagrancy Act ['veɪgrənsi ækt] — Obdachlosengesetz

Unit 11 ▪ Changing nature

genetic modification (GM) [dʒə,netɪk ,mɒdɪfɪ'keɪʃn] — Gentechnik
combination [,kɒmbɪ'neɪʃn] — Kombination
gene [dʒiːn] — Gen
genetic code [dʒə,netɪk 'kəʊd] — genetischer Code
disease [dɪ'ziːz] — Krankheit, Erkrankung
to clone [kləʊn] — klonen
experiment [ɪk'sperɪmənt] — Versuch, Experiment

uncontrollable [,ʌnkən'trəʊləbl] — unkontrollierbar
foe [fəʊ] — Feind/in
to estimate ['estɪmeɪt] — schätzen
pest [pest] — Schädling
erosion [ɪ'rəʊʒn] — Erosion
malnutrition [,mælnjuː'trɪʃn] — Unterernährung
starvation [stɑː'veɪʃn] — Hunger
to resist [rɪ'zɪst] — widerstehen
yield [jiːld] — Ertrag, Ernte
usable ['juːzəbl] — nutzbar
salty ['sɔːlti] — salzig
nutritional [njuːtrɪʃənl] — Nahrungs-
deficiency [dɪ'fɪʃnsi] — Mangel
quarter ['kwɔːtə] — Viertel
allergy ['ælədʒi] — Allergie
slightly ['slaɪtli] — leicht, geringfügig
drastic ['dræstɪk] — drastisch
complex ['kɒmpleks] — kompliziert
balance ['bæləns] — Gleichgewicht
mink [mɪŋk] — Nerz
brutal ['bruːtl] — brutal
to poison ['pɔɪzn] — vergiften
unwanted [,ʌn'wɒntɪd] — unerwünscht
weed [wiːd] — Unkraut
corn [kɔːn] — Mais
attacker [ə'tækə] — Angreifer
mainstream ['meɪnstriːm] — vorherrschende Meinung
breed [briːd] — sich fortpflanzen
the wild [ðə 'waɪld] — die freie Natur
mutant ['mjuːtənt] — verändert, durch Mutation entstanden
superweed ['suːpəwiːd] — Unkraut mit mehreren Resistenzen
alike [ə'laɪk] — gleichermaßen
science fiction [,saɪəns 'fɪkʃn] — Sciencefiction
tropical ['trɒpɪkl] — tropisch
marine [mə'riːn] — Meeres-, maritim
research laboratory [rɪ,sɜːtʃ lə'bɒrətri] — Forschungslabor(atorium)
plant life ['plɑːnt laɪf] — Pflanzenleben
plant-eating ['plɑːnt iːtɪŋ] — Pflanzen fressend
marine life [mə'riːn laɪf] — Meeresfauna und -flora
food chain ['fuːdtʃeɪn] — Nahrungskette
elsewhere [,els'weə] — anderswo

creation [kri'eɪʃn] — Schöpfung, Erschaffung, Erzeugung
to populate ['pɒpjuleɪt] — bevölkern
populous ['pɒpjələs] — dicht besiedelt
destruction [dɪ'strʌkʃn] — Zerstörung, Vernichtung
to erode [ɪ'rəʊd] — austrocknen
to starve [stɑːv] — verhungern
resistant to [rɪ'zɪstənt tə] — widerstandsfähig gegen
protective [prə'tektɪv] — Schutz-
sweet potato [swiːt pə'teɪtəʊ] — Süßkartoffel
species ['spiːʃiːz] — Art(en)
belief [bɪ'liːf] — Glaube

124

genetics [dʒə'netɪks]	Genetik
moral ['mɒrəl]	moralisch
blueprint ['blu:prɪnt]	Blaupause, Bauplan
conception [kən'sepʃn]	Empfängnis, Befruchtung
to get married [get 'mærɪd]	heiraten
genetic test [dʒə,netɪk 'test]	Gentest
to conceive [kən'si:v]	empfangen
womb [wu:m]	Mutterleib
embryo ['embriəʊ]	Embryo
to consist of [kən'sɪst əv]	bestehen aus
cell [sel]	Zelle
defective [dɪ'fektɪv]	fehlerhaft
genetic engineering	Gentechnik
[dʒə,netɪk ,endʒɪ'nɪərɪŋ]	
implication [,ɪmplɪ'keɪʃn]	Auswirkung
bioethics [,baɪəʊ'eθɪks]	Bioethik
nursery school ['nɜːsəri sku:l]	Kindergarten, Vorschule
to indicate ['ɪndɪkeɪt]	(an)zeigen, hinweisen auf
anti-social [,ænti'səʊʃl]	asozial
alcoholism ['ælkəhɒlɪzəm]	Alkoholismus
opponent [ə'pəʊnənt]	Gegner/in
to undermine [,ʌndə'maɪn]	untergraben
civil liberties [,sɪvl 'lɪbəti]	Bürgerrechte
fertility clinic [fə'tɪləti klɪnɪk]	Geburtsklinik
to fertilize ['fɜːtəlaɪz]	befruchten
intelligence [ɪn'telɪdʒəns]	Intelligenz
schooling ['sku:lɪŋ]	Schulung, Ausbildung
to get on better [,get ɒn betə]	besser vorankommen
to head towards	zusteuern auf
['hed təwɔ:dz]	
to divide [dɪ'vaɪd]	teilen
extraordinary [ɪk'strɔ:dnri]	außergewöhnlich, ungewöhnlich
to ring out [,rɪŋ 'aʊt]	ertönen, schallen
courtroom ['kɔ:tru:m]	Gerichtssaal
trial ['traɪəl]	Prozess, Verfahren, Verhandlung
to grip [grɪp]	fest im Griff haben
adrenoleukodystrophy	Fettstoffwechselkrankheit
[ə,dri:nəʊ,lu:kəʊ'dɪstrəfi]	
nervous system	Nervensystem
[,nɜ:vəs 'sɪstəm]	
lawyer ['lɔ:jə]	Anwalt, Anwältin
neglect [nɪ'glekt]	Vernachlässigung
damages ['dæmɪdʒɪz]	Schaden(s)ersatz

125

fundamental [,fʌndə'mentl]	grundsätzlich, wesentlich
social services	Sozialamt
[,səʊʃl 'sɜ:vɪsɪz]	
pregnancy ['pregnənsi]	Schwangerschaft

126

to multiply ['mʌltɪplaɪ]	multiplizieren
century ['sentʃəri]	Jahrhundert
population explosion	Bevölkerungsexplosion
[,pɒpju'leɪʃn ɪkspləʊʒn]	
pharmaceutical	pharmazeutisch
[,fɑ:mə'su:tɪkl]	
to make a breakthrough	einen Durchbruch erzielen
[meɪk ə 'breɪkθru:]	

Part A

to pick up the phone	den Hörer abheben
[,pɪk 'ʌp ðə fəʊn]	

Part B

inefficient [,ɪnɪ'fɪʃnt]	ineffizient
to mix up [,mɪks 'ʌp]	vermischen

127

up to a point [ʌp tu ə 'pɔɪnt]	bis zu einem bestimmten Punkt
to some extent	in gewissem Grade
[tə sʌm ɪk'stent]	
superhuman [,su:pə'hju:mən]	übermenschlich

Unit 11 Further reading

cow [kaʊ]	Kuh
to carry out [,kæri 'aʊt]	durchführen
to omit [ə'mɪt]	weglassen
follow-up question	Anschlussfrage
[,fɒləʊ ʌp 'kwestʃən]	
religious beliefs	Religion, religiöse Anschauungen
[rɪ'lɪdʒəs bɪ'li:fs]	
to interfere with	stören
[,ɪntə'fɪə wɪð]	
distinctiveness	Einzigartigkeit
[dɪ'stɪŋktɪvnəs]	
questionable ['kwestʃənəbl]	fragwürdig
superior [su:'pɪəriə]	hochwertig(er)
vital organ [,vaɪtl 'ɔ:gən]	lebenswichtiges Organ
infertile [ɪn'fɜ:taɪl]	unfruchtbar
gay [geɪ]	schwul, homosexuell, lesbisch
couple ['kʌpl]	Paar

Unit 12 ▪ Europe

129

treaty ['tri:ti]	Vertrag
European Economic Community (EEC)	Europäische Wirtschaftsgemeinschaft (EWG)
[jʊərəpi:ən ,i:kənɒmɪk kə'mju:nəti]	
European Union	Europäische Union
[jʊərəpi:ən 'ju:niən]	
coin [kɔɪn]	Münze
banknote ['bæŋknəʊt]	Geldschein, Banknote
European Central Bank	Europäische Zentralbank
[jʊərəʊ,pi:ən 'sentrəl bæŋk]	
anthem ['ænθəm]	Hymne

130

opinion poll [ə'pɪniən pəʊl]	Meinungsumfrage
single market [,sɪŋgl 'mɑ:kɪt]	Binnenmarkt
investment bank	Investitionsbank
[ɪn'vestmənt bæŋk]	
if only [ɪf 'əʊnli]	wenn nur
crash [kræʃ]	Krach
reserve currency	Reservewährung
[rɪ,zɜ:v 'kʌrənsi]	
euro zone ['jʊərəʊ zəʊn]	Eurozone

immigration [ˌɪmɪ'greɪʃn]	Einwanderung	to fight against ['faɪt əgenst]	kämpfen gegen
skilled [skɪld]	ausgebildet, Fach-	integration [ˌɪntɪ'greɪʃn]	Integration
superpower [ˌsuːpəpaʊə]	Supermacht	mobility [məʊ'bɪləti]	Mobilität
to sound like ['saʊnd laɪk]	sich anhören wie	impracticable	undurchführbar
to come true [ˌkʌm 'truː]	wahr werden	[ɪm'præktɪkəbl]	
trade flow ['treɪd fləʊ]	Handelsstrom	lack [læk]	Mangel
within [wɪ'ðɪn]	innerhalb (von)	other than ['ʌðə ðən]	außer
coal [kəʊl]	Kohle	federalist ['fedərəlɪst]	föderalistisch
to go over to [ˌgəʊ 'əʊvə tə]	übergehen zu	optimistic [ˌɒptɪ'mɪstɪk]	optimistisch
regional ['riːdʒənl]	regional		
specialization [ˌspeʃəlaɪ'zeɪʃn]	Spezialisierung	133	
wheat [wiːt]	Weizen	to be in two minds about	gespaltener Meinung sein
make sense [meɪk 'sens]	sinnvoll sein, Sinn ergeben	[bi ɪn ˌtuː 'maɪndz əbaʊt]	
to be fluent in [bi 'fluːənt ɪn]	fließend sprechen	bathing trunks	Badehose
lingua franca	Verkehrssprache	['beɪðɪŋ trʌŋks]	
[ˌlɪŋgwə 'fræŋkə]		leggings ['legɪŋz]	Leggings
		scissors ['sɪzəz]	Schere
131			
stock exchange	(Wertpapier-)Börse	**134**	
['stɒk ɪkstʃeɪndʒ]		contact lenses	Kontaktlinsen
to standardize ['stændədaɪz]	standardisieren, normieren	['kɒntækt lenzɪz]	
plug [plʌg]	Stecker	steel [stiːl]	Stahl
socket ['sɒkɪt]	Steckdose	nail [neɪl]	Nagel
throughout [θruː'aʊt]	überall (in)	European Commission	Europäische Kommission
appliance [ə'plaɪəns]	Gerät	[ˌjʊərəpiːən kə'mɪʃn]	
to convert to [kən'vɜːt tə]	umstellen auf	to lift a ban [lɪft ə 'bæn]	ein Verbot aufheben
conversion [kən'vɜːʃn]	Umstellung	to look into [ˌlʊk 'ɪntə]	untersuchen, prüfen
		to threaten to ['θretn tə]	drohen zu
flop [flɒp]	Fehlschlag	to break a law [breɪk ə 'lɔː]	ein Gesetz brechen
out of date [aʊt əv 'deɪt]	veraltet	re-use [ˌriː 'juːs]	Wiederverwendung
hairdryer ['heə draɪə]	Fön	in effect [ɪn ɪ'fekt]	tatsächlich
three-pin socket	dreipolige Steckdose	to hinder ['hɪndə]	(be)hindern
[ˌθriːpɪn 'sɒkɪt]			
two-pin plug [ˌtuːpɪn plʌg]	zweipoliger Stecker	**135**	
power cable ['paʊə keɪbl]	Stromkabel	chronological [ˌkrɒnə'lɒdʒɪkl]	chronologisch
washing machine	Waschmaschine	to abolish [ə'bɒlɪʃ]	abschaffen
['wɒʃɪŋ məʃiːn]		import duty ['ɪmpɔːt djuːti]	Einfuhrzoll
exporter [ɪk'spɔːtə]	Exporteur/in	reunification [ˌriːjuːnɪfɪ'keɪʃn]	Wiedervereinigung
to pass on [ˌpɑːs 'ɒn]	weitergeben	GDR [ˌdʒiː diː 'ɑː]	DDR
complicated	kompliziert	internal frontier	Binnengrenze
['kɒmplɪkeɪtɪd]		[ɪnˌtɜːnl 'frʌntɪə]	
traveller ['trævələ]	Reisende/r	expansion [ɪk'spænʃn]	Erweiterung

Unit 12 Further reading

132		**136**	
corporation [ˌkɔːpə'reɪʃn]	(Aktien-)Gesellschaft	veto ['viːtəʊ]	Veto
on the march [ɒn ðə 'mɑːtʃ]	auf dem Vormarsch	ridiculous [rɪ'dɪkjələs]	lächerlich
respondent [rɪ'spɒndənt]	Befragte/r	professional [prə'feʃənl]	professionell
native language	Muttersprache	external [ɪk'stɜːnl]	Außen-
[ˌneɪtɪv 'læŋgwɪdʒ]		tariff ['tærɪf]	Zoll
unstoppable [ˌʌn'stɒpəbl]	unaufhaltsam	to be fed up with	es satt haben
non-native [ˌnɒn'neɪtɪv]	nicht muttersprachlich	[ˌfed 'ʌp wɪð]	
opposition [ˌɒpə'zɪʃn]	Opposition	unelected [ˌʌnɪ'lektɪd]	nicht gewählt
linguistic [lɪn'gwɪstɪk]	linguistisch	bureaucrat ['bjʊərəkræt]	Bürokrat/in
nationalist ['næʃnəlɪst]	Nationalist		
truly ['truːli]	wahrhaftig, wirklich		
united [ju'naɪtɪd]	vereinigt, vereint		

Alphabetisches Wörterverzeichnis

Diese Liste enthält alle Wörter in *New Focus on Success* in alphabetischer Reihenfolge.
Nicht aufgeführt sind Wörter, die zum **Grundwortschatz** gehören.
Wörter aus den Hörverständnisübungen sind mit einem *H* gekennzeichnet.

A

ability *85* Fähigkeit, Können
able-bodied *113* nicht behindert
to abolish *135* abschaffen
Aboriginal *48* (austral.) Ureinwohner/in
Aborigine *116* (austral.) Ureinwohner/in
above *6* über
absolutely *50* absolut, völlig
absurd *62* absurd
to abuse *120* missbrauchen
academic *43* akademisch
to accept *7* akzeptieren
to access *63* zugreifen auf
accessory *47* Accessoire
accommodation *9* Unterkunft
according to *27* laut, nach
account manager *33* Kundenbetreuer/in
accounting *40* Rechnungswesen, (Bilanz-)Buchhaltung
accounts department *101* Buchhaltung
accounts *40* Buchhaltung
to act as *48* dienen als
to act *58* sich verhalten, handeln
action group *40* Aktionsgruppe
action *35H* Aktion, Handlung
activist *138* Aktivist/in
activity *42* Aktivität, Tätigkeit
actual *33* tatsächlich
actually *35H* eigentlich, tatsächlich
ad *8* Anzeige
adapt *58* adaptieren
to add *21* hinzufügen
addicted to *69* süchtig nach, abhängig von
admission *80* Eintritt
to admit *108* zugeben, gestehen
adrenoleukodystrophy *124* eine Fettstoffwechselkrankheit
advanced *18* fortgeschritten
adventure *6* Abenteuer
to advertise *6* inserieren, werben
advertisement *32* Reklame, Werbung, Anzeige
advertisers *36* Werbeleute
advice *26* Ratschlag, (guter) Rat
to advise *12* raten
adviser *102* Berater/in
affair *45* Angelegenheit

to affect *42* beeinflussen
affirmative *113* zustimmend, bejahend
affluent *88* wohlhabend
affordable *69* erschwinglich
after all *101* schließlich doch
agent *14* Vertreter/in
aggressive *84* aggressiv
agreement *34* Vertrag, Vereinbarung
agri-chemical *86* Agrarchemikalie
agricultural *48* landwirtschaftlich
ahead *53H* nach vorne, voraus
to aim to do *32* beabsichtigen zu tun
air pollution *88* Luftverschmutzung
airline *79, 116* Fluggesellschaft
alcoholism *124* Alkoholismus
alike *122* gleichermaßen
allergy *122* Allergie
allowance *47* finanzielle Unterstützung
Alpine *67* alpin
alternative *37* Alternative
although *6* obwohl
altogether *53H* insgesamt
among *81* unter
amount *6* Menge, Ausmaß
amusing *71* lustig, amüsant
to analyze *119* analysieren
ancestor *69* Vorfahr
anchorman *54* Fernsehmoderator
ancient *112* (sehr) alt, historisch
anger *73* Zorn, Ärger
to announce *60* verkünden
announcement *103* Durchsage
annual *40, 106* jährlich
to answer back *63* antworten, reagieren
anthem *129* Hymne
anti-drugs campaign *37* Kampagne gegen Drogen
antique *112* antik
anti-social *124* asozial
anyhow *79* jedenfalls, sowieso
apart from *34* außer, abgesehen von
apart *58* getrennt
apartment (AE) *29* Wohnung
apparent *61* anscheinend
to appear *59* scheinen
appearance *44* Auftreten, äußere Erscheinung
appliance *131* Gerät
applicant *7* Bewerber/in

application *8* Bewerbung
to apply for *33* sich bewerben um
to apply to *16* gelten für, zutreffen auf
appointment *29* Termin, Verabredung
approach *37* Ansatz
appropriate *74* passend
approx(imate) *48, 97* ungefähr, etwa
aptitude *42* Eignung
architect *18* Architekt/in
architecture *17* Architektur
area *43* Bereich
armed robbery *105* bewaffneter Raubüberfall
to arouse *35H* wecken
to arrest *116* verhaften
arrival *99* Ankunft
art department *40* Kunstabteilung
arts and crafts *85* Kunsthandwerk
as well *6* auch (noch), ebenfalls
aspect *65* Aspekt, Seite
assault *105* (tätlicher) Angriff
association *79* Verband
asylum *138* Asyl
at a guess *34* schätzungsweise
at all times *41* jederzeit
at all *26* überhaupt
at large *114* als Ganzes
at least *7* mindestens
at present *6* zurzeit, derzeit
athlete *118* (Leicht-)Athlet/in, Sportler/in
athletics *57* Leichtathletik
attachment *7* Anlage
to attack *63* angreifen
attacker *122* Angreifer
to attend *27* teilnehmen an
attention *35H* Aufmerksamkeit
attitude *44* Einstellung, Haltung
to attract *10* anziehen
attractive *89* attraktiv, anziehend
attractiveness *92* Attraktivität
authorities *67, 99* Behörden
automatic save function *65* automatische Speicherfunktion
available *44* verfügbar
avalanche *67* Lawine
average *51* durchschnittlich
to avoid *25* vermeiden
award-winning *21* preisgekrönt
aware of *81* bewusst
awareness *90* Bewusstsein

B

to backpack *6* als Rucksacktourist reisen
backpacker *116* Rucksacktourist/in
bacteria buster *58* Bakterienschreck
bacteria *58* Bakterien
bad-tempered *42* schlecht gelaunt
baggage *9* Gepäck
balance *122* Gleichgewicht
balanced *50* ausgeglichen, ausgewogen
to ban *36* verbieten
banknote *129* Geldschein, Banknote
bargain *120* günstiges Angebot, Schnäppchen
based on *85* basierend auf
basic *18* einfach, schlicht
basically *65* im Grunde
basics *17* das Wesentliche
bathing trunks *133* Badehose
battle *88* Kampf
to be fed up with *136* es satt haben
to be fluent in *130* fließend sprechen
to be good at sth *34* etw. gut können
to be in two minds about sth *133* gespaltener Meinung sein
to be on top of sth *42* etw. im Griff haben
to be sick of *116* (etwas) satt haben
to be to blame *108* schuld sein, verantwortlich sein
to beam *116* strahlen
beggar *120* Bettler/in
to begin with *19* zunächst, um es vorauszuschicken
to behave *104* sich verhalten, sich benehmen
belief *123* Glaube
believable *61* glaubhaft
beneath *67* unter
benefit *43* zusätzliche Leistung
to beware of *23* aufpassen auf, Vorsicht vor
billion *139* Milliarde
bio-degradable *96* biologisch abbaubar
bioethics *124* Bioethik
biological *117* biologisch
to black out *65* verdunkeln
to blacklist *90H* auf eine schwarze Liste setzen
to blame *54* die Schuld geben
blessing *97* Segen
to block out *99* verdunkeln
blueprint *124* Blaupause, Bauplan
body paint *116* Körperbemalung
bogus *120* falsch, unecht
bonus *20* Zulage
to boom *6* boomen
boomerang *116* Bumerang
border *22* Grenze

border zone *88* Grenzbereich
bowl *58* Schale, Schüssel
bracket *10* Klammer
brain *60* Gehirn
branch *21* Filiale, Zweigstelle
brand *35H* Marke, Typ
brand-new *98H* nagelneu
breach of the law *111* Gesetzesbruch
to break a law *134* ein Gesetz brechen
to break down *61* zusammenbrechen
to break in *79* unterbrechen
to break into *33* „einsteigen" in
to break up with *107H* Schluss machen mit
breath analyser *60* Atemprüfgerät
to breed *122* sich fortpflanzen
brief *48* kurz
bright *35H* leuchtend, hell
to bring out *116* herausbringen
to bring up *45* aufziehen
to broadcast *25* übertragen, senden
brochure *32* Broschüre, Prospekt
brutal *122* brutal
BSc degree *7* (Universitäts-) Abschluss als Bachelor of Science
budget *7* preisgünstig
bureaucrat *136* Bürokrat/in
burglar *112* Einbrecher/in
burglar alarm *106* Alarmanlage
burglary *105* Einbruch
burst *33* Serie, „Salve"
to bury *65* begraben
business empire *36* Wirtschaftsimperium
button *6* Taste, Knopf
by *98* um
by air *25* mit dem Flugzeug
by the way *51* übrigens, nebenbei

C

cadmium *97* Cadmium
to call at *6* vorbeischauen bei
call centre operator *41* Telefonist/in in einem Callcenter
to call for *64* verlangen
to calm down *11* (sich) beruhigen
calories *50* Kalorien
campaign *33* Kampagne
cancer *86* Krebs
candidate *114* Bewerber/in, Kandidat/in
to canoe *6* mit dem Kanu fahren
capital *79* Kapital
car boot *111* Kofferraum
car pool *69* Fahrgemeinschaft
caravan park *99* Campingplatz für Wohnwagen
carbohydrates *50* Kohlenhydrate
carbon dioxide *69* Kohlendioxid
carbon *69* Kohlenstoff

carbon-based *69* durch Kohlenstoff verursacht
to care for *115H* versorgen, sorgen für
career *33* Karriere, Beruf
careful *9* sorgfältig
carer *41* Pfleger/in
to carry around *66* herumtragen
to carry out *128* durchführen
cartoon *68* Karikatur
cartoonist *59* Karikaturist/in
case study *91* Fallstudie
catalytic converter *104* Katalysator
catchphrase *106* Motto
category *96* Kategorie, Klasse
catering manager *54* Gastronom/in
cattle *48* Rinder, Vieh
to celebrate *26* feiern
cell *124* Zelle
cement *98H* Zement
censor *63* Zensor/in
central *116* zentral
to centre on *99* sich konzentrieren auf
century *126* Jahrhundert
cereals *50* Getreideflocken, Cornflakes
certificate *53H* Zeugnis, Urkunde
chain *93* Kette
to chair *94* leiten
chalet girl *67* Hausmädchen
chalet *67* Landhaus
challenge *114* Anfechtung, Ablehnung
championship *53H* Meisterschaft
changing room *52* Umkleideraum
chaos *67* Chaos
to charge *60* belasten
charisma *44* Charisma
charity *120* Wohltätigkeitsorganisation
checklist *9* Checkliste
chef *93* Küchenchef
chief executive officer *90H* geschäftsführende/r Direktor/in
chief *67* Leiter
childcare *48* Kinderbetreuung
choice *17* Wahl, Auswahl
Christmas Day *80H* 1. Weihnachtsfeiertag
chronological *135* chronologisch
citizen *11* (Staats-)Bürger/in
civil liberties *124* Bürgerrechte
civil service *114* öffentlicher Dienst
civilization *12* Zivilisation
to claim *13* (als) Schadensersatz fordern
classified ad *32* Kleinanzeige
to clean out *23* leeren
to clean up *139* sauber machen
clerk *41* Angestellte/r, Kaufmann/frau

client *33* Kunde, Kundin
to climb *112* ersteigen
to clone *121* klonen
to close a circle *86* einen Kreis schließen
closed-circuit TV (CCTV) *106* Kamera-überwachung
closeness *35* Nähe
coal *77, 130* Kohle
cocoa *91* Kakao
co-director *35* Vorstandskollege/kollegin
coffee pot *60* Kaffeekanne
coffee table *60* Couchtisch
co-founder *35* Mitbegründer/in
coin *129* Münze
to collapse *36* zusammenbrechen
colleague *41* Kollege, Kollegin
to collect *12* abholen
column *24* Spalte
combat jacket *81* Kampfanzug
combination *121* Kombination
to combine *69* verbinden, kombinieren
to come down to *114* darauf hinaus laufen
to come into contact with *58* in Kontakt kommen mit
come off it *115H* hör auf (damit)
come on *79* komm (schon)
to come out *86* erscheinen
to come true *130* wahr werden
to come up to *107H* zukommen auf
comfort *18* Komfort, Bequemlichkeit
comfortable *12* bequem
comment on *63* Kommentar zu
commentary *58* Kommentar
commentator *88* Kommentator/in
commercial *27* Geschäfts-, gewerblich
commissioner *72* Kommissar
to commit a crime *110* ein Verbrechen begehen
common sense *60* gesunder Menschenverstand
to communicate *59* kommunizieren
communications *59* Kommunikation
communicator *44* jd., der gut mit Leuten umgehen kann
community policing *107* Polizeiarbeit auf der Straße
community service *111* gemeinnützige Arbeit
community *48, 95* Gemeinde
community *95* Gemeinde
to commute *68* pendeln
commuter *69* Pendler/in
company *6* Unternehmen, Firma
to compete against *114* konkurrieren mit
competition *36* Wettbewerb
competitive *90H* konkurrenzfähig

competitor *30* Konkurrent/in, Wettbewerber/in
to complain *11* (sich) beschweren
complaint *12* Beschwerde
completely *21* völlig
complex *122* kompliziert
complicated *131H* kompliziert
compost heap *102* Komposthaufen
compostible *102* kompostierbar
compromise *90H* Kompromiss
compulsory *81* obligatorisch
computer screen *65* Computerbildschirm
computing *40* Computer-
to conceive *124* empfangen
to concentrate on *40, 46* sich konzentrieren auf
conception *124* Empfängnis, Befruchtung
concerned *73* betroffen
to conclude *46* (ab)schließen
conclusion *65* (Schluss-)Folgerung
concrete *69* Beton
to condemn *120* verurteilen
condemnation *120* Verurteilung
conference *36* Konferenz, Tagung
confidence *71* Selbstvertrauen
to conform *81* entsprechen
to congratulate sb on *109* jdm. gratulieren zu
to connect *89* (miteinander) verbinden
connecting flight *103* Anschlussflug
to consider *42* nachdenken über
considerably *106* beträchtlich
to consist of *124* bestehen aus
conspiracy theory *63* Verschwörungstheorie
constantly *45* ständig
to consume *69* verbrauchen
consumer watchdog *86* Verbraucherschutzorganisation
consumer *25* Verbraucher/in
consumer-friendly *86* verbraucherfreundlich
consumerism *81* Konsumdenken
consumer-related *106* konsumbedingt
contact lenses *134* Kontaktlinsen
to contact *12* sich wenden an
to contain *63* enthalten
container *102* Container
to contaminate *58* verseuchen
contract *62* Vertrag
contrast *116* Gegensatz, Kontrast
to contribute to *51* beitragen zu
controversial *32* kontrovers, umstritten
convenient *79* bequem
conventional *70* herkömmlich, konventionell
conversion *131* Umstellung

to convert into *98H* umwandeln in
to convert to *131* umstellen auf
cooker *97* Herd
cookery *82* Kochen
to cooperate *84* zusammenarbeiten
cooperation *92* Zusammenarbeit
co-owner *21* Mitbesitzer/in
cop (AE) *107H* Polizist
corn *122* Mais
corporation *132* (Aktien-)Gesellschaft
correctness *94* Richtigkeit
correspondence *63* Korrespondenz
correspondent *45* Korrespondent/in
corridor *53H* Gang, Korridor
to corrupt *63* korrumpieren
cost-cutting *54* kostensenkend
council *76H* Gemeinderat
councillor *76H* Ratsmitglied
counselor (AE) *42* Berater/in
counter *42* Ladentisch
couple *128* Paar
courier *40* Kurier
courtroom *124* Gerichtssaal
to cover the cost of *95* die Kosten decken von
to cover up *42* bedecken
cow *128* Kuh
crash *130* Krach
to crawl *68* kriechen
to create *8* bilden, erstellen
creation *123* Schöpfung, Erschaffung, Erzeugung
creative *7* kreativ, schöpferisch
creativity *7* Kreativität
credit *90H* Kredit
credit card fraud *105* Kreditkartenbetrug
Creuzfeldt-Jakob Disease *54* Creutzfeldt-Jakob-Krankheit
crime figures *83* Kriminalitätsstatistik
crime rate *106* Verbrechensrate
criminal record *111* Strafakte
critic *14* Kritiker/in
critical *21* kritisch
to criticize *117* kritisieren
crocodile *48* Krokodil
crop *91* Ernte
to cross *22* überqueren
crossroads *76* Kreuzung
crowded *12* überfüllt
crowding *69* dichter Verkehr
cruel *54* grausam
to crush *67* zerquetschen, zerdrücken
cultural *48* kulturell, Kultur-
currency *9* Währung
currently *7* momentan
curse *97* Fluch
to cut a long story short *48* um es kurz zu machen

cutlery *104* Besteck
cutting board *58* Schneidebrett
CV *7* Lebenslauf
cycling pants (AE) *81* Radfahrhosen
cynical *116* zynisch

D

dairy products *50* Milchprodukte
to damage *28* beschädigen
damages *124* Schaden(s)ersatz
dance troupe *116* Tanzgruppe
to dare *68* (es) wagen, sich trauen
daring *32* kühn, wagemutig
darkness *67* Dunkelheit
data package *91* Datenpaket
day-care centre *72* Kindertagesstätte
to deal with *11* sich befassen mit
deal *33* Geschäft, Abkommen
dealer *112* Händler/in
debt *73* Schuld(en)
decent *113* anständig
to decide on *111* sich entscheiden für
to decline *69* abnehmen
to decorate *18* schmücken
to decrease *38* abnehmen
defective *124* fehlerhaft
deficiency *122* Mangel
to define *81* definieren, bestimmen
definitely *20* bestimmt
definition *22* Definition
delay *60* Stau
delegate *97* Delegierte/r
delighted *40* (sehr) erfreut
to deliver *19* abliefern
delivery service *61* Lieferservice
to demand *54* fordern
democracy *81* Demokratie
to demonstrate *92* demonstrieren, vorstellen
demonstration *111* Demonstration, Vorführung
to deny *86* abstreiten
department store *57* Kauf-, Warenhaus
to depend on *64* angewiesen sein auf, abhängen von
dependent (on) *81* abhängig (von)
deposit *80* Kaution
depth *99* Tiefe
desert *87* Wüste
to deserve *111* verdienen
to design *8* entwerfen, konstruieren
desire *35H* Wunsch
desperate *67, 94* verzweifelt
despite *69* trotz
destination *21* Reiseziel
to destroy *54* zerstören, vernichten
destruction *123* Zerstörung, Vernichtung
to detect *60* entdecken
to deter sb from *111* jdn. abhalten von

deterrent *111* Abschreckung
to develop *33* entwickeln
development *61* Entwicklung
diabetes *51* Zuckerkrankheit, Diabetes
diagnostic *117* diagnostisch
to dial *62* wählen
diamond necklace *111* Diamantenkollier
dictator *63* Diktator/in
didgeridoo *116* Didgeridoo (Holzblasinstrument)
to differ from *117* sich unterscheiden von
difficulty *6* Schwierigkeit
digital *97* digital
diplomatic *74* diplomatisch
director *37* Direktor/in, Geschäftsführer/in
disability *8* Behinderung
disabled *80* (körper)behindert
disadvantaged *114* benachteiligt
to disagree *21* anderer Meinung sein, widersprechen
disappointed *21* enttäuscht
disappointment *12* Enttäuschung
disaster *92* Katastrophe, Unglück
disastrous *72* katastrophal
discovery *73* Entdeckung
to discriminate against *113* diskriminieren
discriminatory *113* diskriminierend
to discuss *11* besprechen, erörtern
disease *121* Krankheit, Erkrankung
dish *58* (flache) Schale
dishonest *25* unehrlich
dishwasher *97* Geschirrspüler
to dislike *10* nicht mögen
to dismiss *108* einstellen
display *15* Anzeige
to dispose of *96* beseitigen, entsorgen
dissatisfied *22* unzufrieden
distinctiveness *128* Einzigartigkeit
to distinguish *79* unterscheiden
to distribute *74* verteilen
district *91* (Verwaltungs-)Bezirk
to divide *124* teilen
division *119* Teilung
divorce *111* Scheidung
to do a good turn *51* etwas Gutes tun
to do well *56* gut gehen
to do your bit *104* seinen Beitrag leisten
dome *18* Kuppel
domestic chores *42* Arbeit im Haushalt
domestic *97* Haus-
doom *99* (Welt-)Untergang
doorstep salesman *86* Vertreter an der Haustür
dot painting *116* pointillistisches Gemälde

downside *69* Nachteil
down-to-earth *40* pragmatisch
dozen *116* Dutzend
dramatic *69* dramatisch
drastic *122* drastisch
to draw *52* zeichnen
dress code *42* Kleiderordnung
drinks can *104* Getränkedose
driverless *69* führerlos
driving licence *66* Führerschein
to drop *92* fallen
drought *91* Dürre(periode)
drug-related *106* im Zusammenhang mit Drogen
drug-taking *105* Drogenkonsum
drug-trafficking *105* Drogenhandel
drunk driving *105* Trunkenheit am Steuer
dry-cleaner's *72* chemische Reinigung
due to *34* wegen, aufgrund von, dank
dumb (AE) *36* dumm, doof
to dump *96* abladen, verklappen
during *11* während
dustbin *102* Mülltonne

E

each other *31* einander
to earn a living *41* den Lebensunterhalt verdienen
earnings *99* Einkünfte
earplug *108* Ohrstöpsel
to ease *76* lindern
to echo *77* wieder aufnehmen
ecological *104* ökologisch
economic *73* wirtschaftlich
economist *11* Wirtschaftswissenschaftler/in
economy *7* Wirtschaft
eco-warrior *104* Umweltaktivist
edge *12* Rand
edition *60* Ausgabe
editor *63* Redakteur/in, Herausgeber/in
educational *63* Ausbildungs-, erzieherisch
effect *73* (Aus-)Wirkung, Einfluss
efficiently *69* wirksam
either *9* entweder
elastic *52* elastisch
to elect *113* wählen
electoral candidate *114* Wahlkandidat/in
electronic *60* elektronisch
electronic guidance system *69* elektronisches Navigationssystem
elegance *36* Eleganz
elegant *36* elegant
element *14* Element
elsewhere *122* anderswo
embryo *124* Embryo

emergency *62H* Notfall
emission *69* Emission
emperor *18* Kaiser
to employ *8* beschäftigen
employee *6* Angestellte/r
employer *43* Arbeitgeber/in, Unternehmer/in
employment *44* Beschäftigung
to enable *85* befähigen
encl *12* Anlage
to enclose *12* beilegen, beifügen
to encourage *69* motivieren, auffordern
encouragement *70* Unterstützung
to end up *91* enden, landen
to endanger *61* gefährden
enemy *40* Feind
energetic *52* kraftvoll, energisch
energy *52* Energie
energy source *91* Energiequelle
engine *69* Motor
engineer *69* Ingenieur/in, Techniker/in
to enjoy oneself *48* sich amüsieren, Spaß haben
enjoyable *34* angenehm
enormous *98* enorm, gewaltig
enthusiasm *42* Begeisterung
entire *119* ganz, vollständig
environmental *68* Umwelt-
epidemic *106* Epidemie
episode *51* Episode
equal *114* gleich
equipment *9* Ausrüstung
to erode *123* austrocknen
erosion *122* Erosion
erotic *32* erotisch
error *13* Fehler, Irrtum
escape *44H* Entkommen
especially *33* besonders
essential *44* (unbedingt) erforderlich
to estimate *122* schätzen
ethnic *106, 113* ethnisch
euro zone *130* Eurozone
European Central Bank *129* Europäische Zentralbank
European Commission *134* Europäische Kommission
European Court of Human Rights *114* Europäischer Gerichtshof für Menschenrechte
European Economic Community (EEC) *129* Europäische Wirtschaftsgemeinschaft (EWG)
European Union *129* Europäische Union
even so *42* trotzdem
evidence *27* Beweis(mittel)
to exaggerate *37* übertreiben
exaggeration *22* Übertreibung
exam certificate *44* Abschlusszeugnis

exchange *48, 95* Austausch; Tausch
exclusive *120* exklusiv
executive *94* Manager/in
exhausted *45* erschöpft
exile *63* Exil
to exist *63* existieren
exotic *6* exotisch
to expand *34* expandieren
expansion *135* Erweiterung
to expect *6* erwarten
expectation *22* Erwartung
to expel *108* ausweisen
expenditure *40* Ausgabe(n), (Un-) Kosten
expenses *101* Spesen, Unkosten, Ausgaben
experienced *18* erfahren
experiment *121* Versuch, Experiment
explosive *99* explosiv
export earnings *139* Exporteinkünfte
to export *69* ausführen, exportieren
exporter *131H* Exporteur/in
expression *22* Ausdruck
to extend *76H* ausdehnen, erweitern
extent *103* (Aus-)Maß, Umfang
external *136* Außen-
extract *114* Auszug
extra-curricular *42* außerlehrplanmäßig
extraordinary *124* außergewöhnlich, ungewöhnlich
extreme *51* extrem
eye contact *71* Blickkontakt
eye-witness *67* Augenzeuge/zeugin

F

faced with *97* konfrontiert mit
facility *40* Vor-, Einrichtung
facsimile *88* Nachbildung
factor *73* Faktor
factory *44* Fabrik
factory farming *54* industrielle Landwirtschaft
factual *86* sachlich
to fail *46* scheitern, versagen
fairly *39* ziemlich
to fantasize *61* sich erträumen
fantastic *61* fantastisch
fantasy *61* Fantasie
fare *48* Fahrgeld
farm worker *41* Landarbeiter/in
farmers' lobby *86* Bauernlobby
farming *54* Landwirtschaft
farmland *54* landwirtschaftlich genutzte Fläche
farmwork *48* Landarbeit
far-off *11* weit entfernt, entlegen
to fascinate *111* faszinieren
fascination, with ~ *63* fasziniert
fast-food store (AE) *93* Imbissladen

fear *67* Angst, Furcht
to fear *108* (be)fürchten, Angst haben vor
feature *35* Merkmal, Kennzeichen, Eigenschaft
Federal Ministry for Consumer Protection, Food and Agriculture *86* Bundesministerium für Verbraucherschutz, Ernährung und Landwirtschaft
Federal Ministry of Agriculture *86* Bundeslandwirtschaftsministerium
federalist *132* föderalistisch
fee *48* Gebühr
to feel like *109* Lust haben auf
fencing *57* Fechten
ferrous *103* eisenhaltig
fertiliser *91* Dünger
fertility clinic *124* Geburtsklinik
to fertilize *124* befruchten
to fetch *18* holen
fewer and fewer *81* immer weniger
fierce *72* heftig
to fight against *132* kämpfen gegen
figure *30* Zahl
file name *7* Name der Datei
to fill in *35H* ausfüllen
to fill up *30* füllen, auftanken
final destination *9* Zielort
finally *24* zum Schluss
finance *90H* Finanz(en)
financially *17* finanziell
fingerprint *66* Fingerabdruck
firearm *111* Feuerwaffe
firm *64* fest
first name *35* Vorname
fitness centre *29* Fitnessstudio
flight *10* Flug
flight of stairs *51* Treppe
flood *21* Flut
floodlight *67* Flutlicht
flop *131H* Fehlschlag
fluent *7* fließend
fluid *103* Flüssigkeit
to fly out *87* ausfliegen
focus group *66* Fachgruppe
to focus on *106* sich konzentrieren auf
foe *122* Feind/in
follow-up question *128* Anschlussfrage
food chain *86, 122* Nahrungskette
food shop *31* Lebensmittelladen
food-borne illness *58* durch Nahrung übertragene Krankheit
foolish *22* dumm, töricht
foot of the stairs *112* unteres Ende der Treppe
for a start *76H* zunächst einmal
for heaven's sake *115H* um Himmels willen
for the first time *33* zum ersten Mal

for this reason *8* aus diesem Grund
to force *36* zwingen
to forecast *86* vorhersagen
foreign travel *73* Auslandsreisen
forest *99* Wald
form *42* Formular
form of address *35* Anrede(form)
formal *35* formell, förmlich
former *48* ehemalig, früher
formula *35* Formel
fortunate *34* glücklich (Umstände)
fortunately *33* glücklicherweise
fossil *69* fossil
to found *102* gründen
frank *25* offen, aufrichtig
free speech *63* Meinungsfreiheit
free trade *88* Freihandel
freedom *31* Freiheit
freely *76H* frei, ungestört
freepost *35H* Porto zahlt Empfänger
freeway *12* Autobahn
frequent *69* häufig
fresh *99* frisch
friction *84* Reibung
fridge *58, 97* Kühlschrank
frustrated *76H* frustriert
to fry *21* (in der Sonne) grillen
fuel *68* Kraftstoff, Benzin
fuel cell *69* Brennstoffzelle
full-time *6* Ganztags-
fumes *112* Dämpfe, Abgase
fundamental *125* grundsätzlich, wesentlich
fur *81* Pelz
furious *19* wütend
further *24* weitere/r/s
futurologist *60* Futurologe/-login

G

to gain *41* gewinnen
gap year *17* ein Jahr Pause
garbage *98H* Müll, Abfall
gas *69* Gas
gate-crasher *26* ungebetener Gast
gay *128* schwul, homosexuell, lesbisch
GDR *135* DDR
gene *121* Gen
general *33* allgemein
generally *9* im Allgemeinen
to generate *98* erzeugen
generation *97* Generation
generosity *120* Großzügigkeit
generous *85* großzügig
genetic code *121* genetischer Code
genetic engineering *124* Gentechnik
genetic modification (GM) *121* Gentechnik
genetic test *124* Gentest
genetics *124* Genetik
gentle *107* sanft, leicht

to get a kick out of *42* Spaß an etw. haben
to get about *8* herumkommen
to get around *51* sich bewegen
to get away from *73* wegkommen von
to get into shape *52* in Form kommen
to get married *124* heiraten
to get off *51* aussteigen
to get on better *124* besser vorankommen
to get on with *11* vorankommen mit
to get rid of *36* beseitigen, abschaffen
to get the message *104* es begreifen
to get the most out of *104* den größten Nutzen ziehen aus
to get up *56* aufstehen
to get used to *56* sich gewöhnen an
giant *94* Riese
to give sb a call *76H* jdn. anrufen
to give sb a ring *31* jdn. anrufen
glad *26* froh
glass ceiling *113* unsichtbare Beförderungssperre
glitzy *86* strahlend
Global Positioning Satellite *60* Navigationssatellit
global *36, 73* global, Welt-
global warming *69* Erderwärmung, Erwärmung der Erdatmosphäre
globalization *88* Globalisierung
glue-sniffing addict *112* klebstoffschnüffelnde/r Süchtige/r
to go along with *55* einverstanden sein mit
to go bankrupt *72* Konkurs machen
to go for it *42* es machen
to go mad *61* durchdrehen
to go over to *130* übergehen zu
to go to extremes *81* bis zum Äußersten gehen
to go well *6* gut gehen
gold chain *81* Goldkette
gonna *77* = going to
good heavens *26* ach du meine Güte
goods *36* Ware(n)
government *11* Regierung
government handout *116* staatliche Unterstützung
government official *94* Regierungsbeamter/beamtin
grade (AE) *42* Note
gradually *38* allmählich
graphics *40* Grafik
greedy *86* gierig
greenhouse gas *69* Treibhausgas
gridlock *68* Verkehrsinfarkt
grim *116* schlimm
to grip *124* fest im Griff haben
grotesque *108* grotesk
ground beef (AE) *58* Rinderhack
ground water *99* Grundwasser

to guarantee *9* garantieren
guard *107H* Wache
guide *9* Führer/in
guilty *45* schuldig
guy *52* Kerl, Typ
gym *52* Sportstudio, Fitnessraum

H

habitat *54* Lebensraum
hairdryer *131H* Fön
halogen bulb *81* Halogenlampe
halter *81* Träger
hamburger patty *58* Fleischklops
to hand out *94* austeilen, verteilen
handcuff *107H* Handschelle
handshake *71* Händedruck
handyman *95* Heimwerker
hard sell *36* aggressives Verkaufsverhalten
hard-hitting *32* zur Sache gehend
hardline *106* hart durchgreifend
hardly ever *9* fast nie
hardware *27* Hardware, Geräte
harmless *71* harmlos
harsh *106* hart, streng
haulage contractor *72* Transportunternehmen
haulage industry *72* Transportgewerbe
to have in common *43* gemeinsam haben
to have to do with *25* zu tun haben mit
hazardous *97* risikoreich, gefährlich
to head for *99* zusteuern auf
to head towards *124* zusteuern auf
heading *34* Überschrift
health care *118* Gesundheitsfürsorge
health club *56* Fitnessklub
heart attack *111* Herzinfarkt, -anfall
heart disease *51* Herzkrankheit
heart rate *51* Herzschlag
heavily *45* stark
heavy-handed *106* scharf vorgehend
hedge *95* Hecke
height *66* Höhe, Größe
hell *21* Hölle
high and dry *99* auf dem Trockenen
high school (AE) *42* Oberschule, Gymnasium
high street *76H* Hauptgeschäftsstraße
highly *21* äußerst
high-rise *99* Hochhaus-
hijacking *105* (Flugzeug-)Entführung
to hinder *134* (be)hindern
to hire *9* einstellen
hit and miss *58* russisches Roulette
hi-tech *107* Spitzentechnik
to hold a meeting *93* eine Sitzung abhalten
hold on *114* Vormachtstellung in

to hold the whip hand *88* das Sagen haben

holidaymaker *21* Urlauber/in

hollow *88* hohl

Home Affairs *138* Innenministerium

home country *85* Heimatland

home repair *82* Haushaltsreparatur

home worker *8* Heimarbeiter/in

homeless *120* obdachlos

homemaker *46* Hausfrau

honour *118* Ehre

horrified *63* entsetzt

hourly rate *43* Stundenlohn

house extension *95* Hausanbau

to house *99* unterbringen

household equipment *97* Haushaltsgeräte

household *119* Haushalt

housework *45* Hausarbeit(en)

housing *138* Unterbringung, -kunft

huge *6* riesig

human being *45* Mensch

human rights *138* Menschenrechte

hybrid car *60* Auto mit Benzin- und Elektroantrieb

hydrogen *69* Wasserstoff

hype *21* Rummel, Reklame

I

ID card *66* Personalausweis

ideally *7* idealerweise

identification *60* Identifizierung

to identify *113* erkennen, identifizieren

identity *67, 84* Identität

ie *86* d.h.

if only *130* wenn nur

illegal *96* illegal

image *33* Image, Bild

immediately *16* sofort, umgehend

immigrant *66* Einwanderer, Einwanderin

immigration *130* Einwanderung

implication *124* Auswirkung

to import *98* einführen, importieren

import duty *135* Einfuhrzoll

impracticable *132* undurchführbar

to impress *106* beeindrucken, imponieren

to improve *69* verbessern

improvement *73* Verbesserung

in a way *21* in gewisser Weise

in addition to *43* zusätzlich zu

in all *26* insgesamt, alles in allem

in any case *79* jedenfalls

in charge *36* in leitender Position

in effect *134* tatsächlich

in exchange *85* zum Ausgleich

in fact *12, 36* tatsächlich

in full *75* vollständig

in other words *86* anders ausgedrückt

in return (for sth) *85* als Gegenleistung (für etw.)

in spite of *103* trotz

in the dead of night *112* mitten in der Nacht

in the long term *73* auf Dauer

in the meantime *74* in der Zwischenzeit

in the short term *73* kurzfristig, auf kurze Sicht

in their hands *21* in ihren Händen

in their teens *51* zwischen 13 und 19

in time *96* rechtzeitig, mit der Zeit

in turn *95* als Gegenleistung

in view of *111* angesichts

inappropriate *81* unpassend

Inc *94* Kapitalgesellschaft

incineration *96* Verbrennung

incinerator *98* Verbrennungsanlage

to include *6* enthalten, einbeziehen

income *40, 95* Einkommen

to increase *36* erhöhen

increasing *45* zunehmend

independence *69* Unabhängigkeit

independent *41* unabhängig

to indicate *124* (an)zeigen, hinweisen auf

indirect *52* indirekt

indirectness *62* Indirektheit

individual *19* einzeln, individuell

individuality *84* Individualität

industrial espionage *105* Industriespionage

industry *28* Industrie, Gewerbe

inefficient *126H* ineffizient

infamous *108* berüchtigt

infertile *128* unfruchtbar

informal *35* ungezwungen, informell

information desk *103* Informationsschalter, Auskunft

informative *61* informativ

infrastructure *68* Infrastruktur

initial *7* Initiale(n)

to injure *28* verletzen

injustice *118* Ungerechtigkeit

in-law *116* angeheiratete/r Verwandte/r

insecure *41* unsicher

insert *35H* Ein-, Beilage

to insert *60* einführen

to insist on *54* bestehen auf

to inspect *139* kontrollieren, überprüfen

inspection *139* Kontrolle, Inspektion

to install *6* installieren, einrichten

instead *11* stattdessen

instructor *9* Lehrer/in, Ausbilder/in

insurance *9* Versicherung

integration *132* Integration

intelligence *124* Intelligenz

to intend *110* beabsichtigen, vorhaben

intensive *40* intensiv

intention *25* Absicht

to interfere with *128* stören

internal *58* innere

internal frontier *135* Binnengrenze

internet access *40* Internetzugang

Internet Service Provider *63* Internetprovider

to interrupt *80* unterbrechen

interviewee *73* Interviewpartner/in, Befragte/r

to invent *61* erfinden

invention *60* Erfindung

inventive *61* erfinderisch

to invest *73, 139* investieren

investment *90H* Investition

investment bank *130* Investitionsbank

invitation *30* Einladung

invoice *75* Rechnung

involved in *90H* beteiligt an

iris *60* Iris

irregular *41* unregelmäßig

issue *54* aktuelle Frage

IT *6* Informationstechnologie

item *81* Artikel, Gegenstand

J

jail *106* Gefängnis

to jam *63* stören

jewellery *23* Schmuck(stücke)

job board *42* Brett mit Stellenanzeigen

job center (AE) *42* Arbeitsamt

job cut *73* Stellenkürzung

job loss *104* Arbeitsplatzverlust

to join *14* eintreten (in)

to join in *51* mitmachen

journalist *26* Journalist/in

journey *22* Reise, Fahrt

to juggle *45* miteinander vereinbaren

to jumble *67* vermischen

junction *76* (Straßen-)Kreuzung

jungle *87* Dschungel, Urwald

junior *35* untergeordnet

junior year (AE) *42* vorletztes Schuljahr

junkie *69* Süchtige/r

to justify *36* rechtfertigen

juvenile *108* Jugend-

K

to keep an eye on *40* ein (wachsames) Auge haben auf

to keep house *67* den Haushalt führen

to keep to *52* sich halten an

kennel *80* Hundehütte

keyboarding *40* Texteingabe, -erfassung

kidnapping *105* Entführung

killing *63* Tötung, Mord
to knife *111* mit einem Messer verletzen
to knock down *76H* abreißen
to knock over *112* niederschlagen
knowledge *60* Wissen

L

laboratory *60* Labor(atorium)
Labour (Party) *114* Labour Party
labour costs *88* Lohnkosten
lack *132* Mangel
lack of *51* Mangel an, Fehlen von
to land *101* landen
landfill site *96* Deponie
lane *60* (Fahr-)Spur
laser beam *60* Laserstrahl
laser sensor *60* Lasersensor
latest *53H* neueste/r/s
launch *33* Start(kampagne)
to launch *20* starten, einführen
law *68* Gesetz
law-breaking *105* Gesetzesbruch
lawsuit *108* Verfahren
lawyer *124* Anwalt, Anwältin
layout *75* Layout, Anordnung
to lead to *51* führen zu
lead *97* Blei
leading *139* führend
leaflet *9* Broschüre, Prospekt
league *33* Liga
to lean over *112* sich lehnen über
leftovers *58* Reste
leg *103* Strecke
legal *114* gesetzlich, juristisch, legal
leggings *133* Leggings
leisure time *11* Freizeit
to lend *29* leihen
lenient *111* milde
leopard *36* Leopard
to let so off *111* jdn. laufen lassen
life expectancy *116* Lebenserwartung
life skills *81* Alltagsfertigkeiten
life-changing *120* lebensverändernd
life-saving *53H* Lebensrettungs-
to lift a ban *134* ein Verbot aufheben
likely *27* wahrscheinlich
lingua franca *130* Verkehrssprache
linguistic *132* linguistisch
link *60* Verbindung
lithium *97* Lithium
litter-bug *104* Umweltverschandler
to live on social security *111* von Sozialhilfe leben
lively *7* lebendig, lebhaft
livestock *54* Vieh
to load *12* (be)laden
loads *36* jede Menge
loaf *27* Laib
loan *80* Verleih

lobbyist *97* Lobbyist/in
loneliness *13* Einsamkeit
long-distance running *51* Langstreckenlauf
long-distance travel *77* Fernverkehr
long-term *51* langfristig
to look forward to *44H* sich freuen auf
to look into *134* untersuchen, prüfen
to look out for *42* achten auf, suchen nach
loss *71* Verlust
low *54* niedrig
lower-cost *88* Niedriglohn-
Ltd *12* (Gesellschaft) mit beschränkter Haftung, GmbH
luck *11* Glück
lucky *33* glücklich
luggage *27* Gepäck
lunch hour *51* Mittagspause
lyrics *77* (Lied-)Text

M

machinery *139* Maschinen
madam *12* gnädige Frau
made up of *97* bestehend aus
magazine *33* Zeitschrift, Magazin
magic *60* magisch, Zauber
mail order catalogue *78* Versandhauskatalog
main entrance hall *103H* Haupteingangshalle
mainly *23* hauptsächlich, vor allem
mains power *104* Stromnetz
mainstream *122* vorherrschende Meinung
to maintain *76H* aufrechterhalten
maintenance *48* Pflege
major *7* größer, wichtig
to make a breakthrough *126* einen Durchbruch erzielen
to make a note of *62H* sich notieren
to make an impression *42* einen Eindruck machen
to make arrangements *103* Vorkehrungen treffen
to make profit *54* Gewinn machen
to make sense *130* sinnvoll sein, Sinn ergeben
to make up for *11* wettmachen, ausgleichen
to make up *116* bilden
mall (AE) *107H* (Einkaufs-)Passage
malnutrition *122* Unterernährung
to manage *6* leiten
to manage to *35* (es) schaffen
management *29* Verwaltung
manslaughter *105* Totschlag
to manufacture *87* herstellen, produzieren

manufacturer *36* Hersteller/in, Produzent/in
manufacturing operation *88* Produktionsvorhaben
marble *18* Marmor
marine *122* Meeres-, maritim
marine life *122* Meeresfauna und -flora
market stall *78* Marktstand
mass *54* Masse
mass tourism *99* Massentourismus
massacre *108* Massaker
massive *91* riesig
to match *34* zuordnen
math (AE) *42* Mathe(matik)
matter *51* Sache, Angelegenheit
maybe *7* vielleicht
mayor *99* Bürgermeister/in
meanwhile *6* inzwischen
media planner *33* Medienplaner
media planning *34* Medienplanung
mediator *94* Vermittler/in
medical *66* medizinisch
membership *48, 66* Mitgliedschaft
memory *60* Gedächtnis, Speicher
to mend *81* ausbessern
to mention *37* erwähnen
mercury *97* Quecksilber
metal *97* Metall
midday *67* Mittag
Middle Ages, the *36* das Mittelalter
might *26* könnte
milestone *86* Meilenstein
military *81* militärisch
military ruler *63* Militärmachthaber
mind, to my ~ *52* meiner Meinung nach
miniature *60* Miniatur-
minibus *12* Kleinbus
mini-roundabout *76* kleiner Kreisel
ministry of transport *68* Verkehrsministerium
mink *122* Nerz
minor *111* unbedeutend, klein
minority *113* Minderheit
miracle *69* Wunder
mirror *60* Spiegel
to mislead *21* irreführen
to miss out *112* auslassen, überspringen
missing *77* fehlend
mission *45* Auftrag, Mission
misunderstanding *6* Missverständnis
mitigating circumstances *111* mildernde Umstände
to mix up *126H* vermischen
mixture *50* Mischung
mobile *81* Handy
mobility *132* Mobilität
monthly *62H* monatlich
moral *124* moralisch

Mother Earth *104* Mutter Erde
motor *69* Motor
motorway *21* Autobahn
to move on *35H* weitergehen
to move to *39* umziehen nach
movement *52* Bewegung
movement-sensitive lighting *106*
   Außenbeleuchtung mit Bewegungs-
   melder
MP *54* Parlamentsmitglied
Ms *8* Frau/Fräulein
mugging *105* Straßenraub
multinational *87* multinational
to multiply *126* multiplizieren
muscle *51* Muskel
musical instrument *120*
   Musikinstrument
muslim *18* moslemisch
mutant *122* verändert, durch
   Mutation entstanden

N

nail *134* Nagel
nanny *45* Kindermädchen
narrow *76* eng, schmal
nasty *13* unangenehm
nation *115* Nation
nationalist *132* Nationalist
nationwide *21* landesweit
native language *132* Muttersprache
neat *42* ordentlich, sauber
neglect *124* Vernachlässigung
to negotiate *94* aushandeln
neither *44* keiner
neon sign *32* Neonreklame
nervous system *124* Nervensystem
net *103* netto
network *43* Netz(werk)
neutral *99* neutral
newcomer *11* Neuling
newsflash *67* Kurzmeldungen
newsletter *40* Rundschreiben,
   Informationsblatt
no longer *46* nicht mehr
No. *75* Nr.
noble *116* edel
noisy *14* laut
non-degradable *96* nicht abbaubar
non-essentials *106* nicht notwendige
   Dinge
non-ferrous *103* nicht eisenhaltig
non-native *132* nicht muttersprach-
   lich
non-profitmaking *48* gemeinnützig
non-recyclable *98* nicht wiederverwertbar
nonsense *25* Unsinn
normally *9* normalerweise
North Atlantic Free Trade Area *88*
   Nordatlantische Freihandelszone
nose ring *42* Nasenring

nostalgia *87* Nostalgie
to note down *62H* aufschreiben,
   notieren
nothing like *35* nicht zu vergleichen
   mit
nuclear fusion *91* Kernfusion
nuclear waste *111* Atommüll
nurse *17* Krankenschwester, -
   pfleger/in
nursery school *124* Kindergarten,
   Vorschule
nutritional *122* Nahrungs-

O

to obey *84* gehorchen, befolgen
objective *22* objektiv
observer *99* Beobachter/in
obvious *8* offensichtlich
occasionally *9* gelegentlich
offence *106* Straftat, Vergehen
offender *106* Straftäter/in
official *99, 138* Beamter/Beamtin
off-piste skiing *67* Skilaufen abseits
   der Pisten
oil tanker *74* Öltanker
oil-rig *120* Bohrinsel, Ölplattform
old banger *68* alte Klapperkiste
Olympic flame *116* olympisches
   Feuer
Olympics *116* Olympische Spiele
Olympic-size *53H* in Olympia-Größe
to omit *128* weglassen
on average *116* im Durchschnitt,
   durchschnittlich
on balance *65* alles in allem
on impulse *78* spontan
on offer *62H* im Angebot
on the doorstep *78* an der Haustür
on the march *132* auf dem Vormarsch
on the other hand *17* andererseits
on their way *28* unterwegs
on top of that *76H* darüber hinaus
once-only *107* einmalig
one *35* eins, man
one-sided *37* einseitig
one-way system *76* System von
   Einbahnstraßen
online banking *79* Online-Banking
to open up *40* öffnen, erschließen
opening *42* offene Stelle
opening ceremony *116*
   Eröffnungszeremonie
opening hours *80* Öffnungszeiten
opinion poll *130* Meinungsumfrage
opponent *124* Gegner/in
opposition *132* Opposition
optimistic *132* optimistisch
order *8, 97* Reihenfolge; Zustand
ordinary *36* gewöhnlich, normal
organic *48* ökologisch
organization *69* Organisation

organized crime *97* organisierte
   Kriminalität
original *46* Original
osteoporosis *51* Osteoporose,
   Knochenschwund
other day, the ~ *52* vor ein paar
   Tagen
other than *132* außer
otherwise *18* sonst
ought *44H* sollte/n
out of breath *51* außer Atem
out of control *61* außer Kontrolle
out of date *131H* veraltet
out of place *108* ungewöhnlich
out of shape *51* übergewichtig
outdoors *85* im Freien
outer packaging *102* äußere Verpackung
outlet *78* Verkaufsstelle
outrage *120* verletzen, schockieren,
   entrüsten
outrageous *103* empörend
outskirts *67* Außengebiete, Stadtrand
to outweigh *65* überwiegen
to overcome *115H* überwinden
overcrowded *21* überfüllt
overhead *60* darüber
overnight *13* Übernachtungs-
overtime *43* Überstunden
overweight *51* übergewichtig
overwhelmed *112* überwältigt
owing to *103H* wegen, aufgrund
own, of one's ~ *33* eigen
own, on one's ~ *11* allein
owner *20* Besitzer/in
ownership *103* Besitz
oxygen *51* Sauerstoff

P

package holiday *14* Pauschalreise
packaging *37* Verpackung
paint *28* Farbe
pair of earrings *107H* ein Paar Ohr-
   ringe
panel of experts *36* Expertenrunde
panic *72* Panik
paper qualifications *43* Zeugnisse
paper-maker *98H* Papierhersteller
paragraph *34* Absatz, Abschnitt
parking lot (AE) *80* Parkplatz
parking space *29* Parkplatz, -lücke
parliamentary seat *114* Parlamentssitz
particularly *6* besonders
partly *37* teilweise
partnership *115H* Partnerschaft
part-time *42* Teilzeit-, Halbtags-
to pass by *7* vorübergehen
to pass laws *118* Gesetze verabschieden
to pass on *104, 131H* weitergeben,
   -leiten

passport to paradise *21* Pass ins Paradies

past *12* vorbei (an)

pay as you go *62* Zahlung nach Verbrauch

to pay back *56* zurückzahlen

payment *60* Zahlung

PE (= physical exercise) *52* Sport(unterricht)

peace *48, 90H* Frieden, Ruhe

peak *62* Spitze(nzeit)

pedestrian precinct *76* Fußgänger-zone

pedestrianized *76* für Fußgänger/in

pentathlon event *57* Fünfkampf

people skills *44* Fähigkeiten im Umgang mit Menschen

percentage *97* Prozentsatz

performance *70* Leistung(en)

permanent *43* ständig, dauerhaft

personal *19* persönlich

personal space *71* Diskretions-abstand

personality *81* Persönlichkeit

personalized *60* personalisiert, indivi-duell gestaltet

personally *37* persönlich

personnel *88* Personal

to persuade *32* überzeugen, überre-den

pest *122* Schädling

pet store *56* Zoohandlung

petrol station *72* Tankstelle

petrol *28* Benzin

petroleum *69* Petroleum

pharmaceutical *126* pharmazeutisch

philosophy *93* Philosophie

phone line *63* Telefonleitung

phrase *75* (Rede-)Wendung, Ausdruck

to pick up the phone *126H* den Hörer abheben

pie chart *69* Kreisdiagramm

PIN code *81* PIN-Nummer

to place orders *79* Bestellungen auf-geben

plain text *7* nur Text

plant extract *87* Pflanzenauszug

plant life *122* Pflanzenleben

plantation *91* Plantage

plant-eating *122* Pflanzen fressend

to play down *97* herunterspielen

playschool *45* Kindertagesstätte

pleasant *12* angenehm, nett

pleasure *76H* Vergnügen, Freude

plenty of *20* viele

plug *131* Stecker

pocket money *85* Taschengeld

point of view *62H* Standpunkt

to point out *15* hinweisen auf

pointless *107* sinnlos

to poison *122* vergiften

poisonous *55* giftig

police officer *28* Polizeibeamter/beamtin

police record *66* Polizeibericht

policing *84* Einsatz von Polizeikräften

policy *18* (Firmen-)Politik

politeness *62* Höflichkeit

political refugee *63* politischer Flüchtling

pollutant *89* Schadstoff

to pollute *68* (die Umwelt) verschmutzen

pollution *69* (Umwelt-)Verschmutzung

pool table *53H* Poolbillardtisch

to populate *123* bevölkern

population explosion *126* Bevölkerungsexplosion

populous *123* dicht besiedelt

pornographic *63* pornographisch

position *46* Lage

positive discrimination *114* positive Diskriminierung

to possess *81* besitzen

possibility *66* Möglichkeit

pot *95* Topf

potential *40* Potenzial

potter *95* Töpfer/in

poultry *26* Geflügel

power cable *131H* Stromkabel

power cut *65* Stromausfall

power unit *69* Antriebsaggregat

powerful *20* leistungsstark

powerless *106* machtlos

practical *7* praktisch

to practise *8* (ein)üben

to pray *77* beten

preacher *77* Prediger/in

to predict *69* vorhersagen

pregnancy *125* Schwangerschaft

prejudice *118* Vorurteil

pre-paid *35H* vorher bezahlt

preparation *40* Vorbereitung

presence *114* Anwesenheit

president *106* Präsident/in

press release *94* Pressemitteilung

press *20* Presse

to pretend *77, 120* vorgeben, so tun als ob

to prevent *58, 63* verhindern, verhü-ten

previous *38* vorhergehend

primary school *48* Grundschule

to print *74* drucken

to print out *60* ausdrucken

prison sentence *106* Haft-, Gefängnisstrafe

prison *108* Gefängnis

privilege *115H* Privileg

to process *87* (weiter)verarbeiten

producer *21* Produzent/in

production *33* Produktion

professional *136* professionell

profile *60* Porträt, Beschreibung,

profit *88* Profit, Gewinn

profitable *97* Gewinn bringend

programmer *20* Programmierer/in

progress *34* Fortschritt/e

project consultant *60* Projekt-berater/in

to promote *32* anpreisen

propaganda *63* Propaganda

properly *45* richtig, korrekt

property *106* Eigentum

prophet *99* Prophet/in

to prosecute *107H* strafrechtlich belangen

prosperity *116* Wohlstand

protective *123* Schutz-

protective clothing *88* Schutzkleidung

protein *50* Protein

prototype *60* Prototyp

to provide *9* bieten, sorgen für

to provide with *84* versorgen mit

psychologist *81* Psychologe/Psycho-login

psychology *79* Psychologie

publication *64* Veröffentlichung, Verbreitung

publicity *21* Publicity, Werbung

to publish *63* veröffentlichen

to pull back *60* zurücksteuern

to pull from *67* herausziehen aus

to punish *84* bestrafen

punishment *107* Strafe

pure *18* rein, pur, echt

purpose *63* Zweck

purse (AE) *107H* Handtasche

pushy *71* sich vordrängend

to put into practice *7* in die Praxis umsetzen

to put on *28* anziehen

to put on probation *111* auf Bewährung entlassen

to put out a message *63* eine Nachricht verbreiten

to put out of business *86* arbeitslos machen

to put sb in danger *110* jdn. in Gefahr bringen

to put to use *40* einsetzen, gebrau-chen

to put together *33* zusammenstellen

Q

qualification *7* Qualifikation, Fähigkeit

to qualify *8* (sich) qualifizieren

quality *36* Qualität, Eigenschaft

quantity *112* Menge, Quantität

to quarrel *6* streiten

quarter *122* Viertel

quarterly *40* vierteljährlich

questionable *128* fragwürdig
questionnaire *104* Fragebogen
queue *72* (Warte-)Schlange
quota *113* Quote
to quote *62H* angeben

R

racial tension *106* Rassenunruhen
radar *60* Radar
radical *86* radikal
rail shipment *111* Bahntransport
rainfall *99* Niederschlag
to raise *46, 69* aufziehen; erhöhen
ramp *118* Rampe
random selection *114* Zufallsprinzip
range *69* Radius
rape *105* Vergewaltigung
rapid *34* schnell, rasch
rare *115H* selten
rarely *9* selten
to rate *58* abschneiden
rate *80* Tarif
rather than *19* anstelle von, anstatt
ration book *74* Bezugscheine
to ration *74* rationieren
raw *58* roh
raw material *95* Rohstoff(e)
Re *75* Betr., Betrifft
to react to *13,* reagieren auf
realistic *37* realistisch
reality *116* Wirklichkeit
to realize *86* erkennen
reasonable *25* vernünftig
receipt *86* Quittung, Beleg
to receive *75* erhalten
receiver *60* Empfänger
recent *35H* letzte, jüngst
recently *30* in letzter Zeit, vor
  kurzem
reception *20* Empfang
receptionist *23* Empfangsdame, -chef
recession *14* Rezession,
  Wirtschaftsflaute
to recharge *69* aufladen
rechargeable battery *104* aufladbare
  Batterie
to recognize *110* erkennen
to recommend *111* empfehlen
recyclable *96* wiederverwertbar,
  recyclebar
red herring *79* Ablenkungsmanöver,
  falsche Fährte
to reduce *37* reduzieren, verringern
reduction *40* Ermäßigung
redundancy pay *88* Arbeitslosengeld
to refer to *48* sich beziehen auf
reference *42* Referenz
reference number *62H* Bestell-
  nummer
reform *86* Reform
refreshments *103* Erfrischungen

to refrigerate *87* kühlen
refrigerator *88* Kühlschrank
refund *12* Rückzahlung, (Rück-)Er-
  stattung
to refuse *66* ablehnen
regards, With best ~ *8* Viele Grüße
region *25* Gebiet, Gegend
regional *130* regional
regularly *9* regelmäßig
relationship *31* Beziehung, Verhältnis
relative *97* relativ
to relieve *51* lindern
religious beliefs *128* Religion,
  religiöse Anschauungen
to rely on *45* sich verlassen auf
to remain *24* bleiben
remains *102* (Über-)Reste
to remind *70* (jdn. an etw.) erinnern
to remove *76* entfernen, beseitigen
to replace *27* ersetzen, austauschen
repressive *81* repressiv
to reprocess *96* wiederverarbeiten
request *62* Bitte
rescue work *67* Rettungsarbeit(en)
rescuer *67* Retter
research laboratory *122* Forschungs-
  labor(atorium)
to resell *106* wieder verkaufen
reserve currency *130* Reserve-
  währung
residence *66* Wohnsitz
resident *66* Einwohner/in
resident population *99* Wohnbevölke-
  rung
residential *66* den Aufenthalt betref-
  fend
to resist *122* widerstehen
resistant to *123* widerstandsfähig
  gegen
resort *15* Ferien-, Urlaubsort
resource *36* Mittel, Reserve
respectful *118* ehrfürchtig
respondent *132* Befragte/r
response *69* Reaktion, Antwort
responsibility *12* Verantwortung
resumé (AE) *42* Lebenslauf
retail *73* Einzelhandels-
retail sector *112* Einzelhandels-
  bereich
retailer *79* Einzelhändler/in
retailing consultant *79*
  Einzelhandelsberater/in
retaliation *108* Vergeltung
to retire *20* in den Ruhestand gehen
to retrain *93* sich umschulen lassen
retreat *45* sich zurückziehen
return air ticket *49* Hin- und
  Rückflugticket
return flight *85* Rückflug
returnable *102* Mehrweg-
reunification *135* Wiedervereinigung

re-use *134* Wiederverwendung
to reveal *81* enthüllen, zeigen
to revise *103H* überarbeiten
revolution *86* Revolution
rewarding *85* lohnend
to rewrite *34* umschreiben
ridiculous *136* lächerlich
right to *66* Berechtigung zu
to ring out *124* ertönen, schallen
to rip *81* (zer)reißen
road rage attack *68* Angriff wütender
  Autofahrer
roadworks *60* Straßenbauarbeiten
to rob *112* ausrauben
robbery *28* Raub
rock-bottom price *54* Niedrigstpreis
to rocket *72* kräftig steigen
role *18* Rolle
to roll *112* rollen
romanticized *116* romantisiert
roof over one's head *120* Dach über
  dem Kopf
room temperature *58* Raumtempe-
  ratur
to rot away *96* verrotten
roughly *97* ungefähr
route *52* Route, Strecke
rubber *103* Gummi
rude *62* unhöflich
to run out *17* ausgehen, zu Ende
  gehen
to run over *62H* durchgehen
run-up *116* Vorlauf
rural *107* ländlich
rush-hour traffic *68* Berufsverkehr
rusty *12* rostig

S

sack, the ~ *88* die Entlassung
safety *58* Sicherheit
salary *20* Gehalt, Lohn
sale *36* Verkauf
sales agreement *86* Kaufvertrag
sales manager *117* Verkaufsleiter/in
salty *122* salzig
satisfaction *42* Befriedigung,
  Zufriedenheit
satisfactory *119* befriedigend
satisfied *12* zufrieden
sauce *31* Soße
sauna *52* Sauna
savage *116* Wilde/r
savings *98* Ersparnisse
to scan *60* scannen, einlesen, erfassen
scandal *54* Skandal
scarce *99* knapp
scare story *99* Horrorgeschichte
scared *42* verstört, ängstlich
sceptical *79* skeptisch
scheme *95* Programm, Projekt

school party *80* Schulklasse
schooling *124* Schulung, Ausbildung
school-leaver *17* Schulabgänger/in
schoolwork *42* Schularbeiten
science fiction *122* Sciencefiction
scissors *133* Schere
scooter *104* (Motor-)Roller
Scotland Yard *120* die Londoner Polizei
search *34* Suche
seashore *60* Strand, Meeresufer
seawater *99* Meerwasser
secret *93* geheim, heimlich
section head *44* Abteilungsleiter/in
secure *8* sicher, fest
security *23* Sicherheit
to seek *42* suchen
seldom *6* selten
to select *21* auswählen
selection *26* Auswahl, Angebot
selection committee *114* Wahlausschuss
self-confidence *85* Selbstsicherheit, -vertrauen
self-employed *72* selbstständig
selfish *104* egoistisch, selbstsüchtig
to send off *35H* abschicken
senior citizen *40, 80H* ältere/r Mitbürger/in, Senior/in
senior *35* vorgesetzt, leitend
to sense *60* wahrnehmen
sensible *76H* vernünftig
sensitive *61* empfindlich, sensibel
sensor *88* Sensor
sentimental *32* gefühlsmäßig, sentimental
separate *23* getrennt
separately *96* getrennt
to serve *18* bedienen
service provider *81* Dienstleister
set buffet *26* kaltes Büfett
to set up *19* einrichten
several *11* einige, mehrere
severe *84* streng, hart
sex object *36* Sexobjekt
shack *116* Hütte, Schuppen
to shake *44* schütteln
to share *29* (sich) teilen
sharp *38* stark
sheep *48* Schaf
shift *47* Schicht
shipyard *93* Schiffswerft
shocked *107H* schockiert
shocking *32* schrecklich, schockierend
to shoot up *73* in die Höhe schießen
shop assistant *41* Verkäufer/in
shoplifting *105* Ladendiebstahl
shopping mall *31* Einkaufszentrum
shortage *11* Mangel
shortly *44H* in Kürze

sick *81* krank
similar *6* ähnlich
simplistic *90* (zu) stark vereinfachend
since *8* seit
single market *130* Binnenmarkt
single mother *111* allein erziehende Mutter
sir *12* mein Herr
site, website *6* Website
site *23* Ort
sketch pad *120* Skizzenblock
ski slope *67* Skihang
skier *67* Skiläufer/in
skill *40* Fertigkeit, Fähigkeit
skilled *130* ausgebildet, Fach-
to sleep rough *120* im Freien schlafen
sleeping bag *48* Schlafsack
slice *27* Scheibe
slightly *122* leicht, geringfügig
to slow down *11* nachlassen
smart card *60* Kreditkarte
to smuggle *97* schmuggeln
snow slide *67* Schneeabgang
snowfall *67* Schneefall
so far *33* bis jetzt
soapy *58* seifig
so-called *54* so genannt
social security *42* Sozialversicherung
social security payment *66* Sozialhilfezahlung
social services *125* Sozialamt
socket *131* Steckdose
soft drink *26* alkoholfreies Getränk
software engineer *7* Softwareentwickler/in
solarium *52* Solarium
solitaire *15* Patience
solitude *12* Einsamkeit
to some extent *127* in gewissem Grade
sophisticated *36* raffiniert, differenziert
sort *32* Art, Sorte, Typ
to sort out *90H* klären, lösen
to sound like *130* sich anhören wie
sour *60* sauer
source *54* Quelle
souvenir shop *116* Souvenirladen
to speak out *104* aussprechen, seine Meinung sagen
special offer *35H* Sonderangebot
specialist *6, 21* Spezialist/in, Fachmann/frau
specialization *130* Spezialisierung
to specialize in *6* sich spezialisieren auf
species *123* Art(en)
speed *68* Geschwindigkeit
spirits *26* Spirituosen
to spoil *104* verderben
spokesman *81* Sprecher

spokesperson *21* Sprecher/in
sponsorship *32* Sponsorentum
sports and leisure centre *51* Sport- und Freizeitzentrum
sportswear *94* Sportkleidung
spread *58* Verbreitung
squash court *52* Squashplatz
staff *6* Angestellte, Personal
stage *46* Phase, Stadium
to stand for *35* stehen für
to stand out from *42* sich abheben von
standard *18* Niveau
to standardize *131* standardisieren, normieren
stand-by switch *104* Bereitschaftsschalter
to stare *68* starren
to start with *79* zunächst
starvation *122* Hunger
to starve *123* verhungern
state benefit *66* staatliche Unterstützung
statement *7* Aussage
statistics *42* Statistiken, statistische Angaben
to stay off work *101* der Arbeit fernbleiben
steady *38* gleichmäßig
steel *112, 134* Stahl
to stick to *112* festkleben an
to sting *88* brennen
stock exchange *131* (Wertpapier-)-Börse
stomach ache *58* Magenschmerzen
to store up *51* ansammeln
storefront (AE) *42* Ladenfront
straight *14* direkt
street crime *81* Straßenkriminalität
stress-free *41* stressfrei
stressful *41* sehr anstrengend, stressig
to stretch *72* sich (er)strecken
strike *90H* Streik
strip *99* Streifen
stroller (AE) *80* Buggy, Sportwagen
to struggle *63* kämpfen
stuck *68* eingeklemmt
studio audience *54* Studiogäste, -publikum
to sub-contract *81* weitervergeben
subjective *16* subjektiv
submachine gun *111* Maschinenpistole
subsidiary *88* Tochtergesellschaft
to subsidize *73* subventionieren
subsistence farmer *91* nur für den eigenen Lebensunterhalt anbauender Landwirt
subtle *36* raffiniert, subtil
suburb *107* Vorort, Außenbezirk

to succeed in *18* Erfolg haben mit
sudden *65* plötzlich
to sue *108* verklagen, (gerichtlich) belangen
to suffer *54* leiden
to suggest *35* vorschlagen
suggestion *57* Vorschlag
suit of armour *112* Rüstung
to suit *8* passen, recht sein
suitable *28* geeignet, passend
summer camp *85* Sommerlager
summer job *33* (Sommer-) Ferienjob
superhuman *127* übermenschlich
superior *128* hochwertig(er)
superpower *130* Supermacht
superweed *122* Unkraut mit mehreren Resistenzen
supplier *86* Anbieter/in, Lieferant/in
supplies *112* Vorräte
to supply *9* liefern
to support *21* Unterstützung
to support a habit *112* seine Sucht befriedigen
to suppress *84* unterdrücken
surely *114* sicherlich
surface *58* Arbeitsfläche
Surgeon-General (AE) *86* Oberster Amtsarzt der USA
survey *69* (Meinungs-)Umfrage, Untersuchung
to survive *120* überleben
survivor *67* Überlebende/r
to suspend *111* aussetzen
to swallow *67* verschlucken
to swap *71* tauschen
sweet potato *123* Süßkartoffel
to switch to *54* sich umstellen auf
switch *88* Schalter
to sympathize *75* sympathisieren
synonym *13* Synonym

T

tailback *68* Rückstau
to take a break *6* eine Pause machen
to take a message *101* eine Nachricht entgegennehmen
to take a seat *35* Platz nehmen
to take action *93* Schritte unternehmen
to take apart *98* auseinander nehmen, demontieren
to take away *52* wegnehmen
to take charge of *34* übernehmen
to take in *52* zu sich nehmen
to take into account *111* in Betracht ziehen, berücksichtigen
to take notice of *98* beachten
to take off *12* abheben, starten
to take on *36* annehmen
to take out *42* herausnehmen
to take over *69* übernehmen

to take sb to court *63* gegen jdn. gerichtlich vorgehen, jdn. verklagen
to take seriously *104* ernst nehmen
to take up *6* beanspruchen
to take up space *76H* Platz beanspruchen
talent *115* Talent, Begabung
talk time *62* Sprechzeit
to tap into *60* eingeben
target *106* Ziel
target audience *39* Zielgruppe
tariff *136* Zoll
task *36* Aufgabe
tax *36* Steuer
tax cut *69* Steuersenkung
tax evasion *106* Steuerhinterziehung
to tear out *63* herausreißen
technical *18* technisch
technician *41* Techniker/in
technology *60* Technik, Technologie
techno-waste *97* Elektronikschrott
teen (AE) *42* Teenager, Jugendliche/r
telecommuter *70* Telearbeiter/in
telematics *69* Fernsteuerung
telephone sales *62* Telefonverkauf
to tell on sb *108* jdn. verpetzen
temporary *8* vorübergehend, zeitlich befristet
tennis court *52* Tennisplatz
terminal *103H* Abfertigungsgebäude
terrible *54* schrecklich, furchtbar
terrific *58, 104* großartig, phantastisch
terrifying *33* erschreckend
text messaging *62H* SMS schicken
theft *81* Diebstahl
themselves *14* (sie) selbst
then again *35H* dann wiederum
therapist *95* Therapeut/in
thermometer *58* Thermometer
these days *28* heutzutage
thief *23* Dieb/in
third, a ~ *42* ein Drittel
though *44H* jedoch
to threaten to *134* drohen zu
threatening *81* bedrohlich
three-pin socket *131H* dreipolige Steckdose
thrill *106* Kitzel, Gefühl
throughout *48, 131* überall (in)
throughout *86* die ganze Zeit über
to throw away *97* wegwerfen
tight *88* streng
timeline *86* Zeitachse
tin *27* Dose
T-junction *76* (Kreuzung mit) Rechts- und Linksabbieger
tobacco company *86* Tabakfirma
token *95* Marke, Chip
tolerant *111* tolerant
ton *97* Tonne

to top up *68* auffüllen
to toss a coin *114* eine Münze werfen
totally *37* völlig
tour *56* Rundgang
tourist class *103H* Touristenklasse
towards *76H* auf ... zu, in Richtung auf
toxic *96* giftig, toxisch
trade flow *130* Handelsstrom
trader *116* Händler/in
traditional *41* traditionell
traffic jam *76H* Verkehrsstau
tragedy *67, 108* Tragödie
tramp *120* Tramp
transaction *60* Überweisung
to transfer *103H* umsteigen
to translate into *97* hinauslaufen auf
transmitter *60* Sender
transport *18* Verkehr(smittel)
to trap *67* fangen
travel agency *6* Reisebüro
travel documents *103H* Reisedokumente
travel pass *69* Fahrausweis
traveller *131H* Reisende/r
to treat *21* behandeln
treaty *129* Vertrag
trial *124* Prozess, Verfahren, Verhandlung
trivial *111* trivial, geringfügig
to trivialize *36, 120* trivial machen, trivialisieren
tropical *122* tropisch
trouble *12* Schwierigkeit, Ärger
truck driver (AE) *72* Lkw-Fahrer/in
truly *132* wahrhaftig, wirklich
to trust *21* vertrauen
truthful *63* wahrhaftig
to try a case *108* einen Fall behandeln
to turn a blind eye *97* ein Auge zudrücken
to turn into *36* verwandeln in, machen zu
to turn over *56* sich umdrehen
two-pin plug *131H* zweipoliger Stecker
type *50* Art, Typ, Sorte
typing *48* Maschineschreiben
tyre *103* Reifen

U

umbrella *29* (Regen-)Schirm
unauthorized possession *111* unbefugter Besitz
unclear *37* unklar
uncomfortable *71* ungemütlich
uncontrollable *122* unkontrollierbar
undemocratic *82* undemokratisch
under construction *99* im Bau
under pressure *7* unter Druck

to undercut *54* unterbieten
to underline *10* unterstreichen
to undermine *124* untergraben
understanding *31* Verständnis
unelected *136* nicht gewählt
unemployed *6* arbeitslos, ohne Beschäftigung
unemployment *84* Arbeitslosigkeit
unfit *51* nicht fit
unfortunate *25* unglücklich
unfree *81* Unfreie/r
unhealthy *82* ungesund
unhelpful *90* nicht hilfreich, irreführend
uniform *81* Uniform
uninvited *27* nicht (ein)geladen
Union *73* (Europäische) Union
unique *67* einzigartig
united *132* vereinigt, vereint
unknown *67* unbekannt
unnatural *54* unnatürlich
unofficial *26* inoffiziell
unpleasant *120* unangenehm
unreasonable *86* unvernünftig
unsafe *82* unsicher
unscrupulous *116* skrupellos
unsocial *41* unsozial
unstable *139* instabil
unstoppable *132* unaufhaltsam
unsuitable *84* ungeeignet, unpassend
unsurprisingly *72* erwartungsgemäß
unusable *103* nicht zu gebrauchen
unusual *6* ungewöhnlich
unwanted *122* unerwünscht
unwelcome *64* nicht willkommen
up to *66* bis zu
up to a point *127* bis zu einem bestimmten Punkt
update *76H* letzter Stand
to upset *36* verwirren, aufregen
upside *69* Vorzug
urban *48, 69* städtisch, Stadt-
urgent *65* dringend, eilig
usable *122* nutzbar
used *104* gebraucht
user *8* Benutzer/in
utensil *58* Gerät

V

Vagrancy Act *120* Obdachlosengesetz
vagrant *120* Obdachlose/r
valley *67* Tal
valuables *23* Wertgegenstände

to value *70* (ab)schätzen
van *12* Transporter
vandalism *105* Vandalismus
variety *26* Auswahl
various *33* verschiedene
VCR (AE) *104* Videorekorder
veggie, vegetable *58* Gemüse
vehicle *69* Fahrzeug
vehicle number *60* Kfz-Kennzeichen
verdict *111* Urteil
versus *90* gegen(über)
veto *136* Veto
via *60* über
victim *63, 67* Opfer
victory *88* Sieg
videotape *26* Videokassette
viewpoint *75* Standpunkt
vigorous *51* kräftig, kraftvoll
violence *108* Gewalt
violent *82* gewalttätig
vision *60* Vision
vital *36* (lebens)wichtig, wesentlich
vital organ *128* lebenswichtiges Organ
voice-activated *62* sprachgesteuert
volunteer *14* Freiwillige/r
vote *66* Wahl

W

wages *43* Lohn, Gehalt
waiter *44* Kellner
waitress *41* Kellnerin, Serviererin
to walk around *76H* herumlaufen
warehouse *62* Lager(haus)
washing machine *131H* Waschmaschine
waste *37* Abfall, Müll
waste disposal *97* Abfallbeseitigung, Müllentsorgung
wasteful *36* verschwenderisch
to watch out *60* aufpassen
weapon *108* Waffe
website designer *7* Webdesigner, Internetprogrammierer
weed *122* Unkraut
to weigh *52* wiegen
weight *29* Gewicht
well-paid *7* gut bezahlt
what's more *36* zudem
What's the story now? *103* Wie geht's jetzt weiter?
whatever *35H* was auch immer
wheat *130* Weizen

wheelchair *8* Rollstuhl
whenever *138* immer wenn
white wine *31* Weißwein
to widen *76* erweitern, verbreitern
wild, the ~ *122* die freie Natur
wilderness *12* Wildnis
willing *48, 84* arbeitswillig, gewillt (sein)
willingness *94* Bereitschaft, Bereitwilligkeit
to win back *107H* zurückgewinnen
window dressing *116* Schau, Augenwischerei
window-shopping *78* Schaufensterbummel
windpower *73* Windkraft
windscreen *60* Windschutzscheibe
wiring *88* Verkabelung
to withdraw from *86* zurücktreten von
within *67, 130* innerhalb (von)
without *14* ohne
womb *124* Mutterleib
to wonder *44H* sich fragen
word processing *40* Textverarbeitung
to work on *33* arbeiten an
to work out *50* ausarbeiten, sich ausdenken
work visa *85* Arbeitserlaubnis
workcamp *48* Arbeitscamp
workforce *90H* Belegschaft
working week *11* Arbeitswoche
workplace *45* Arbeitsplatz
worktop *58* Arbeitsplatte
worldwide *60* weltweit
worried *21* besorgt, beunruhigt
worryingly *112* beängstigend
to wound *110* verwunden
wristwatch *60* Armbanduhr
wrong *113* Unrecht

Y

yield *122* Ertrag, Ernte
Y-junction *76* Gabelung
Yours faithfully *12* Mit freundlichen Grüßen, Hochachtungsvoll
Yours sincerely *75* Mit freundlichen Grüßen
youth *36* Jugend

Z

zero tolerance *105* Null-Toleranz

Geographische Namen

Africa ['afrɪkə]   Afrika
Alabama [ˌælə'bæmə]   Alabama
Alps [ælps]   Alpen
Alsace [æl'sæs]   Elsass
Amazon ['æməzən]   Amazonas
Amsterdam ['æmstədæm]   Amsterdam
Arab ['ærəb]   arabisch; Araber/in
Asia ['eɪʃə]   Asien
Asian ['eɪʃn]   asiatisch; Asiate/Asiatin
Australia [ɒ'streɪliə]   Australien
Austria ['ɒstriə]   Österreich
Balkans ['bɔːlkənz]   Balkan
Belgian ['beldʒən]   belgisch; Belgier/in
Belgium ['beldʒəm]   Belgien
Berlin [bɜː'lɪn]   Hauptstadt Deutschlands
Britain ['brɪtn]   Britannien, Großbritannien
British ['brɪtɪʃ]   britisch; Brite/Britin
Briton ['brɪtn]   Britanne/ Britannin (hist.), Brite/Britin
Brussels ['brʌslz]   Brüssel
Bulgaria [bʌl'geəriə]   Bulgarien
California [ˌkælə'fɔːniə]   US-Bundesstaat an der Pazifikküste
Canada ['kænədə]   Kanada
China ['tʃaɪnə]   China
Chinese [tʃaɪ'niːz]   chinesisch; Chinese/Chinesin
Cuba ['kjuːbə]   Kuba
Cyprus ['saɪprəs]   Zypern
Czech Republic [tʃek rɪ'pʌblɪk]   Tschechische Republik
Denmark ['denmɑːk]   Dänemark
Dublin ['dʌblɪn]   Hauptstadt der Republik Irland
Dutch [dʌtʃ]   holländisch; Holländer/in
Edinburgh ['edɪnbərə]   Hauptstadt Schottlands
Eastern Europe [ˌiːstən 'jʊərəp]   Osteuropa
EU [ˌiː 'juː]   Europäische Union
Europe ['jʊərəp]   Europa
Finland ['fɪnlənd]   Finnland
France [frɑːns]   Frankreich
French [frentʃ]   französisch; Franzose/Französin
Germany ['dʒɜːməni]   Deutschland
Greece [griːs]   Griechenland
Hungary ['hʌŋgəri]   Ungarn
India ['ɪndiə]   Indien
Indian ['ɪndiən]   indisch; Inder/in
Indonesia [ˌɪndəʊ'niːziə]   Indonesien
Indonesian [ˌɪndəʊ'niːziən]   indonesisch
Ireland ['aɪələnd]   Irland
Irish ['aɪrɪʃ]   irisch; Ire/Irin
Israel ['ɪzreɪl]   Israel

Italian [ɪ'tæljən]   italienisch; Italiener/in
Italy ['ɪtəli]   Italien
Japan [dʒə'pæn]   Japan
Japanese [dʒæpə'niːz]   japanisch; Japaner/in
Kenya ['kenjə]   Kenia
Korean [kə'rɪən]   koreanisch; Koreaner/in
LA [ˌel 'eɪ]   Los Angeles
Latin America [ˌlætɪn ə'merɪkə]   Lateinamerika
Luxembourg ['lʌksəmbɜːg]   Luxemburg
Malaysia [mə'leɪziə]   Malaysia
Manchester ['mæntʃɪstə]   Großstadt in Nordwestengland
Mediterranean [ˌmedɪtə'reɪniən]   mediterran; Mittelmeer(länder)
Mexico ['meksɪkəʊ]   Mexiko
Mexico City [ˌmeksɪkəʊ 'sɪti]   Hauptstadt von Mexiko
Middle East [ˌmɪdl 'iːst]   Naher Osten
Midwest [mɪd'west]   mittlerer Westen
the Netherlands [ðə 'neðələndz]   die Niederlande
New York [ˌnjuː 'jɔːk]   größte Stadt in den USA
North-Rhine Westphalia [ˌnɔːθraɪn west'feɪliə]   Nordrhein-Westfalen
Paris ['pærɪs]   Hauptstadt Frankreichs
Parisian [pə'rɪziən]   Pariser/in
Poland ['pəʊlənd]   Polen
Portugal ['pɔːtʃʊgl]   Portugal
Rhine [raɪn]   Rhein
Romania [ru:'meɪniə]   Rumänien
Rome [rəʊm]   Rom
Russia ['rʌʃə]   Russland
Russian ['rʌʃn]   russisch; Russe/Russin
the Sahara [ðə sə'hɑːrə]   die Sahara
Scandinavia [ˌskændɪ'neɪviə]   Skandinavien
Scotland ['skɒtlənd]   Schottland
Scottish ['skɒtɪʃ]   schottisch
Singapore [ˌsɪŋə'pɔː]   Singapur
Slovakia [sləʊ'vækiə]   Slowakei
Spain [speɪn]   Spanien
Spanish ['spænɪʃ]   spanisch
Sweden ['swiːdn]   Schweden
Swedish ['swiːdɪʃ]   schwedisch
Texas ['teksəs]   US-Bundesstaat
Tokyo ['təʊkiəʊ]   Tokio (Hauptstadt von Japan)
Uganda [ju'gændə]   Land in Afrika
UK [ˌjuː 'keɪ]   Vereinigtes Königreich
(the) Ukraine [ðə ju'kreɪn]   die Ukraine
USA [ˌjuː es 'eɪ]   die Vereinigten Staaten von Amerika

Unregelmäßige Verben

Infinitive	Past Tense	Past Participle	
arise	arose	arisen	entstehen
be	was/were	been	sein
become	became	become	werden
begin	began	begun	starten, anfangen
bind	bound	bound	binden
break	broke	broken	brechen, kaputt-machen
bring	brought	brought	bringen
broadcast	broadcast	broadcast (-ed)	senden
build	built	built	bauen
burn	burnt	burnt (burned)	brennen
buy	bought	bought	kaufen
catch	caught	caught	fangen
choose	chose	chosen	wählen
come	came	come	kommen
cost	cost	cost	kosten
cut	cut	cut	schneiden
deal	dealt	dealt	handeln, sich be-schäftigen mit
dig	dug	dug	graben, bohren
do	did	done	tun, machen
draw	drew	drawn	zeichnen
drink	drank	drunk	trinken
drive	drove	driven	fahren
eat	ate	eaten	essen
fall	fell	fallen	fallen
feel	felt	felt	fühlen
fight	fought	fought	(be)kämpfen
find	found	found	finden
fly	flew	flown	fliegen
forget	forgot	forgotten	vergessen
freeze	froze	frozen	(ein-)frieren
get	got	got	bekommen
give	gave	given	geben
go	went	gone	gehen
grow	grew	grown	wachsen
have	had	had	haben
hear	heard	heard	hören
hide	hid	hidden	(sich) verstecken
hit	hit	hit	schlagen
hold	held	held	halten
hurt	hurt	hurt	wehtun
keep	kept	kept	behalten
know	knew	known	wissen, kennen
lay	laid	laid	legen
lead	led	led	führen
learn	learnt	learnt (learned)	lernen
leave	left	left	(weg)gehen, (ver)lassen

Infinitive	Past Tense	Past Participle	
let	let	let	lassen, erlauben
light	lit	lit (lighted)	erleuchten, entzünden
lose	lost	lost	verlieren
make	made	made	machen, tun
mean	meant	meant	bedeuten
meet	met	met	treffen
pay	paid	paid	bezahlen
put	put	put	legen, stellen
read	read	read	lesen
ride	rode	ridden	fahren, reiten
rise	rose	risen	steigen, sich erheben
ring	rang	rung	klingeln
run	ran	run	laufen, verwalten
say	said	said	sagen
see	saw	seen	sehen
seek	sought	sought	suchen
sell	sold	sold	verkaufen
send	sent	sent	senden
set	set	set	setzen, stellen, legen
shake	shook	shaken	schütteln
show	showed	shown (showed)	zeigen
shut	shut	shut	schließen
sing	sang	sung	singen
sink	sank	sunk	(ver)senken
sit	sat	sat	sitzen
sleep	slept	slept	schlafen
smell	smelt	smelt (smelled)	riechen
speak	spoke	spoken	sprechen
speed	sped	sped (speeded)	rasen
spend	spent	spent	ausgeben
stand	stood	stood	stehen
steal	stole	stolen	stehlen
swim	swam	swum	schwimmen
take	took	taken	nehmen
teach	taught	taught	unterrichten
tear	tore	torn	zerreißen
tell	told	told	erzählen
think	thought	thought	denken
throw	threw	thrown	werfen
understand	understood	understood	verstehen
wake	woke	woken	wecken
wear	wore	worn	tragen
win	won	won	gewinnen
write	wrote	written	schreiben

Quellenverzeichnis

Fotos

Titel: Corbis Stock Market: Vasco DaGama Brücke, Lissabon/M. Mastrorillo; K. Owaki (Sonnenblumen); Premium: Datené Photography (Tastatur); BAVARIA Stock/L. Lefkowitz (Autos);

action press, Hamburg: S. 6/Sunshine, S. 17/R. Unkel, S. 67/ARC;

Advertising Archive, London: S. 32, S. 36;

AP Photos, Frankfurt/Main: S. 106/News Sentinel-Ellie Bogue, S. 121/Rodney White;

Argus Fotoarchiv, Hamburg: S. 13/K. Andrews, S. 91/R. Giling, S. 96/P. Frischmuth;

A. Austin: S. 110;

Australian Tourist Commission: S. 49;

BBC, London: S. 54, S. 72;

Bill Bachman, Victoria, Australien: S. 116/Australian Geographic;

C. Buckstegen, Berlin: S. 41–f, S. 78–6;

J. Chipps, London: S. 14; S. 16; S. 17; S. 21; S. 26; S. 68, S. 102, S. 111 (3), S. 113;

COMSTOCK, Luxemburg: S. 4 (3), S. 5 (2), S. 33, S. 34, S. 40 (3), S. 41 (2), S. 50, S. 58, S. 78, S. 81, 87 (2) S. 111 (2), S. 113(6);

Corbis Stock Market, Düsseldorf: S. 6/D. Stoecklein, S. 16/DiMaggio, S. 40/Mug Shots, S. 41/J.Feingersh–a, S. 59/Straus/Curtis, S. 78/M. Keller–1, C. Savage–2, Mug Shots–5, S. 79/M. Keller, S. 85/T. Stewart/A. Skelley/R. Kaufman, S. 87/H. Prinz, S. 91/R. Duchaine/T&D.A. McCarthy, S. 96/L. Lefkowitz–5/A. Beck–7, S. 105/R. Lewine/C. Savage–1/I. Bradshaw–4/R. Gayle–5/R. Morsch–6+8, S. 121/D. Scott;

Das Fotorchiv, Essen: S. 17/J. Scheibner, S. 18/J. Tack, S. 41/J. Meyer–c, A. Riedmiller–e, P. Hollenbach–g, B. Nimtsch–h; S. 51/C. Karp, S. 78/K. Müller–4, A. Riedmiller–7, T. Mayer–8, S. 81/M. Matzel, S. 96/O. Baumeister–2/R. Oberhäuser–4/B. Nimtsch–6;

dpa-Bildarchiv, Berlin: S. 30, S. 72, S. 99, S. 105–3, S. 108, S. 116, S. 121–a;

FOCUS, Hamburg: S. 121/Rosenfeld Images Ltd/J. King-Holmes (c–2)/Eye of Science/F. Norman–d, S. 124/ Y. Nikas, S. 128/V. Habbick Visions;

Getty Images/Bavaria, München: S. 45/D. Anthony, S. 111/Photomondo, S. 105–2, S. 119/L. Bray;

Getty Images/Stone, München: S. 6/T. Powell, S. 12/C. Condina, S. 59/P. Banko, S. 77/J. Corwin;

Getty Images Creative, Hamburg: S. 87, 96–1;

S. & R. Greenhill, London: S. 41–b;

S. Hughes, Rodborough: S. 95 (2);

IFA-Bilderteam, Düsseldorf: S. 105/International Stock–7;

The Image Bank, Berlin: S. 95/M. Melford;

Andrew Meares, Lilyfield, Australien: S. 116;

Picture Press, Hamburg: S. 88/Sygma, S. 93/R. Townshend, S. 120/Sygma;

PREMIUM, Düsseldorf: S. 15/B. Wittlington, S. 91/G. Huszar, S. 96/GGF, S. 124/Images Colour;

Stockfood, München: S. 26;

Wir bedanken uns bei folgenden Firmen, die uns freundlicherweise Material für dieses Lehrwerk zur Verfügung gestellt haben:
The Body Shop
GRUNDIG AG, Nürnberg
SIEMENS Elektrogeräte, München
Volkswagen AG, Wolfsburg

Illustrationen

Oxford Designers & Illustrators

Texte

S. 58: Choices Magazine, Scholastic, March 2000; S. 60: Visions by Michio Kaku, OUP, 1998; S. 77: California Dreamin' Words & Music by John Phillips & Michelle Gillian ©1965 Wingate Music Corp. USA. Universal/MCA Music Ltd. London. Used by permission of Bosworth GmbH. All Rights Reserved. International Copyright Secured; S. 116: The Sunday Telegraph, 17.9.2000; S. 120: The Guardian, 27.8.2001;

Nicht alle Copyright-Inhaber konnten ermittelt werden; deren Urheberrechte werden hiermit vorsorglich und ausdrücklich anerkannt.